What Educators Say About Dr. Borba

"Over the last three years I have used a lot of self-esteem materials. Michele Borba's are the best for the classroom teacher! They are hands-on and easy to put into use in the classroom. Her ideas and centers are being used . . . and they are working!"
—Catherine Graham, Mentor Teacher
San Jose, California

"The Oak Hill teachers were unanimous in considering [Dr. Borba's] materials the most timely, useful and motivating they have experienced during their teaching careers. They will make a significant difference for students and teachers."
—Harold King, Principal
Converse, Indiana

"We have been using many of the materials and ideas presented by Dr. Michele Borba. Our teachers and even students themselves report positive things. . . . We have all grown in being more sensitive to others' self-esteem."
—Dr. Marilyn Skinner
Assistant Superintendent for Instruction
Kokomo, Indiana

"Michele is wonderful! She stimulated and excited my entire staff with her research, her ideas and her materials. (This workshop helped us start our school year in a very positive mode.) We are regularly using her materials in our classrooms now."
—Shirley Baker, Principal
Colorado Springs, Colorado

"My early training in self-esteem building was as a parent aide in Dr. Borba's classroom. I saw the impact on the kids! They came in at the beginning of the year scared and confused. They left happy and confident!"
—Mary Grace Galvin
Self-Esteem Consultant
Dellwood, Minnesota

"During the first week of school, I walked through the classrooms and was gratified and surprised by the immediate impact of [Dr. Borba's] workshop. Every classroom had at least one of her charts and I caught a large percentage of the teachers engaging students in the activities she had suggested. . . . It will positively affect the lives of hundreds of children. . . ."
—William Knight, Ph.D., Principal
Newport Beach, California

"The Monday morning after Michele Borba left here, we had in place numerous centers and ideas throughout the five grades. The ripple effect is definitely happening in the area of self-esteem!"
—Barbara Tarbet, Principal
Aspen, Colorado

"It gives me great personal pride to tell you that Dr. Borba's ideas provided our instructional and support staff with a true desire to change our perspectives on educating youngsters for the twenty-first century."
—Loraine Brown, Coordinator
Multicultural Education
Sacramento, California

ESTEEM BUILDERS

A K-8 Self-Esteem
Curriculum for
Improving Student
Achievement, Behavior
and School Climate

Dr. Michele Borba
EDITED BY BINAH TAYLOR-McMILLAN

Forewords by Jack Canfield,
Dr. Hanoch McCarty and
Robert Reasoner

JALMAR PRESS
ROLLING HILLS ESTATES
CALIFORNIA

Jalmar Press
45 Hitching Post Dr., Bldg. 2
Rolling Hills Estates, CA 90274
Tel: (213) 547-1240

ISBN 0-91519053-2 (Paperback)
ISBN 0-91519088-5 (Spiral-Bound)

Library of Congress number: 88-80769

Editing by Binah Taylor-McMillan
Additional copy editing by Jackie Melvin
Consulting Dr. Craig Borba
Cover painting by Luis R. Caughman
Illustrations by Michele Borba and Taylor Measom
Design and page composition by Highpoint Type and Graphics, Inc., Claremont, CA
Manufactured in the United States of America

First edition
Printing: 10 9 8 7 6 5

Dedication

This book is dedicated with love to my sons Jason, Adam and Zachary. Each of you, just because you're you, has brought constant joy and meaning to my life. May each year give you even greater awareness of what incredibly special and unique individuals you are. You are my Esteem Builders!

Acknowledgments

ESTEEM BUILDERS is the culmination of seventeen years of research and development in finding ways to enhance students' self-esteem. A project of this scope involves countless special people who have guided or supported me through the years.

In particular I owe thanks to the following people:

Greg and Cindy Morse, Nancy Shipcott, Barbara Namian, Mary Grace Galvin, Bev Takeda and Jack Smith—my special colleagues who were there at the beginning (and now!) lending their support to my early efforts in applying it all to kids. And to new colleagues of today: Chris Nelson and Susan Hurst—for their endless suggestions and encouragement—and to Carol Friedenberg for her constant sources of inspirational quotes and uplifting comments.

To Jack Canfield, Hanoch McCarty and Robert Reasoner—your work has been an inspiration not only to this book but to all of us in the field of self-esteem. Thanks for the invaluable suggestions, subtle mentoring and also for the fun.

To the very special students at Congress Springs and Brownell schools who were my true source of feedback that *this really works!*

To Ione Farmer, my master teacher, and to Aileen Fredrickson, my first teacher, who will always be my inspirations of how to apply esteem building to kids.

To Brad Winch, my publisher, for his dedication to self-esteem and unflinching support on this project from start to finish. Michael Heilpern, project manager, for giving this book the look I wanted. And especially to Binah Taylor-McMillan, editor, for organizing the text, giving invaluable feedback and making it run smoothly. Thanks to all of them for their amazing tenacity and vision, and for helping me put it all together.

To Joseph A. Guzicki, Michael Goodman and Nicholas Rayder, practicing psychologists who reviewed the assessment tools.

To the hundreds of teachers and parents who have shared their ideas and techniques in esteem building with me at the seminars I have conducted.

To Ernest and Lorayne Borba for their endless encouragement and support.

To Daniel and Treva Ungaro, the real self-esteem experts (and my parents), who just instinctively knew how to do it all along. Their never-ending support and love have always been my beacon and model. Thank you for teaching me to believe in myself.

And especially to my husband, Craig, the creative idea force and my personal esteem builder who has continually filled my days with encouragement and love while keeping my thoughts of tomorrow bright.

Table of Contents

Foreword

by Jack Canfield, Hanoch McCarty and Robert Reasoner

JACK CANFIELD *is the author of* 100 Ways to Enhance Self-Concept in the Classroom *and* Self-Esteem in the Classroom: A Curriculum Guide. *He is President of Self-Esteem Seminars and President of the Foundation for Self-Esteem. He is a member of the California Task Force to Promote Self-Esteem, and Personal and Social Responsibility and a member of the Board of Trustees of the National Council for Self-Esteem.*

I have a dream—that someday every child in every school and at every grade level will have a class entitled "Self-Esteem and Effective Living Skills." It will show up on their schedule every day somewhere between English and math. I have this dream because I think it is the major missing link to educational reform in America today. Kids and teachers both need to expand their self-esteem, increase their interpersonal communication skills, and learn the affective and behavioral skills necessary for creating success in all areas of their lives.

While many people are working on making this dream come true, I believe it will be a long time coming. Like all things that are of deep value and lasting in nature, it will take hard work over a long time to build it—I'm guessing ten years at least. However, you don't have to wait that long to start teaching these things to your kids, because the basics are all here in this book: teaching kids to love themselves, to realize their basic worth, to respect the needs and feelings of others, to set and achieve goals, to think positively, to honor their feelings and to go for their most cherished dreams.

Michele Borba has done a herculean job in gathering together some of the finest ideas and activities ever collected in one volume. She has provided the K–8 teacher with one of the most valuable resources on self-esteem that I have ever seen. You have in your hands a veritable treasure chest of ways to make your love and caring for kids come alive. It will take you at least two years to use all of this material— maybe more. But I'll make you a promise. If you use even half of these activities with your kids, you will get to know them—and yourself—in a deeper way than you ever have before. I'll make you another promise, too. You will see miracles happen in your class.

Kids will pay attention more because they have more attention paid to them.

Kids will become more responsible because they have been responded to more.

Kids will become more achievement-oriented because their basic human needs have been achieved.

Kids will become more understanding of others because they have come to understand themselves more.

Kids will discover a new love for learning because they have learned to love and be loved.

I promise you nothing short of miracles. No kidding!

That's the good news. The bad news is you have to use the activities—every day if possible. You have to make a commitment to make self-esteem a priority in your classroom. But that really isn't bad news. Using these activities will change the quality of your teaching. You'll have more fun, you'll see greater results, you'll feel more successful, and you'll end up feeling better about yourself as well.

I believe every child and every teacher should leave school at the end of the day feeling better about themselves than when they came to school in the morning. Unfortunately, all the statistics indicate just the opposite happens. But now you can change all of that for yourself and for your students. Just start using this book today...and use all of the other resources Michele offers us as well. She lists hundreds of children's books that embody the themes of self-esteem. She provides enough work-sheets to keep anyone busy, and she provides you with a solid structure to pull it all together.

This is probably three books disguised as one, but Michele has always given more value than expected in her books as well as at her fantastic workshops. As I said earlier, you have a real treasure chest here. I suggest you open it and start sharing the treasure as soon as possible. You are in for a real treat!

Good luck and have fun!

—*Jack Canfield*

DR. HANOCH McCARTY *is a member of the Executive Board of the National Council for Self-Esteem and is past President of the Association for Humanistic Education. He received the 1988 Golden Apple Award, presented by the Foundation for Self-Esteem for significant work in the development of self-esteem enhancement in the United States. His most recent text is entitled* Growing Pains in the Classroom *and was published by Reston.*

Do you believe, as I do, that *self-esteem is the 'bottom line' underlying school achievement?* Has your experience taught you that low self-esteem children will be found clustered at the bottom of the achievement scale in most classrooms? Little by little, the evidence accumulates connecting self-esteem and school achievement; self-esteem and school misbehavior; self-esteem and suicide, drug abuse, delinquency, arrest records, child abuse. The list goes on.

It would be so nice to be able to assume that most children come from homes which are nurturing, caring, warm and sustaining. Children need affirmation for their specialness; for their curiosity; for their growing abilities and uniqueness. What schools we could run if, indeed, the children came to us all in that condition: believing implicitly in their own worth and value. And wouldn't it be a grand world if the classrooms they came to were all equally supportive of that growth and of that positive image of self?

Alas, anyone who has worked with children knows the sad truth that many homes send more and stronger messages of disapproval than of acceptance. Many children have received literally thousands of negative comments, predictions of future failure, dismissals of current success and improvement, withdrawals of affection. On a recent visit to a supermarket, I saw a little child, sitting in the basket, reach out to touch and inspect items from nearby shelves. "What this, Mommy?" "I want it." This was repeated several times down the aisle. The mother looked harried, overworked, strained. Each time she ignored the child's question and snatched the item from the child's hands and replaced it on the shelf. "Stop it!" she hissed angrily. "Don't take those things, I'm warning you." "Why?" asked the child. "Can I have this one?" Suddenly, the mother reached her limit. Shaking the child roughly and repeatedly by the shoulders, she shouted, "IF YOU TOUCH ANOTHER THING, I'LL RIP YOUR HEAD OFF!!!" The child began screaming. The other adults in the aisle looked away embarrassedly. (Shamefully, so did I.) And the mother was even more upset by the crying. She pushed her cart down the aisle toward the checkout. I've seen such events many times, haven't you? And I worry: can self-esteem develop in such a family relationship? Does the mother understand her role in the child's developmental process? I've watched verbal abuse so often. I've witnessed children showing beautiful curiosity and desire to learn—and seen those critically important processes punished by angry adults. Sometimes those adults were the parents and sometimes the teachers of those children. So we know all too well how many children come to us as 'damaged goods' rather than as 'valuable merchandise.' We in the schools are, for many children, the first and last best hope to repair the damage; to enable and empower children to become functioning adults and attain some reasonable measure of happiness. We are the only ones, in most cases, who have a chance to break the cycle of child abuse in which the abused become the abusers because it is their only model of parenting. The schools are the crossroads of our society. Not everyone goes into the army, not everyone visits city hall. But everyone (or as close to everyone as we can conceivably ensure) comes to school. Not everyone can get counseling to undo years of neglect, abuse or attacks on their emotional health. But everyone comes to school sometime. This is our society's window of opportunity.

My work with teachers, counselors, administrators and parents has for many years focused on self-esteem as the basis for all learning and growth. If a child does not believe in herself, how can she grow, learn, succeed? It has been heartbreaking to see children who clearly had ability not be able to organize, mobilize, utilize that ability because their self-perception is one of inadequacy, inability, failure. In the many workshops for schools I've conducted around the United States and Canada for the past twenty years, I have emphasized this crucial connection. And teachers agree, "Yes, we really must enhance student self-concept in order to build their school achievement. But how shall we proceed?"

This book, *Esteem Builders*, by Michele Borba, is a major step toward answering that question. What Dr. Borba has given us all is the greatest gift—a complete resource for the improvement of instruction in the area of building self-esteem. She has done our homework for us. She has empowered the caring teacher in a unique way. There are books on the theory of self-esteem. There are other books of "recipes" filled with great quantities of lesson plans on self-esteem affirming strategies. But no one, to my knowledge, has done what she has here. She has gone beyond *strategies* to offer us a *method* of teaching.

Repeatedly we hear the phrase "methods of teaching" misused as synonymous with "teaching strategies." I'd like to clarify this in order to describe this book more fully. A strategy is the activity or lesson plan you might do on Tuesday afternoon from 1:00 to 1:50 p.m. It may be an excellent strategy and fully appropriate to the children and to the curriculum and to your goals. A *method* is something much larger. A method is your reason for doing that strategy and all the others you have chosen. A method includes your philosophy, your values, your vision, your goals, your intent. It is partly chosen because of your training and pedagogic rationale, and partly chosen because of who you are and what you believe, feel and need as a person. It is either congruent with or in conflict with the society of the school and the society of the community. A method, then, implies, suggests, urges us to select those strategies we may use on a particular day with children. The method is always in control of our choices of strategy.

This may be part of the reason why some classrooms are ultimately confusing to children: each lesson may be well-taught but poorly chosen. Or, each lesson may be well-taught but not clearly and meaningfully connected to those which came before and those which follow. The *intent* of the lesson may be incomprehensible to the students and even to the teacher. It is my experience, in working with many teachers, that there are those who teach beautifully (if teaching is seen as a daily performance in front of an audience) who are teaching *intuitively* and yet cannot articulate or explain why they choose this particular strategy or that specific set of rules, procedures and expectations. These are people focusing on strategies without ever becoming clear about their method.

Esteem Builders gives us more than strategies. Dr. Borba has provided for us a clear rationale, a philosophy explaining why we need to work on student self-esteem, and many sources and resources which offer supportive research data and conceptual frameworks by a number of important thinkers in this field. She then supplies a structure for this method through the "five components of self-esteem." These components are generally recognized throughout the field of self-esteem enhancement as being most important. The building blocks are offered to help teachers create their own curricular plans including lessons, appropriate children's literature on all grade levels, activities, strategies—all presented within the framework of the five components. The organizational plan is very understandable, which enables the teacher to immediately find what is needed.

Not neglected is the school climate—the self-esteem of teachers and principals and others within the building. It is hard to help someone else with their self-esteem if yours is in question. And there is even a companion book aimed at helping parents to support the self-esteem development of their children at home.

It is therefore a pleasure to hold a copy of this book because it is one of the most complete sources for self-esteem enhancement I have ever seen. I know that I will be using it for years to come. I will be adopting it for my graduate classes and recommending it everywhere for those who work in the helping professions. It is a masterpiece of its genre: thorough, thoughtful, complete. The strategies which come from her method are very well-chosen and there is such a wide variety of them in each of the several areas that a teacher can easily find some which will fit her style and be suitable for her students.

I have known Dr. Borba as a colleague and friend for several years. She is an extraordinary presenter of in-service workshops and addresses. Her work is lively, humorous, and especially filled with practical ideas. It is from her extensive work with and for teachers that this extraordinary book comes. Its ideas are teacher-tested and classroom-proved. These are no "ivory tower theories." These really work! I welcome you to this book and urge you to make a commitment to implement this method in your classroom, in your school. I urge you to be a missionary for this method with friends and colleagues. As a member of the Board of Trustees, I invite you to join us in the National Council for Self-Esteem. Join us in the quest for the improvement of children's lives and abilities. Write to us at: *National Council for Self-Esteem, P.O. Box 3728, Palo Alto, CA 94309-3728.* Our national and regional conferences and our excellent publications are designed to be helpful to all those who wish to work in self-esteem enhancement.

—*Hanoch McCarty*

ROBERT REASONER *is Superintendent of the Moreland School District in San Jose, California. He is President of the National Council for Self-Esteem, Director of the Center for Self-Esteem, and author of* Building Self-Esteem: A Comprehensive Program.

As a school administrator with more than 34 years of experience, I am convinced that attention to self-esteem may be one of the most significant things we can do in school. Experienced teachers have seen remedial students suddenly blossom into highly motivated achievers under the right conditions. They have seen other students achieve well beyond normal expectations, and gifted students with great potential achieve well below what one might expect, all because of the attitudes they hold about themselves.

Unfortunately, a high percentage of students enter our schools today from deprived and impoverished home conditions. Others carry the emotional scars of family strife and divorce. They lack feelings of significance, belonging, personal worth, or competence. It is, therefore, no wonder that they fail to enter into the learning process with confidence and perseverance. To enable children to achieve their full potential every teacher needs to address the issue of self-esteem and strive to establish the conditions that enhance those attitudes conducive to learning. I am convinced that by creating climates in our schools and classrooms that foster self-esteem we can significantly improve the level of functioning of our students.

In *Esteem Builders* Michele Borba has identified those key conditions and has provided teachers with the resources and ideas that build self-esteem. As an author, she demonstrates why she is considered one of the top authorities on self-esteem in the United States. *Esteem Builders* is well grounded in research and is full of creative and innovative ideas for applying this research. The wealth of information presented enables the classroom teacher to understand the concepts underlying self-esteem so that the activities can be prescribed on an individual or group basis, according to defined needs. It can also be used either as a complete program or as an integrated part of the regular curriculum.

Educators wishing to build self-esteem in their classroom or school will find *Esteem Builders* to be a valuable resource and an effective guide.

Preface

ESTEEM BUILDERS is about a topic of vital importance for today's classrooms: how to increase the self-esteem of our students. Self-esteem, which is a key factor in improving student behavior and academic achievement, can no longer be ignored in education. Many educators recognize the urgency in these findings, but have been curtailed in their efforts to implement a program due to lack of effective self-esteem curricula. This book is designed to remedy this dilemma.

ESTEEM BUILDERS is the culmination of seventeen years of research and exploration in the area of self-esteem. Each year has brought new reflection and refinement until this work finally evolved.

The research really started in a classroom at Congress Spring School in Saratoga, California, while I was a special education teacher. Instead of teaching, however, I found myself more often being caught up in two quite different kinds of roles: either behavior management technician or counselor—or both. If I wasn't interrupting my lesson plans to intervene in a behavior dispute, I was wearing the hat of "amateur counselor" and trying to encourage students that they could indeed do the activity if they'd just give it a try.

While brewing over my dilemma in the faculty room one afternoon, I came upon an article in an educational journal that described the correlation between how students feel about themselves (their self-esteem), their academic performance and their behavior. I can still hear myself saying, "Aha, that's it!" From that moment on, my goal was to develop research-based activities and strategies that could be used to build self-esteem in a school or classroom. The most successful of these were field-tested and published in two volumes, co-authored with my husband, Dr. Craig Borba.[1] The books are still used by educators worldwide and formed the basis of an educator seminar on building student self-esteem that I've conducted nationally and throughout Canada for the past six years.

ESTEEM BUILDERS really was formed by the invaluable feedback offered by teachers at these seminars. Although the activities were widely accepted and praised, more and more educators voiced the need for a framework in which to use the strategies. "Where do I start?" was a commonly voiced concern, as was the need to have a system by which to identify students with possible low self-esteem.

These concerns were certainly legitimate. If self-esteem is to become a viable component used in classrooms on an everyday basis, it must consist of elements that are found in any other "serious" subject area. Therefore, it should consist of a research-based curriculum, daily lessons from a sequential plan, a developmental framework from which to teach, grade level activities categorized by subject area, a plentiful supply of easy-to-use activities and, finally, an evaluation tool to determine growth. Obviously much reflection, research and reorganization went into developing such a framework; but it certainly would never have been achieved without the constant support and feedback from educators across the country.

---

1. Borba, Michele and Craig. *Self-Esteem: A Classroom Affair; 101 Ways to Help Students Like Themselves* (San Francisco: Harper & Row, 1981), Vol. 1.
    _____. *Self-Esteem: A Classroom Affair; More Ways to Help Students Like Themselves* (San Francisco: Harper & Row, 1983), Vol. 2.

A major source of inspiration for the building blocks in ESTEEM BUILDERS must go to my friend and colleague, Robert Reasoner. His work, *Building Self-Esteem*,[2] identifies five components that individuals with high self-esteem appear to possess. These include the feelings of security, identity, belonging, purpose and competence. All my research concurred with Reasoner's findings; therefore, I have used his components as the basis for my model, which comprises Security, Selfhood, Affiliation, Mission and Competence. Bob's contributions both to the field of self-esteem and to me are enormous.

Once the activities and framework for ESTEEM BUILDERS were designed, classroom effectiveness had to be proved. All the strategies have been field-tested for six years and used in over 60,000 classrooms covering with a wide range of student abilities. To list the hundreds of teachers and counselors who used the activities would be too lengthy; these activities have been used in preschools through middle schools (as well as alternative high school programs), in public and private settings, and in regular classrooms as well as special education and gifted programs. The evidence points to the ease with which they can be incorporated into classroom settings.

At present too many students exist in the shadows. Their potential and capabilities will never shine because they are clouded by self-doubt or by lack of self-worth, which affects all aspects of their being. Such self-defeating attitudes certainly are not left at home or in the hallway but quickly find themselves inside the classroom door, and pollution of learning occurs. Low self-esteem has been cited over and over again as a key factor in behavior problems as well as poor academic performance. For example, let's consider the first grade students of fall 1988 who will graduate in the year 2000. If the current trend continues, according to the National Dropout Prevention Center only 70 percent of these students will graduate from high school.[3]

We now know, however, that the forecast need not be so gloomy—that the sunlight can shine through. This is what ESTEEM BUILDERS is about: to provide a curriculum that raises the self-esteem of our students and thereby increases the likelihood of success and happiness both inside and outside the schools walls, which in turn positively affects our students' future endeavors.

The real success of the program, though, rests on YOU. As an educator you are in an incredible position of being able to invite students to see themselves as capable human beings. You have the power to turn the tide of your students' lives by helping them reach their potential as learners. Keep in mind a key principle: self-esteem can be changed both positively and negatively. Your role as an esteem builder is critical in making this distinction. Henry Adams perhaps best summarized the immense power and significance you hold with students when he said:

"A teacher affects eternity; he can never tell where his influence stops."

Don't ever stop. Just keep influencing. What a difference you'll make!

Michele Borba
Palm Springs, California
March 1989

---

2. Robert W. Reasoner. *Building Self-Esteem: A Comprehensive Program* (Palo Alto, CA: Consulting Psychologists Press, 1982).
3. *National Dropout Prevention Newsletter*, Vol. 1, No. 2, Fall 1988.

An Outline of ESTEEM BUILDERS

ESTEEM BUILDERS is a complete curriculum for enhancing student self-esteem and is divided into the following sections:

INTRODUCTION _____
Laying the groundwork; the background and research-based data as to why esteem building is essential for today's students.

COMPONENTS OF SELF-ESTEEM _____
An explanation of the five building blocks of self-esteem.

ESTEEM BUILDER'S GUIDE _____
A detailed plan of daily, weekly, monthly and yearly activities that are grade level specified and cross-referenced to all major curriculum areas.

SECURITY _____
Activities and strategies to build the student's feelings of trust, safety and security.

SELFHOOD _____
Activities and strategies to build the student's feelings of individuality and acquisition of self-knowledge.

AFFILIATION _____
Activities and strategies to increase the student's feelings of belonging as well as enhance social skills.

MISSION _____
Activities and strategies to help the student gain a sense of purpose and aim in his/her life. Covers goal-setting, measuring past performance and decision-making skills.

COMPETENCE _____
Activities and strategies to help the student recognize successes and internalize feelings of accomplishment.

CONCEPT CIRCLES _____
Activities in which students work as cooperative teams to build each of the five feelings within themselves and others. These may be done in large groups, small teams or pairs. Of use especially for counselors and psychologists, but also for educators favoring team- or group work.

JOURNAL WRITING _____
Daily language development assignments and topics. Covers all the five components and is especially compatible with Concept Circle work.

SCHOOL-WIDE ESTEEM BUILDERS _____
Activities done on a school-wide basis to increase each of the five self-esteem components. Presents spirit and climate energizers as well as activities for principals.

To facilitate application, each activity in ESTEEM BUILDERS has been coded as to grade level appropriateness and major curriculum areas.

In addition, a companion volume to ESTEEM BUILDERS is available. Titled HOME ESTEEM BUILDERS, it overviews parent/school cooperation and how this can be so effective in enhancing a student's self-esteem. There are 40 activities for students to do at home with their parents.

The Building Blocks of Self-Esteem

The following building blocks, based on the five feelings found in students with high self-esteem, are the sequential esteem-building steps incorporated in the curriculum.

BUILDING BLOCK
(Acquired Feeling)

STEPS FOR ESTEEM BUILDER
(Adult Functions)

SECURITY
A feeling of strong assuredness. Involves feeling comfortable and safe; knowing what is expected; being able to depend on individuals and situations; and comprehending rules and limits.

1. Build a trusting relationship.
2. Set reasonable limits and rules that are consistently enforced.
3. Create a positive and caring environment.

SELFHOOD
A feeling of individuality. Acquiring self-knowledge, which includes an accurate and realistic self-description in terms of roles, attributes and physical characteristics.

1. Reinforce more accurate self-descriptions.
2. Provide opportunities to discover major sources of influence on the self.
3. Build an awareness of unique qualities.
4. Enhance ability to identify and express emotions and attitudes.

AFFILIATION
A feeling of belonging, acceptance or relatedness, particularly in relationships that are considered important. Feeling approved of, appreciated and respected by others.

1. Promote inclusion and acceptance within the group.
2. Provide opportunities to discover interests, capabilities and backgrounds of others.
3. Increase awareness of and skills in friendship making.
4. Encourage peer approval and support.

MISSION
A feeling of purpose and motivation in life. Self-empowerment through setting realistic and achievable goals and being willing to take responsibility for the consequences of one's decisions.

1. Enhance ability to make decisions, seek alternatives and identify consequences.
2. Aid in charting present and past academic and behavioral performances.
3. Teach the steps to successful goal-setting.

COMPETENCE
A feeling of success and accomplishment in things regarded as important or valuable. Aware of strengths and able to accept weaknesses.

1. Provide opportunities to increase awareness of individual competencies and strengths.
2. Teach how to record and evaluate progress.
3. Provide feedback on how to accept weaknesses and profit from mistakes.
4. Teach the importance of self-praise for accomplishments.

Introduction

Laying the Groundwork for High Self-Esteem

"I regard self-esteem as the single most powerful force in our existence...the way we feel about ourselves affects virtually every aspect of our existence: work, love, sex, interpersonal relationships of every kind."
—DR. NATHANIEL BRANDEN

The Psychology of Self-Esteem

As September draws around each year it would be difficult to find an educator who has not thought twice about the possible makeup of the "infamous" class list. And, if pressed, these same educators would admit to having a secret desire for the list to be filled with "winners." These are the students whose track record alone puts them in the "winner" category and gives them high visibility even before they arrive in the classroom. They are motivated and eager, responsive to ideas and suggestions. Above all, they are students who succeed in learning. Judging by the comments in faculty rooms, such students are far fewer than could possibly fill the lists. Typical teacher statements are: "Students just aren't like they used to be," "More of my time is spend disciplining than teaching," "They're so unmotivated lately!" and "How can I make any difference when the home is the way it is?" Many students are far from the ones we dreamed about.

The student of the '80s and '90s is a unique educational challenge, because the economic and social factors of today contribute to a "different student." Observe a few statistics depicting contemporary American youth:

- *Broken homes.* Three in five born today will live with a single parent by age 18.

- *Child care.* Two out of four children aged 13 and under live with parents who both work.

- *Drugs.* One student in six by ninth grade has tried marijuana, and one in three alcohol.

- *Sex.* The percentage of girls under 15 who have had sex has tripled in two decades. Of every 100 children born today, 13 will be born to teen-age mothers and 20 will be born out of wedlock.[1]

- *Poverty.* The percentage of children living in poverty in the United States has increased from one in seven 20 years ago to one in five today.[2]

- *Dropouts.* Of every three students who start school only two will complete high school. The National Dropout Prevention Fund reports that every day about 3,500 students quit school. This means at the present time 28 percent of students fail to complete high school.[3]

---

1. *Children's Defense Fund Fact Book 1988.*
2. *A Nation At Risk*, National Commission on Excellence in Education, April 1983, p. 8.
3. National Dropout Prevention Fund, 1988.

- *Performance.* Average achievement of high school students on most standardized tests is now lower than 26 years ago when the Sputnik was launched. International comparisons of student achievement, completed 10 years ago, reveal that on 19 academic tests American students were never first or second and, in comparison with other industrialized nations, were last seven times.[4]

- *Suicide.* Between 1950 and 1984 the rate of suicide for individuals between 15 and 24 years of age, the second leading cause of death in this age group, rose by nearly 178 percent. Suicide now constitutes the second leading cause of deaths among all people of this age group. The rate for youths under 15 has tripled since 1980.[5]

Taking the above into account, the American educational system can be summed up as follows:

- a decline in national test scores;
- an increase in student drug and alcohol dependency;
- an increase in student dropouts and absenteeism;
- an increase in violence and vandalism in the schools;
- an increase in student behavior problems;
- an increase in juvenile crime both on and off campus;
- an increase in the numbers of qualified teachers choosing to leave the field.

A Student-Centered Approach

Despite the fact that more money has been allocated to education than at any other time in history, the results have been less than satisfying. Some critical element, therefore, is missing from the endless lists of goals, objectives, checklists, test scores and progress charts...something that just may hold the greatest educational promise. That something is *the student.*

Many educators now recognize that a student's attitude toward learning can no longer be separated from the process. A powerful educational force is a thorough repertoire of knowledge and skills combined with the feeling, *I am a capable student.*

Too many students arrive at the school doors void of the feelings needed to build self-esteem—such as security, selfhood, affiliation, mission and competence. In all too many cases the absence of these crucial self-esteem builders accelerates a downward spiral of low self-worth. And the student with poor self-esteem becomes another tragic social statistic. The good news, however, is that this cycle need not continue its downward plunge because:

- self-esteem can be changed, regardless of age;
- the year spent with you in the classroom can provide enough security to make the difference for the student from an abusive home;
- self-esteem is learned; therefore, you can teach it.

By creating environments that engender security and develop strength, educators can help students acquire the feelings needed to build self-esteem. ESTEEM BUILDERS provides activities, suggestions, contracts, centers, activity sheets in a sequential, research-based process to help students acquire greater self-esteem.

---

4. "Children Under Stress," *U.S. News and World Report*, Vol. 101, No. 17, Washington, D.C., pp. 58–64.
5. International Center for Health Statistics, 1986.

1

The Components of Self-Esteem: Looking at the Whole Picture

1

The Components of Self-Esteem:
Looking at the Whole Picture

*Building self-esteem in children can be viewed
as a sequential, step-by-step process.*
—ROBERT REASONER

As a child grows and has more experiences, his/her inner picture of self expands. This inner picture comprises all the descriptions an individual attaches to himself/herself and is called *self-concept*. All of the five components of the self—Security, Selfhood, Affiliation, Mission and Competence—serve to mold the student's inner portrait, which is subjective and therefore not necessarily the same as how another perceives him/her.

How the student experiences each component is crucial, because each forms the basis for self-evaluation—which can be either positive or negative. This process of evaluating or judging inner self-descriptions is called *self-esteem*. It basically means how a person feels about him- or herself from within. *Esteem builders* should strive to do the following:

1. Help the student form an accurate inner picture of the self, because an individual with low self-esteem generally carries an inaccurate inner picture. Esteem builders need to provide opportunities—and give concrete examples—that will illuminate more realistic descriptions of the self in each of the five components.

2. Provide positive, successful, achievable experiences within each of the five components of

self-esteem, particularly in areas where students struggle.

BECOMING A SIGNIFICANT OTHER

A very large determiner of students' self-esteem is the external forces in their lives. Repeated patterns or experiences (positive or negative) help mold self-opinions. Whether or not another individual can change a student's current self-esteem depends on how significant the individual is to the student. By becoming a "significant other," or esteem builder, an educator plays a critical role in self-esteem enhancement.

An esteem builder is defined as someone who:

- has the ability to change a student's self-opinion for the better;

- has an enormous influence on a student's self-esteem;

- must be considered worthy, important or significant to the student in order to be effective.

It is important to win a student's trust and respect. Therefore, the esteem builder's attitude should invite and nurture positive self-enhancement in the students. Any individual who desires to help another improve his/her self-image should possess these qualities:

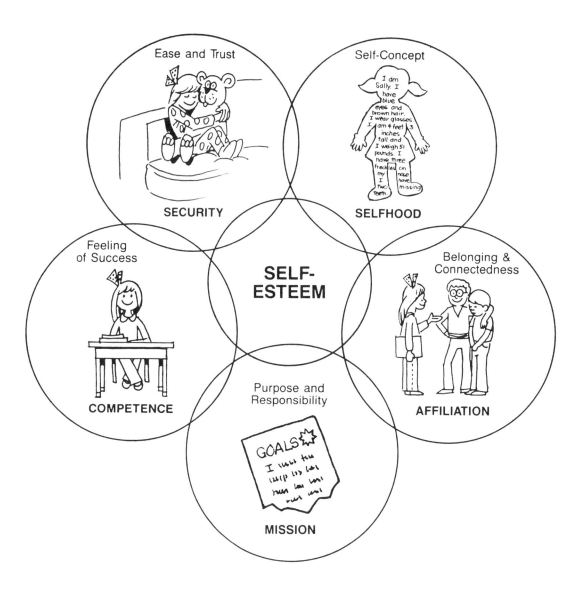

- a sincere interest and concern for the student;

- a personal rapport such that the student feels significant to the esteem builder;

- a genuine recognition of the positive qualities of each individual;

- a real belief that the student's self-image can change and the ability to communicate that to him/her with confidence;

- a willingness to make the effort and take the time to help individuals feel better about themselves;

- the willingness to "open up" to students and share genuine personal qualities/experiences with them;

- the desire to build a trusting relationship and be someone who is both reliable and trustworthy;

- the willingness to review one's own self-picture periodically, being aware that the esteem builder's role model is vital to esteem building.

THE ESTEEM-BUILDING ENVIRONMENT

The esteem builder as a significant other must create an environment conducive to positive self-esteem building. Only when that exists will specific self-esteem activities be effective. Even the most expensively packaged kit with its many alternatives for self-esteem raising will be rendered useless by an improper environment.

> Environments that promote positive self-esteem usually can be described with these words:
> caring   nonthreatening   accepting
> supportive   trusting   encouraging
> secure   comfortable   inviting
> warm   nonjudgmental   positive

Coopersmith's Findings

Stanley Coopersmith, a child psychologist at the University of California at Davis, devoted his life's work to the study of self-image. His book, *The Antecedents of Self-Esteem*,[1] has become a landmark in this area. One of Coopersmith's research goals was to try and ascertain what family conditions help to promote high self-esteem. His research team studied over 1700 boys and their families and found that these boys' self attitudes were formed either by how their parents or significant others saw them or by how they thought they were seen by parents and/or significant others. Coopersmith's study also revealed three critical elements common to the homes of those individuals with high self-esteem, namely:

1. They came from backgrounds where they experienced the kind of love that expresses respect, concern and acceptance. As children they were accepted for their strengths and capacities as well as for their limitations and weaknesses. It was clearly "love with no strings attached."

2. Their parents were significantly less permissive than were parents of children with lower self-esteem. Within the household there were clearly defined limits, standards and expectations and, as a result, children felt secure.

3. The families functioned with a high degree of democracy. The children were encouraged to present their own ideas and opinions for discussion (even ones that deviated from those of their parents).

Consequently, environments that are most effective in enhancing self-esteem and self-image are those in which children or students:

• perceive a sense of warmth and love;
• are offered a degree of security that allows them to grow and to try new things without an overriding concern about failure;

• are respected as individuals;
• are encouraged to have ideas and opinions;
• recognize that there are clear and definite limits within the environment;
• are given rules and standards that are reasonably and consistently enforced;
• have a chance to succeed at their own levels;
• are accepted "with no strings attached."

THE FIVE COMPONENTS

The five components of self-esteem (Security, Selfhood, Affiliation, Mission and Competence) are derived from Robert Reasoner's exhaustive review of self-theory.[2] These are the basis for the process of building self-esteem in this book. Each component is determined an esteem builder based on the following criteria.

> The component must be:
> • a general characteristic felt by individuals with high self-esteem;
> • well substantiated as a major element of self-esteem in major self-esteem research;
> • one that an esteem builder could enhance using well-defined tasks and roles.

Coopersmith notes that positive self-esteem can be acquired with less than all five of the feelings intact; although, in general, the higher the number of feelings possessed, the higher the overall self-esteem. To begin the process, it is important to note the following:

1. Security is the prerequisite to the other components; therefore it should be the first building block unless it is already well established in the individual. Selfhood, Affiliation, Mission and Competence follow sequentially. Sometimes, however, you will need to bring in some activities from another component to enhance the one you're working on: For example, several affiliation activities where students get to know each other are also ideal for establishing security in the classroom. Be flexible, and exercise your own judgment.

1. Coopersmith, Stanley. *The Antecedents of Self-Esteem* (San Francisco: W.H. Freeman, 1967).

2. Reasoner, Robert. *Building Self-Esteem: A Comprehensive Program* (Palo Alto, CA: Consulting Psychologists Press, 1982).

2. Change takes place slowly...don't expect dramatic results overnight. Remember, students have had many years to form their self-perceptions. Be patient.

3. Consistency is critical. The esteem builder must be willing to make a conscious effort each day to help the student develop more positive feelings about him-/herself.

4. The esteem builder's attitude and the environment play significant roles in helping a student form a more positive self-picture.

ESTEEM COMPONENT CHARACTERISTICS

Security
(abbreviated throughout as S)

A student with a high level of security conveys a strong sense of assuredness and can handle change or spontaneity without undue discomfort. This individual feels safe, knowing there are people he/she can count on.

In a classroom setting, students generally feel secure if they can trust and depend on the teacher and when they comprehend the rules and limits expected in the situation.

Students with successful security experiences might make comments like these:

The rules in my school are necessary and fair.

I can count on my teacher.

Mrs. Bilmore is my principal. She always listens to me.

I like my classroom. I always feel good when I'm there.

On the other hand, students who experience insecurity might say:

I can't trust Mrs. Thomas.

I'd never write any secret thoughts in my journal. My teacher would tell.

I never know what they want out of me. Sometimes they're strict and sometimes they're easy.

Psychologists Erik Erikson and Abraham Maslow both emphasize how important a sense of security is in creating the foundation for subsequent healthy emotional development. Students must first feel secure in their setting, and they must be able to trust the adult who is attempting to enhance their self-esteem. Only then can the esteem builder begin the process of building self-esteem.

Selfhood
(abbreviated throughout as SH)

When a good sense of self-knowledge is obtained, the student has an accurate and realistic description of his/her roles and attributes. This student has a strong sense of individuality, and feels adequate and worthy of praise. He/she will produce statements like these:

Everyone says I look nice in my new outfit.

I am a lot of things...a boy, a soccer player, a son, a grandson, a nephew, an artist and a brother.

I'm five feet tall with brown hair, freckles and a nice smile. I have a lot of good ideas and like to help other people.

I'm not as good-looking as a movie star, but when I smile I know I'm beautiful.

On the other hand, a student with a weak sense of selfhood might say:

I don't want to take my coat off; I'm too ugly.

I don't want to look in the mirror. There's nothing good to look at.

I don't care what anybody else says, I've had nothing but bad things ever happen to me.

I know that people don't think much of me.

An esteem builder who helps students recognize their unique qualities and special contributions will be strengthening each one's sense of self.

Affiliation
(abbreviated throughout as A)

When a student is in relationship to another—be it family members, classmates, peers or friends/acquaintances—there is potential for affiliation or belonging. A student who feels good about his/her social experiences generally feels connected to others and accepted.

This individual not only seeks out others but is able to maintain friendships. He/she is able to cooperate and share as well as show compassion toward others. This student is likely to make the following statements:

Can Johnny come over to play?

I like being with my family.

I sure have a lot of good friends.

Most people like me.

School is a fun place to be; all my friends are here.

I felt sad for Jane when she fell down and broke her arm.

It's OK with me if you share my pens and pencils.

On the other hand, a student who feels a low sense of affiliation might say:

Why do I have to go to school? Nobody likes me.

There's never anyone to play with; I'm always left out.

I don't want to go with you on a vacation. Everybody always fights.

Do I have to talk to her? She won't like me anyway.

I don't want to share with Johnny; I never win.

Friends have enormous bearing on a student's feelings about who he/she is. Through friendships, students can enter into an interaction of mutual support. They can share problems, joys and experiences with others of the same age. They can also learn to relate to others as equals. As with the other components of self-esteem, gaining a sense of affiliation requires many positive successes. Esteem builders can do much in their environments to help provide opportunities for students to experience successful peer interactions, which are critical for positive self-esteem.

Mission
(abbreviated throughout as M)

A student with a strong sense of mission is one who not only sets realistic and achievable goals, but is also able to follow through on plans. This student takes initiative, is responsible for his/her actions, seeks alternatives to problems, and evaluates him-/herself according to past performance. Such a motivated individual might make remarks such as:

Yesterday I got 15 spelling words right. Tomorrow I'm going to try for 17.

I may not be good at soccer right now, but I know what I can do to change it.

This year I am going to learn how to do two more tricks on my skateboard.

I know that if I spend 10 minutes a day cleaning my room, I can keep it tidy.

On the other hand, a student who lacks a sense of mission and direction might say:

Life is so bad, but there's nothing I can do about it.

I don't have any control over my life, so why should I bother?

Yesterday I got 5 spelling words right. Tomorrow I'm going to try for 25.

Students who set realistic goals generally achieve them. This in turn increases their motivation and willingness to take risks. But before students can gain a thorough sense of competence, they must first be aware of what it is they wish to achieve and go through the process of getting there. Therefore, it is essential that students experience and complete this level before going on to the next component.

Competence
(abbreviated throughout as C)

The experience of success usually results in an individual feeling capable and, therefore, willing to take risks as well as share opinions and ideas. However, the success must come from experiences that the individual sees as valuable and important to him/her.

An individual who feels competent is not only aware of his/her strengths but is also able to accept his/her weaknesses. Failure is generally not an issue; in fact, these students perceive mistakes as valuable learning tools. A competent student is likely to make the following remarks:

I am good at a lot of things, although I sometimes put things off to the last minute.

I learn fast.

Sure, I'll try it.

When I messed up that time, I really discovered what I needed to know.

However, students who experience frequent failures, or are not brought to recognition of their success, produce these kinds of statements:

Why can't I learn like everyone else?

I'm not going to try that...I'll just goof up again.

I can't do anything right!

How do I know what my strengths are?

I don't like to share in class, I feel so dumb.

These students obviously feel incapable; therefore, they are unwilling to try, and give up quickly when the first sign of difficulty emerges. Feeling successful is critical to self-esteem and positive behavior.

When this final feeling of self-esteem is achieved, the student is self-empowered. The individual is now capable of internally controlling him-/herself as well as internally acknowledging successes.

ORIGIN OF THE COMPONENTS

The following theories were particularly helpful in determining the components necessary for enhancing self-esteem:

Clemes, Harris, and Bean, Reynold. "Connectedness, Uniqueness, Power, and Models." *Self-Esteem: The Key to Your Child's Well-Being* (New York: Kensington, 1981).

Felker, Donald. "Belonging, Competence, and Worth." *Building Positive Self-Concepts* (Minneapolis: Burgess, 1974). (Felker based "Belonging, Competence, and Worth" on the theories of Erikson, 1963; Diggory, 1966; and Jersild, 1963, respectively.)

Coopersmith, Stanley. "Power, Significance, Virtue, and Competence." *The Antecedents of Self-Esteem* (San Francisco: W.H. Freeman and Co., 1967).

Reasoner, Robert. "Security, Identity, Belonging, Purpose, and Competence." *Building Self-Esteem: A Comprehensive Program* (Palo Alto: Consulting Psychologists Press, 1982).

Samuels, Shirley. "Body Image, Social Self, Cognitive Self, and Self-Esteem." *Enhancing Self-Concept in Early Childhood* (New York: Human Sciences Press, 1977).

Erikson, Erik. *Identity, Youth and Crisis* (New York: Norton, 1968).

Maslow, Abraham. *Toward a Psychology of Being* (New York: Van Nostrand Reinhold, 1968).

(The work of both Erikson and Maslow has provided important material for self-esteem theory. Both psychologists emphasize security [trust and safety] as the foundation for healthy emotional development.)

2

The Esteem
Builder's Guide:
How to Use
This Curriculum

- The Implementation
- The Esteem Builder's Attitude
- Esteem Builder Planning
- Esteem Builder Planner—
  A 40-Week Lesson Plan

2

The Esteem Builder's Guide: How to Use This Curriculum

Education is helping the child realize his potentialities.
—ERICH FROMM

ESTEEM BUILDERS provides a collection of ideas, activities, centers and contracts to help enhance students' self-esteem. The activities can and should be used to fit your needs as well as those of your students. Each activity is based on substantiated research and has been classroom-tested for use as an assignment or free-choice activity. The book is specifically designed for students of many ages in a wide variety of situations and settings that include:

* the entire school/district;
* counseling groups;
* individual esteem building for special students;
* the entire class;
* home esteem building (see HOME ESTEEM BUILDERS companion booklet).

Abbreviations. The key components of Esteem Building are abbreviated on the planning calendar, activity sheets and in lists throughout the book.

S = Security
SH = Selfhood
A = Affiliation
M = Mission
C = Competence
CC = Concept Circles

J = Journal Writing
SW = School-wide

Ages. The activities in this book have been developed for students from grades K through 8. As this encompasses a wide age-span, wherever possible activities are marked with more specific grade level suitability. Some activities are adaptable for older students who require more sophisticated and complex procedures. Or, they can be scaled down for younger, nonreading/writing students by using pictorial answers and/or writing down their responses for them. Taping their responses is another option.

For ease of use, each chapter on the self-esteem components has an accompanying activity list with grade level suitability and subject areas covered. Choose those most suitable for your situation.

Props. Many activities call for props as activity motivators. Often these are tailored for younger students. Simply eliminate them for the older grades.

Materials. Make substitutes according to availability and your grade level.

Team Builders. Many teachers find it beneficial to permanently place their students in groups of five or six students. Since one of the prime purposes of grouping is to build a sense of affiliation for its participants, it is important that members feel comfortable with each other.

A suggestion from Jeanne Gibbs in her *Tribes* program[1] is to ask each student to print the names of six other classmates he/she would like to have on the team. Collect the cards and then begin to balance each team using the following guidelines from Slavin's research on cooperative learning:[2]

1. Balance the number of boys and girls in each group.
2. Assign a leader/achiever type to each group.
3. Distribute low self-esteem students among the groups, which could include those who are behaviorally disruptive, socially isolated and excessively shy.

Each team should have between four and six students, each of which has at least one chosen friend in the group. For a more detailed description of team activities, see Concept Circles, Chapter 8. Once teams have been formed, consider using them for the following:

Esteem activities. Any of the activities in ESTEEM BUILDERS can be done as Team Builders. By remaining in the same group, students are more likely to gain a sense of affiliation as they find out about the strengths, interests and characteristics of one another.

Assignments. One of the first team activities is for team members to find out the phone number of each of the teammates. If a student is absent, he/she may call other team members for the assignments. (Kindergarten may be too young to participate in this.)

Questions. Many educators using Team Builders have a class rule: If you have a question, you must first ask every member of your team before you ask the teacher. This rule has cut down on the amount of questions directed to teachers and put more responsibility on the students.

Affirmations. As teams gain a sense of affiliation they will also begin to care about each member.

This is the time to take advantage of the group cohesiveness and use it toward esteem building. Encourage team members to give recognition to deserving teammates, make cards to recognize special occasions (moving, get well, congratulations, thank you's, etc.) and express positive, supportive statements to one another.

THE IMPLEMENTATION

Evaluation. Many of the esteem-builder activities can also serve as evaluations of progress within the particular self-esteem component. As you begin a component, students complete one of the activity sheets suitable for their grade level and date it. The sheet should then be kept at school. On the back of it you may write any observation notes about how they completed it ("Very hesitant," "Whizzed through quickly and confidently"). These can augment the *Student Self-Esteem Assessment* (B-SET) charts, see Appendix II.

All contracts, observation sheets and selected activity sheets should go in a permanent manila folder that you have provided. Near the end of the component, students complete an activity sheet identical to the first one. If growth has occurred, an obvious difference between the first and last sheet will be noted.

Self-Esteem Observation. Use the *Self-Esteem Prescriptive Plan* form in Appendix II as your record of student progress. Duplicate a form for each student and set up your own "Self-Esteem Folder." As you form observations, based on each of the five components of self-esteem, write them on the student's form. You may make your assessment based on observations of student behavior, parent conferences, student journal entries, performance on an activity sheet or student/teacher dialogue. (These forms should be confidential; they are for your use, not the student's.)

Checklist of Educator Behaviors. ESTEEM BUILDERS includes a checklist of "esteem-building behavior" for each component. This can be found in the beginning material of Chapters 3-7 and 10. You may either fill out each form individually or make it a staff activity. Consider filling out each checklist two or more times a year to evaluate your esteem enhancing progress.

1. Gibbs, Jeanne. *Tribes: A Process for Social Development and Cooperative Learning* (Santa Rosa, CA: Center Source Publications, 1987).
2. Slavin, Robert. *Cooperative Learning: Student Teams* (Washington, D.C.: National Education Association, 1982).

Essential Materials. In most cases, the activities in ESTEEM BUILDERS require the use of commonly used materials that are available in most classrooms. Where less readily available materials are needed, they are listed and described near the beginning of the activity. For your convenience you may wish to have an ample supply in your classroom of the following materials:

- pencils
- crayons
- marking pens
- paints
- paint brushes
- scissors
- paste or glue
- writing paper
- drawing paper
- construction paper
- decorating items: rickrack, lace, yarn, buttons, macaroni, seeds, glitter, assorted stickers, stamp pads and stamps, sequins
- material, felt and construction paper scraps
- catalogs, magazines and calendar pictures

Many teachers choose to set up a permanent activity center for esteem building in which students can find these supplies and where they can work on their projects. Whenever these items are hard to find, ask the parents. They are often willing to provide additional supplies for activity centers. Duplicate a letter with a checklist of needed items and send it home with each student.

Awards for Contests. Many activities in ESTEEM BUILDERS suggest giving awards for recognition. There are so many possibilities; however, often the simplest ones are best. Begin by considering what you already have available. Also enlist the support of local businesses and parents. They can be a tremendous source of ideas and materials. Here are some suggestions:

School Spirit Ideas

Consider imprinting with your school name and mascot.

- pencils, pens
- shoelaces
- bookmarks
- bumper stickers
- backpacks
- T-shirts
- book covers
- notebooks/folders
- rulers
- ribbons
- posters
- banners
- awards/certificates
- calendars
- hats, visors
- scrapbooks
- year books
- erasers
- stickers

Special Events/Situations

- pass/free time
- extra recess
- rented VCR movie to view
- name in principal's newsletter
- name on bulletin board
- name in newspaper ad
- lunch with staff member
- free ice cream

Special Purchases

- badge maker
- button maker
- computer certificate maker

Trinkets

May be purchased in large quantity.

- pencils
- erasers
- bracelets
- small games
- whistles
- magic tricks
- small cars
- small vehicles
- stickers
- crayons
- colored pens
- coloring books
- sticker books

Books

- quality comic books
- reading books
- coloring books
- sticker books
- drawing paper (stapled)
- blank journal books

Rummage Sale Items

Left-over items.

- toys
- stuffed animals
- vehicles
- books
- puzzles
- sports equipment

Local Businesses

Items supplied free of charge.

- food certificates/coupons
- poster certificates
- tape/record certificates
- book certificates
- toy certificates
- movie tickets
- amusement park tickets
- sports event tickets

ACTIVITIES AWARDS

The following reinforce student achievement, performance and behavior:

Spirit Awards

Recognize spirit, positivism or behavior.

C24 Newsflash/Proud Gram
C31 Now Hear This!
C34 Design an Award
C35 Badges
C39 Positive Wristbands
C40 Pride Center Awards
S2 From Me to You
S3 I Just Wanted You To Know
S4 Special Recognition
S5 I Like Gram
S26 Super Sparkle Gram
S32 Sparkle Compliments
S33 Sparkle Cover
S34 A Special Message to You
S35 Add a Compliment
SW1 Spirit Tickets
SW2 Spirit Award
SW4 Positive Performance Award
SW5 Gotcha Tickets
SW6 Sparkle Gram
SW7 Good Guy Award
SW8 Pass the Buck
SW14 Good News Report
SW22 Principal's Birthday Card
SW29 Positive Comments Contest

Achievement Awards

Recognize achievement, effort or performance.

C4/5 Attention!/Strength Awards
C24 Newsflash/Proud Gram
C31 Now Hear This!
C33 Pat-on-the-Back Handprints
C37 Blue Ribbon Award
C39 Positive Wristbands
C40 Pride Center Awards
S2 From Me to You
S3 I Just Wanted You To Know
S4 Special Recognition
S5 I Like Gram
S26 Super Sparkle Gram
SW2 Spirit Award
SW5 Gotcha Tickets
SW14 Good News Report

SW15/16 Student of the Week
SW25 Koala-T Efforts
SW26/27 Book of Winners

THE ESTEEM BUILDER'S ATTITUDE

Because self-esteem is learned, those who possess it themselves will be more effective in conveying principles of self-esteem to students than those who don't. It is no coincidence that teachers with high self-esteem are more successful at producing students with high self-esteem. Individuals who have a strong self-attitude are able to bring out the best in others because they have such confidence in themselves. They can encourage and challenge students to set goals and reach their true potential because they've done so themselves. An esteem builder or educator with high self-esteem is a powerful role model for the students.

The staff member with low self-esteem, though, is quite a different picture. Too often such individuals use their own sense of insecurity and negative self-attitudes in their interactions with others. Such reverse modeling can have serious consequences on students. It is vital to recognize that it is just as easy to build self-esteem as it is to decrease self-esteem. Crucial to an esteem-building program, therefore, is to increase the esteem of staff members.

This involves the same framework that is entailed for enhancing student esteem. The administrator (or other staff member) who wishes to improve staff self-attitudes should begin by fostering the five components of esteem as described throughout the book.

ESTEEM-BUILDING GROUPS

Trying to enhance self-esteem all on your own is a difficult (if not impossible) task. Good results in esteem building have generally come from a group setting. This thought holds true for esteem building: "Together we can do so much more." The following esteem-building groups have successfully been used in schools for self-esteem enhancement. You may wish to consider adopting some of the ideas for your classes.

Parent Aides

With the proper training, parent aides can be extremely beneficial to an esteem-building program.

You will find it will give you extra time to give personal support to children who need your full attention, as well as to do those extra projects you thought you would never get finished. Parent aides have also been found to be wonderful esteem builders! When asked to give special positive strokes to particular students, you may find wonderful results. These few hints may be helpful:

1. It is best to introduce the use of aides gradually to your classroom structure. Be selective: choose only those helpers with whom you feel comfortable. This will ensure a better esteem-enhancing environment. If you do not feel a particular parent will be just right, instead ask him/her to do clerical tasks at home—such as correcting papers or making new dittos.

2. Parent aides will, of course, be more effective for you if you clearly let them know what you want them to do. Meet with parents to explain your teaching methods and classroom arrangements in detail. Acquaint them with where all the supplies are kept. Let them know your standards and rules.

3. Explain in depth your esteem-building program. Tell parent aides how vital their comments are toward the students. You could show them an ongoing list of builder-upper statements so that they are aware of the type of comments students and staff are saying to each other. Usually your own modeling of positive statements is enough. A teacher was overheard explaining her curriculum to parent aides with this message, which you may wish to pass on: "Please remember that you are very important and appreciated in this classroom. Maybe the most significant thing you can do while you are here is to say a positive statement to as many students as you can while you work with them. I can't always do that and it certainly makes a difference!"

Cross-Age Tutors

A program that has been effective in enhancing self-esteem is the use of cross-age tutors. These "helpers" are typically two to three grade levels ahead of the students whom they tutor. They can provide you with extra classroom assistance, helping to build the self-esteem of the students with whom they work. Many teachers who pair a cross-age tutor with a younger student report that the bond which develops between the two of them during each session is a delight to observe. Invariably the younger student looks up to his/her older friend with awe and respect. Oftentimes, this is the first occasion in which the tutor is the recipient of awe and respect. Consider the following guidelines before implementing the program in your class or school:

1. Organization is a must! Set aside a special place in the room as a "check-in" spot and provide any materials the tutor may need to use with a student—such as an evaluation form for the tutor to fill in and any specific notes you have for the student(s). Often you will not have enough time to tell the tutor everything you would like; therefore, write it down! This will make things much more official.

2. A training session before you begin is desirable. Ask the teacher whose students you plan to use as cross-age tutors to exchange classes with you for 20 minutes. Their teacher watches your class as you talk with the potential cross-age tutors, during which time you explain to them exactly what you expect of them. Inform them of your discipline policy and what they should do if a problem emerges. Most important, explain clearly your esteem-building approach. Show students where all the materials will be located and where they can check in for their assignments.

3. Consider an after-school training session. This would be an in-class discussion for tutors on ways to help students, specific behavioral goals you are working toward, and the location of new materials. It will give tutors a chance to ask questions about how to help their students.

4. The task of cross-age tutors is to reinforce skills that you have already presented. Teach the tutors game techniques to use as support during their tutoring sessions. The tutors will often create stimulating and motivating games of their own. Encourage them to devise activities that reinforce skills. However, ask the tutors to check out their ideas with you before using them in the tutoring sessions.

5. Arrange regular talks with the tutors. Remember to praise them, answer any questions they ask, discuss any problems they are having, and give them constructive suggestions for future sessions.

6. Finally, consider using cross-age tutors that have low self-esteem. So often, teachers send students with positive self-attitudes; yet numerous studies have pointed out how beneficial being a tutor can be toward self-enhancement. How wonderful for a sixth grader with a first-grade reading ability to be able to tutor a six-year-old with sound concepts! Not only will it be beneficial to the younger student, but it will also enhance the competence of the older student who begins to feel special and unique. In his studies at Stanford University on shyness, Philip Zimbardo reported that one of the best techniques for enhancing the esteem of the very shy child is to pair him/her with children much younger.[3] You may wish to consider Zimbardo's findings as you pair tutors with partners.

Foster Grandparents

Grandparents, as well as parents, can be effective aides. The former generally have more available time (particularly if they are retired) and can help as an aide on a more consistent and regular basis. Many teachers report that not only are grandparents patient and loving, in many cases they often develop a close bond with a student and become an important esteem builder.

Staff Adopt-a-Student

Do not overlook the possibilities of using staff members. Many schools have instituted an Adopt-a-Student program with great success. Each staff member is assigned one "high-risk" student (a student with low self-esteem who needs special attention and esteem building). The job of the staff member is to support that student in any way possible. Often this entails just taking the extra time to say hello. This extra personal contact can have miraculous results. Many high-risk students have completely turned around, apparently just because someone was there to care. This may be particularly beneficial on a large campus where students tend to feel more anonymous.

In addition to the Adopt-a-Student program, you may call upon special staff members to help individual students by providing special support or

expertise. The following support staff could be very helpful as mentors for students with low self-esteem.

Art Teacher. The artistically inclined student may be able to gain recognition and achieve a sense of competence for an artistic ability that might otherwise go unnoticed.

Librarian. A student with a high reading ability will benefit from library participation. Ask the student to read to lower-grade students.

Physical Education Teacher. Students who flounder on the playground will benefit from being taught a physical skill that will help them "fit in" better with their peers.

Principal. This is positive for any student who needs an extra pat on the back. Ask for a convenient time to send the student to the office (for being good!).

The possibilities are endless. If you tap into the available resources of each other, your esteem-building environment will be that much more effective.

Special Resources

"Peer Facilitator Quarterly," a newsletter that is available from Educational Media Corp., P.O. Box 21311, Minneapolis, MN 55421 (a book and film catalog is also available).

Student Specialist Packet, information on the Milwaukie, Oregon, peer helper program is available from N. Hersey, Ickes Junior High, Milwaukie, OR 97222.

Myrick, R.D., and Bowman, R.P. *Becoming a Friendly Helper: A Handbook for Student Facilitators* (1981). Available from Educational Media Corp., see above.

Children Helping Children: Teaching Students to Become Friendly Helpers. Manual and film; available from Educational Media Corp., see above.

Mastroianni, M., and Dinkmeyer, D. "Developing an Interest in Others Through Peer Facilitation." *Elementary School Guidance and Counseling*, Vol. 14, 1980, pp. 214–221.

ESTEEM BUILDER PLANNING

ESTEEM BUILDERS is purposely designed to be used in many ways, which include:

3. Zimbardo, Philip. *The Shy Child: A Parent's Guide to Overcoming and Preventing Shyness from Infancy to Adulthood* (New York: Doubleday, 1982).

- on a *daily* or *month-by-month* basis, particularly for high-risk students, or when the school or district has a major goal of improving student self-esteem;
- on a *weekly* or *biweekly* basis, where lessons are taught either by the homeroom teacher or an outside trained staff member;

- on a *periodic* basis, where these activities can serve as enrichment.

To simplify implementation, ESTEEM BUILDERS provides a series of prearranged day-to-day lessons. The *Esteem Builder Planner* is designed to focus on each self-esteem component for two months (or eight school weeks). The flow sequence is as follows:

Monthly Planner										
	Sep	Oct	Nov	Dec	Jan	Feb	Mar	Apr	May	Jun
Security	XXXXXXX									
Selfhood			XXXXXXXX							
Affiliation					XXXXXXX					
Mission							XXXXXXXX			
Competence									XXXXXXXX	

This is merely a suggested framework to simplify implementation. Please use your professional judgment and trust your intuition. Many students are particularly low in one component area and will need much more time focusing on that component. If you feel you need to move more slowly, *do so.* Always remember: the focus is on the *students,* not the lessons; your goal should be to meet their needs first.

Increasing self-esteem is a sequential process; therefore, it is critical that each foundation component be sufficiently developed before moving on. Some components, however, might work together for certain activities or in particular situations. For example, you might consider an activity from the Mission component to complement the work you're doing on Selfhood. And if you do Concept Circles early on in the year, an activity from the Affiliation section could be helpful in enhancing group awareness. But for the most part, the components are designed to follow on from each other in the order presented. Consider them a whole, a "power cycle," which students may pass through more than once. Each time they go through the cycle it is at a higher level—in the same way as a spiral.

If you plan to use ESTEEM BUILDERS on a day-to-day basis or a few times a week, the *Esteem Builder Planner* provides a model for implementing the activities into the daily curriculum. The charts are definitely *not* intended to tell you what your students should be doing at any given point. They are meant only as an idea source. A solid self-

esteem curriculum is by definition a highly individual plan related to the personal needs of students. By focusing on your unique classroom/school situation, you will develop a self-esteem plan appropriate for your students. Before you begin the planning, read the introduction to acquaint yourself with the five components and glance through the entire book for an overview. Then read through Chapter 3 on Security, which will prepare you for planning the first component.

You may find that many students are very low in the security component; still others may have had few opportunities to express their feelings or to have others actually listen to their opinions. There may even be students who are uncomfortable working in teams or small groups. All these elements will need to be addressed. Give clear guidelines right from the start and set rules that you are able to monitor consistently. Above all, students need to be reminded that *you are to be trusted.* This will take time to be developed and *should not be rushed.* That is why it is essential to take your time in the planning, allowing as much time as necessary to establish a firm sense of trust and safety for the students.

PLANNING SUGGESTIONS

Plan for one week at a time. Each day reconsider what you have planned for the next day. You may find that many students will need a much longer period of focus in each component area than is provided in the *Esteem Builder Planner*, so use your discretion. Younger students, or those with very low self-esteem, may need to have an adjusted plan, such as:

Monthly Planner for Younger or Low Self-Esteem Students									
	Sep	Oct	Nov	Dec	Jan	Feb	Mar	Apr	May	Jun
Security	XXXXXXXXXXXXX									
Selfhood		XXXXXXXXXXXXX								
Affiliation				XXXXXXXXXXXXXXXXXXX						
Mission									XXXX	
Competence									XXXXXXXXX	

For this type of student, introduce goal-setting strategies and problem-solving skills from the Mission component at a surface level only.

Older students, or students who already possess feelings of security and selfhood, will be able to move through the program much more quickly. Their plan will be very different:

Monthly Planner for Older or More Proficient Students									
	Sep	Oct	Nov	Dec	Jan	Feb	Mar	Apr	May	Jun
Security	XXXX									
Selfhood		XXXX								
Affiliation			XXXXXXXXXXXXXXX							
Mission					XXXXXXXXXXXXXXXXXXXX					
Competence							XXXXXXXXXXXXXXXXXXXXXX			

Individual Planning

For students with particularly low self-esteem you may need to plan on an individual basis. Use the *Self-Esteem Prescriptive Plan* form in Appendix II to accommodate specific self-esteem needs. Low self-esteem students may not be able to keep up with the structured classroom plan for esteem building.

Ongoing Activities

Several activities in ESTEEM BUILDERS are on-going, which means they can be used on a daily or weekly basis throughout the school year, regardless of the component in which they are listed. C10 Favorite Work Folder, for example, is an activity where students keep a record of one piece of classroom work they are proud of for each week of the school year. Though the activity helps students gain a feeling of competence, the activity is not beneficial if it is only started in May, when Competence activities are suggested on the *Esteem Builder Planner*. To plan esteem-building activities on monthly themes, use the *Monthly Planner* form on page 42. Other ongoing activities you may wish to consider implementing at the *beginning* of the school term are:

For Progress Improvement

A31 Friendship Goal
C6 Class Strength Book
C7 Student Strength Book
C9 Recording Progress
C10 Favorite Work Folder
C11 Friday Timer Writing Task
C13 Mastery Devices
C14 Paper Chains
C19 Academic Progress Charts
J10 Writing Center
M13 Homework Assignments
M19 Daily Goal-Setting
M20 Weekly Goal Card
M22 Goal Wheels
M23 Goal Passbook
M28 A Month of Goals

S1 Teacher/Student Exchange Topics
SW26/27 Book of Winners

For Student Recognition

A11 V.I.P. Center
A13 Friendly Letter
A14 King/Queen for the Day
A15 Dandy Lion
A35 Card Friendship Center
C32 Pride Center
S37 A Month of Positivism
S38 Happy Happenings
SH19 Seeing Myself
SW1 Spirit Tickets
SW3 Positive Performers
SW8 Pass the Buck
SW9 Spirit Tree
SW14 Good News Report
SW15/16 Student of the Week
SW19 Birthday Recognition
SW20 Principal's Birthday Party
SW21 Birthday Poster
SW22 Principal's Birthday Card
SW23 Birthday Pencils
SW25 Koala-T Efforts

For Positivism

A35 Card Friendship Center
C34 Pride Center
S37 A Month of Positivism
S38 Happy Happenings
SW1 Spirit Tickets
SW8 Pass the Buck
SW14 Good News Report

WEEKLY ESTEEM BUILDER IMPLEMENTATION

You may also use the *Esteem Builder Planner* if you plan to use the program only once or twice a week. The same sequence of feeling components will follow for each month. From the suggestions of daily activities that appear on the planner, you merely select one or two activities you would like your class to do for the week. If you use HOME ESTEEM BUILDERS (which is available as a companion booklet), you can send those activities home each week. And you may also wish to include the school-wide activity suggestion that appears on the bottom section of each month of the planner.

Periodic Use of Activities

Even if you only occasionally use the program, it is still preferable to present the activities to your students in the order they are given within each component. All activities are organized sequentially according to the esteem builder steps within each component. As time becomes available, continue to implement more activities into your program.

Esteem Builder Planner Contents for Each School Week

Each month's plan contains complete day-by-day esteem builder suggestions. The five self-esteem components all have two months of planned ideas and suggested strategies for implementation. Activities are purposely structured for different types of classroom groupings and formats that allow for teacher flexibility. Each school week, in addition to activities listed for each component, includes:

- Two Concept Circle activities.
- School-wide activities.

Each plan also includes suggested school-wide esteem builders and a staff esteem activity for the month. These may be done in any of the following group formats: large, half-class, small teams or partners. Activity procedure roughly falls into two categories:

- **Total Group Activity** to enhance the component.
- **Independent Learning Idea** for students to use on their own or to include as part of an individualized learning program.

	MONDAY	TUESDAY	WEDNESDAY
WEEK 1	**ESTEEM BUILDER #1:** **Build a Trusting Relationship** **S15 - Rules** **A11 - V.I.P. Center:** Set up a V.I.P. Center about yourself. Describe Center. Assign new school students a "buddy." **S1 - Teacher/Student Letter Exchange:** Write a personal note to each student at the beginning of the journal. **S17 - Time for Friends** *Begin the daily practice of greeting students at the door.*	**CC1 - Beginning Circle:** Make Sparkle Name Tags **S15 - Rules** (Review) **S1:** "Tell me something you're looking forward to in school this year." *Are your class rules clearly posted?*	**SW10 -** Begin procedure for **School-wide Friendship Assembly** Read the *Original Warm Fuzzy Tale* by Steiner. **S1:** "My favorite part of the summer was..." *Students choose H, H or H—"Hug, Handshake or High Five"—from you as they enter classroom.*
WEEK 2	**ESTEEM BUILDER #2:** **Set Reasonable Limits and Rules That Are Consistently Enforced** **S16 - Scholar Dollars:** Introduction. **A11 - V.I.P. Center** (Set up) **S1:** "If I could ask my teacher one thing, it would be..." *Never stop building a trusting relationship with students. It's an ongoing process.*	**CC2 - How Do You Do?** **S16 - Scholar Dollars** **S1:** "When I'm alone, my favorite thing to do is..." *"Who teaches me for a day is my father for a lifetime."* —*Chinese Proverb*	**S22 - Interest Search** (K-3) *or* **S23 - Find a Friend** (3-8) **S16 - Scholar Dollars** **S1:** "One part of school I don't understand is..." *Consider visiting a student at home.*
WEEK 3	**S16 - Scholar Dollars** **A11 - V.I.P. Center** (Set up) **S1:** "My favorite TV show is... because..." *How are you letting students know you care?*	**CC3 - Listen Up!** **S16 - Scholar Dollars** **S1:** "My favorite book is... because..." *Send home positive grams S2, S3, S4, S5.*	**S18 - Name Bingo** *or* **S20 - Personality Trivia** **S16 - Scholar Dollars** **S1:** "My favorite movie star is... because..." *Call one parent each night to report the good things his/her child is doing.*
WEEK 4	**ESTEEM BUILDER #3:** **Create a Positive and Caring Environment** **S14 - Significant Others:** Adapt form, using construction paper circles for younger students. **S16 - Scholar Dollars** **A11 - V.I.P. Center** (Set up) **S1:** "Something I'd like to share with the teacher is..." *Consider starting a Teacher V.I.P. board.*	**CC2 - How Do You Do?** **S16 - Scholar Dollars** **S1:** "I wish the teacher would tell my parents..." *Start a journal topic suggestion box or section on the board where students can add topic ideas.*	**S13 - List of People I Can Depend On** **S16 - Scholar Dollars** **S1:** "One question I'd like to ask the principal is..." *Send a happy gram to a staff member.*

SCHOOL-WIDE ACTIVITIES
SW10 - Friendship Assembly.
Birthday celebrations ongoing throughout school year: **SW19, SW20, SW21, SW22, SW23.** Choose one as a staff.
Ongoing student recognition activities: **SW12 - Who's New?** *or* **SW13 - Meet Our Kids.**
Consider using **S16 - Scholar Dollars** as a school-wide activity.

THURSDAY	FRIDAY	NOTES / PLANS
Review rules for Concept Circles CC1 - Favorite TV Show S1: "My favorite part of the school day is…" *Post a chart of your Concept Circle Rules.*	S18 - Name Bingo *or* S21 - Student Interview A11 - V.I.P. Center: Presentation. Share yourself with the students. A12 - V.I.P. Letter to Parent: Randomly pick a student's name from a hat; assign him/her to be next V.I.P. S1: "The best part of this school week was…" *Do students understand the consequences of broken class rules?*	**SECURITY:** *A feeling of strong assuredness. Involves feeling comfortable and safe; knowing what is expected; being able to depend on individuals and situations; and comprehending rules and limits.* Read chapter on **Security.** S1: Bind pages together for a Teacher-Student Letter Exchange booklet for each student. Page options: J2, J3 or J13. Continue to reinforce the first three Security Esteem Builders throughout the school year. Security is the foundation of self-esteem.
Concept Circle: Review rules CC1 - Favorite Color S16 - Scholar Dollars S1: "I wish this classroom…" *Respect students who don't like to be touched. Begin by standing in close proximity.*	SW11 - Name Tag Exchange Make name tags. S16 - Scholar Dollars A11 - V.I.P. Center (Presentation) A12 - V.I.P. Parent Letter S1: "I'm glad this classroom…" *Greet as many students as you can personally.*	**ONGOING ACTIVITIES** **Name Awareness Activities:** To help students discover each other's names: S17, S18, S19, S20, S22, S23. Begin **S16 Scholar Dollars** Continue activity as long as needed. With some classes this may mean well into the next school month. This activity could be extended as a school-wide activity.
S16 - Scholar Dollars **Concept Circle: Student Interview (S21)** S1: "My favorite place to be is…" *Consider having a student help you greet other students at the door.*	SW10 - School-wide Friendship Assembly S16 - Scholar Dollars C10 - Favorite Work Folder: Design cover. A11 - V.I.P. Center (Presentation) A12 - V.I.P. Parent Letter S1: "My favorite person is…" *Do students know when they can approach you for private conferences?*	**C10 - Favorite Work Folder:** To help students gain evidence of their yearly work progress, start work folder for *each* student. Each week throughout the remainder of the school year each student chooses one page of work he/she is most proud of and places it in the folder. Older students must keep track of their *own* progress and present it to the teacher at the grading period. Other options: C9, C11, C12, C18, C19.
S16 - Scholar Dollars **Concept Circle Topic:** "A person I can always depend on is…because…" Students may use S13 form if needed. S1: "Sometime this year I wish we could learn about…" *Keep track of the growth of one problem student.*	S19 - Name Exchange S16 - Scholar Dollars C10 - Favorite Work Folder Choose one sample of work to be kept. A11 - V.I.P. Center (Presentation) A12 - V.I.P. Parent Letter S1: "The best part of this month of school was…" *Are you documenting student gains?*	**All V.I.P.** Each Friday randomly choose one student to be the "featured student" for the following week. Send home **A12 V.I.P. Parent Letter** with student explaining program to his/her parents. On Monday the V.I.P. student brings in a display of him-/herself. The display can be done as a poster, bulletin board, carrel or table top display. On Friday the student verbally describes the display. Older students may write an autobiography.

POSITIVELY RECOGNIZED STUDENTS

STAFF ESTEEM BUILDER
Consider setting up a bulletin board display for a "staff member" of the week. A staff member is recognized each week just for being a member of the staff. With larger staffs you may need to have more than one member displayed.

This guide is only a suggested framework for Esteem Building.

	MONDAY	TUESDAY	WEDNESDAY
WEEK 5	SW3 - Positive Performers: Start and continue through next month. A11 - V.I.P. Center (Set up) S37 - A Month of Positivism (Introduce) *Continue to build a trusting relationship with each student.*	Concept Circles: Brainstorm list of ways students can demonstrate positive performances. Each team designs a poster of examples (pictures or words). SW3 - Positive Performers S37 - A Month of Positivism *Provide students with specific feedback for improvement in an area.*	S14 - Significant Others SW3 - Positive Performers S37 - A Month of Positivism *Have a time for a standing ovation each day (or week) for deserving students.*
WEEK 6	S27 - Secret Friendly Hello Person: Introduce and model; code word "Hello." A11 - V.I.P. Center (Set up) SW3 - Positive Performers S37 - A Month of Positivism *Informally ask each student if he/she can name class rules and consequences.*	CC6 - Body Tracings (1st Team Member) S27 - Secret Friendly Hello Person SW3 - Positive Performers S37 - A Month of Positivism *Set up a signal code of red and green paper indicating when talking is permitted (red=no; green=permitted).*	S27 - Secret Friendly Hello Person SW3 - Positive Performers S37 - A Month of Positivism *Consider setting aside a 5-minute conference time for each student, discussing specific progress and ways to improve.*
WEEK 7	S12 - Someone Special S25 - Smile Book (Introduction) A11 - V.I.P. Center (Set up) SW3 - Positive Performers S37 - A Month of Positivism *Consider assigning a student with low self-esteem as a cross-age tutor.*	CC6 - Body Tracings (3rd Team Member) S25 - Smile Book SW3 - Positive Performers S37 - A Month of Positivism *How about a class motto, slogan or colors?*	S10 - Letter to a Significant Other S25 - Smile Book SW3 - Positive Performers S37 - A Month of Positivism *Discuss with faculty members: Do all students have the opportunity to be recognized?*
WEEK 8	S8 - Significant Other Biographies: Based on compiled information (2-8) or S9 - Significant Other Sharing (K-4) S27 - Secret Friendly Hello Person Code: "How are you?" A11 - V.I.P. Center (Set up) SW3 - Positive Performers S37 - A Month of Positivism *Mark papers with a yellow highlighter to highlight correct answers.*	Concept Circle: "Share what you've learned about a significant other." or S9 - Significant Other Sharing S27 - Secret Friendly Hello Person SW3 - Positive Performers S37 - A Month of Positivism *"Those who bring sunshine to the lives of others cannot keep it from themselves."* —Sir James Barrie	S8 - Significant Other Biographies or S9 - Significant Other Sharing S27 - Secret Friendly Hello Person SW3 - Positive Performers S37 - A Month of Positivism *"Deal with the faults of others as gently as your own."* —Chinese Proverb

SCHOOL-WIDE ACTIVITIES
Continue **SW12 - Who's New?** or **SW13 - Meet Our Kids.**
Birthday Celebrations: **SW19, SW20, SW21, SW22** or **SW23.**
SW9 - Spirit Tree in hall by office or some other accessible location (Middle School, adapt to a bulletin board display). Use leaf or other cut-out paper shapes for names of positive students. Hang leaves on the tree.

THURSDAY	FRIDAY	NOTES / PLANS
CC5 - Partner Interview (New partner)	S10 - Letter to a Significant Other	SECURITY: "A feeling of strong assuredness. Involves feeling comfortable and safe; knowing what is expected; being able to depend on individuals and situations; and comprehending rules and limits."
SW3 - Positive Performers	SW3 - Positive Performers	
S37 - A Month of Positivism	A11 - V.I.P. Center (Presentation)	
	A12 - V.I.P. Parent Letter	**ONGOING ACTIVITIES**
	S37 - A Month of Positivism	C10 - Favorite Work Folder
	C10 - Favorite Work Folder	
Ask students to write individual notes thanking deserving staff members for special deeds.	*Is it time for a "class celebration" (popcorn, a video, an outing to a park)?*	A11 - V.I.P. Center: Student set-up and presentation.
		S15 - Review rules as needed.
CC6 - Body Tracings (2nd Team Member)	S27 - Secret Friendly Hello Person	S16 - Scholar Dollars: Continue as needed.
S27 - Secret Friendly Hello Person	A11 - V.I.P. Center (Presentation)	C21, C22 - Reading recording options for younger students.
SW3 - Positive Performers	A12 - V.I.P. Parent Letter	
S37 - A Month of Positivism	SW3 - Positive Performers	**POSITIVE CLASS HAPPENINGS** Introduce and continue on a daily basis:
	S37 - A Month of Positivism	S31 - Sparkle Line *or* S34 - A Special Message to You
Are your activities providing opportunities for students to be successful?	*Wear school colors.*	S37 - A Month of Positivism: Each student keeps track of positive happenings in classroom.
CC6 - Body Tracings (4th Team Member)	S7 - Significant Other Interview: Compile list of questions in class. Homework: interview.	
S25 - Smile Book	S25 - Smile Book	**JOURNAL WRITING** Continue S1 Teacher/Student Letter Exchange Books daily. See J14 for topics.
SW3 - Positive Performers	A11 - V.I.P. Center (Presentation)	
S37 - A Month of Positivism	A12 - V.I.P. Parent Letter	
	SW3 - Positive Performers	
	S37 - A Month of Positivism	**SIGNIFICANT OTHER AWARENESS** S8 - Significant Other Biographies (2-8). Students compile information they've gathered about their significant others in biography form *or*
	C10 - Favorite Work Folder	
Increase your internal time between asking a question and calling on a student.	*"People have a way of becoming what you encourage them to be— not what you nag them to be."* —Scudder N. Parker	
S8 - Significant Other Biographies: Share your "draft" with your team or a partner *or*	S8 - Significant Other Biographies Final version *or*	S9 - Significant Other Sharing Assign a day/time for each student to share something special about a Significant Other. In some cases Significant Others can be brought to class.
S9 - Significant Other Sharing	S9 - Significant Other Sharing	
S27 - Secret Friendly Hello Person	S27 - Secret Friendly Hello Person	
SW3 - Positive Performers	A11 - V.I.P. Center (Presentation)	
S37 - A Month of Positivism	A12 - V.I.P. Parent Letter	**POSITIVELY RECOGNIZED STUDENTS**
	SW3 - Positive Performers	
	C10 - Favorite Work Folder	
"Look for strength in people, not weakness; good, not evil. Most of us find what we search for." —Anonymous	S37 - A Month of Positivism *Have a crazy hat day; students design their own crazy hats and wear them.*	

STAFF ESTEEM BUILDER
Set up a "Teacher's Pride Bulletin Board" in your faculty room. Teachers may highlight or display special projects and suggestions currently being used in classrooms.

This guide is only a suggested framework for Esteem Building.

MONDAY	TUESDAY	WEDNESDAY
WEEK 9 **ESTEEM BUILDER #1: Reinforce More Accurate Self-Descriptions** SH3 - A Self-Portrait J8: "The part of me I like the best..." A11 - V.I.P. Center (Set up) SW1 - Spirit Tickets (Positive behavior) *Remember: Praise should be highly specific!*	CC8 - Names *or* CC9 - Design-a-Logo J8: "The part of me I'd most like to change..." SW1 - Spirit Tickets *"Man lives more by affirmation than by bread."* —Victor Hugo	SH2 - Me Riddles (K-3) SH4 - Focus on Me (2-6) CC10 - Me Bag: Do as homework assignment; send home to decorate. J8: "When I look in the mirror..." SW1 - Spirit Tickets *Review S15 Rules.*
WEEK 10 **ESTEEM BUILDER #2: Provide Opportunities to Discover Major Sources of Influence on the Self** SH14 - Time-Line Center/Significant Events (2-8) SH8 - Me Shape Book (K-3) A11 - V.I.P. Center (Set up) SW1 - Spirit Tickets *Respect students who cannot handle public praise—do so privately.*	**Concept Circle Topic: S28** *or* **S35.** Practice activity first in small groups. S28 - Smile File *or* S35 - Add a Compliment *Try putting on the board names of students who demonstrate positive behavior.*	S28 *or* S35 SH15 - A Movie of My Life (K-5) SH14 - Focus on a significant milestone in Time-Line (5-8) (Use as journal topic.) SW1 - Spirit Tickets *Read* Dandelion *or* Be a Perfect Person in Just Three Days.
WEEK 11 S28 *or* S35 SH6 - Me Dolls (K-1) SH24 - Begin **All-About-Me Center;** S25 Contract SH26 - Dioramas (1-5) Begin **Autobiography** (4-8) A11 - V.I.P. Center (Set up) SW1 - Spirit Tickets *Do students clearly understand your expectations?*	S28 *or* S35 CC12: "If I Could Replay One Part of My Life, I'd Choose..." (5-8) SH26 - Dioramas (cont.) **Autobiography** homework (4-8): Interview a . . . SW1 - Spirit Tickets *"He that knows himself knows others."* —Charles Caleb Colton	S28 *or* S35 SH6 - Me Doll (K-1) SH16 - The Many Parts of Me (2-8) SH27 - Letter to a Friend Continue autobiography (4-8) SW1 - Spirit Tickets *Are your rules posted?*
WEEK 12 **ESTEEM BUILDER #3: Build an Awareness of Unique Qualities** SH18 - My Identity Shield SH30 - Measuring Me A11 - V.I.P. Center (Set up) SW1 - Spirit Tickets *Consider pairing a student with low self-esteem with a much younger student.*	S28 *or* S35 CC12 - Topic: Share Identity Shield in small group or with partner SH31 - Me Mask SW1 - Spirit Tickets *Continue to offer specific feedback to help students form accurate self-descriptions.*	S28 *or* S35 SH20 - Playing Favorites SH32 - Life Story SW1 - Spirit Tickets *Keep track of students you are positively recognizing.*

SCHOOL-WIDE ACTIVITIES
SW1 - Spirit Tickets; Emphasis: "positivism."
Begin **Cross-Age Tutoring Program** if you haven't already done so. Begin with an "explanation meeting" for students and staff. Be sure to clearly state expectations.
Continue student recognition ideas **SW12** or **SW13** and birthday celebrations **SW19-SW23**.
SW9 - Spirit Tree or bulletin board display; use appropriate theme (pumpkins, ghosts, etc.).

THURSDAY	FRIDAY	NOTES / PLANS
CC10 - Me Bag **J8:** "I wish I were..." **SW1 - Spirit Tickets** *Have each student identify one physical attribute about him-/herself to focus on.*	**SH6 - Me Doll** **J11 - Your Thoughts About...** (3-8) "What do TV commercials say about physical beauty..." **J8:** "Three words that describe how I look are..." **C10 - Favorite Work Folder** **A11 - V.I.P. Center** (Presentation) **A12 - V.I.P. Parent Letter** **SW1 - Spirit Tickets** *Emphasize the concept of inner beauty.*	**SELFHOOD:** *A feeling of individuality. Acquiring self-knowledge, which includes an accurate and realistic self-description in terms of roles, attributes and physical characteristics.* Read chapter on **Selfhood.** Some students may need extra time in Security material. Extend the time devoted to Esteem Builder #1 for younger students. Additional activity options include **SH1-SH13.**
CC12 - Share Yourself (5-8) "Share a key milestone in your life." **CC11 - I Like** (K-4) Topic: Describe favorite place to visit. Make **SH9 Walking Me Puppet** to do talking. **SW1 - Spirit Tickets** *Include a reaction statement at the conclusion to a concept circle or journal writing: "I learned...," "I discovered..."*	**SH15 - A Movie of My Life** (cont.) **SH5 - Measure Up** (1-3) **C10 - Favorite Work Folder** **A11 - V.I.P. Center** (Presentation) **A12 - V.I.P. Parent Letter** **SW1 - Spirit Tickets** *Continue to have students add specific complimentary statements to a list. Statements can be referred to during S28 or S35 activity.*	Prepare **S28 Smile File** or **S35 Add a Compliment:** Continue to do the activity daily until all students are recognized. **A11 - V.I.P. Center:** Continue as a weekly activity. **A12 - V.I.P. Parent Letter:** Send home on Friday preceding V.I.P.'s week.
S28 *or* **S35** **CC15 -** Share a page or memory from your **Autobiography** *or* **SH6 - Me Doll** *or* **SH16 - The Many Parts of Me** **SH28 - I Like Mobile** **SW1 - Spirit Tickets** *"The secret of education lies in respecting the pupil."* *—Ralph Waldo Emerson*	**S28** *or* **S35** (Complete projects) **C10 - Favorite Work Folder:** Complete autobiography. **SH29 - Commercial About Me** **A11 - V.I.P. Center** (Presentation) **A12 - V.I.P. Parent Letter** **SW1 - Spirit Tickets** *Effective praise is earned or deserved.*	**J5 - Journal Topics:** List ideas for daily journal writing or concept circle starters. Set up **SH24 All-About-Me Center, SH25 All-About-Me Contract:** Students may work as a group or as individuals. Choose one of the suggested activities for each day, appropriate for older or younger student. Students may write an autobiography based on the first two Selfhood esteem builders. Younger students can dictate the information and use **SH8 Me Shape Book.**
S28 *or* **S35** **CC12 -** Topic: Share **Playing Favorites** **SH 33 - Me Banner** **SW1 - Spirit Tickets** *Continue to suggest complimentary statements students can say to one another for S28 or S35.*	**S28** *or* **S35** **C10 - Favorite Work Folder** **SH18** or **SH20:** Enlarge as a poster or color in with marking pens and cut out for bulletin board. **SH34 - I Collage** **A11 - V.I.P. Center** (Presentation) **A12 - V.I.P. Parent Letter** *"The teacher gives not of his wisdom, but rather of his faith and lovingness."* *—Kahlil Gibran*	**C10 - Favorite Work Folder:** Continue each Friday. **POSITIVELY RECOGNIZED STUDENTS** (table)

STAFF ESTEEM BUILDER
Keep a scrapbook of school- and class-wide happenings that highlight teacher efforts.

This guide is only a suggested framework for Esteem Building.

MONDAY	TUESDAY	WEDNESDAY
WEEK 13		
S28 - Smile File *or* S35 - Add a Compliment	SW5 - Gotcha Tickets	SW5 - Gotcha Tickets
SW5 - Gotcha Tickets: Emphasis: kindness. Post a list of kind deeds. Encourage students to add to list.	S28 *or* S35	S28 *or* S35
SH35 - Puppet Bag	CC14 - Identity Bag	SH17 - Who Am I? *or* SH19 - Seeing Myself
A11 - V.I.P. Center (Set up)	SH36 - My Dreams	SH37 - Want Ad
Review S15 Rules. Add or delete as needed.	*"We learn by doing."* —Aristotle	*Stand in closer proximity to low esteem students.*
WEEK 14		
SW5 - Gotcha Tickets	SW5 - Gotcha Tickets	SW5 - Gotcha Tickets
S28 *or* S35	S28 *or* S35	S28 *or* S35
SH17 - Who Am I? *or*	CC12 - Topic: Share one "I am..." (SH17)	SH17 - Who Am I?
SH19 - Seeing Myself		SH21 - Wanted Poster
SH40 - Time Capsule	SH41 - Like Me	SH42 - Me Hanging
A11 - V.I.P. Center (Set up)		
"We become what we habitually contemplate." —George Russell	*Keep track of students you positively recognize.*	*"What we are is what we have thought for years."* —Buddha
WEEK 15		
SW5 - Gotcha Tickets	SW5 - Gotcha Tickets	SW5 - Gotcha Tickets
S28 *or* S35 **ESTEEM BUILDER #4: Enhance Ability to Identify and Express Emotions and Attitudes**	S28 *or* S35	S28 *or* S35
SH45 - Dictionary of Feelings	CC18 - Happy-Sad Beanbag (K-2) *or* "A time when I felt happy" (2-8)	SH47 - Sending I Messages: Introduce as a group (3-8) *or*
SH47 - Sending I Messages	SH45 - Dictionary of Feelings	SH45 - Dictionary of Feelings
A11 - V.I.P. Center (Set up)		
Remember: You make a difference!	*Post a list of "builder-upper" words.*	*Inform students you will answer only one question per group.*
WEEK 16		
SW5 - Gotcha Tickets	SW5 - Gotcha Tickets	SW5 - Gotcha Tickets
S28 *or* S35	S28 *or* S35	S28 *or* S35
SH44 - The Gift of Self (K-3); (4-8) Tell students: Keep track in your journal of kind deeds you've done for others.	**Concept Circle: Share My Interests and Hobbies SH23** (3-8)	SH45 - Dictionary of Feelings (K-3): (Complete) Work in teams or partners to develop lists of "feeling" words. (4-8)
A11 - V.I.P. Center (Set up)	CC19 - Emotion Hats (K-2)	
"So much is a man worth as he esteems himself." —Francois Rabelais	*Make a positive phone call home.*	*"Who can say more than this rich praise; that you alone are you?"* —Shakespeare

SCHOOL-WIDE ACTIVITIES
Introduce **SW5 - Gotcha Tickets** or continue **SW1 - Spirit Tickets**; Emphasis: "kindness."
SH23 - My Interests and Hobbies; consider having a school **Hobby Day (C1)**.
Continue student recognition ideas **SW12** or **SW13** and birthday celebrations **SW19-SW22**; also, **A24 - Word Gifts**.
SW9 - Spirit Tree or bulletin board display; use appropriate theme (turkeys or trees).

THURSDAY	FRIDAY	NOTES / PLANS
S28 *or* S35 SW5 - Gotcha Tickets CC14 - Identity Bag SH38 - Sparkles *Consider sending a note of praise to a student who cannot handle public praise.*	S28 *or* S35 SW5 - Gotcha Tickets C10 - Favorite Work Folder SH17 - Who Am I? *or* SH19 - Seeing Myself A11 - V.I.P. Center (Presentation) A12 - V.I.P. Parent Letter SH39 - Special People *"No one can make you feel inferior without your consent."* *—Eleanor Roosevelt*	**SELFHOOD:** *A feeling of individuality. Acquiring self-knowledge, which includes an accurate and realistic self-description in terms of roles, attributes and physical characteristics.* Continue reading chapter on **Selfhood.** Many students (particularly younger or those with lower self-esteem) will need more time with Esteem Builder #4. Continue to help them identify and express emotions throughout the year.
S28 *or* S35 SW5 - Gotcha Tickets CC12 - Topic: Share one " I am…" SH17 SH22 - Resumé (5-8): Share qualities in a group or with a partner. SH43 - Me Poster *Send home to a different student each day unique characteristics you've discovered about him/her.*	S28 *or* S35 SW5 - Gotcha Tickets SH17 - Who Am I? *or* SH19 - Seeing Myself SH22 - Resumé (Complete form) C10 - Favorite Work Folder A11 - V.I.P. Center (Presentation) A12 - V.I.P. Parent Letter SH24 - Continue All About Me Center until completed. *Praise the student's behavior, not the student.*	Continue S28 *or* S35 until students have mastered the concept. **ON-GOING ACTIVITIES** A11 - V.I.P. Center: Student set-up and presentation. S15 - Rules: Review as needed. C10 - Favorite Work Folder: Continue each Friday choosing one work sample. Older students need the opportunity to practice sending I Messages to each other. They also may practice/brainstorm appropriate strategies to verbalize anger.
S28 *or* S35 SW5 - Gotcha Tickets Concept Circle Topic (3-8) SH47 - Sending I Messages Practice in partners or "A time when I felt sad." SH45 - Dictionary of Feelings *Make a positive phone call home.*	S28 *or* S35 SW5 - Gotcha Tickets C10 - Favorite Work Folder SH23 - My Interests and Hobbies (3-8) SH45 - Dictionary of Feelings A11 - V.I.P. Center (Presentation) A12 - V.I.P. Parent Letter *Consider allowing each student to display a hobby or interest.*	J8 - Sentence Completion Topics on Selfhood: writing or talking starters. **LITERATURE SELECTIONS** *Dandelion* (Freeman) *Frosted Glass* (Cazet) *I Wish I Were a Butterfly* (Howe) *Be a Perfect Person in Just Three Days* (Manes) *Tuck Everlasting* (Babbitt)
S28 *or* S35 SW5 - Gotcha Tickets CC5 - Partner Interview CC19 - Emotion Hats (K-2) *Examine your list of "Positively Recognized Students." Which students' names are missing?*	S28 *or* S35 SW5 - Gotcha Tickets SH46 - Feelings Wheel (K-3) C10 - Favorite Work Folder Work in teams to brainstorm appropriate ways to display or verbalize anger. (4-8) A11 - V.I.P. Center (Presentation) A12 - V.I.P. Parent Letter *Display student-generated list of appropriate ways to handle anger.*	**POSITIVELY RECOGNIZED STUDENTS** (table)

STAFF ESTEEM BUILDER
Present staff members with buttons or badges inscribed with "I Make A Difference," "Proud to Teach" or "Significant Other."

This guide is only a suggested framework for Esteem Building.

MONDAY	TUESDAY	WEDNESDAY
WEEK 17		
ESTEEM BUILDER #1: **Promote Inclusion and Acceptance Within the Group** SW8 - Pass the Buck: Introduce as a school-wide activity. J1 - Journal Cover J8 - Sentence Completion Topics: Affiliation A11 - V.I.P. Center (Set up) A1 - Books on Belonging and Acceptance: Choose an appropriate book from the suggested list. Address the questions relating to Affiliation on A1. *Consider assigning each student to a support team—a team of 4 students who affirm each other.*	Concept Circle: A4 - Paired Name Collage (3-8) *or* CC35 - Glasses Circle (K-3) J5 *or* J8 - Journal Topics *or* Dictation on Affiliation *Keep a list of friendly deeds posted in your classroom.*	A2 - Common Points J5 *or* J8 - Journal Topics *or* Dictation on Affiliation *"Recipe for having friends: be one."* —Elbert Hubbard
WEEK 18		
ESTEEM BUILDER #2: **Provide Opportunities to Discover the Interests, Capabilities and Backgrounds of Others** A11 - V.I.P. Center (Set up) A5 - Class Discovery Book J5 *or* J8 - Journal Topics *or* Dictation on Affiliation *Allow students the opportunity of working in a team.*	CC31 - Riddles (K-8) A5 - Class Discovery Book J5 *or* J8 - Journal Topics *or* Dictation on Affiliation *Encourage students to use eye contact when they talk to others.*	A10 - Friendly Riddles A5 - Class Discovery Book J5 *or* J8 - Journal Topics *or* Dictation on Affiliation *Periodically ask students: "Who's had someone do something nice for you today? What was it?"*
WEEK 19		
A6 - Solve the Riddle *or* A9 - Mystery Person A11 - V.I.P. Center (Set up) J5 *or* J8 - Journal Topics *or* Dictation on Affiliation *"People are lonely because they build walls instead of bridges."* —Joseph Newton	A19 - Friend Interviews J5 *or* J8 - Journal Topics *or* Dictation on Affiliation *Have a school-wide smile contest. Post photos of great smiles.*	A6 - Solve the Riddle *or* A9 - Mystery Person J5 *or* J8 - Journal Topics *or* Dictation on Affiliation *Teach students a phrase or two to use in initiating a conversation.*
WEEK 20		
ESTEEM BUILDER #3: **Increase Awareness of and Skills in Friendship Making** A17 - Friendly Class Actions A11 - V.I.P. Center (Set up) J5 *or* J8 - Journal Topics *or* Dictation on Affiliation *Teach students how to respond to a compliment.*	Concept Circle Task: A18 - Helping Each Other J5 *or* J8 - Journal Topics *or* Dictation on Affiliation *"No man can become rich without himself enriching others."* —Andrew Carnegie	A20 - What Is A Friend? Adapt for younger students by doing as a class. Form one list to make a poster "What Is A Friend?" J5 *or* J8 - Journal Topics *or* Dictation on Affiliation *Ask students to clip out news articles of friendly and caring deeds of others.*

SCHOOL-WIDE ACTIVITIES
SW8 - **Pass the Buck:** Emphasis: recognizing positive deeds of others.
Continue **SW5 - Gotcha Tickets** or **SW1 Spirit Tickets;** Emphasis: "courtesy."
SW19-SW23 — birthday recognitions; also, **A24 - Word Gifts.**
SW9 - **Spirit Tree** or bulletin board display.
SW12 - **Who's New?** or SW13 - **Meet Our Kids.**

THURSDAY	FRIDAY	NOTES/PLANS
CC25 - Sunshine Statements	**A3 - Getting to Know You Wheel** (2-8)	**AFFILIATION:** *A feeling of belonging, acceptance or relatedness in relationships that are considered important. Feeling approved of, appreciated and respected by others.*
J5 *or* **J8 - Journal Topics** *or* **Dictation on Affiliation**	**A11 - V.I.P. Center** (Presentation)	
	A12 - V.I.P. Parent Letter	Read chapter on **Affiliation.**
	C10 - Favorite Work Folder	
	J5 *or* **J8 - Journal Topics** *or* **Dictation on Affiliation**	
"Competition brings out the best in products and the worst in people." —David Sarnoff	*"A friend is a present you give yourself."* —Robert Louis Stevenson	**JOURNAL WRITING OR DICTATION** Construct a journal for each student to use in daily writing concerning the topic of Affiliation. J1 - cover; J2 or J3 - pages; J4 - binding; J8 - Affiliation sentence completion topics.
CC29 - Picture Puzzles (2-8)	**A5 - Class Discovery Book** Report discoveries to the class.	
J5 *or* **J8 - Journal Topics** *or* **Dictation on Affiliation**	**A11 - V.I.P. Center** (Presentation)	
	A12 - V.I.P. Parent Letter	
A5 - Class Discovery Book	**C10 - Favorite Work Folder**	**CLASSROOM POSITIVE ACTIVITIES** Consider using any of the following activities on a daily basis to encourage peer support: S24, S26-S35. Choose one and consistently do the activity daily. Modeling appropriate behavior and providing specific suggestions are critical points for activity effectiveness.
	J5 *or* **J8 - Journal Topics** *or* **Dictation on Affiliation**	
Ask students to write in their journals each day a friendly deed they've observed.	*"One learns about people through the heart, not the eyes or the intellect."* —Mark Twain	
CC27 - Banners	**A6 - Solve the Riddle** *or* **A9 - Mystery Person**	
	A11 - V.I.P. Center (Presentation)	**ONGOING ACTIVITIES** **A11 - V.I.P Center** (Presentation)
J5 *or* **J8 - Journal Topics** *or* **Dictation on Affiliation**	**A12 - V.I.P. Parent Letter**	
	C10 - Favorite Work Folder	**A12 - V.I.P. Parent Letter**
	J5 *or* **J8 - Journal Topics** *or* **Dictation on Affiliation**	
	Provide cut paper strips for students to use to write names of friendly classmates. Paste the names to form a chain.	**C10 - Favorite Work Folder:** Document successes.
"Friendship is a sheltering tree." —Samuel Taylor Coleridge		**A5 - Class Discovery Book:** Continue throughout month.
Concept Circle Task: A19 - Friend Interviews	**A21 - Friendship Recipes:** Adapt for younger students by doing as a class.	
J5 *or* **J8 - Journal Topics** *or* **Dictation on Affiliation**	**A11 - V.I.P. Center** (Presentation)	**A9 - Mystery Person** *or* **A10 - Friendly Riddles**
A37 - Care Ropes	**A12 - V.I.P. Parent Letter**	
	C10 - Favorite Work Folder	**POSITIVELY RECOGNIZED STUDENTS**
Give a rope length to each student and have him/her tie it to a chair or backpack. Each time they do a friendly deed, they tie a knot in the rope.	**J5** *or* **J8 - Journal Topics** *or* **Dictation on Affiliation** *"The antidote for fifty enemies is one friend."* —Aristotle	

STAFF ESTEEM BUILDER
Tape a long length of butcher paper to the staff wall. Write a caption that reads: "Write something nice to a colleague."

This guide is only a suggested framework for Esteem Building.

	MONDAY	TUESDAY	WEDNESDAY
WEEK 21	**A38 - Compliment Hanging** or other daily classroom positive activity. *(See Notes/Plans)* **A22 - Friendship Wheel:** Adapt for older students by having them keep a list in a folder. **A11 - V.I.P. Center** (Set up) *Remember to catch behavior when it's good.*	**A38 -** *(See Notes/Plans)* **A22 - Friendship Wheel:** Each student spins completed wheel as he/she enters class and does "friendly deed" designated by wheel's arrow for a randomly selected classmate. **A25 -** Continue activity for the week. **Concept Circle Topic:** Report friendly behaviors observed in others. *"Your friend is the man who knows all about you, and still likes you."* —*Elbert Hubbard*	**A38 -** *(See Notes/Plans)* **A22 - Friendship Wheel** **A21 - Friendship Recipes** *Don't assume anything. Make sure students know exactly what you expect.*
WEEK 22	**A38 -** *(See Notes/Plans)* **A28 - Recording Good Deeds** **A11 - V.I.P. Center** (Set up) *Have a friendship book week. Read nothing but books about friends.*	**A38 -** *(See Notes/Plans)* **Concept Circle:** **A23 - Friendship Openers** Adapt for younger students *or* **CC26 - Sparkle Box** *Consistency is essential.*	**A38 -** *(See Notes/Plans)* **A31 - Friendship Goal** *"Clapping with the right hand only will not produce a noise."* —*Malay Proverb*
WEEK 23	**ESTEEM BUILDER #4:** **Encourage Peer Approval and Support** **A38 -** *(See Notes/Plans)* **A33 - Caring Words** **A11 - V.I.P. Center** (Set up) *Positive energizers need to be frequently charged.*	**CC33 - Word Gifts** (K-4) **CC34 - Word Power** (3-8) **A38 -** *(See Notes/Plans)* *Praise students with low self-esteem often.*	**A38 -** *(See Notes/Plans)* **A32 - Sunrays** (K-3) **A31 - Friendship Goal** (4-8) *Periodically send deserving students to the principal's office.*
WEEK 24	**A38 -** *(See Notes/Plans)* **A37 - Care Ropes** (K-3) **A39 - Autographs** (2-8) **A11 - V.I.P. Center** (Set up) *Set up a plan to help a new student feel affiliated.*	**A38 -** *(See Notes/Plans)* **CC38 - Me Bag Compliments** *Tell students exactly what they did well.*	**A38 -** *(See Notes/Plans)* **CC39 - Name Poster** Do as teams. *Tell students exactly how they can improve.*

SCHOOL-WIDE ACTIVITIES
SW14 - Good News Report: Begin if you haven't already done so. Use a positive recognition activity such as **SW1, SW5, SW8** to recognize "friendliness."
Continue **SW19-23**; **SW12** *or* **SW13**.
SW9 - Spirit Tree: "friendliness."

THURSDAY	FRIDAY	NOTES / PLANS
A38 - *(See Notes/Plans)*	A38 - *(See Notes/Plans)*	**AFFILIATION:** *A feeling of belonging, acceptance or relatedness in relationships that are considered important. Feeling approved of, appreciated and respected by others.*
A22 - **Friendship Wheel**	A22 - **Friendship Wheel**	
	A21 - **Friendship Recipes** (Complete)	
	A11 - **V.I.P. Center** (Presentation)	
A18 - **Helping Each Other** (Review)	A12 - **V.I.P. Parent Letter**	Read chapter on **Affiliation.**
	C10 - **Favorite Work Folder**	
	Ask students for suggestions about positive energizers.	**JOURNAL WRITING OR DICTATION** Continue daily journal writing using **J8**-Affiliation sentence completion topics.
Use specific praise frequently.		
A38 - *(See Notes/Plans)*	A38 - *(See Notes/Plans)*	
CC33 - **Word Gifts** (K-4)	A11 - **V.I.P. Center** (Presentation)	**CLASSROOM POSITIVE ACTIVITIES** Continue to use any of the following activities to encourage peer support: **CC41, S24, S26-S35, A38.** Choose one and consistently do the activity daily. Modeling appropriate behavior and providing specific suggestions are critical points for activity effectiveness.
CC34 - **Word Power** (3-8) *or* A31 - **Friendship Goal:** Share in Concept Circle	A12 - **V.I.P. Parent Letter**	
	C10 - **Favorite Work Folder**	
Review school-wide rules.	*Send notes of praise home for deserving students.*	**ONGOING MONTHLY CLASSROOM ACTIVITIES**
A38 - *(See Notes/Plans)*	A38 - *(See Notes/Plans)*	A11 - **V.I.P. Center** (Presentation)
CC37 - **Me Bags by Others**	A11 - **V.I.P. Center** (Presentation)	A12 - **V.I.P. Parent Letter**
	A12 - **V.I.P. Parent Letter**	
	C10 - **Favorite Work Folder**	C10 - **Favorite Work Folder:** Document successes.
"Hold a true friend with both your hands." —Nigerian Proverb	*Celebrate class successes.*	A22 - **Friendship Wheel**
A38 - *(See Notes/Plans)*	A38 - *(See Notes/Plans)*	
	CC40 - **Compliments:** Do as teams or as a class.	A35 - **Card/Friendship Center** *or* A36 - **Team Member Center**
CC38 - **Me Bag Compliments**	A11 - **V.I.P. Center** (Presentation)	
	A12 - **V.I.P. Parent Letter**	**POSITIVELY RECOGNIZED STUDENTS**
	C10 - **Favorite Work Folder**	
Praise each student every day.	*Reinforce students for cooperative behavior.*	

STAFF ESTEEM BUILDER
Begin **Secret Pals.** Each staff member pulls the name of another staff member and secretly does kind deeds for the staff member. The activity may last for any length of time and pals try to keep their identity secret for as long as possible.

This guide is only a suggested framework for Esteem Building.

	MONDAY	TUESDAY	WEDNESDAY
W E E K 25	**ESTEEM BUILDER #1:** **Enhance Ability to Make Decisions, Seek Alternatives and Identify Consequences** SH6 - Me Doll (K-2) M1 - What I Like...What I Want to Change A11 - V.I.P. Center (Set up) *How about a clean campus crusade?*	Concept Circle Topic: M1 - What I Like...What I Want to Change **Homework:** Bring home form to significant other. *Is your philosophy displayed as a banner or motto in your classroom?*	M2 - Problems As a group, generate solutions to possible school-wide problem. Go through the problem steps as a class. *"It may be those who do most, dream most."* —Stephen Leacock
W E E K 26	M3 - Problem/Solution Report (3-8) *or* M4 - Pictorial Problem/Solution Report (K-2): Introduce one of the forms to the class and practice filling it out using a mock problem. A11 - V.I.P. Center (Set up) *"Vision is the art of seeing the invisible."* —Jonathan Swift	**Concept Circle** CC44 - Brainstorming Solutions: (4-8) Use *Dear Abby* problems. (K-3) Adapt activity and use picture problems glued on cards. Assign roles and brainstorm steps 1-4. *Make it a policy: For every negative call, make two positive phone calls home.*	M7 - Booklist to Enhance Mission: Choose a selection that can be read in one sitting; *Jumanji*, *The Shrinking of Treehorn* are appropriate for older students. Stop before the problem is solved to brainstorm solutions. *Post the steps for goal-setting.*
W E E K 27	**ESTEEM BUILDER #2:** **Aid in Charting Present and Past Academic and Behavioral Performances** CC44 - Brainstorming Solutions: Introduce a Problem Box. Supply index cards. Ask students to be anonymous. A11 - V.I.P. Center (Set up) M10, M11, M12 *or* M13 *Periodically give out an unexpected award.*	CC44 - Brainstorming Solutions: Teams choose from the Problem Box and brainstorm solutions. Be sure to add problems to the box. M10, M11, M12 *or* M13 *Set aside time to describe student behaviors you observed that are appropriate.*	M5 - Brainstorming (in teams) M10, M11, M12 *or* M13 *"Hold fast to dreams, for if dreams die, life is a broken winged bird that cannot fly."* —Langston Hughes
W E E K 28	M10, M11, M12 *or* M13 J2 *or* J3 - Journal Writing: Students each choose one of the progress charts and every day analyze progress in their journal... "Yesterday I performed _____; today I performed _____. A11 - V.I.P. Center (Set up) *Display your teaching certificates in frames.*	M10, M11, M12 *or* M13 J2 *or* J3 - Journal Writing: Yesterday I performed _____; today I performed _____; tomorrow I'll try for _____. *"In order for a goal to be effective, it must effect change."* —Anonymous	M10, M11, M12 *or* M13 J2 *or* J3 - Journal Writing: Yesterday I performed _____; today I performed _____. I made (didn't make) what I shot for; tomorrow I'll try for _____. *Repeat specific praise for a behavior intermittently.*

SCHOOL-WIDE ACTIVITIES
SW14 - Good News Report; SW19-SW23, SW12 or SW13
SW24 - School Problem Report
SW25 - Koala-T Efforts (Introduce)

THURSDAY	FRIDAY	NOTES/PLANS
CC43 - Would You Rather? (K-3)	**M2 - Problems** Students now review process from Wednesday and practice the brainstorming steps using the form. **(M5)**	**MISSION:** *A feeling of purpose and motivation in life. Self-empowerment through setting realistic and achievable goals and being willing to take responsibility for the consequences of one's decisions.*
Concept Circle Topic: (4-8) **M2 - Problems:** Practice steps to brainstorming as a team. **(M5)**	**A11 - V.I.P. Center** (Presentation)	
	A12 - V.I.P. Parent Letter	Read chapter on **Mission.**
	C10 - Favorite Work Folder	
"The task ahead of us is never as great as the power behind us." —Ralph Waldo Emerson	*Encourage students to seek their own solutions.*	**ONGOING ACTIVITIES** **C10 - Favorite Work Folder**
CC44 - Brainstorming Solutions Continue task from Tuesday doing steps 5-6.	**M8 - Super Sleuth Book Report** (1-4) *or* **M9 - Problem Map** (4-8) Use the questions **(M7)** as a guide or make a ditto. Students work individually or in teams to generate solutions to a new book selection.	**A11 - V.I.P. Center:** Student set-up and presentation. **S15 - Rules:** review as needed. **A12 - V.I.P. Parent Letter**
	A11 - V.I.P. Center (Presentation)	**PROBLEM SOLVING** Younger students will need many problem-solving opportunities. Extend problem-solving to real-life problems. Continue the suggested tasks for as long as necessary. Some tasks may need to be extended over a week's time. Remember to model the problem-solving steps. Adapt the activities for younger students by using pictures.
	A12 - V.I.P. Parent Letter	
	C10 - Favorite Work Folder	
Set up a Problem Box for students to add personal problem suggestions.	*Whenever possible, allow students to share in the decision-making.*	
CC44 Brainstorming Solutions: Solution Graphs	**M6 - Strategy Sheet of Solution Consequences**	**CHARTING PERFORMANCE** Although students may have been charting their performances throughout the year, these activities are designed to help students *reflect* on their performance. You may need to set aside time with individual students for conferences. Students should continue charting their academic or behavioral performances throughout the year (**M10, M11, M12** *or* **M13**).
	A11 - V.I.P. Center (Presentation)	
M10, M11, M12 *or* **M13**	**A12 - V.I.P. Parent Letter**	
	C10 - Favorite Work Folder	
	M10, M11, M12 *or* **M13**	
Teach students to brainstorm alternatives.	*"Action may not always bring happiness, but there is no happiness without action."* —Benjamin Disraeli	**CLASSROOM POSITIVE ACTIVITIES** Choose one of the following each day to recognize a different student: **S33 - Sparkle Book/Cover**
M10, M11, M12 *or* **M13**	**M10, M11, M12** *or* **M13**	**S34 - A Special Message to You**
J2 *or* **J3 - Journal Writing:** Yesterday I performed _____; today I performed _____. I made (didn't make) what I shot for; tomorrow I'll try for _____.	**J2** *or* **J3 - Journal Writing:** Yesterday I performed _____; today I performed _____. I made (didn't make) what I shot for; tomorrow I'll try for _____.	**POSITIVELY RECOGNIZED STUDENTS**
	A11 - V.I.P. Center (Presentation)	
	A12 - V.I.P. Parent Letter	
	C10 - Favorite Work Folder	
Focus on only one or two problem behaviors at a time.	*Avoid confronting in anger.*	

STAFF ESTEEM BUILDER
At a faculty meeting cut out a construction paper heart for each participant. Take five minutes to write something nice about each person on their "heart." Tape the corresponding heart to the back of the recipient.

This guide is only a suggested framework for Esteem Building.

	MONDAY	TUESDAY	WEDNESDAY
WEEK 29	**ESTEEM BUILDER #3:** Teach the Steps to Successful Goal-setting **M14 - Goal-setting Step-By-Step** (Introduce chart) **J8 - Journal Sentence Completion Topics: Mission** **A11 - V.I.P. Center** (Set up) *"Hitch your wagon to a star."* *—Ralph Waldo Emerson*	**M15 - Group Goal-setting** **J8 - Journal Sentence Completion Topics: Mission** *Review school/class rules. Add or delete if needed.*	**M15 - Group Goal-setting** **J8 - Journal Sentence Completion Topics: Mission** *"I can give you a six-word formula for success: 'Think things through—then follow through.'"* *—Edward Rickenbacker*
WEEK 30	**M16 - Goal-setting, Charting the Course** Use completed M1 for the activity. **A11 - V.I.P. Center** (Set up) **M27 - Goal Achievement Journal** *Be descriptive in your praise.*	**Concept Circle Topic: M16** Each student has two minutes to share his/her proposed goal with the team. Teammates are then given two minutes to brainstorm resources and approaches that could lead to successful goal attainment. *Teach students how to send "I Messages."*	**M17 - Overcoming Obstacles to Goals** *Provide suggestions for coping strategies.*
WEEK 31	**M19 - Daily Goal-setting** (2-8) *or* **M22 - Goal Wheel** (K-3) **A11 - V.I.P. Center** (Set up) *Read* The Hurried Child *by David Elkind.*	**CC46 - Goal Sharing** **M19 - Daily Goal-setting** *or* **M22 - Goal Wheel** *"If you're not sure where you are going, you're liable to end up someplace else."* —Robert F. Mager	**M19 - Daily Goal-setting** *or* **M22 - Goal Wheel** *Describe to the problem student the problem behavior.*
WEEK 32	**M20 - Weekly Goal Card** (2-8) *or* **M23/24 - Goal Passbook** (1-6) **A11 - V.I.P. Center** (Set up) *Remember: Praise the behavior, not the student.*	**CC48 - Goal Accomplishment** **M20 - Weekly Goal Card** *or* **M23/24 - Goal Passbook** *Tell the student what effect the behavior has on the situation.*	**M20 - Weekly Goal Card** *or* **M23/24 - Goal Passbook** *Ask students, "Did you remember to tell yourself 'You did a good job' for deserved actions?"*

SCHOOL-WIDE ACTIVITIES
SW24 - School Problem Report
SW25 - Koala-T Efforts (Introduce)
SW14 - Good News Report; SW19-SW23; SW12 or SW13

THURSDAY	FRIDAY	NOTES / PLANS
M15 - Group Goal-setting (Set up team goal for Concept Circle discussion) J8 - Journal Sentence Completion Topics: Mission *Hold a school read-a-thon.*	M15 - Group Goal-setting J8 - Journal Sentence Completion Topics: Mission A11 - V.I.P. Center (Presentation) A12 - V.I.P. Parent Letter C10 - Favorite Work Folder *"Part of the problem today is that we have a surplus of simple answers and a shortage of simple problems."* *—Syracuse Herald*	**MISSION:** *A feeling of purpose and motivation in life. Self-empowerment through setting realistic and achievable goals and being willing to take responsibility for the consequences of one's decisions.* Read chapter on **Mission.** **ONGOING ACTIVITIES** C10 - Favorite Work Folder S15 - **Rules:** Review as needed. A11 - **V.I.P. Center:** Student set-up and presentation.
CC45 - I Wish I Could . . . *"Goals are not only absolutely necessary to motivate us. They are essential to really keep us alive."* *—Robert Schuller*	M17 - Overcoming Obstacles to Goals (Review) A11 - V.I.P. Center (Presentation) A12 - V.I.P. Parent Letter C10 - Favorite Work Folder *Have students tally how many negative and positive statements they hear.*	A12 - **V.I.P. Parent Letter** **GOAl-SETTING ACTIVITIES** Introduce goal-setting gradually. Use the goal-setting steps (**M14**) as a suggested sequence. Keep in mind that a characteristic of low self-esteem students is that they don't know how to evaluate their performance realistically. They often set unattainable goals. A key to success is helping students first keep track of their performances. Continue M10, M11, M12 *or* M13.
CC47 - How Will You Make It? M19 - Daily Goal-setting *or* M22 - Goal Wheel *Invite dialogue with students.*	M19 - **Daily Goal-setting** *or* M22 - **Goal Wheel** A11 - V.I.P. Center (Presentation) A12 - V.I.P. Parent Letter C10 - Favorite Work Folder *Encourage students to clip articles relating to "decision-making."*	M29 - **Goal Award Grams:** Use to recognize goal attainment. M27 - **Goal Achievement Journal:** Bind together several pages and have students keep track of goal successes. Continue the project into the next 2 months. M25 - **Goal Results:** Use with individual students when needed to help them keep track of goal successes.
CC48 - Goal Accomplishment M20 - Weekly Goal Card *or* M23/24 - Goal Passbook *Have a school beautification day.*	M20 - **Weekly Goal Card** *or* M23/24 - **Goal Passbook** A11 - V.I.P. Center (Presentation) A12 - V.I.P. Parent Letter C10 - Favorite Work Folder *"You must know from which harbor you are headed if you are to catch the right wind to take you there."* *—Seneca*	**CLASSROOM POSITIVE ACTIVITIES** Choose one of the following each day to recognize a different student: CC40 - **Compliments** CC41 - **Compliment Hanging** S31 - **Sparkle Line** **POSITIVELY RECOGNIZED STUDENTS**

STAFF ESTEEM BUILDER
Give each staff member a package of Lifesavers attached to a note describing why they are a lifesaver.

This guide is only a suggested framework for Esteem Building.

	MONDAY	TUESDAY	WEDNESDAY
WEEK 33	**ESTEEM BUILDER #1:** Provide Opportunities to Increase Awareness of Competencies and Strengths C1/2 - Hobby Day: Share your hobby. M28 - A Month of Goals A11 - V.I.P. Center (Set up) *"What the human mind can conceive and believe, it can accomplish." —David Sarnoff*	C3 - Strength Profile (Begin individually) M28 - A Month of Goals *Set up specific times when you and the student can evaluate school progress together.*	C6 - Class Strength Book (Introduce) M28 - A Month of Goals *"As soon as you trust yourself, you will know how to live." —Goethe*
WEEK 34	C7 - Student Strength Book C6 - Class Strength Book M28 - A Month of Goals A11 - V.I.P. Center (Set up) *Write specific messages as often as you are able on corrected work.*	Concept Circle Topic: C1/2 - Hobby Day Sharing C6 - Class Strength Book M28 - A Month of Goals *"Failure is the only opportunity to more intelligently begin again." —Henry Ford*	SH44 - The Gift of Self C6 - Class Strength Book M28 - A Month of Goals *"Self-trust is the first secret of success." —Ralph Waldo Emerson*
WEEK 35	**ESTEEM BUILDER #2:** Teach How to Record and Evaluate Progress C16 - I Can or C15 - Add a New Success C6 - Class Strength Book M28 - A Month of Goals A11 - V.I.P. Center (Set up) *Remember to be a model of positive self-talk.*	C15 or C16 Concept Circle Topic: C1/2 - Hobby Day Sharing or CC58 - I Can C6 - Class Strength Book M28 - A Month of Goals *Ask students to write one thing they achieved in school each day.*	C15 or C16 C6 - Class Strength Book M28 - A Month of Goals *"Nurture your mind with great thoughts." —Benjamin Disraeli*
WEEK 36	C15 or C16 C6 - Class Strength Book M28 - A Month of Goals A11 - V.I.P. Center (Set up) *"Men never plan to be failures; they simply fail to plan to be successful." —William A. Ward*	C15 or C16 Concept Circle Topic: Share one page from C10 that you're proud of. C6 - Class Strength Book M28 - A Month of Goals *Have students write letters to the principal: "I'm proud of my school because..."*	C15 or C16 C6 - Class Strength Book M28 - A Month of Goals *Keep a positive spirit.*

SCHOOL-WIDE ACTIVITIES
SW14 - Good News Report; SW19-SW23
SW24 - School Problem Report
SW26/27 - Book of Winners (introduce) or continue SW25 - Koala-T Efforts

THURSDAY	FRIDAY	NOTES / PLANS

| | CC36 - Sun Rays (Class activity) | **COMPETENCE:** *A feeling of success and accomplishment in things regarded as important or valuable. Aware of strengths and able to accept weaknesses.* |

THURSDAY

Concept Circle Topic:
C1/2 - Hobby Day Sharing

C6 - Class Strength Book

Begin the day by sharing a success.

FRIDAY

CC36 - Sun Rays
(Class activity)

C6 - Class Strength Book

A11 - V.I.P. Center (Presentation)

A12 - V.I.P. Parent Letter

C10 - Favorite Work Folder

"Success or failure is caused more by mental attitude than by mental capacity." —Sir Walter Scott

---

THURSDAY

Concept Circle Topic:
C1/2 - Hobby Day Sharing

C6 - Class Strength Book

M28 - A Month of Goals

"To accomplish great things, we must not only act but also dream, not only dream but also believe."
—Anatole France

FRIDAY

C8 - Strength Barbell

C6 - Class Strength Book

M28 - A Month of Goals

A11 - V.I.P. Center (Presentation)

A12 - V.I.P. Parent Letter

C10 - Favorite Work Folder

Have a read-a-thon sleepover.

THURSDAY

C15 *or* C16

Concept Circle Topic:
C1/2 - Hobby Day Sharing *or*
CC58 - I Can

C6 - Class Strength Book

M28 - A Month of Goals

Provide the opportunity for students to practice praise as a group chant.

FRIDAY

C15 *or* C16

C6 - Class Strength Book

M28 - A Month of Goals

A11 - V.I.P. Center (Presentation)

A12 - V.I.P. Parent Letter

C10 - Favorite Work Folder

Have a backwards day.

THURSDAY

C15 *or* C16

CC49 - Strength Book

C6 - Class Strength Book

M28 - A Month of Goals

Write individual notes stating a special memory you have about the student.

FRIDAY

C15 *or* C16

C6 - Class Strength Book

M28 - A Month of Goals

A11 - V.I.P. Center (Presentation)

A12 - V.I.P. Parent Letter

C10 - Favorite Work Folder

To many students—you are the difference!

NOTES / PLANS

Read chapter on **Competence.**

ONGOING ACTIVITIES
C10 - **Favorite Work Folder**

A11 - **V.I.P. Center:** Student set up and presentation.

S15 - **Rules:** Review as needed.

A12 - **V.I.P. Parent Letter**

GOAL-SETTING ACTIVITIES
M28 - **A Month of Goals** (2-8):
Review the concept of goal-setting by having students practice the goal-setting skills.

M27 - **Goal Achievement Journal** (Continue)

M29 - **Goal Award Grams** (Continue)

STRENGTH AWARENESS
C3 - Use the **Strength Profile** to keep an ongoing record of each student's strengths and competencies.

C1/2 - **Hobby Day:** Assign day for each student to share his/her hobby.

C4/5 - **Attention/Strength Awards:** Distribute awards as earned.

C6 - **Class Strength Book:** Introduce, then continue to add student's individual strengths to their respective pages.

CLASSROOM POSITIVE ACTIVITIES
Choose one of the following activities to do each day as a classroom activity to increase positivism:
S37 - **A Month of Positivism**

S38 - **Happy Happenings**

POSITIVELY RECOGNIZED STUDENTS

STAFF ESTEEM BUILDER
Purchase a large papier mache egg. Each week choose one deserving staff member to receive the egg. Write a message describing what the recipient did to deserve the award and present it to the honoree.

This guide is only a suggested framework for Esteem Building.

	MONDAY	TUESDAY	WEDNESDAY
WEEK 37	**ESTEEM BUILDER #3:** Provide Feedback on How to Accept Weaknesses and Profit from Mistakes C32 - Pride Center (Introduce) A11 - V.I.P. Center (Set up) C18 - Accomplishment Journal *"For they can conquer who believe they can." —John Dryden*	CC50 - Brag Time C32 - Pride Center C18 - Accomplishment Journal *Keep a list of each student's strengths.*	C25 - Strengths and Weaknesses C32 - Pride Center C18 - Accomplishment Journal *Point out successes as they occur.*
WEEK 38	C26 - Accomplishment Banner C18 - Accomplishment Journal C32 - Pride Center A11 - V.I.P. Center (Set up) *Provide opportunities for students to share individual strengths.*	CC55 - Me Commercials C18 - Accomplishment Journal C32 - Pride Center *Have a "Collection Day" when students share their collections.*	C26 - Accomplishment Banner (Complete) C18 - Accomplishment Journal C32 - Pride Center *"He who would climb the ladder must begin at the bottom." —English Proverb*
WEEK 39	**ESTEEM BUILDER #4:** Teach the Importance of Self-Praise for Accomplishments C27 - Be a Model of Self-Talk C18 - Accomplishment Journal C30 - Blue Ribbon Book C32 - Pride Center *Focus on one or two specific strengths of a low self-esteem student.*	CC59 - Self Introduction *or* CC57 - I Thought I Could C18 - Accomplishment Journal C32 - Pride Center *"Nothing is good or bad, but thinking makes it so." —William Shakespeare*	C32 - Pride Center Students make awards for themselves to recognize a special accomplishment in the year. C18 - Accomplishment Journal *"The reward of a thing well done is to have done it." —Ralph Waldo Emerson*
WEEK 40	A39 - Autographs C18 - Accomplishment Journal C32 - Pride Center *"The whole secret of the teacher's force lies in the conviction that men are convertible." —Ralph Waldo Emerson*	**Concept Circle Topic:** Share the paper you are most proud of from **C10 - Favorite Work Folder** A39 - Autographs C18 - Accomplishment Journal C32 - Pride Center *"It matters not what you are thought to be, but what you are." —Publilius Syrus (1st C. B.C.)*	A39 - Autographs C18 - Accomplishment Journal C32 - Pride Center *"He that knows himself knows others." —Charles Caleb Colton*

SCHOOL-WIDE ACTIVITIES
SW14 - Good News Report; SW19-SW23
SW24 - School Problem Report
SW26/27 - Book of Winners, continue *or* continue SW25 Koala-T Efforts.

THURSDAY	FRIDAY	NOTES / PLANS
CC54 - One Good Thing About Me **C32 - Pride Center** **C18 - Accomplishment Journal** *Assign each student to be a "Positive Finder." Students report positive observations.*	**C32 - Pride Center** **C18 - Accomplishment Journal** **A11 - V.I.P. Center** (Presentation) **A12 - V.I.P. Parent Letter** **C10 - Favorite Work Folder** *"Great works are performed not by strength but by perseverance."* *—Samuel Johnson*	**COMPETENCE:** *A feeling of success and accomplishment in things regarded as important or valuable. Aware of strengths and able to accept weaknesses.* Read chapter on **Competence.** **ONGOING ACTIVITIES** **C10 - Favorite Work Folder**
CC56 - I'm Proud **C32 - Pride Center** **C18 - Accomplishment Journal** *"Do not bring me your successes; they weaken me. Bring me your problems; they strengthen me."* *—Charles F. Kettering*	**C41 - Books to Enhance Competence:** Choose a selection **C18 - Accomplishment Journal** **C32 - Pride Center** **A11 - V.I.P. Center** (Presentation) **A12 - V.I.P. Parent Letter** **C10 - Favorite Work Folder** *Have a crazy-sock day.*	**A11 - V.I.P. Center** (Assign students) **A12 - V.I.P. Parent Letter:** Continue until all students have been recognized. **S15 - Rules:** Review as needed. **STRENGTH AWARENESS** **C32 - Pride Center** (Introduce)
CC52 - Blue Ribbon *or* **CC50 Brag Time** **C18 - Accomplishment Journal** **C32 - Pride Center** *Have students compile a group collage of school/class memories.*	**C18 - Accomplishment Journal** **C32 - Pride Center** **C10 - Favorite Work Folder** *"Potential: It's all there. You've just got to work to get it out."* *—Glenn Van Ekeren*	**C18 - Accomplishment Journal:** Students keep track of their accomplishments for one month. Add extra pages to the journal to encourage continued writing when school lets out. Additional journal topics, see **J8.** **C41 - Books to Enhance Competence:** Read and/or get written assignment after discussion.
C18 - Accomplishment Journal **A39 - Autographs** **C32 - Pride Center** **Concept Circle Topic:** Students choose favorite topic. *Have each student share one special memory they have of the school year.*	**C18 - Accomplishment Journal** **A39 - Autographs** **C32 - Pride Center** **C10 - Favorite Work Folder** *"Life is a lively process of becoming."* *—General Douglas MacArthur*	**CLASSROOM POSITIVE ACTIVITIES** Choose one of the following activities to do each day as a classroom activity to increase positivism: **S35 - Add a Compliment** **S30 - Builder-Uppers** **POSITIVELY RECOGNIZED STUDENTS** |	
---	---

STAFF ESTEEM BUILDER
Set up a "Compliment Hanging" board, adapted from **A38,** for staff members to write positive notes to one another.

This guide is only a suggested framework for Esteem Building.

Monthly Planner

Coordinator/Team:_____

Esteem Component:_____

Theme (if any):_____

Purpose:

School-wide Activity:

Classroom Activities:

• Language Arts/Literature:

• Math:

• Social Studies/Science:

• Other:

Resources:

| Week 1 |
| Week 2 |
| Week 3 |
| Week 4 |

3

A Strong Foundation: Building Security

ESTEEM BUILDERS
- Build a Trusting Relationship
- Set Reasonable Limits and Rules That Are Consistently Enforced
- Create a Positive and Caring Environment

SUMMARY OF SECURITY

Definition: *A feeling of strong assuredness. Involves feeling comfortable and safe; knowing what is expected; being able to depend on individuals and situations; and comprehending rules and limits.*

SUPPORT DATA

- "In general, only a child who feels safe dares to grow forward healthily. His safety needs must be gratified." Abraham Maslow. *Toward a Psychology of Being*, 2nd Ed. (New York: Van Nostrand Reinhold, 1968).
- "Attitude substantially affects the motivation of every individual." Stanley Coopersmith. *The Antecedents of Self-Esteem* (San Francisco: W.H. Freeman, 1967).
- "A sense of security is the first prerequisite to positive self-esteem. Children need this sense of security before they look at themselves realistically or risk the possibility of failure." Robert Reasoner. *Building Self-Esteem: A Comprehensive Program* (Palo Alto, CA: Consulting Psychologists Press, 1982).
- "Everything the teacher does, as well as the manner in which he does it, incites the child to respond in some way or another and each response tends to set the child's attitude in some way or another." John Dewey. *How We Think* (Lexington, MA: D.C. Heath, 1933).
- "The concepts which the teacher has of the children become the concepts which the children come to have of themselves." C.H. Patterson. *Humanistic Education* (Englewood Cliffs, NJ: Prentice-Hall, 1973).

ESTEEM BUILDERS

- Build a Trusting Relationship
- Set Reasonable Limits and Rules That Are Consistently Enforced
- Create a Positive and Caring Environment

POSSIBLE INDICATORS OF WEAK SECURITY

- avoids situations or environment;
- withdraws from close physical contact even with known persons;
- distrusts others; avoids or hesitates in forming close personal attachments;
- exhibits stress or anxiety symptoms (that is, nail biting, thumb sucking, hair twirling, teeth grinding, shaking, crying without apparent reason);
- challenges authority;
- displays excessive and/or unfounded fears;
- is uncomfortable with new experiences;
- lacks knowledge of who can be counted on.

POSSIBLE INDICATORS OF STRONG SECURITY

- knows who to count on and trust;
- generally feels safe and secure, therefore risks separating from trusted sources for brief periods;
- displays few symptoms of stress and anxiety (see above);
- has formed a trusting, personal relationship with a significant other;
- is comfortable with close physical contact from known persons;
- handles change and spontaneity with relative ease.

Most students will not conform exactly to the profiles listed above but are more likely to be stronger in some areas and weaker in others. In order to determine the degree to which a student feels secure, complete the student self-esteem assessment (B-SET) chart located in Appendix II. The chart may be referred to periodically or updated as a way of measuring progress. These charts are also useful in determining which activities are appropriate for your class.

Security Activities List

Code	Grade	Title	Soc. Studies	Sci.	Writ. Lang.	Oral Lang.	Math	Art	Lit.
S1	2–6	Teacher/Student Letter Exchange			✔				
S2	K–8	From Me to You Gram			✔				
S3	K–8	I Just Wanted You to Know Gram			✔				
S4	K–8	Special Recognition Gram			✔				
S5	K–8	I Like Gram			✔				
S6	K–8	Tool Day	✔		✔	✔			
S7	K–8	Significant Other Interview	✔		✔	✔			
S8	2–8	Significant Other Biographies	✔		✔				
S9	K–4	Significant Other Sharing				✔			
S10	2–8	Letter to a Significant Other			✔				
S11	K–8	Special Books on Significant Others			✔				✔
S12	3–8	Someone Special			✔	✔			
S13	1–8	List of People I Can Depend On			✔				
S14	2–8	Significant Others			✔	✔		✔	
S15	2–8	Rules	✔		✔	✔			
S16	1–8	Scholar Dollars				✔	✔		
S17	1–8	Time for Friends			✔	✔	✔		
S18	1–5	Name Bingo			✔	✔			
S19	1–8	Name Exchange			✔	✔		✔	
S20	4–8	Personality Trivia			✔	✔			
S21	2–8	Student Interview			✔	✔			
S22	K–3	Interest Search			✔	✔		✔	
S23	3–8	Find a Friend			✔	✔			
S24	2–8	Sparkle Statements			✔	✔		✔	
S25	2–5	Smile Book	✔		✔	✔	✔	✔	
S26	K–6	Super Sparkle Gram			✔	✔			
S27	K–8	Secret Friendly Hello Person				✔			
S28	K–4	Smile File			✔	✔		✔	
S29	K–4	Smile Cans			✔	✔		✔	
S30	3–8	Builder-Uppers			✔	✔			
S31	K–4	Sparkle Line			✔	✔		✔	
S32	K–4	Sparkle Compliments			✔	✔			
S33	K–3	Sparkle Book/Cover			✔	✔		✔	
S34	2–8	A Special Message to You			✔				
S35	3–8	Add a Compliment			✔				
S36	K–4	Sparkle Greeting/Bags			✔	✔		✔	
S37	2–8	A Month of Positivism			✔		✔		
S38	1–6	Happy Happenings			✔				

Affiliation Activities That Enhance Students' Awareness of Each Other

A1	K–8	Books on Belonging and Acceptance
A2	2–6	Common Points
A3	2–8	Getting to Know You Wheel
A4	3–8	Paired Name Collage
A5	K–6	Class Discovery Book
A6	1–4	Solve the Riddle
A7	K–4	Friendship Graphs
A8	K–3	Our Favorite Books
A9	2–6	Mystery Person
A10	2–8	Friendly Riddles

Affiliation Activities That Create a Positive and Caring Environment

A23	4–8	Friendship Openers
A24	1–4	Word Gifts
A33	K–8	Caring Words

Concept Circle Activities That Promote Security

Code	Grade	Title	Grouping
CC1	K–8	Beginning Circle	Full
CC2	K–8	How Do You Do?	Full/Team
CC3	K–8	Listen Up!	Full/Team
CC4	K–3	Ball Pass	Full/Team
CC5	2–8	Partner Interview	Full/Partner
CC6	2–8	Body Tracings	Team
CC7	2–8	The One-Cent Interview	Partner

School-wide Activities That Promote Security

Code	Grade	Title	Element
SW1	K–8	Spirit Tickets	Security
SW2	K–8	Spirit Award	Security

Outstanding Friendliness

Code	Grade	Title	Element
SW3	K–8	Positive Performers	Security
SW4	K–8	Positive Performance	Security Award
SW5	K–8	Gotcha Tickets	Security
SW6	K–4	Sparkle Gram	Security/Selfhood
SW7	3–8	Good Guy Award	Security/Selfhood
SW8	K–8	Pass the Buck	Security
SW10	K–8	Friendship Assembly	Security/Affiliation
SW11	K–8	Name Tag Exchange	Security/Affiliation

Checklist of Educator Behaviors
That Promote SECURITY

Directions: For a self-evaluation of your skills in enhancing students' sense of security, complete the following items:

Never 1	Sometimes 2	Frequently 3	Always 4	
				As an educator:
_____	_____	_____	_____	1. Do I let each student feel he/she is accepted, welcomed and important?
_____	_____	_____	_____	2. Do I share my own thoughts and feelings with my students?
_____	_____	_____	_____	3. Do I provide time to listen to my students?
_____	_____	_____	_____	4. Do I respect the privacy and confidentiality of my students?
_____	_____	_____	_____	5. Do I convey realistic and reasonable expectations to my students (high enough to be challenged and still capable of being met)?
_____	_____	_____	_____	6. Do students see me as an individual that they can depend on and trust?
_____	_____	_____	_____	7. Do I make an effort to personalize my relationships with students (i.e., send personal notes, phone home, greet students personally)?
_____	_____	_____	_____	8. Do I set reasonable and meaningful rules and limits within my learning environment?
_____	_____	_____	_____	9. Are my students clearly aware of these rules and limits? Do they understand the consequences/ rewards?
_____	_____	_____	_____	10. Does my attitude convey a positive model to my students?

_____ + _____ + _____ = _____   Total:_____

Areas I could improve in to increase the development of a student's sense of security:____

_____

_____

Esteem Builders. Jalmar Press
Rolling Hills Estates, CA

3

A Strong Foundation: Building Security

Only a child who feels safe dares to grow forward healthily.
His safety needs must be gratified.
—ABRAHAM MASLOW

The first step toward enhancing a student's self-esteem is to create an environment that supports self-attitudes. The most essential component to this framework is a sense of security. This feeling is so crucial that without it, the development of a strong, healthy sense of self is extremely limited. Students must feel safe and assured in their environment in order to grow. They must perceive the atmosphere as a nonthreatening place where "I can grow and learn." Only when the student feels a firm sense of security will he/she be comfortable enough to take chances, explore new options and challenges, ask questions and risk failure.

This need for security has been chronicled by many psychologists, including Abraham Maslow in his self-actualization theory.[1] A basic tenet of Maslow's personality theory is his "need hierarchy," which consists of five types of human needs. Those on the base must be satisfied first in order for individuals to progress to the next higher level. The natural direction of growth is toward the top of the hierarchy, which includes self-esteem and, finally, self-actualization.

Maslow contends that the three lower order needs that must first be met include: physiological needs, safety and belonging (love). These three needs are certainly ones that the educator should keep in mind when creating an environment for learning, because these are the building blocks that help the child to grow toward a sense of healthy selfhood and, therefore, to become an efficient learner.

Maslow's Hierarchy of Needs

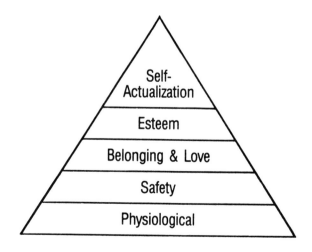

---

1. Maslow, Abraham. *Toward a Psychology of Being* (New York: Van Nostrand Reinhold, 1968).

Higher-Order Needs	*Self-Actualization* The need to know, understand, create and appreciate beauty. *Self-Esteem* The need to feel competent, independent and worthy.
Lower-Order Needs	*Belonging and Love* The need to belong to a family, group; to love and be loved. *Safety* The need to avoid pain, escape fear and be secure. *Physiological Necessities* The need to obtain food, water, oxygen and shelter.

When a student feels insecure and unsafe, he/she may indicate this in a variety of behaviors, such as:

- avoids situation or environment;
- withdraws from close physical contact even with known persons;
- distrusts others; is hesitant or avoids forming close personal attachments;
- exhibits stress or anxiety indicators (nail biting, hair twirling, thumb sucking, teeth grinding, shaking, crying without apparent reason);
- challenges authority;
- displays excessive and/or unfounded fears;
- is uncomfortable with new experiences;
- lacks knowledge of who can be counted on.

All these behaviors greatly reduce the student's capacity to learn.

On the other hand, a student with a strong sense of security is likely to display the following behaviors:

- knows who to count on and trust;
- generally feels safe and secure, therefore risks separating from trusted sources for brief periods;
- displays few symptoms of stress and anxiety (see above);
- has formed a trusting, personal relationship with a significant other;
- is comfortable with close physical contact from known persons;
- handles change and spontaneity with relative ease.

SUMMARY

A sense of security is prerequisite to all other components of self-esteem; therefore, it is essential that the educator create an environment where such a feeling is paramount. There are three steps the esteem builder can take to increase the sense of security for the student:

1. Build a trusting relationship.
2. Set reasonable limits and rules that are consistently enforced.
3. Create a positive and caring environment.

=ESTEEM BUILDER #1=

Build a Trusting Relationship

"We really are teaching human beings, not test scores."
—ROBERT REASONER

A student/esteem builder relationship that is warm and trusting can contribute to student development academically as well as increase self-esteem. For a trusting relationship to evolve, an esteem builder needs to demonstrate to the student acceptance, respect, realness and realistic expectations.

ACCEPTANCE

Coopersmith's research found acceptance from others to be one of the three major conditions

associated with the development of a child's positive self-image.[2] True acceptance means the student is accepted not only for his/her strengths but also for weaknesses—that is, the relationship must be one in which the student feels appreciated with "no strings attached." For example, through being accepted by others, Johnny can grow because he perceives that "they like me for what I am" and not for "what I should be." In this environment, *he has the necessary emotional support to change and even try new ways of behaving.*

---

2. Coopersmith, Stanley. *The Antecedents of Self-Esteem* (San Francisco: W.H. Freeman and Co., 1967).

RESPECT

Coopersmith's work also showed that children with high self-esteem generally were raised in environments in which they were treated respectfully, which included being heard by adults. This does not mean that the educator necessarily agrees with the student's opinions and ideas, but that the pupil has the chance to be heard. This type of treatment conveys the message "my ideas and opinions count," which in turn enhances self-esteem.

A particularly important element of respect is that the esteem builder honor the student's privacy. Students need to feel as though they can count on the adult to keep confidential comments just that— confidential! For some students this level of the relationship may take a long time to develop. It is essential that there be no breach of faith.

REALNESS

Psychologist Carl Rogers expressed his conviction that one of the essential qualities to facilitate learning is for the esteem builder to radiate a feeling of "realness or genuineness."[3] This enables the educator to be much more effective in the relationship. In order to build trust, we must be willing to give of ourselves: to open up and show our true colors and feelings. Ample opportunities for this arise in situations with students. It might include actively participating in a self-esteem activity, being willing to share your own thoughts and feelings, or just sharing a concerned and interested ear. Whatever the activity or situation, students must feel the esteem builder's sincere interest and genuine concern toward them. Only then will they be more willing to open up and trust.

REALISTIC EXPECTATIONS

There is clear-cut evidence that teachers who expect children to learn, and believe they are capable of succeeding, produce marked increases in student performances. The student receives the message, "You care about my learning and because you care I'm going to try harder." Good speculated that teachers' expectations may become a self-fulfilling prophecy to the student: he/she learns as little or as much as the teacher expects.[4]

One of the most famous classroom studies illustrates just how critical teacher expectations really are. This study, conducted by Robert Rosenthal and Lenore Jacobson,[5] began by giving a learning ability test to a group of kindergarten through fifth-grade students in a lower socioeconomic neighborhood.

The following fall, the new teachers were each given the names of five or six students from the test group and told that they had the capacity to make large scholastic improvements during the coming school year. The test supposedly revealed that these "high-potential" students had exceptional learning ability. What the teachers did not know was that the names of these "high-potential" students had been chosen entirely at random. When the students were retested at the end of the school year, there were astonishing results. The students whom the teachers thought had "exceptional learning ability" actually made significant progress and had gained as many as 15 to 27 I.Q. points. When interviewed by the experimenters, the teachers also indicated that the "high potential" students were happier, more curious, better adjusted, more affectionate than average, and were more likely to be successful in their future lives than were other students.

The only difference that year was that the teachers' expectations of the students were changed. Because they had been led to expect more of certain students, a spiraling effect occurred. Those students came to expect more of themselves. The teachers' beliefs and attitudinal changes toward them probably provided a climate in which they felt themselves to be more successful, more capable and more worthy—in short, to have "greater potential."

A teacher's attitude toward a student is therefore a powerful tool in creating change in his/her self-portrait. It is vital, however, to keep in mind that it is just as easy to slip into negative building as it is into positive building. A positive esteem builder conveys *reasonable* expectations.

Another function of being a positive esteem builder is to give praise where deserved. This form of approval, given sincerely, is a powerful technique for enhancing self-esteem. The most effective praise generally has the following characteristics:

3. Rogers, Carl. *Freedom To Learn* (Columbus, OH: Charles E. Merrill, 1969), p. 106.
4. Good, T.L. "How Teachers' Expectations Affect Results," *American Education*, Vol. 18, No. 10, Dec. 1982, pp. 25–32.
5. Rosenthal, Robert, and Jacobson, Lenore. *Pygmalion in the Classroom* (New York: Holt, Rinehart & Winston, 1968).

SECURITY

Effective Praise

- Deserved
- Immediate
- Behavior-Centered
- Individual
- Specific
- Repeated
- Spontaneous

1. **Deserved.** Students are quite perceptive and know if they really earned the praise they received. Be sure that the praise you give is deserved, or your statements will seem insincere.

2. **Immediate.** The best time to give praise is on the spot. Keep in mind that the longer you delay your praise, the less effective your comment is. Younger students, or low self-esteem students, tend to forget their praiseworthy moments. If possible, praise as soon as the action is performed.

3. **Behavior-Centered.** To begin, limit your praise to specific student behaviors instead of positive attributes. Stick to what the student *did*. Telling a low self-esteem student he/she is "cute," "sweet" or "nice" often does not fit the student's existing inner self-image; consequently, the praise will be met with disbelief. For these students, it's important to relate the praise to a behavior. Consider limiting praise to one or two student behaviors in the beginning. Any more may reduce the effectiveness of your remarks.

4. **Individual.** Effective praise is individual. Keep in mind that many students cannot easily accept praise and display their uneasiness in behaviors such as: being embarrassed, denying it, acting out (being silly) or disregarding it. Instead of verbalizing praise to these students, many teachers choose to write it down in the form of a gram, note or in the student's journal. It's sometimes less threatening this way.

5. **Specific.** The most effective praise is very concrete and lets the individual know exactly what was done well. When you observe good behavior, don't say "good job"; but, instead, word your message specifically, like this: "Ryan, you did a great job on this writing paper today because you used the margin and stayed inside

the lines!" Specific praise lets students know what they did well and, as a result, they're more likely to repeat the behavior.

6. **Repeated.** Giving praise one or two times is not enough for individuals with low self-esteem. Their internal image is so ingrained you may need to repeat the praise for similar behaviors 10–15 times before the message is internalized and accepted. Don't feel you're becoming a broken record; but do praise frequently for the same observed behavior.

7. **Spontaneous.** Although the keyword for effectiveness is "repeated praise," it is not advisable to always praise the same behavior every time it occurs. For instance, if you praise David every time he turns in quality work, he may begin to take your comments for granted and grow to expect it. When your praise of the same earned behavior comes across as spontaneous (that is, you may sometimes choose not to praise it), the comment is more effective.

ESTEEM BUILDER GUIDELINES TO PROMOTE A TRUSTING RELATIONSHIP

1. Start the year on a positive note by sending a letter to each student with the message: "I can't wait to see you!" A personal message sets a good tone.

2. Try to greet students each day at the door with an obvious "I'm glad to see you" face.

3. Consider having at least one conference during the year at the student's home.

4. Consider inviting students to your home. Special event!

5. Save a shoe box and make a slot on the top. Decorate the box and inscribe it with the words "Private Letters." Encourage students to write letters or cards (or draw pictures) to you. Be sure to answer each letter individually. Some students may use the Letter Box as an opportunity to write more personal notes to you in which they describe their feelings, thoughts or problems. Remember to respect the confidentiality of the letters.

6. Keep in touch with parents through frequent phone calls and messages sent home. For

younger students, place a plastic phone on a different student's desk each day. Tell students that you appreciate their efforts and that you will be giving their parents a *Sunshine Call* during the day to let them know about their child's efforts.

7. Send special notes and messages to students recognizing their efforts, achievements and specialness. Also remember special occasions (birthdays, moving away, get well, congratulations, new students, thank you's). You may copy special message grams (S2–S5) and distribute them to students.

8. Share yourself. Make your own self-esteem activities each time the students do; these will make wonderful samples for the class as well as convey special information about you.

9. Share your feelings with your students. If you provide a space on the chalkboard for students to write their names down when they're having a trying day, remember to include your own name from time to time.

10. Allow students opportunities to be heard. You could set up "One Minute and Be Heard" sessions. Students need to realize that someone will listen to them, but set boundaries too.

11. Make sure the students know your desk is a place where they can talk and confer with you. Designate a place in the room (the chalkboard or a sheet of paper on your desk) where students can schedule conference times with you.

12. Invite a student(s) to lunch. This need not be to a restaurant. Both of you could bring a bag lunch that day. The important thing is that you're taking time for each other.

13. Set individual goals for your students that are reachable—both academically and behaviorally. Don't underestimate their capabilities, but don't over-challenge them either. Praise them for their accomplishments.

ACTIVITIES: GROUP 1

There is nothing more critical in your role as an esteem builder than to foster a relationship based on trust with each individual student. A large portion of your success in changing a student's self-feelings depends on this essential first premise.

There are endless ways to build rapport and trust with students; keep in mind, though, that the activities need not be complex or time consuming. Whatever you do with your students, the key is to convey the critical message that you care about them as individuals.

The following activities help form a close, trusting teacher/student relationship.

Grades 2–6	Teacher/Student Letter Exchange	S1

Purpose: To provide the opportunity for an ongoing teacher/student dialogue.

One of the bigger challenges for a teacher is trying to maintain personal daily contact with students. As class sizes increase, this responsibility becomes more and more difficult to fulfill adequately. One technique many teachers have found useful is "Teacher/Student Letter Exchange."

Similar to a journal, students write daily in their booklets about differing topics, keeping a personal ongoing dialogue with the teacher. For a complete description of daily letter exchange topics, and Let's Write to Each Other forms, refer to Chapter 9, Journal Writing.

Grades K–8	Special Recognition Grams	S2/3/4/5

Purpose: To recognize students' special school accomplishments and increase teacher/student communication.

Materials: Copies of the 4 recognition grams.

Procedure: Make an ample supply of the four recognition grams on light-colored construction paper and cut them along the center and outer margins as indicated. Whenever a student deserves recognition for school behavior, accomplishments or "just because," fill out the form and hand it to the deserving person. You may wish to keep track of who receives the award so that all students have the chance to receive one.

SIGNIFICANT OTHERS

One of the characteristics of secure individuals is that they know there are others who they can count on and trust. The following group of activities encourage students to explore the major sources of influence in their life.

Grades K–8	Tool Day	S6

Purpose: To help students reflect on their family member roles.

Materials: An object and photograph, brought from the student's home, that represents a particular family member.

Procedure: Ask students to think about each family member (or key significant others). What object do they associate with each member? On appointed days, students bring in an object they think best represents their chosen family member, as well as a photograph of that person. They then show the class the photograph and share why they chose that particular object.

Follow-up: Students write their stories in a "Tool Book." (Younger students can either dictate to you or a class aide.)

Grades K–8	Significant Other Interview	S7

Purpose: To provide an opportunity for students to discuss issues with a significant other. To practice interviewing skills.

Materials: A list of interview questions compiled by the students. Type these up on a ditto so that each student has a copy.

A brief explanation letter to the interviewee regarding the activity and its purpose. Make copies for students to give to the potential interviewee.

Procedure: Following a discussion about what a "significant other" is, each student chooses an individual who fits the description for them. Tell the students they are to interview the person and find out things about him/her that they did not know until now. As a class you may compile a list of questions, such as:

- What was it like growing up?

- Where did you grow up? How was it similar to/different from now?

- What was the hardest/easiest thing about school?

- How was going to school then different from now?

- Who was your favorite teacher? Tell me about him/her.

- What were your favorite things to do then? Now?

Print answers on the interview form and use as the background material for Significant Other Biographies (S8). This activity could be adapted for younger students by allowing them to tape the interview.

Grades 2–8	Significant Other Biographies	S8

Purpose: To expand students' knowledge about the significant others in their lives.

Materials: Completed interview questions from S7.

Procedure: Students write, in biography form, the information learned from the Significant Other Interview. The length and sophistication of the assignment will depend upon time constraints and grade level. You may wish to display copies of published biographies of famous Americans as a guide to the concept of a biography.

Grades K–4	**Significant Other Sharing**	**S9**

Purpose: To help students reflect upon significant others currently in their lives.

Materials: Send a letter or make a phone call to students' chosen significant other in which you explain the program and ask for convenient times and dates for a classroom visit.

Procedure: Students bring a significant other of their choice to share with the class. The individual stays for a designated time (or no time constraints). To assign one particular day may prove awkward for many working adults; in which case, set up a flexible schedule with several choices of times and days.

Adapt for older students. Ask them to invite a significant other to the classroom to share a particular expertise, profession, skill, hobby or just him-/herself.

Grades 2–8	**Letter to a Significant Other**	**S10**

Purpose: To help students define the role significant others play in their life.

Materials: Writing paper and a writing instrument.

Procedure: Students each choose a significant other who is particularly special to them. Ask students to think carefully why they chose this person. What specific things did the person do that were so special? (See S12 Someone Special form.) Each student writes a formal, personal letter to the significant other expressing in words how special this person is to him/her and why.

Grades K–8	**Special Books on Significant Others**	**S11**

Purpose: To enhance students' awareness of the significant sources of influence on their lives.

Materials: One of the following book selections:

What Mary Jo Shared, Janice May Udry (Scholastic, 1967). Mary Jo chose to share her father. Good for follow-up activities.

Guess Who My Favorite Person Is? Byrd Baylor (Atheneum, 1977). Two characters discuss favorite things in their lives. (Grades 2–6)

In Grandpa's House, Philip Sendak (Harper & Row, 1985). A story written by Maurice Sendak's father, of early immigrant values and beliefs that he wished to pass on to his own children and grandchildren. (Grades 6–8)

Procedure: Read, or assign as independent reading, one of the above-mentioned books dealing with significant others. The selections have wonderful possibilities for follow-up activities and discussions.

Grades 3–8	**Someone Special**	**S12**

Purpose: For students to gain greater appreciation of their significant others.

Materials: A copy of S12 Someone Special form for each student.

Procedure: Students reflect upon people who are special to them and fill in the form. Use the completed form as a guide for students to describe their "special someone" to their partners or teammates.

Grades 1–8	**List of People I Can Depend On**	**S13**

Purpose: To help students recognize the people they can trust.

Materials: A copy of S13 List of People I Can Depend On form for each participating student.

Procedure: Students write the names of people whom they can trust. You may need to discuss the

SECURITY

concept of "trust" by defining it as people they can always count on; who are there when they need them; can keep a secret; and can always be depended upon to help. On the line under the name of each listed individual, students write why that person is special to them. Younger students, or those who don't read, can dictate their answers.

| Grades 2-8 | **Significant Others** | **S14** |

Purpose: To help students discover which individuals are the sources of influence in their life.

Materials: A copy of the S14 Significant Others form for each student.

Procedure: Begin by discussing the term "significant other" with students unless they're already familiar with the concept. Describe a significant other as someone who can be depended on and trusted; someone who is very special, whose company they enjoy. You may wish to describe significant others in your life to illustrate.

Students begin the task by putting their name in the center circle. In the circles surrounding their name they write the names of those people they consider to be their significant others.

To adapt to younger students. Make a facsimile of the form by cutting out 5" circles from light-colored construction paper. On a large piece of butcher paper, students glue the circles around their name circle—in the same formation as the S14 Significant Other form. They may draw pictures of their significant others inside the circles, using crayons or marking pens.

Idea suggested by Robert Reasoner; Superintendent, Moreland School District, San Jose, California.

ESTEEM BUILDER #2

Set Reasonable Limits and Rules That Are Consistently Enforced

"People have a way of becoming what you encourage them to be, not what you nag them to be."
—SCUDDER N. PARKER

In his intensive investigation of what environmental conditions enhance self-esteem, researcher Stanley Coopersmith also found that clearly defined and enforced limits and standards are essential to well being and security. But in order to be effective, esteem builders must enforce limits consistently.

Coopersmith's research[6] offers the following guidelines for establishing limits within the self-enhancing environment:

1. Base limits on reasonable and realistic grounds.

2. Set a small number of limits at a time. They can then be maintained more easily without making enforcement into a burdensome way of life.

3. Regulate boundaries with consistency and firmness.

4. Establish clear behavioral consequences when limits are exceeded. Since students inevitably test limits, continue to clarify and elaborate on them.

5. Only enforce limits nonphysically. Never threaten with loss of acceptance.

6. In order for limits to make sense to the students, they must first be meaningful to the teacher. As an esteem builder you must genuinely believe and expect that the limits set will be observed.

7. Establish rewards for students who do well within the structure.

ACTIVITIES: GROUP 2

The following activities are designed to enhance students' awareness of their boundaries. They may be given intermittently throughout the year. In addition, School-wide esteem activities SW1 through SW9 may easily be adapted for classroom use in order to recognize students for positive behavior. See Chapter 10, School-wide Esteem.

---

6. Coopersmith, Stanley. *The Antecedents of Self-Esteem* (San Francisco: W.H. Freeman, 1967).

Grades 2–8	**Rules**	**S15**

Purpose: To familiarize students and parents with class and school rules.

Materials: A copy of the S15 Rules form for every student.

Adapt for younger students by making a rule chart on a large piece of posterboard or chart paper.

The activity is best done as a group where students suggest and discuss appropriate classroom rules.

Procedure: Many researchers feel that it is critical for students to take an active role in the formation of any rules that might affect them. Constructed in this way, rules are then seen by the students as "owned." This activity helps students formulate classroom rules that will guide their behavior. Robert Ellington, a consultant, suggests incorporating five general concepts as a format for the rules:

> 1. Truth
> 2. Trust
> 3. Responsibility
> 4. Active Listening
> 5. No Put Downs

Add any other categories you consider important to your environment. Encourage students to come up with the wording for rules using each of the concepts. Write these rules on a chalkboard or large chart (a large facsimile of the Rules form could be transposed on posterboard and kept in the classroom as a permanent class reminder of the rules).

Students may vote on the rule wording that they feel best suits each category. Students then write these finalized rules on their Rules form (for younger or nonwriting students you'll need to write the finalized list on the form). You may wish to have each student meet with you briefly to describe the rules back to you. When you recognize that the student understands the rules, sign the form together. The student then brings the form home to discuss the rules with a parent or guardian, who in turn signs the form. The student returns the signed form, which is kept in a student folder.

The second critical aspect of rule making is to ensure students understand the consequences of any rule infringement. Consider having students go through the same procedure as above, but this time list clear consequences to each infringement. Be sure to make the consequences fit the crime! Remember that it is much easier to change behavior through positive means than negative. As often as you can, "catch them being good" when they are in compliance with the rules. The S16 Scholar Dollar activity helps reinforce positive behavior.

Grades 1–8	**Scholar Dollars**	**S16**

Purpose: To familiarize students with school/class rules. To reinforce positive behavior with concrete rewards.

Materials: *Scholar Dollars.* Have on hand a plentiful supply of S16 Scholar Dollars. Make copies of the form on ditto paper. Use a paper cutter to cut individual dollars along the lines. Store the cut dollars in an accessible box or basket.

Rules Poster. Each classroom rule will require one piece of 12" x 18" light-colored posterboard. Using thick colored marking pens, print the classroom rule on the posterboard. For younger students you may wish to depict the rule in pictorial form. Use either a hand-drawn picture or Polaroid picture of students correctly demonstrating the rule.

Formulate rules from the student-guided S16 Rules activity. Assign each rule a number. Depending on the number of rules you have, print the assigned number on each poster so that it is clearly visible.

Scholar Dollar Wallet. Make a wallet from a piece of light-brown construction paper for each student to store their "dollars." Fold and cut it as described in the directions.

Various Awards. Make available various "awards" for students to buy with their Scholar Dollars. Each award should be clearly marked with a price tag or sticker as to how much it would cost. Set prices in relation to how often you plan to distribute Scholar Dollars and the cost of the item.

Procedure: Discuss each rule again with the students. Post the rules around the room at a visible location. Explain that you will be watching for students who follow the rules. Whenever you see such behavior, hand the student a Scholar Dollar. The student must now correctly identify which of the rules he/she was in compliance with. The student quickly checks the posted rules, then writes the number of the rule in the center of the Scholar Dollar, as well as what he/she thinks the rule was that the teacher was reinforcing with him/her, and signs the form.

The dollar should be kept by the student in the wallet. (It may be better for younger students to give their dollars to you for safekeeping.) At a convenient time, consider having a quick Scholar Dollar evaluation time. Each student who earned a dollar now reports to the class which rule they think they were demonstrating when they were awarded the dollar. Students keep all awarded dollars until they wish to "spend them" at the class store. Assign special "buying times."

ESTEEM BUILDER #3

Create a Positive and Caring Environment

"If you think in positive terms, you will achieve positive results."
—NORMAN VINCENT PEALE

A sense of security only exists in a positive environment, that is, one in which the student immediately perceives he/she is welcomed and appreciated. Students will bond to such an atmosphere. They will feel that it is their classroom; it is where they are cared for and belong. Such feelings are obviously conducive to learning because the student is more willing to participate, attend and behave in an appropriate classroom manner. A student's learning attitude cannot be separated from education; it is the combination of these two factors that creates a powerful force for learning.

Helping students maintain a positive attitude is no easy task, particularly when we deal with the negative student. One of the reasons why such an individual is so difficult is that no matter how positive we are, his/her negative attitude ("I don't want to," "I'm dumb!", "I can't do this!") just perpetuates itself. Negativism is just like the domino effect: it spreads wherever negative statements are made. By the same token, positive statements are contagious. Therefore, it is easier to maintain a positive environment when positive models are available.

One of the ways we maintain our ideas about ourself is through a self-referent speech system. For this reason, negative statements are particularly detrimental to self-esteem. Rarely do we stop to think about our inner language as it is largely automatic and internal, but it is nonetheless powerful. Continuous negative self-statements ("I can't do anything right," "I'm ugly") obviously do little to promote a positive sense of self. How can we turn this around and help students make more positive self-statements and build a more positive environment? The following ideas may be helpful to bear in mind as you examine your own esteem-building atmosphere.

STRATEGIES TO USE TO ACCENTUATE POSIVITISM

Accentuate the Positive
1. Model positive statements.
2. Accentuate the positive.
3. Build awareness of esteem-building language.
4. Label appropriate esteem-building language.
5. Reinforce positive statements.
6. Practice positive skills.
7. Teach how to receive compliments.

Eliminate the Negative
1. Draw awareness to negativity.
2. Label the negative.
3. Rule: one put down = one put up.
4. Teach positive self-talk.

Steps to Accentuate the Positive

1. **Model Positive Statements.** Never forget your own impact on your students, and don't downplay your influence as a role model for them. So watch the self-statements you verbalize in front of others. You may wish to purposefully say positive self-statements so that the class may hear you: "I am really pleased with myself today. My lesson turned out well." Or, "I like the bulletin board. I worked hard on it and it does look nice."

2. **Accentuate the Positive.** In any environment, establish a firm commandment. "Thou shalt not talk negatively about thyself or others." Put it in your own words, if you like; but post it in a highly visible location, such as on the door, along the length of the chalkboard or on a bulletin board.

3. **Build Awareness of Esteem-Building Language.** Some students do not know what a positive statement is and need to be taught the skill. As a group, compile a list of builder-upper statements on a large sheet of paper. As new statements are said or learned, add them to the list. Students may refer to these statements.

4. **Label Appropriate Esteem-Building Language.** Many students need help in distinguishing between appropriate language and destructive language. They may have said put-down statements so often they've actually conditioned themselves to say the negative. It is helpful to label appropriate and inappropriate language for the student. Terms that could be used to depict appropriate language include: *fuzzy, compliment, builder-upper* or *sparkle*. Inappropriate language could be labeled by terms such as: *zinger, put down, prickly* or *killer*. Choose one term from each category, teach it to students and then consistently use it to label esteem-building language. For example: "That's a zinger." Or, "That's a put up."

5. **Reinforce Positive Statements.** Reinforce what you want to be repeated. Try to key in on the student's positive statements and forget the negative ones for awhile. It's easier to change behavior by focusing on the positive aspects instead of the negative. Some students, however, make that very tough to do and will almost provoke you to put them down. If you remember that you're only hooking into their game if you do, it'll be easier to stay focused on the positive.

Try reinforcing positive statements and actions with more than verbal statements of recognition every once in a while. A pat on the back, a phone call home and a message gram are just a few different ways to acknowledge deserving statements. Use the positive message gram awards (S2, S3, S4, S5). Make ample copies of them and stock an activity center with additional message grams. Students can then

be encouraged to give them out to one another. Remember, peers can be a powerful force in making positivism an epidemic in your environment.

6. **Practice Positive Skills.** A list of builder-upper statements on a poster, while helpful, is not enough to change a student's behavior. Students must be provided with opportunities to practice positive behaviors. Many activities in ESTEEM BUILDERS are designed for this purpose. Keep in mind that some students may not be comfortable saying positive statements. These students should be allowed to choose the kinds of statements that they feel safe saying. "Hello," "Hi," "How are you?" or a smile and eye contact are appropriate first steps for these students. Forcing someone to say a positive statement causes it to be insincere.

7. **Teach How to Receive Compliments.** Finally, if students are to be recipients of positive statements, they should be taught how to correctly receive the compliment. Make a list of concrete responses students could use, such as the following: Thank you; Thanks; Thanks for noticing; I appreciate that; That made me feel good. Students may choose a response to return to the sender.

Ways to Eliminate the Negative

When students are negative toward themselves or others, there are several techniques to use:

1. **Draw Awareness to Negativity.** When a student goes against the positive commandment, be careful not to be negative toward his/her already negative disposition. Casually mention, "Remember, we only say positive things about ourselves," and be quick to point out the positive statements of others. Some teachers use a private code or signal between themselves and their students. Each time a student states a negative comment, the teacher says a code word like "Zap!" or uses a signal (such as raising a hand) to remind the student.

Often students are not aware of how many negative self-statements they are saying; therefore, you will need to bring them to an awareness of the growing number. One way to do this is a simple tally system on paper. Designate one column for positive statements, the other for negative ones. Each time a student makes either a positive or negative comment, he/she adds a stamp or mark to the appropriate side.

Another way to reward positive statements is to use tokens such as marbles, poker chips, peanuts, etc. A student holds tokens in the left pocket. When he/she makes a negative statement, a token is transferred to the right pocket. Often just one reminder will get the message across.

2. **Label the Negative.** Teach students to recognize a put down by saying a code word or making a sound immediately back to the sender. This should be previously agreed upon by all students so that they recognize the code. These could include such words as: "put down," "pricklie," "killer," "zinger" or sounds such as "ouch," "buz-z-z" or "ding-a-ling." This also makes the sender aware that the statement was inappropriate.

3. **Rule: One Put Down = One Put Up.** Make it a class rule that put-down statements are not allowed. Whenever a put down is said, teach the rule that the sender must then change the put down into a "put up." In some schools this rule is even more stringent: for every put down there must be three put ups. Whatever your number, it must be consistently enforced.

4. **Teach Positive Self-Talk.** Try pointing out positive attributes to the negative student and have him/her verbalize them back to you. Be sure the attribute you're pointing out, though, really does deserve recognition. For example: "Rory, you did such a nice job on your paper today. Your letters are written clearly and they are in the spaces. You should be proud of your work. Tell yourself you did a good job."

Rory then quietly verbalizes the positive self-statement aloud. Always conduct this interaction between only you and the student. An individual with low self-esteem humiliates very quickly and if you do it in front of others, it may only exacerbate the behavior problem.

ACTIVITIES: GROUP 3

The following group of activities relates to building positive behavior in students by promoting a positive, secure environment. This includes activities to help students learn the names of their classmates as well as each others' interests. A class in which students feel connected to each other is more likely to be a positive environment.

Note: There are also activities that support students learning about each other in Chapter 5, Affiliation. They are: A1 through A10, all designed to help a student gain a sense of belonging within the group, which in turn enhances individual security.

| Grades 1–8 | **Time for Friends** | **S17** |

Purpose: To allow students to personally interact with each other.

Materials: A copy of S17 Time for Friends worksheet for each student; pencil.

Procedure: For each hour of the clock, students fill in a different classmate's name. Encourage them to initiate the meeting with the classmate by introducing themselves. For example, "Hi, my name is _____. What's yours? Do you have anything available at _____ o'clock?" You may model to the students how to make introductions to classmates.

The student then writes the classmate's name in the available time slot, and the greeted classmate writes the name of the student who initiated the conversation on his/her form. Each classmate continues the activity until the forms are completely filled.

Each student now has a predetermined partner. You may wish to use this information throughout the year for building teams or any paired activities. For example, "Today, everyone should team up with their 8 o'clock partner" is all that is needed for class organization.

| Grades 1–5 | **Name Bingo** | **S18** |

Purpose: To familiarize students with each other's names and practice the skill of introductions.

Materials: Set of name cards. Print the name of each student in large, manuscript letters on a 3" x 5" index card.

Grid Construction: Make a ditto of a grid containing 1" x 1" squares. There should be as many boxes in the grid as students, rounded off to the nearest higher number and in any combination—5 x 5, 4 x 6, 6 x 5, etc. Draw the grid at least 2 1/2" from the margin. List students' names in the margin. Write "Name Bingo" on the top.

Procedure: Inform the class that you will be playing Name Bingo. Pass the grids out to each student. Ask them to first write their own name in the upper left-hand corner. If there are more squares than students, tell them to put an "X" through the extra number. These may be in any location. Inform students that these squares are "Free."

Students now have the job of filling up their grid with each other's names. Tell the class that they are to walk around and trade names with another classmate who signs his/her name in an empty box. The rule is: "Every time I trade my name, you trade yours." Encourage students to cross off the friend's name in the margin column as they receive the signature. If students need it, model introductions for them.

Now you're ready to play bingo. Draw class names from the name cards. Tell students that if they have the name, to mark an X over it. If you wish to reuse the grid, you may want to use beans or paper markers instead. The first student with four in a row (or five, depending on grid size) wins the game.

Variation: As students become familiar with peer names, change the strategy to "Interest Bingo." Students must now determine which student has which interest.

Idea suggested by Pam Plancich; Enatai Elementary School, Bellevue, Washington.

| Grades 1–8 | **Name Exchange** | **S19** |

Purpose: To provide the opportunity for students to learn each other's names.

Materials: Copies of S19 Name Exchange form, 1 per student, run off on light-colored construction paper and cut along the outside border; marking pens, crayons or pencils.

Procedure: Give each participant a copy of the Name Exchange form. Ask students to write their name in the center shape. Encourage them to colorfully decorate their name letters and the form using marking pens, crayons or colored pencils. In the spaces provided, they then include a few words, pictures or symbols that describe them (interests, strengths, favorite place or pastime). Instruct students to color only to the center rectangle, and not to color in the space that contains their name.

Explain to students that they are now to find out the names of each of their classmates by referring to everyone's decorated name tag. The object of the activity is to fill in each classmate's name in the spaces provided. Model to students how to initiate the meeting with classmates. They are to introduce themselves by stating their name and showing their name tag. Students take a moment to explain a few symbols they've used on their own tag. The introducing student then writes the classmate's name in an available space, and the greeted student writes the name of the initiator in an available space on his/her name tag. Classmates continue the activity until the forms are completely filled out. Students may wear completed name tags; laminate them if they are to be used over and over again.

| Grades 4–8 | **Personality Trivia** | **S20** |

Purpose: To increase students' awareness of each other. To find out student likes.

Materials: 3" x 5" index cards on which you have written 3 randomly selected numbers between 1-44 in the top left-hand corner—1 card per student; copies of the S20 Personality Trivia questionnaire (see page 68).

Procedure:

1. Hand each student an index card and a questionnaire.

2. Students write the answers to the three questions that correspond to the numbers on the questionnaire. For instance, if a student has numbers 9, 10 and 15 written on the card, these are the questions he/she should answer. The student then signs the back of the card when completed and turns it in to the teacher.

Variation: Duplicate the questions on a sheet for each student, who picks a partner. Within a set time period, students are to answer as many of the questions as possible and then exchange partners. You can also set up teams of four to six students.

1. Now make another questionnaire based on the answers on the index cards. Type these questions onto one page. For example, if a student has answered that his/her favorite actor is Tom Selleck, the question on the questionnaire would read: "Which student's favorite actor is Tom Selleck?"

2. Pass out the new questionnaires to students for them to complete. Students could also work in teams.

Idea suggested by Gary Edwards; San Jose, California.

Grades 2–8	**Student Interview**	**S21**

Purpose: To increase students' awareness of others.

Materials: A copy of the S21 Student Interview form for each student; pencil.

Procedure: Assign each student a partner, or use the S17 Time for Friends partners as a guide. Each student receives an interview form and conducts an interview with a partner based on the interview questions. The interview may be timed if desired. At the conclusion, each student introduces his/her partner to the rest of the class.

Grades K–3	**Interest Search**	**S22**

Purpose: To increase students' awareness of each other. To discover shared likes and interests.

Materials: A copy of S22 Interest Search form for each student; pencil.

Procedure: Students read the "favorite categories" in the left-hand column. They then write or draw their response to each category in the middle column. Finally, each student interviews a classmate to find a friend who shares the same favorite. When the student has found the "right"

friend, he/she writes the name down in the final column. Students go through the same procedure for each category.

Grades 3–8	**Find a Friend**	**S23**

Purpose: To enable students to know more about their classmates.

Materials: A copy of S23 Find a Friend form for each student; pencil or other writing instrument.

Procedure: Each student must locate a classmate who qualifies for at least one of the categories in the left-hand column. The student must interview classmates to determine their interests. When he/she finds a classmate who qualifies, that person signs his/her name next to the category. Encourage students to find as many classmates as they can for the categories.

Grades 2–8	**Sparkle Statements**	**S24**

Purpose: To increase students' awareness of the positive statements they can say to each other.

Materials: A copy of S24 Sparkle Statement form; marking pens; long length of butcher paper.

Procedure: Before students can say positive statements to others they must be taught what positive statements are. Make a copy of the S24 Sparkle Statement form accessible to each student; it also could be the basis of an ongoing Sparkle Statement bulletin board.

To construct, cover a bulletin board, door or carrel with butcher paper. Introduce the board by telling students that statements we say to one another are powerful: they either build us up or tear us down. Tell them that those that build others up are called "sparkles," "builder-uppers," "compliments" or "fuzzies" (choose a term that is appropriate to your students' age). You may make copies of the statements from the form onto the butcher paper. When students hear positive statements, you or they add them to the butcher paper list. You may want to have ongoing school lists in areas other than classrooms, such as halls, cafeterias, gyms and offices.

| Grades 2–5 | Smile Book | S25 |

Purpose: To increase students' awareness of the importance of smiles and to observe smiles in others.

Materials: S25 Making a Smile Book instruction sheet per student. As the student completes each task, which is checked of by the teacher/aide, he/she may color the number space on the sheet corresponding to the task finished.

Smile Book. To make each book, place 5 sheets of writing paper on top of a 12" x 9" piece of colored construction paper. Fold the pages in half lengthwise and staple along the creases. Number the pages front and back.

Students will use the book to write in their responses to each task.

Procedure:

1. Provide students with glue, scissors and an assortment of magazines. Students look through the magazines and find people who smile in ways that appeal to them. They cut out the smiles and glue them to the cover of their Smile Book. Using a thin-tipped black marking pen, students may write the words "Smile Book" and their name on the cover. They may also use the first blank page as a title page.

2. Each student brings a photograph from home that shows off his/her great smile. They can also draw a self-portrait. Or, you can use a Polaroid camera to photograph their smiles in the classroom. Students glue their photograph or self-portrait on page 2. On the following page, they write about things that make them smile.

3. This task requires a measuring tape and pencil. Students each choose three friends to measure. You may want to pull names from a box to make sure that everyone will be chosen. Students measure the length and width of their classmates' smiles. They write their findings on pages 4 and 5 of the Smile Book.

4. For this task students will need a newspaper, pencil and paste. They read through the newspaper to find a story that makes them smile, then cut it out and paste it on page 6. On page 7 they write why the story made them smile.

5. Students each find four people on the school grounds whose smiles they admire. They choose from these four categories: adult male, adult female, student male and student female. Students write their choices and why they picked these people on pages 8 and 9 of the Smile Book.

| Grades K–6 | Super Sparkle Gram | S26 |

Purpose: To acknowledge students' positive words and deeds.

Materials: S26 Super Sparkle form duplicated on bright-colored paper. Use construction or cardstock-weight paper.

Procedure: Duplicate an ample supply of the awards. When students perform positive actions or say particularly positive statements to others, reward them with a Super Sparkle gram.

| Grades K–8 | Secret Friendly Hello Person | S27 |

Purpose: To increase classroom positivism.

Materials: Copies of S26 gram; SW6 or SW7 gram (see Chapter 10, School-wide Esteem).

Badge. Make from construction paper, or pin-making machine, a badge that reads, "Hello! I was the Secret Friendly Hello Person."

Procedure:

1. Begin the activity by assigning one student to be the Secret Friendly Hello Person for the day. The appointed student has two tasks:
   a) To keep their appointment a secret from the other students.
   b) To count the number of times classmates extend verbally friendly statements toward him/her. Statements that qualify include: Hi, Hello, How do you do? How are you? Glad to see you, You look great, etc.

2. The teacher then tells the class that there is a Secret Friendly Hello person in their midst whose job it is to keep his/her identity secret and count the number of times he/she is told

the code word/phrase for the day. Tell the class what the code word/phrase is.

Note: Consider using simple, nonthreatening terms to begin with so that all students are comfortable participating. If verbalizing positive statements is difficult for them, try starting with nonverbal exchanges, such as: pats on the back, handshakes, smiles, eye contact.

3. When the fifth classmate says the code word/phrase to the Secret Friendly Hello Person, he/she lets everyone in on the secret. This could be performed in a variety of ways:
   • the person calls out the code word/phrase or "Hello!";
   • the person writes the above on the chalkboard;
   • the person calls out "I'm the one!"

4. The teacher then gives the badge saying "Hello! I was the Secret Friendly Hello Person" to that student to wear for the rest of the day. The fifth person who greeted the student receives the S26, SW6 or SW7 grams. (For older students you may wish to increase the count to 10 or 15 greetings.)

5. Assign a new Secret Friendly Hello Person for the following day. Change the code each time to reflect a different positive statement or gesture. The class may enjoy introducing the activity to the classroom next door. Soon the class activity will become a school-wide one.

Grades K-4	Smile File	S28

Purpose: To increase positivism.

Materials: Run off the two pages of S28 form back-to-back on heavy construction or cardstock-weight paper. Fold along dotted lines where indicated on the worksheets.

Staple the file at the outside edges of "In" and "Out" to make pockets.

Cut 1" x 5" strips out of light-colored construction paper. Each student needs the same number of strips as there are students in the class. Students write the name of each classmate on a different strip and put them in the "In" side of the assembled file.

Procedure: Begin the activity by having each student hold their smile files and randomly choose three strips from the In pocket. They read the names and place them in the Out pocket, keeping the names a secret. Sometime during the day students must tell a builder-upper statement to the friends whose names were pulled.

Since much of positivism is learned through modeling, be sure to have a pack of your own. At the end of the day, ask students if they could guess which classmates pulled their names. Ask questions such as:

• How did you know _____ pulled your name?

• What builder-upper statement did your friend tell you?

• Did you hear a builder-upper statement you like that you'd want to use tomorrow?

The following day, each student chooses three new names and repeats the process until all names have been drawn from the In pocket.

Grades K-4	Smile Cans	S29

Purpose: To help students learn to say positive comments to each other as well as making sure all students are recipients of compliments.

Materials: 3 empty juice cans (same size, cleaned with tops removed); popsicle or tongue depressor sticks (1 for each class member including teacher and 15 extra); glue, scissors; contact or construction paper; permanent thin-tipped black and red marking pens; Xeroxed class photo, each one circling a different student (optional, recommended particularly for nonreaders or younger students).

Note: Smile Cans may be made for each class member or used as a class activity, in which case only one can is needed. You may wish to first introduce the project as a group task and as students become familiarized with the activity, change it so that each student has his/her own can.

Procedure: Connect the three juice cans by cutting a piece of contact or construction paper their height, width and length. Join the three cans with the paper. Use the thin-tipped marking pen to write the words "In" on one can, "Out" on the second can and "Smile Words" on the third.

Name sticks: Use a thin-tipped permanent black marking pen to print vertically the name of each student on the side of each stick. For nonreading students you may wish to glue a Xeroxed class photo to the top of each stick. Place all the name sticks in the can marked "In."

Positive Comment sticks: On the remaining 15 sticks use a permanent marking pen to print a separate positive comment. Ask the students to generate ideas for the comments. Remind them that you should be able to make the comment to anyone (for example, "I like your brown shoes" would not be a good comment) and *it must put a smile on someone's face.* All comments should be ones you can *say,* not do, to someone in the class or school.

Spray paint all the positive comment sticks a pale color, or use a different colored marking pen, to distinguish them from the name sticks.

These are some suggestions for positive comments:

- It's good to see you.
- I like being with you.
- I like you.
- You're a good friend.
- You've got good ideas.
- Have a great day.
- You're fun to be with.
- I'm glad you're here.
- Let's play together.
- Thanks a lot.

Add these sticks to the Smile Words can.

Activity procedure: Begin by randomly electing a student each day to pull one to three names from the In can. Sometime during the day each classmate should be encouraged to say a comment to the chosen peers. Any student who needs a suggestion for a positive comment should pull one from the Smile Words can. The pulled names are put in the Out can. When no names remain in the In can, all the sticks are placed back in the In can to begin the process again.

Variations:

1. Students have individual Smile Cans. Each day a student pulls one name from the In can and adds it to the Out can when he/she verbalizes a friendly comment to that person.

2. As students enter the room they pull a name from the In can, read it and place it in the Out can. That person is their Secret Name Pal for the day, to whom they are responsible for saying a positive comment. This way each day every student will give and receive a positive statement.

3. Using the variations above, students pull a name but write or draw a positive comment back to their friend. Keep a large supply of message slips by the Smile Can for students to use during the activity.

| Grades 3–8 | **Builder-Uppers** | **S30** |

Purpose: To increase student's positive comments to each other.

Materials: S30 Builder-Upper form.

Procedure: Type or write the names of each student on the left column of the form, then duplicate a copy for all class members. Alternatively, students may print the names of their classmates themselves.

Every day each student chooses a different classmate from the left-hand column and a builder-upper statement from the right. The student checks off the statement and classmate's name. Sometime during the day (or at a designated time) each student says a builder-upper to the chosen person.

Continue the activity until all students have had an opportunity to interact positively with each one

SECURITY

of their classmates. Add more positive statements as they are heard or suggested by others.

Grades K-4   Sparkle Line   S31/32

Purpose: To create a permanent, visual reminder of the importance of builder-upper statements.

Materials: To create a "clothesline of compliments": long cord or rug yarn of desired length; 1 clip or clothespin for each participant; S31 Sparkle Boy and Girl patterns to trace; heavy paper, such as tag, for boy and girl patterns; thin-tipped black and colored marking pens; crayons, glue, scissors; construction paper scraps, rickrack (optional); metal hooks for attaching clothesline (if needed); large supply of duplicated S32 Sparkle Greeting.

Procedure: Begin with each student creating a figure according to their likeness:

1. Trace the boy and girl patterns onto heavy paper and cut out.
2. Students decorate their figures with paper scraps, rickrack, crayons, etc.
3. Write the student's name clearly on the figure (preferably with a thin-tipped black marking pen).
4. Glue the completed figures onto the clothespins, which are clipped somewhere along the length of the hanging clothesline.

The actual compliment activity may be carried out in a number of ways. In each of the suggestions below, the complimenter takes a Sparkle Compliment, fills it out and clips it on the recipient's clothespin figure. (This part of the activity applies to those students who can write.)

1. Each day students choose a Secret Pal by randomly pulling a name of a peer from a box containing all the classmates' names on slips of paper (or you can use the Smile Cans, S29). The puller is responsible for writing a compliment to that student sometime during the day and clipping it to the appropriate figure on the clothesline.
2. Students may also send a positive message to any peer of their choice—particularly someone who has said or done something kind to them.
3. Another way is to choose a student to be the recipient of the Sparkle Greeting for the day. Each classmate writes a compliment to the chosen person and clips it to his/her clothespin. At the end of the day, the recipient collects all the messages from the class.
4. Encourage students to write messages on special occasions to a peer (thank you's, birthday, get well, we miss you, etc.)

Idea adapted from Chick Moorman and Dee Dishon: Our Classroom: We Can Learn Together *(Englewood Cliffs, NJ: Prentice-Hall, 1983).*

Grades K-3   Sparkle Book/Cover   S33

As students become more proficient in the language of positive statements, start group activities in which students support each other verbally—such as the Sparkle Book.

Purpose: To increase students' positive comments and deeds toward one another.

Materials: Yellow construction paper; scissors and hole-punch; 24" yarn lengths; writing paper.

Procedure: Make a copy of the Sparkle Book/Cover on a double piece of yellow construction paper. Cut around the shape to form the back and front cover of the book. Cut a piece of writing paper for each student from the same pattern.

Each day, choose one student to be the Sparkle Book recipient of the day. Classmates draw, write or dictate positive comments to their peer on their writing page. At the end of the day, collect all the pages and staple them between the cover. The booklet may be worn by the proud recipient by punching out the two top holes and then stringing it with a 24" piece of yarn.

| Grades 2–8 | A Special Message to You | S34 |

Purpose: To provide the opportunity for students to write positive comments to classmates.

Materials: S34 Special Message to You form duplicated on the front and back of cardstock-weight paper.

Procedure: Older students, or those more proficient in writing, may enjoy this activity. Each day, choose a different student to be the message recipient. Pass the card around the class to each student who, in turn, writes a positive comment to the chosen student and signs his/her name. Present the completed card to the proud recipient to take home.

| Grades 3–8 | Add a Compliment | S35 |

Purpose: To provide the opportunity for students to write positive comments to classmates.

Materials: Duplicate on colored paper enough copies of the S35 Add a Compliment form for each student.

Procedure: Each day, choose one student to become the compliment recipient. This activity is also suitable for special occasions, such as a student's birthday or return from sickness. Instruct the classmates to quickly write a compliment to the student. They will not have enough time to read everyone's comments. As soon as they have written a compliment and signed their name, they pass it to the next classmate until everyone has signed the form.

| Grades K–4 | Sparkle Greeting Bags | S36 |

Purpose: To increase positive statements. To practice receiving positive statements from others.

Materials: Lunch-size paper bag, one per student; S33 Sparkle Cover—duplicated so that each student receives one from another classmate; copies of S32 Sparkle Greeting duplicated on construction paper, one per student; glue, scissors, crayons.

Procedure:

1. Students decorate their bags by gluing the Sparkle figure to the front. Tape bags to students' desks or pin up on a bulletin board at their eye level.

2. Each day choose a student (or several) to receive a Sparkle Greeting from their friends.

3. Classmates write the messages on the Sparkle Greeting and insert them inside the appropriate bag(s).

4. The recipients receive the messages and respond with verbal or written thank you's.

| Grades 2–8 | A Month of Positivism | S37 |

Purpose: To help students keep track of their own positive actions.

Materials: A copy of S37 A Month of Positivism form for each student.

Procedure: Instruct students to fill in the corresponding dates for the current month writing with small numbers in the upper right-hand column of the squares. At the end of each class day ask students to reflect upon what positive things they have done throughout the day for themselves or for others. Students quickly note the deed they are most proud of in the corresponding box. Younger students can keep track by drawing a happy (or sad) face in the box that depicts their actions.

| Grades 1-6 | Happy Happenings | S38 |

Purpose: To enhance students' awareness and appreciation of the daily positive occurrences in the classroom.

Materials: Several copies of S38 Happy Happenings form; construction or cardstock-weight paper for the cover; stapler.

Procedure: Each week appoint a different student to become class secretary. Every day of the week the secretary records positive happenings that have taken place during class time. These could include positive deeds and sayings of classmates as well as special occasions, occurrences or accomplishments of students.

Staple or bind the pages together to form a class journal. (See Chapter 9, Journal Writing.)

Variation: Individual students could also record their "happy happenings." Make a copy of the form for each student to complete for himself/herself.

S20

Name   Date

Personality Trivia

1. Favorite toy as a child?
2. Your middle name?
3. Where born?
4. Favorite toy/activity now?
5. Name of street living on?
6. Father's first name?
7. Childhood nickname?
8. Names of pets?
9. Favorite possession?
10. Favorite TV show?
11. Favorite food?
12. Favorite drink?
13. Favorite animal?
14. Favorite song?
15. Favorite actor?
16. Favorite radio station?
17. Favorite color?
18. Favorite car?
19. Favorite sport?
20. Best school subject?
21. Favorite place?
22. Favorite person?
23. Favorite season?
24. Favorite hobby?
25. Favorite rock group?
26. Favorite male singer?
27. Favorite female singer?
28. Favorite sports star?
29. Favorite flower?
30. Things you like to do most?
31. Life's ambition?
32. Favorite book?
33. Favorite board game?
34. Favorite ice cream flavor?
35. Favorite pizza topping?
36. Favorite candy?
37. Favorite day of the week?
38. Favorite name?
39. Favorite amusement park?
40. Favorite chips?
41. Favorite holiday?
42. Favorite football team?
43. Favorite month?
44. Favorite age?

Esteem Builders, Jalmar Press
Rolling Hills Estates, CA

From Me to You

S2

_____

_____

_____

_____

_____

_____

Signed: _____

Date: _____

I Just Wanted You to Know

S3

_____

_____

_____

_____

_____

Signed: _____

Date: _____

Special Recognition!

S4

To: _____

For: _____

_____

_____

_____

Congratulations!

Signed: _____

Date: _____

I Like: _____

S5

_____

Because: _____

_____

_____

_____

_____

Signed: _____

Date: _____

— 69 —

Esteem Builders. Jalmar Press
Rolling Hills Estates, CA

| Name | Date |

Someone Special

Who is someone extra special in your life? Someone whom you look forward to seeing, whom you really care about, whom you'd miss greatly if he/she was gone. Write about your someone:

Someone special in my life is_____

I have known him/her for _____

I first met this person (when) _____

When I'm with him/her I feel _____

_____

I feel this way because_____

_____

This person is very special to me because _____

_____

_____

A special time I had with him/her was_____

_____

_____

_____

_____

Three things I enjoy doing most with my special person are _____

_____

_____

Esteem Builders. Jalmar Press
Rolling Hills Estates, CA

Name   Date

List of People I Can Depend On

People you can trust are people you can count on. They are there when you need them, can keep a secret, and can always be depended upon to help. Who are the people you can trust?

Directions: Make a list of people you can trust. Under each name write why the person is so special. Why can you count on them?

1. _____

_____

_____

2. _____

_____

_____

3. _____

_____

_____

4. _____

_____

_____

5. _____

_____

_____

6. _____

_____

. . .and who can depend on me!

Esteem Builders. Jalmar Press
Rolling Hills Estates, CA

Name	Date

Significant Others

A "Significant Other" is someone who is extra special to you—someone whom you look forward to seeing, whom you really care about, whom you'd miss greatly if he/she was gone. This person may have told you how much he/she believes in you; it is someone who has had a great impact on you.

Task: Put your name in the center circle. In the circles surrounding your name, write the names of those people whom you consider to be the most "significant others" to you—those persons who mean the most to you.

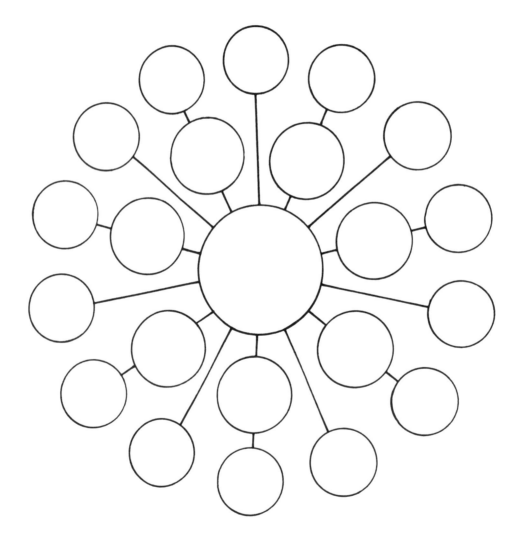

Put a ☆ by those you consider to be the most important people in your life.

Adapted from a group activity conducted by Robert Reasoner.

Esteem Builders. Jalmar Press
Rolling Hills Estates, CA

OUR RULES

_____

_____

_____

_____

_____

_____

_____
Student

_____
Teacher

_____
Parent

Esteem Builders. Jalmar Press
Rolling Hills Estates, CA

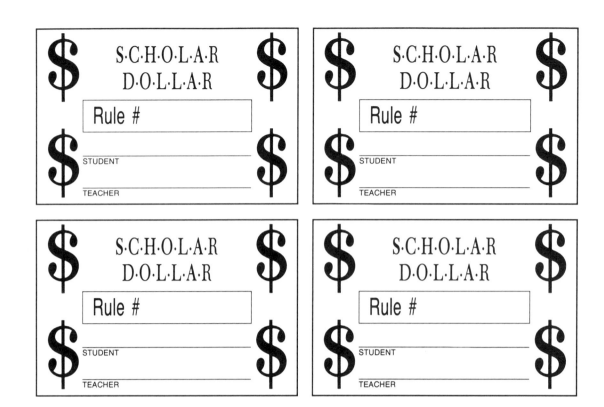

SCHOLAR DOLLAR WALLET

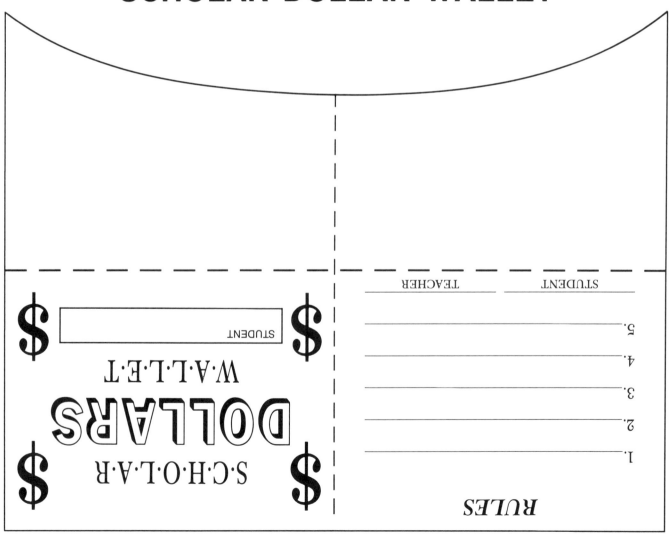

Permission to Reprint for Classroom Use.
© 1989 by Michele Borba

Esteem Builders. Jalmar Press
Rolling Hills Estates, CA

Name	Date

TIME FOR FRIENDS

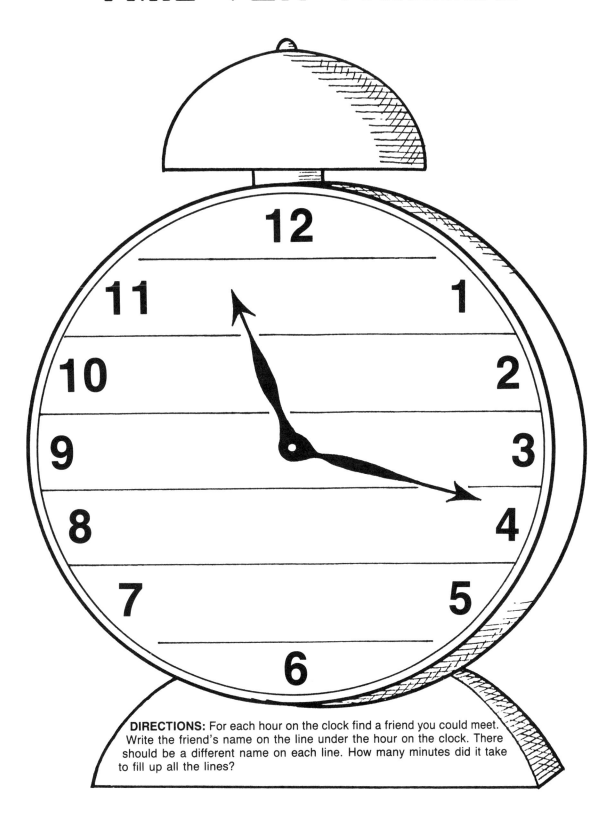

DIRECTIONS: For each hour on the clock find a friend you could meet. Write the friend's name on the line under the hour on the clock. There should be a different name on each line. How many minutes did it take to fill up all the lines?

Esteem Builders. Jalmar Press
Rolling Hills Estates, CA

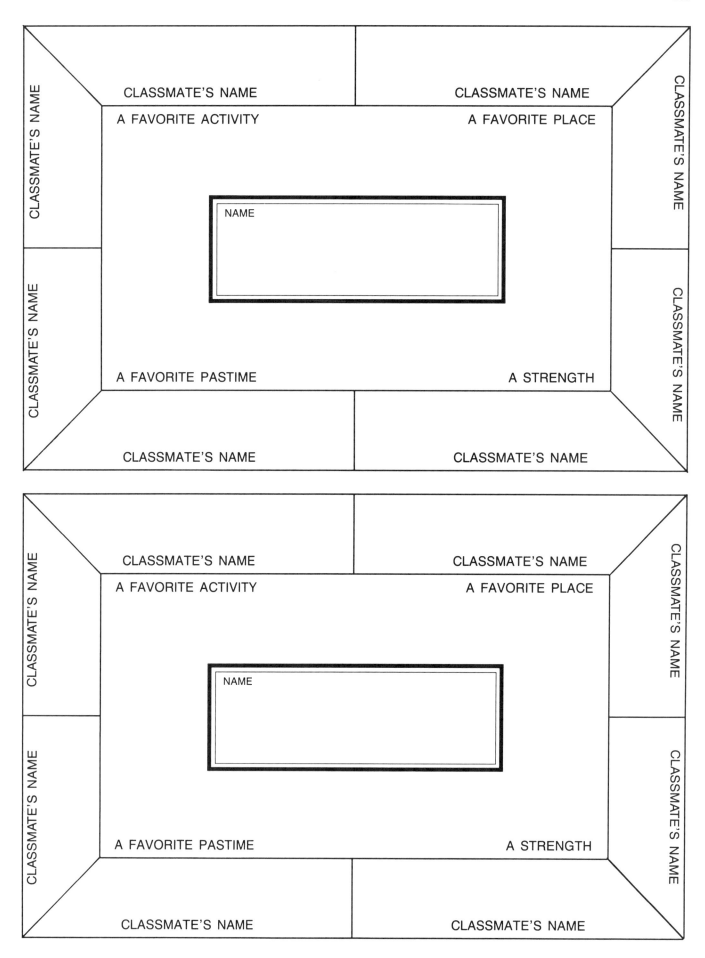

S19

Esteem Builders. Jalmar Press
Rolling Hills Estates, CA

Name	Date

STUDENT INTERVIEW

Interview your partner. Write down your findings.

Partner's full name: _____

Birthdate: _____

Place of birth: _____

Number of brothers and sisters: _____

Favorite TV show: _____

Favorite book: _____

Previous places you've lived: _____

Favorite subjects in school: _____

Favorite song: _____

Favorite movie: _____

Describe your hobbies and interests: _____

_____

Name something about yourself that you're proud of: _____

_____

If you could talk to anyone in the world, who would it be and why?

_____

_____

List three words that are usually used to describe you: _____

_____

_____

What would you like others to know about you that they may not already know?

_____

Esteem Builders. Jalmar Press
Rolling Hills Estates, CA

| Name | Date |

Interest Search

1. Read each category in the left column. Write your answer in the middle column.
2. Find a friend to match each of your answers. Write each friend's name in the right-hand column.

Category	My Favorite	A Friend's Name
Color		
Book		
TV Show		
Movie		
Number		
Ice Cream Flavor		
Indoor Game		
Sport		

Esteem Builders. Jalmar Press
Rolling Hills Estates, CA

Name	Date

Find a Friend

Find a friend who . . .	Friend's name
. . . is an only child.	
. . . has been to a foreign country.	
. . . can operate a computer.	
. . . likes to eat spicy food.	
. . . has two sisters.	
. . . was born in March.	
. . . has earned a trophy.	
. . . knows how to ski.	
. . . is about the same height as you.	
. . . can play a musical instrument.	
. . . has broken a bone.	
. . . has a bird for a pet.	
. . . is the oldest in the family.	
. . . wears the same shoe size as you.	
. . . has one brother.	
. . . is the youngest in the family.	
. . . likes to fish.	
. . . can whistle through his/her fingers.	
. . . has a cat.	
. . . was born the same month as you.	
. . . likes to play baseball.	
. . . takes dancing lessons.	

Esteem Builders. Jalmar Press
Rolling Hills Estates, CA

Name _____   Date _____

Sparkle Statements

You're cool.
Let's play together.
I like knowing you.
You look nice today.
You're a good friend.
Can we work together?
It's fun knowing you.
It's great working with you.
I'd like to know you better.
I like your outfit.
Thanks for being you.
Thanks for being such a buddy.
You're really good at _____ .
I like it when you _____ .
Thank you for _____ .
I like sharing with you.
Can we sit together?
Can I share with you?
I'm proud to know you.
You did a nice job.
I'm glad you're here today.
I like your smile.
You brighten my day.
You're my special friend.
Thanks for sharing yourself.
I'm glad we're in the same class.
I'm glad we're buddies.
Hello!
Hi!
I enjoy you.
Thank you!
You contribute good things.
Thanks for your kindness.
I hope you do well.
I hope we're together today.
Have a good one.
Let's help each other.
You were helpful when you _____ .

I especially appreciated it when you
_____ .
You're fun to be with.
Congratulations on your _____ .
You're clothes look rad!
I feel good when I'm with you.
I'm proud of you.
You make me happy.
You made me laugh.
Thanks for listening.
You're great/neat.
I like you!
It's good to see you.
I like to sit by you.
You're a good team member.
Have a good day.
Will you play with me?
You're special.
I like to be with you.
I thought about you.
You're a good buddy.
Good morning!
I like your _____ .
I'm glad I know you.
Let's get to know each other better.
Thanks for being you.
I'm lucky to know you.
You're my friend.
Thanks for your support.
Hope today is super for you.
Good luck today.
I like the way you _____ .
I hope today is great for you.
I appreciate you.
I look forward to seeing you.
I'm glad we're on the same team.
You deserve a pat on the back for
_____ .

Esteem Builders. Jalmar Press
Rolling Hills Estates, CA

Name	Date

 # Making a Smile Book

Look through magazines. Find pictures of people who have great smiles. Cut out the smiles and paste them on the cover of your book. Now look at the cover. How does it make you feel?

1

At home, look at old photographs of yourself. Find one that shows you with a great smile. Bring it to school with you and glue it in your book on page 2. Write about things that make you smile on page 3.

2

Find three friends. Measure the length of each of their smiles. Write your findings on pages 4 and 5 of your book.
1. Who are your friends?
2. What are the lengths of your friends' smiles?
3. What are the widths of your friends' smiles?

3

Read through the newspaper. Find a story that makes you smile. Cut it out and paste it in your book. What made you choose the story? What was it about it made you smile? Write your reasons on pages 6-7.

4

Make a survey of people in your school whom *you* think have great smiles. Find a smile winner for each category: boy, girl, adult male and adult female. Write your answers on pages 8 and 9. What was special about each winner's smile?

5

Esteem Builders. Jalmar Press
Rolling Hills Estates, CA

SUPER SPARKLE

Presented to:

Date:

Official Signature:

OUT

IN

Esteem Builders. Jalmar Press
Rolling Hills Estates, CA

Nice Things to Say

My Ideas:

Hi
Hello!
I like you.
How are you?
You're a good friend.
You look nice today.
Let's be friends!
You're nice.
I'm glad I know you.
Thanks for helping me.
You're special.
Can I help you?

(Fold up)

(Fold up)

— 84 —

Esteem Builders. Jalmar Press
Rolling Hills Estates, CA

Name	Date

BUILDER-UPPERS

*Things you could say to someone in this class or school that
would put a smile on their face or make them feel happy inside*

Directions: Write the names of your classmates in the spaces under the left-hand column.
Each day, choose a different classmate's name from the list *and* a Builder-Upper Statement
of your choice. Sometime during the day, say the statement to the classmate. Check off
the name and statement as you use them.

Classmates' Names	Builder-Upper Statements
	☆ Hello!
	☆ Have a great day!
	☆ How are you?
	☆ I'm glad you're here!
	☆ I'd like to get to know you better.
	☆ It's fun knowing you.
	☆ I like you.
	☆ I like being with you.
	☆ You're fun.
	☆ Nice to see you!
	☆ It's good to see you.
	☆ You're great!
	☆ Good morning! (afternoon)
	☆ Have a good one!
	☆
	☆
	☆
	☆
	☆
	☆
	☆
	☆

Esteem Builders. Jalmar Press
Rolling Hills Estates, CA

Sparkle Boy and Girl

GIRL
PATTERN

BOY
PATTERN

Esteem Builders. Jalmar Press
Rolling Hills Estates, CA

A Sparkle to: _____

From: _____

Message:_____

A Sparkle to: _____

From: _____

Message:_____

A Sparkle to: _____

From: _____

Message:_____

A Sparkle to: _____

From: _____

Message:_____

Esteem Builders. Jalmar Press
Rolling Hills Estates, CA

SPARKLE BOOK COVER

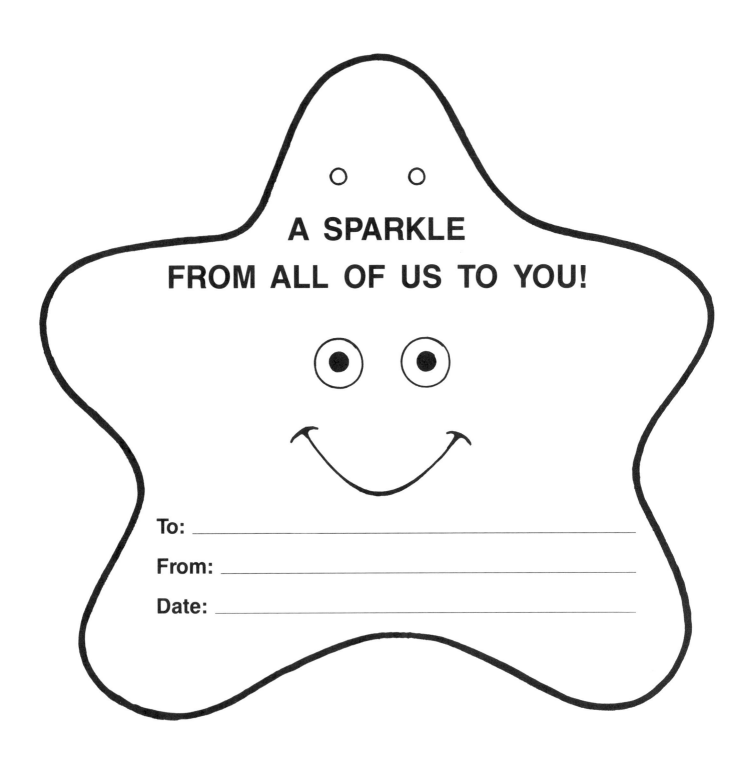

A SPARKLE
FROM ALL OF US TO YOU!

To: _____

From: _____

Date: _____

Esteem Builders. Jalmar Press
Rolling Hills Estates, CA

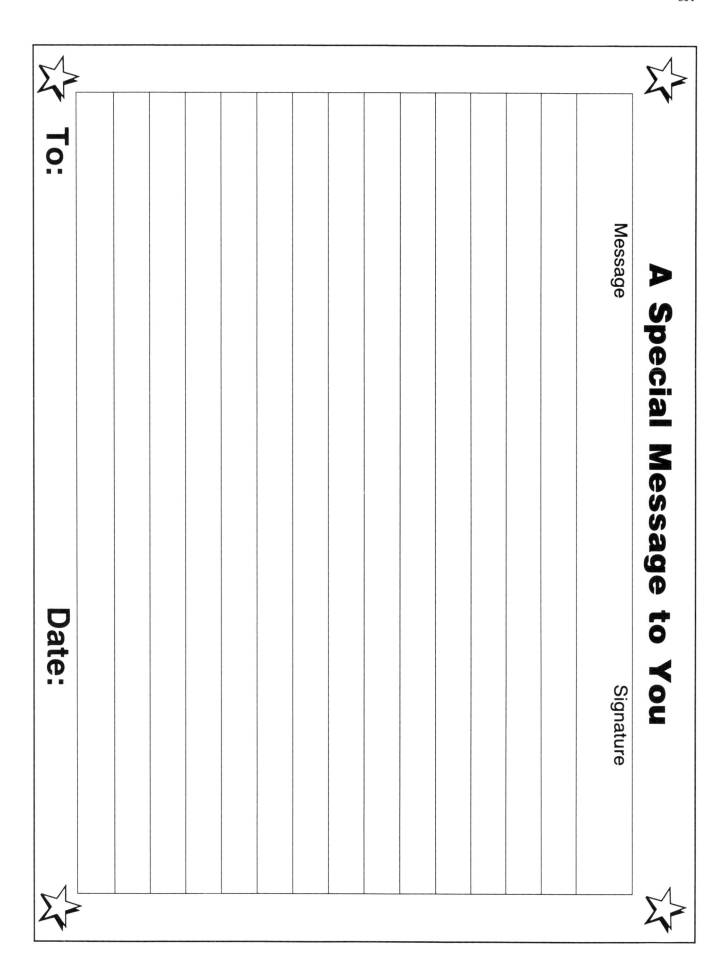

A Special Message to You

Message

Signature

To:

Date:

Esteem Builders. Jalmar Press
Rolling Hills Estates, CA

Name	Date

Add a Compliment

Write a compliment to the owner of this paper on the first empty line. Now pass this page to the nearest classmate, who adds another compliment and passes it on.

Return this paper with a smile to the owner.

Esteem Builders. Jalmar Press
Rolling Hills Estates, CA

S37

| Name | | | | Date |

A Month of Positivism

Keep track of your own positive statements. What did you do or say to put a smile on someone's face?

Monday	Tuesday	Wednesday	Thursday	Friday

Esteem Builders. Jalmar Press
Rolling Hills Estates. CA

Name		Date

HAPPY HAPPENINGS

Monday

Tuesday

Wednesday

Thursday

Friday

Esteem Builders. Jalmar Press
Rolling Hills Estates, CA

4

Clarifying the
Inner Picture:
Building Selfhood

ESTEEM BUILDERS

- Reinforce More Accurate Self-Descriptions
- Provide Opportunities to Discover Major Sources of Influence on the Self
- Build an Awareness of Unique Qualities
- Enhance Ability to Identify and Express Emotions and Attitudes

SUMMARY OF SELFHOOD

Definition: *A feeling of individuality. Acquiring self-knowledge, which includes an accurate and realistic self-description in terms of roles, attributes and physical characteristics.*

SUPPORT DATA

- "A well-defined sense of self and identity provides us with effective strategies for managing psychological stress—the major stress in our society." David Elkind. *All Grown Up and No Place to Go* (Addison Wesley, 1984).
- "The child must first learn self-respect and a sense of dignity that grows out of his increasing self-understanding before he can learn to respect the personalities and rights and differences of others." Virginia Axline. *Dibs: In Search of Self* (Ballantine, 1964).
- "High self-esteem occurs when children experience the positive feelings of satisfaction that result from having a sense of uniqueness. That is, a child acknowledges and respects the personal characteristics that make him special and different, and receives approval and respect from others." Harris Clemes and Reynold Bean. *Self-Esteem: The Key to Your Child's Well Being* (G.P. Putnam, 1977).
- "Most studies suggest that people who have negative feelings about their bodies are likely to have negative feelings about themselves as people and thus have lower self-esteem." Thomas Yawkey. *The Self-Concept of the Young Child* (Brigham Young University Press, 1980).

ESTEEM BUILDERS

- Reinforce More Accurate Self-Descriptions
- Provide Opportunities to Discover Major Sources of Influence on the Self
- Build an Awareness of Unique Qualities
- Enhance Ability to Identify and Express Emotions and Attitudes

POSSIBLE INDICATORS OF WEAK SELFHOOD

- frequently uses negative statements regarding self and others;
- embarrasses easily, oversensitive to criticism;
- lacks confidence in physical self or necessary physical skills, therefore rarely engages in fine or gross motor activities;
- is dependent on adults, anxious to please them;
- is uncomfortable with praise: denies, undermines, disregards or becomes embarrassed;
- conforms or mimics others: is unwilling to express self in own way or risk being different;
- may seek acknowledgment for negative characteristics;
- is misinformed regarding roles, attributes or physical characteristics;
- dresses in extremes, either to attract attention or cover up the body.

POSSIBLE INDICATORS OF STRONG SELFHOOD

- handles fine and gross motor activities with ease;
- expresses uniqueness and individuality, risks being different;
- has an accurate self-description in terms of physical characteristics, capabilities, roles and attitudes;
- generally makes positive statements toward self and others;
- identifies and expresses emotions appropriately;
- is comfortable accepting praise.

Most students will not conform exactly to the profiles listed above but are more likely to be stronger in some areas and weaker in others. In order to determine the degree to which a student feels a sense of Selfhood, complete the student self-esteem assessment (B-SET) chart located in Appendix II. The chart may be referred to periodically or updated as a way of measuring progress. These charts are also useful in determining which activities are appropriate for your class.

Selfhood Activities List

Code	Grade	Title	Soc. Studies	Sci.	Writ. Lang.	Oral Lang.	Math	Art	Lit.
SH1	K–3	My Physical Self		✔	✔	✔		✔	
SH2	K–3	Me Riddle		✔	✔			✔	
SH3	K–8	Self-Portrait		✔	✔	✔		✔	
SH4	1–4	Focus on Me		✔	✔			✔	
SH5	1–6	Measure Up!		✔			✔		
SH6	K–2	Me Doll		✔				✔	
SH7	K–2	Me Doll Lace-up		✔				✔	
SH8	K–3	Me Shape Book		✔	✔	✔		✔	
SH9	K–3	Walking Me Puppet		✔		✔		✔	
SH10	K–2	Photo Stick Puppet	✔	✔		✔		✔	
SH11	K–2	Fabric Crayon Puppet		✔		✔		✔	
SH12	K–1	Paper Bag Face Puppet		✔		✔		✔	
SH13	K–4	Me Puppet		✔		✔	✔	✔	
SH14	2–8	Time-Line Center/Significant Events	✔		✔		✔		
SH15	K–5	A Movie of My Life			✔		✔		
SH16	2–8	The Many Parts of Me			✔				
SH17	2–5	Who Am I?			✔			✔	
SH18	K–8	My Identity Shield			✔	✔		✔	
SH19	K–8	Seeing Myself			✔			✔	
SH20	2–8	Playing Favorites			✔	✔		✔	
SH21	2–8	Wanted Poster			✔			✔	
SH22	5–8	Resumé	✔		✔	✔			
SH23	3–8	My Interests and Hobbies	✔	✔	✔	✔			✔
SH24	1–5	All-About-Me Center	✔	✔	✔	✔	✔	✔	✔
SH25	1–5	All-About-Me Contract			✔		✔		
SH26	1–5	Dioramas						✔	
SH27	1–5	Letter to a Friend			✔				
SH28	1–5	I Like Mobile			✔		✔	✔	
SH29	1–5	Commercial About Me			✔	✔			
SH30	1–5	Measuring Me					✔		
SH31	1–5	Me Mask						✔	
SH32	1–5	Life Story			✔	✔		✔	
SH33	1–5	Me Banner			✔			✔	
SH34	1–5	I Collage			✔			✔	
SH35	1–5	Puppet Bag				✔		✔	
SH36	1–5	My Dreams			✔			✔	
SH37	1–5	Want Ad			✔				
SH38	1–5	Sparkles						✔	

Code	Grade	Title	Soc. Studies	Sci.	Writ. Lang.	Oral Lang.	Math	Art	Lit.
SH39	1–5	Special People	✔		✔		✔	✔	
SH40	1–5	Time Capsule	✔		✔			✔	
SH41	1–5	Like Me			✔		✔	✔	
SH42	1–5	Me Hanging			✔		✔	✔	
SH43	1–5	Me Poster			✔			✔	
SH44	K–3	The Gift of Self	✔		✔			✔	✔
SH45	K–3	Dictionary of Feelings			✔	✔			✔
SH46	K–3	Feelings Wheel				✔		✔	
SH47	3–8	Sending I Messages	✔			✔			
SH48	K–8	Books to Enhance Identity							✔

School-wide Activities That Promote Selfhood

Code	Grade	Title	Element
SW13	K–6	Meet Our Kids	Selfhood/Affiliation
SW14	K–8	Good News Report	Selfhood
SW15/16	K–6	Student of the Week	Selfhood/Affiliation
SW17/18	K–8	Citizen of the Week	Selfhood/Affiliation
SW19	K–8	Spirit Tree	Security/Selfhood

Concept Circles That Promote Selfhood

Code	Grade	Title	Grouping
CC8	2–8	Names	Partner/Team
CC9	1–8	Design-a-Logo	Team
CC10	K–8	Me Bag	Team/Full
CC11	K–4	I Like	Full
CC12	K–8	Share Yourself	Full/Team
CC13	K–3	I Like to Be Me	Full
CC14	2–8	Identity Bag	Full/Team
CC15	K–8	I'm Great!	Team/Full
CC16	K–6	A Me Hanging	Team/Full
CC17	K–5	Feeling Drawings	Team
CC18	K–2	Happy-Sad Beanbag	Full
CC19	K–2	Emotion Hats	Full
CC20	K–3	Feeling Thermometer	Full
CC21	K–3	Individual Thermometers	Full
CC22	K–3	Feeling Masks	Full
CC23	K–4	Wishes	Full
CC24	3–8	Dreams	Full/Team

Checklist of Educator Behaviors
That Develop SELFHOOD

Directions: For self-evaluation of your skills in enhancing your students' selfhood, complete the following items.

Never 1	Sometimes 2	Frequently 3	Always 4	*As an educator:*
_____	_____	_____	_____	1. Do I express to students traits and characteristics that could enhance their feelings of self-worth?
_____	_____	_____	_____	2. Do I provide opportunities for students to discover their interests, attitudes, roles and physical characteristics?
_____	_____	_____	_____	3. Do I create situations for students to reflect upon significant influences in their past and present, and how these have played a role in their self-perceptions?
_____	_____	_____	_____	4. Do I encourage students to express their uniqueness and to risk being different?
_____	_____	_____	_____	5. Do I help students explore feelings and attitudes that promote their awareness of what they value?
_____	_____	_____	_____	6. Do I help students learn to make positive statements and accept praise?
_____	_____	_____	_____	7. Do I accept students for their differences?
_____	_____	_____	_____	8. Do I allow students opportunities to increase their list of self-descriptions?
_____	_____	_____	_____	9. Do I encourage students to develop a sense of pride in their unique qualities?
_____	_____	_____	_____	10. Do I avoid equating the students' work with their self-worth?

_____ + _____ + _____ + _____ = **Total:_____**

Areas I could improve in that will help develop selfhood in my students:_____

_____

_____

Esteem Builders. Jalmar Press
Rolling Hills Estates, CA

4

Clarifying the Inner Picture: Building Selfhood

Selves are not born but made.
—ASHLEY MONTAGU

Once a solid feeling of security has been achieved in your classroom, you can introduce the succeeding components, starting with development of selfhood or self-concept.

Though there are a multitude of different definitions of self-concept, the following best fit the self-esteem model:

- *that which is designated in common speech by the pronoun of the first person singular, "I" or "me"*[1]

- *a person's perceptions of himself [herself]*[2]

- *the description an individual attaches to himself or herself.*[3]

Self-concept is not a value judgment of self, only a series of internal thoughts based on the roles one plays and the attributes one possesses. The description *may* or *may not* be accurate or realistic, but it certainly is real to the perceiver. Self-description is critical to esteem building because it is the basis of self-evaluations.

Students come to school with all sorts of predetermined descriptions about themselves. If they haven't done so already, they very quickly put a personal price tag of worth on each self-description. Their self-esteem is related to the degree to which they are satisfied or dissatisfied within themselves.

All too often students believe their personal tag is "damaged goods" instead of "valuable merchandise." This can have negative repercussions in classroom achievement and behavior. The starting block toward a more positive feeling of self, therefore, is to help students develop an accurate self-description. Any activity that helps students to clarify, sharpen or think more in depth about themselves will enhance self-concept.

A student with a weak sense of selfhood may be identified by the following behavioral characteristics:

- frequently uses negative statements regarding self and others;

- embarrasses easily, oversensitive to criticism;

- lacks confidence in physical self or necessary physical skills, therefore rarely engages in fine or gross motor activities;

- is dependent on adults, anxious to please them;

1. Combs, H.A., and Snygg, D. *Individual Behavior* (New York: Harper & Row, 1959).
2. Shavelson, R., et al. "Self-Concept: Validation of Construct Interpretations," *Review of Educational Research*, Vol. 46, 1976, pp. 407–41.
3. Beane, James, and Lipka, R. *Self-Concept, Self-Esteem and the Curriculum* (New York: Teachers College Press, 1986).

SELFHOOD

- is uncomfortable with praise: denies, undermines, disregards or becomes embarrassed;
- conforms or mimics others: is unwilling to express self in own way or risk being different;
- may seek acknowledgment for negative characteristics;
- is misinformed regarding roles, attributes or physical characteristics;
- dresses in extremes, either to attract attention or cover up the body.

A student with a strong selfhood, on the other hand, may be identified by the following behaviors:

- handles fine and gross motor activities with ease;
- expresses uniqueness and individuality, risks being different;
- has an accurate self-description in terms of physical characteristics, capabilities, roles and attitudes;
- generally makes positive statements toward self and others;
- identifies and expresses emotions appropriately;
- is comfortable accepting praise.

SUMMARY

The esteem builder who is working with students on identity should:

1. Reinforce more accurate self-descriptions.
2. Provide opportunities to discover major sources of influence upon the self.
3. Build an awareness of unique qualities.
4. Enhance ability to identify and express emotions and attitudes.

ESTEEM BUILDER #1

Reinforce More Accurate Self-Descriptions

> *"You cannot teach people anything. You can only help them discover it within themselves."*
>
> —GALILEO

One of the highest tags of self-worth that students place upon themselves is the value of physical attractiveness. We may tell them "Beauty is in the eye of the beholder" or "It's what's inside that counts," but to young minds physical characteristics appear to be much more important than we preach. At quite an early age, they have begun to form a concept of themselves and others based on "outer beauty," and to differentiate between what they consider to be the "attractive and unattractive" appearance of others. This physical concept has a powerful impact on their thinking about themselves and others.

There has been a lot of research in this field. Most studies have found that people who have negative feelings about their bodies are more likely to have negative feelings about themselves as people and thus have lower self-esteem.[4]

In one study, for instance, students were asked to respond to the question, "When you think about yourself, what comes to your mind?" Almost universally they responded with thoughts about their physical being.[5]

In another study conducted by Stenner and Katzenmeyer (1976),[6] 3,700 primary students in grades one through three were asked, "Are you good looking?" Twenty-five percent of the first graders and almost 50 percent of the second and third graders answered negatively. Rosenberg's investigations yielded similar results.[7] When students were asked, "What are you least proud of about yourself?" the largest percentage of responses cited some physical characteristics of their self.

Concern over physical appearance, therefore, occupies an enormous amount of a student's waking hours. When a student feels unattractive, all types of behaviors can manifest. Slumped-over posture

4. Yawkey, Thomas. *Self-Concept in the Young Child: An Anthology* (Provo, UT: Brigham Young Univ. Press, 1980), p. 39.
5. McDonald, Kay. "Enhancing a Child's Positive Self-Concept," *Self-Concept in the Young Child: An Anthology* (Provo, UT: Brigham Young Univ. Press, 1980), p. 52.
6. Stenner, A.J., and Katzenmeyer, W.G. "Self-Concept Development in Young Children," *Phi Delta Kappan*, 58 (1976): 356–57.
7. Rosenberg, Morris. *Conceiving the Self* (New York: Basic Books, 1976), p. 203.

is often one telltale clue. Some students physically cover up their faces while engaged in a school task. Others resort to the "Jacket Annie" syndrome by refusing to take off their jackets regardless of the outside temperature. Stanley Coopersmith commented that the reverse effect can also happen where the student goes to extreme means to be accepted and dresses to eccentric excess.[8]

Studies also reveal that students' concepts of attractiveness may have a powerful impact on their social relationships as well. As early as three years of age, students stereotype others on the basis of physical attractiveness.[9] In countless investigations, attractive peers were thought of in more positive ways than their more unattractive counterparts.[10] Clearly, physical attractiveness influences young children's thinking about themselves and others.

Thus, a child forms his/her physical self-image very early on in life. In fact, it is probably related to the early very intense preoccupation with physical self-discovery. It is also the aspect of the self that appears to preoccupy students' concerns.

Since society places such an enormous emphasis on outward physical appearance, there is a lot of pressure for a student to have an "OK" body even though it might not be realistic. Even as adults we are up against a million dollar advertising business that tells us "blondes have more fun" and that one toothpaste brand will give us "greater sex appeal" than another.

But as changes in outward physical appearance to fit the "American dream image" are not usually possible, a more realistic avenue is to help students become appreciative of personal physical characteristics and traits, recognize their strengths and shortcomings, and from this build a more accurate self-picture with which they can feel comfortable— even proud.

ACTIVITIES: GROUP 1

The following activities are designed to increase self-knowledge, focusing primarily on physical characteristics.

8. Coopersmith, Stanley. *The Antecedents of Self-Esteem* (San Francisco: W.H. Freeman and Co., 1967).
9. Langlois, Judith, and Cookie, Stephen. "The Effects of Physical Attractiveness and Ethnicity on Children's Behavior Attributions and Peer Preferences," *Child Development*, Vol. 48, 1977, pp. 1694–1698.
10. Dion, Karen. "Young Children's Stereotyping of Facial Attractiveness," *Developmental Psychology*, Vol. 9, 1973, pp. 183–188.

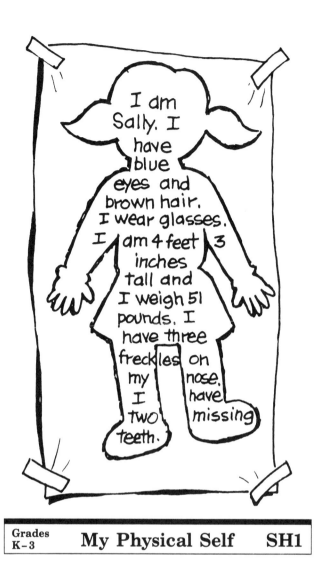

SELFHOOD

| Grades K-3 | My Physical Self | SH1 |

Purpose: To enhance students' feelings about their physical characteristics and capabilities.

Materials: Butcher paper or brown wrapping paper; marking pens.

Procedure: Student lies down on a piece of butcher paper or brown wrapping paper while a classmate draws around his/her body.

Students may color or paint their self-pictures to look like they do today, using a mirror to check the details of clothing and physical characteristics. They then cut out the decorated picture and write an accompanying self-description inside the outline.

Variations:

* Students label the body parts in the correct locations within the outline.

SELFHOOD

- Students color their outlines to look like themselves, cut out a matching outline, and staple around the edge leaving the top open. They stuff the figures with crumpled newspaper and staple closed.

- Outline the student's body on posterboard or cardboard. Cut out the body form and then cut it into shapes for a Me Puzzle.

- Student writes a brief autobiography inside the outline.

Grades K–3	Me Riddle	SH2

Purpose: To enhance students' feelings about their physical characteristics and capabilities.

Materials: Heavy paper of various sizes; baby picture of student; glue, scissors and marking pens.

Procedure: Student creates a description of his/her physical self, answering to Who Am I?, and writes it on the heavy paper. Cut out a matching shape, identical to the cut-out heavy paper, and glue this to the back of the first page. Cut open a doorway and fold back to reveal a baby picture (which is glued to the paper) identifying the author.

Grades K–8	A Self-Portrait	SH3

Purpose: To increase students' awareness of their physical characteristics.

Materials: SH3 A Self-Portrait form for each student; crayons or marking pens; mirror.

Procedure: Students take turns looking into a mirror, then draw and write what they see. Allow younger students to dictate this section. Students could also work as partners: one writes and holds the mirror while the other talks and draws.

Grades 1–6	Focus on Me	SH4

Purpose: To enhance students' awareness of specific aspects of their physical identity.

Materials: SH4 Focus on Me form for each student; scale, mirror; writing instrument, crayons or marking pens.

Procedure: Students fill out the answers (or dictate them to the teacher or parent aide) about individual aspects on the form. Encourage them to look in a mirror before answering some of the questions.

Grades 1–3	**Measure Up!**	SH5

Purpose: To increase students' awareness of their body measurements.

Materials: SH5 Measure Up! form for each student; measuring tape and pencil.

Procedure: Using a measuring tape, students fill in the measurements of the body parts listed on the sheet. Encourage them to pick a partner to help.

Grades K–2	**Me Doll**	SH6

Purpose: To increase students' awareness of their physical characteristics.

Materials: SH6 boy and girl pattern; two pieces of 12" x 18" construction paper per student; wallpaper (or fabric), yarn, buttons, rickrack, sequins, feathers; paint, marking pens, crayons, scissors, glue.

Procedure: Student traces around teacher-made tagboard boy or girl stencil onto two pieces of flesh-colored construction paper (see **Variation**). Using marking pens, crayons, paint or glued-on objects, the student adds physical features that depict him/her. Glued-on objects might include:

• yarn (hair, mouth)

• buttons (eyes, buttons for "clothes")

• rickrack, lace, sequins, feathers (clothes accessories)

• wallpaper, fabric (clothes)

Be sure to keep a hand mirror available for this activity and to have students clothe the front and back of the boy or girl.

Variation: Dolls may be "stuffed" by stapling the dressed figures around the outside edges. Leave the head area open and add crumpled-up newspapers to the doll's insides. Staple closed.

Teacher Directions: Trace the SH6 boy and girl patterns onto tagboard for stencils. The dotted lines indicate the Me Shape Book stencil for the auto-

biography activity (SH8). You may also make clothes patterns into stencils for students to trace.

Grades K–2	**Me Doll Lace-up**	SH7

Purpose: To increase students' awareness of their physical characteristics.

Materials: SH6 boy or girl pattern; large grocery bag, turned inside out, for each student; paint and brushes, pencils and marking pens; scissors, hole-punch and glue; crumpled newspaper, 45" yarn lengths; fabric, wallpaper or construction paper scraps for clothes.

Procedure: This is a variation of the SH6 Me Dolls. The student traces the boy or girl stencil onto two pieces of large grocery bags (with the writing on the inside of the bag). Students complete their figures by adding features and clothes—just like the Me Doll.

When both back and front features are completed, the student uses a hole-punch to punch holes 1/4" from the edge all the way around the figure. The holes should be 1/2" to 1" apart. Stuff the dolls with crumpled paper and then lace-up by using a long piece of yarn.

Both SH6 and SH7 activities make colorful borders around the room. They may also be hung from the ceiling by punching a hole in the top of the "head."

Grades K–3	**Me Shape Book**	SH8

Purpose: To increase students' awareness of their physical characteristics.

Materials: Tagboard stencil of pattern (see SH6 and SH7); heavy paper, writing paper and stapler; colored construction paper or wallpaper; glue, scissors and marking pens.

Procedure: Students each trace one tagboard boy or girl stencil onto a heavy sheet of paper (chart paper works well). They then cut out the figures and add features and clothes as per the SH6 Me Doll and SH7 Me Doll Lace-up.

For this activity, the teacher makes an additional tagboard stencil of the shape represented by the dotted lines in the SH6 pattern. Students each cut one dotted line shape out of colored construction paper (or paper matching the clothes that the student chose). This will be the book's back cover.

Cut several additional dotted line shapes from writing paper. Staple the pages together onto the figure. The student may then write a short autobiography (or draw pictures) in the Me Shape book. Another option is for the student to write a self-riddle. For example: I am 48 inches tall, I have brown eyes and black hair. I like to wear blue and I have two missing front teeth. Who am I?

PUPPETS!

Puppets are an excellent tool and a fun way to increase self-awareness as well as highlight physical characteristics.

Grades K–3	Walking Me Puppet SH9

Materials: SH9 Walking Me Puppet form; a photo portrait of each student; glue, scissors and marking pens; wallpaper, construction and wrapping paper.

Procedure: Duplicate the SH9 Walking Me Puppet onto heavy tagboard. Students decorate the pattern according to their own physical characteristics using marking pens, wrapping paper, wallpaper, crayons, etc. Glue a photo of each student in the center of the "head." Fold the puppet arms forward on the dotted lines. To make the puppet walk, students put their index and middle fingers through the holes.

Grades K–2	Photo Stick Puppet SH10

Materials: A 3" x 5" photograph of the student; tongue depressor or popsicle stick; glue and scissors.

Procedure: Cut out and glue a wallet-size photograph, which students have brought from home, onto a tongue depressor or popsicle stick.

Variation: Students can make a complete set of their family members by bringing in their photographs, each glued onto a separate stick.

Grades K–2	Fabric Crayon Puppet SH11

Materials: SH13 Me Puppet felt pattern; plain drawing paper; fabric crayons, pinking shears; white sheets or fabric; iron and sewing machine.

Procedure: Duplicate the SH13 Me Puppet pattern for each student on plain drawing paper. Using fabric crayons (available at variety stores and large fabric stores), students color pictures of themselves. Encourage them to color as much of the pattern as possible and to press down with the crayons. They should not print words and letters as they will print backwards. Outline the puppet pattern with the crayon.

Using an old white sheet, carefully turn each drawn puppet pattern onto a section of the sheet. The crayon drawing should be touching the sheet. At a low temperature setting, press the iron slowly back and forth over the paper until you see an imprint coming through. (Read the instructions on the box of fabric crayons.)

To Assemble: Cut out the puppet pattern on the sheet with pinking shears. Also cut out (use any fabric) a matching back for each puppet. Stitch the two sides together 1/4" along the edge on the sewing machine. Leave the bottom open as entryway for the hand.

Grades K–1	Paper Bag Face Puppet SH12

Materials: Brown paper lunch bags; marking pens or crayons; scissors and glue; skin-colored construction paper.

Procedure: Duplicate the SH12 Face pattern onto skin-colored construction paper. Students should color the figure so that it resembles their facial features. To help them, you may wish to pass around a hand mirror. Cut around the face and mouth and the hair length as desired.

Provide a small lunch-size paper bag for each student. Tell them to paste the upper part of the face onto the bottom flap of the bag and the chin onto the side of the bag immediately under the bottom flap. When the bag is folded flat, the chin should match up with the rest of the face.

Note: This activity works very well in Concept Circles. See Chapter 8, CC2 How Do You Do?

Grades K–4	Me Puppet	SH13

Materials: SH13 Me Puppet pattern; two skin-colored felt squares per student (or ask students to bring them from home); tacky glue (craft glue, available at variety stores, holds better than regular glue).

Odds and ends:

- material and felt scraps
- buttons, rickrack, sequins
- yarn (hair colors)
- braids, laces, trims

Sewing machine or large needle and thread (embroidery size).

Procedure:

1. Cut out two puppet shapes per student. (This is an activity that parents could do at home and then send back to school.)
2. Students decorate the face of the puppet with odds and ends to represent their features as closely as possible.

Glue or sew on:

eyes...use cut felt scraps, buttons or purchased movable eyes; *eyebrows*...felt scraps, yarn pieces; *hair*...glue on yarn or felt scraps; *mouth*...buttons or felt scraps; *nose*...felt scraps or buttons; *clothes*...material or felt scraps, braid, laces, trims.

You may wish to create separate patterns for clothes.

3. To complete, choose one of the following options:
   a) Send home to parents, who will stitch around outer edge leaving a 1/2" open border along the bottom.
   b) Using craft glue, seal around the outer edges leaving a 1/4" open border along the bottom.
   c) Students stitch the puppets themselves using embroidery thread and a small running stitch.
   d) Younger students may lace-up their puppets if you pre-punch holes along the outer edge.

Note: You can make a special Me Puppet by gluing or stapling on a circle cut slightly smaller than the pattern head shape. Cut the circle from acetate, aluminum foil or any material that is reflective. By holding the puppet so that it faces them, students see their own face talking back to them.

Idea suggested by Susan Swenson; Kohl Elementary, Broomfield, Colorado.

ESTEEM BUILDER #2

Provide Opportunities to Discover Major Sources of Influence on the Self

"All that we are is a result of what we have thought."
—BUDDHA

A large part of our inner picture evolves as a result of the types of experience we have with significant people and events in our life. Some are positive, others, negative. How we as an individual perceive each experience is the critical factor in determining how it will affect feelings about ourself. We evaluate experience internally as either a success or a failure, enjoyable or unenjoyable, positive or nega-tive: we stockpile each evaluation for future reference. Our perception, of course, may or may not be accurate or realistic, but it has been internally logged and may be retrieved for many years to come.

Since significant experiences with events and people may play such a large role in the formation of self-opinions, increasing a student's awareness of them is an important esteem builder. Activities that provide opportunities for students to reflect upon significant experiences, and in the process help shift the existing self-image, are particularly beneficial for the low self-esteem student who commonly has

SELFHOOD

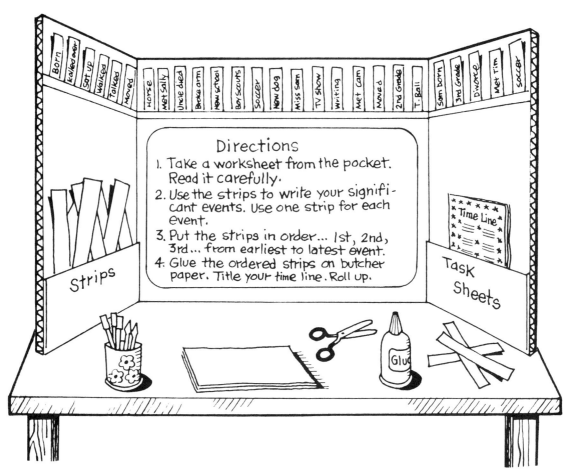

a self-pitying attitude that "no one has as many bad things happen to them as I do." By comparing experiences with fellow classmates, the student gradually builds an awareness that others have their share of negative experiences too. When the low self-esteem student discovers that negative experiences need not always be perceived in the same way, then important learning has taken place. This type of student learns, too, that some individuals do not dwell on the past; they actually turn around a negative experience by reflecting on it positively and seeing the learning value in so-called "mistakes."

ACTIVITIES: GROUP 2

The following activities help students explore the formation of their selfhood.

Grades 2–8	Time-Line Center/ Significant Events	SH14

Purpose: To expand personal awareness of the significant events that have shaped a student's inner self-picture.

Materials:
1–19" x 26" piece of cardboard;
2–13" x 19" pieces of cardboard;
Reinforced tape (1/2");
15–8 1/2" x 1" construction paper strips;
clear contact or laminating machine; butcher paper and colored tagboard; marking pens, scissors and glue.

Center Construction: Build a carrel from the 19" x 26" and two 13" x 19" pieces of cardboard. Cover the cardboard with colored tagboard, butcher paper or colored contact paper. Use marking pens to decorate the carrel and for signage. Make two pockets on the left and right sides of the construction from a folded 12" x 12" piece of tagboard. Cover the finished carrel with clear contact paper for durability. Hinge the carrel together with the tape.

Duplicate the SH14 Time-Line of Significant Events form for each student. Store the sheets in one of the carrel's pockets.

Procedure: Cut light-colored construction paper strips (at least 15 per student) in 8 1/2" x 1" lengths. Store these in the other pocket.

Students carry out the task by completing the Time-Line form: they check and fill out each topic that applies to their life. Parents may help at home by studying it with their child. On each 8 1/2" x 1" strip, students write an important event. They arrange the strips in chronological order and glue them to a 10" x 36" (or longer) piece of butcher paper. If they wish, they may write event dates below each strip.

Younger students may draw events on three to five 5" x 8" colored pieces of construction paper.

teacher only); 3–5 copies of the filmstrip form for each student; marking pens or crayons, glue.

Procedure: Make a theater out of a shoe box. Turn the box on its side. Cut an 8" long slit in the middle of one long side of the box.

Turn the box over and do the same on the other long side. Then cut a rectangle 5 1/4" x 4" in the center of the bottom of the box.

Students cut out the filmstrips along the outside lines and paste them together to form one long strip. They draw pictures in each space to show scenes of their life. They put the film in the "viewer" and pull it!

Note: Older students may make their own viewers.

Grades 2–8	The Many Parts of Me	SH16

Purpose: For students to recall the different experiences that have helped form their personality.

Materials: SH16 Many Parts of Me puzzle sheet for each student.

Procedure: On each puzzle piece students write a different experience that was significant in their life. Tell students: "If you can remember, write how old you were when the experience happened. Some will be easy to think of and others will be much more difficult. It may help you to go through each year of your life."

For example, "When I was six, my grandma came to live with us." Encourage them to use keywords or phrases as the space is limited.

Grades K–5	A Movie of My Life	SH15

Purpose: To increase students' awareness of the significant events that have helped form their inner self-picture.

Materials: Shoe box; knife or sharp scissors (for

ESTEEM BUILDER #3

Build an Awareness of Unique Qualities

"Who can say more than this rich praise, that you alone are you?"
—WILLIAM SHAKESPEARE

School districts should periodically hire a blimp to fly low over playgrounds so that every student can read the banner that says, "You are special . . . be

proud of it!" All students need the opportunity to feel unique and to know their special qualities are appreciated and respected by others. This is how self-worth develops, which is essential to the attainment of high self-esteem. Such a feeling is not inherited, it is learned.

The development of individuality is a gradual process that must begin with the internal clarification of self-descriptions as well as an understanding of differences. As a child gains an awareness of his/her interests, attitudes and roles, he/she also begins to recognize that not everyone shares the same commonalities. The realization sets in that "my self-descriptions may not be the same as another person's." For positive self-esteem to evolve, it's vital that a student not only develop the feeling of being different but being comfortable with that difference. "I recognize I have unique qualities and, as a result, I like myself even more."

Unfortunately, not all students follow this process toward a strong sense of selfhood. The majority are just not comfortable with themselves and resent their differences. Instead of savoring their special qualities, they wallow in their shortcomings. But there are steps the esteem builder can take to help students acknowledge and respect their uniqueness:

1. *Accept the student for his/her unique and distinct differences.* A feeling of self-worth starts with the knowledge that one is fully accepted for all that one is. This is a critical foundation toward any further esteem building.

2. *Build an awareness of interests, roles and attributes that may influence self-descriptions.* Before a student can acknowledge differences between self and others, he/she must first recognize self-characteristics. Helping students clarify or sharpen the content of their self-descriptions will aid in this process.

3. *Suggest new dimensions that might be added to the descriptions.* Often students are unaware of their unique interests, capabilities or traits. You can help them discover themselves through specific feedback that points out such characteristics.

ACTIVITIES: GROUP 3

The following activities help build awareness of unique qualities.

| Grades 2–5 | Who Am I? | SH17 |

Purpose: To increase students' awareness of their inner self-descriptions and help them sharpen or clarify their content.

Materials: Paper fasteners, 2 per student; hole-punch; SH17 Who Am I? form duplicated on heavy-weight paper, such as cardstock, tag or construction paper; SH17 Comment Strips copied onto regular paper; contact paper or laminating equipment.

Book Assembly: Cut out 10–20 Comment Strips per student and punch holes as shown. These will become the body of the booklet, attached at the base of the portrait by paper fasteners. Laminate the back and smaller booklet cover after students have completed working on them.

Materials for self-portrait: Choose either

1. student photograph; or
2. light-colored construction paper for student to draw a self-picture; or
3. scraps of skin-colored paper for students to make a self-portrait collage.

Procedure: Begin the project by discussing with students how everyone is unique and special. For example: "No two people are alike and each of us has our own characteristics and private thoughts."

After each student has created his/her self-portrait—which is placed centrally on the booklet "back" which is then laminated—ask the students to think about themselves. For instance, how would they complete this sentence?: "I am . . ." Some examples are: "I am tall for my age." "I am a baseball player." "I am honest." Younger students will do this on a very concrete level.

Suggest ideas to older students to help them access their inner descriptions in a new way. For example, in relationships: "I am loyal," "I am sympathetic," etc.

Students secure each Comment Strip, one on top of the other, to the booklet with the two paper fasteners. Continue the activity for several days so that students have a good range of self-descriptions. Add the laminated cover to the top of the comments when the booklet is completed.

Grades K-8 — My Identity Shield SH18

Purpose: To reinforce students' sense of selfhood.

Materials: SH18 My Identity Shield form.

Procedure: Students fill in the various sections of the shield. Nonwriting students may draw pictures.

Variation: For older students, divide the class into small groups (five or less) and have them share with each other what they wrote.

Grades K-8 — Seeing Myself SH19

Purpose: To aid students in recognizing their own unique qualities as well as those in others.

Materials: Clear 9" x 12" window for each student; butcher paper.

For Me Figure: Skin-colored paint; yarn or cut paper strips for hair; fabric, wallpaper, wrapping or construction paper for clothes; buttons, rickrack, lace, sequins.

Window Construction: Cut a 9" x 12" piece of construction paper. Create a "frame" by cutting a 7" x 10" shape from the middle of the 9" x 12" piece; a rectangular empty shape with a 1" border all around should result. Place the frame in a laminating machine to create a clear window and trim the edges.

Alternative Window Construction: Make the window by using a 9" x 12" piece of acetate. Tape strips of tagboard on three sides (bottom and sides).

Figure Construction: Students create a 20" figure of themselves from the waist up. (Younger students could trace around their actual body on butcher paper and then decorate the interior to depict their features.) Encourage students to be as creative as they want. Pin each finished figure to the bulletin board.

Staple the window along the bottom and side edges to the chest of each figure.

Procedure: Each week discuss a different aspect of identity. Topics could include any of the ones below or those that the students themselves suggest.

On an 8 1/2" x 11" piece of paper, each student writes about his/her feelings regarding the topic. At a designated time students may verbalize why they chose that particular topic. The activity also helps classmates learn the "inside secrets" of one another.

Variation: Individual students may make large tagboard shields according to a 14" x 20" pattern. Students trace around the pattern onto tagboard. They give their answers to each category in pictures and/or words.

Note: This activity could also be integrated into Affiliation and Concept Circles, Chapters 5 and 8.

Topic Suggestions:

My favorite . . .

- food, toys, game
- movie, book, outdoor sport
- TV show, animal, school subject
- interest, color, clothing

My least favorite...
- food, toys, game, etc.

Idea suggested by Susan Swenson; Kohl Elementary School, Broomfield, Colorado.

Grades 2–8   Playing Favorites   SH20

Purpose: To help students recognize their interests as well as those of others.

Materials: SH20 Playing Favorites Wheel duplicated on construction paper for each student; crayons or marking pens, scissors.

Procedure: In each category space, students draw or write on the wheel favorite things that have special meaning to them. Hang completed wheels from the ceiling or use as a bulletin board.

The wheel may also become a "get-acquainted" activity. Ask students to find another classmate who has written the same interest. The classmate must initial the student's wheel in the designated space. Each space should have a different student's initials.

Note: This activity also fits in well with the Affiliation component.

Grades 2–8   Wanted Poster   SH21

Purpose: To enhance students' awareness of their identity, focusing on interests and special skills.

Materials: A copy of SH21 Wanted Poster form for each student; crayons or marking pens (or an actual 3" x 5" photograph of each student); scale and measuring tape (optional).

Procedure: Students fill out the SH21 Wanted Poster form. You may wish to send the form home to parents so they can help their child fill it out. Or, you can divide the class into teams in which all the members help each student fill in the questions.

Students may need a mirror for the questions on physical characteristics. Provide a scale and measuring tape so that students can determine their correct height and weight. The picture of the "wanted" student may either be self-drawn or an actual photograph glued in place.

Grades 5–8   Resumé   SH22

Purpose: To help students reflect upon their current educational and social accomplishments.

Materials: A copy of SH22 Resumé form for each student.

Procedure: Explain to students that the usual way to get a job is to first submit a resume. Bring in actual resumés and display them as examples. Encourage students to think about past experiences (both educational and social) that would make them desirable for a job position. Students then fill out their "contributions and experiences" on the form.

Students may also role-play job interviews in teams or dyads. The student describes his/her resumé to the partner/teammates.

Note: This activity will also work well in Concept Circles.

Grades 3–8   My Interests and Hobbies   SH23

Purpose: To enhance students' awareness of who they are in relation to their hobbies and interests.

Materials: A copy of SH23 My Interests and Hobbies form for each student.

Procedure: Begin the discussion of interests and hobbies by sharing one of your own. Display something representing this hobby or interest and encourage other staff members or parents to share as well.

Students then fill in the form, after which they sign up for a date and time when they will present their actual hobby or interest to the class. Use the form as an outline for the presentation.

Grades 1–5   All-About-Me Center   SH24-43

Purpose: To increase students' awareness of their individual identity.

Materials for the Center:

Bulletin board, cardboard carrel or table top for the Center; 18 task cards, cut and laminated; shoe box or task-card stand to store task cards; SH25 All-About-Me Contract for each student.

Supplies: glue, scissors, hole-punch, stapler, yarn, construction paper scraps, pencils, crayons or marking pens.

Materials for the tasks:

Task 1 SH26 shoe box.

3 SH28 wire hanger; tagboard templates (at least 6" in size) of the following shapes: circle, triangle, square and diamond.

5 SH30 measuring tape.

6 SH31 tagboard templates of a boy and girl. Enlarge the shapes for students to trace around. Remove eye shapes by cutting out 2 circles 3" in diameter.

7 SH32 3" x 36" strip of butcher paper; 2 pencils.

8 SH33 paper tube from a wire clotheshanger; 36" yarn length; 12" x 18" piece construction paper; wallpaper, burlap or fabric.

9 SH34 tagboard "I" pattern enlarged to 12" x 18" for stencil; 12" x 18" construction paper.

10 SH35 lunch-size paper bag; construction paper scraps (different sizes); 6" x 6" skin-colored construction paper.

11 SH36 overhead projector; 9" x 12" or 12" x 18" black construction paper; 2 1/2" x 5" white paper strips.

13 SH38 12" x 12" yellow construction paper; 11" cardboard star pattern; glitter.

14 SH39 cardboard circle templates of the following diameters: 2", 4", 6", 8", 10", 12"; light-colored construction paper cut from the templates.

15 SH40 cardboard paper towel tube; 10" x 36" butcher paper strip.

16 SH41 9" x 12" construction paper; glue, light-colored construction paper cut into shapes.

17 SH42 8 1/2" x 11" white or flesh-colored construction paper (or make tagboard girl/boy figures for students to trace around); yarn, hole-punch.

18 SH43 12" x 18" piece of construction paper; magazines.

Procedure:

1. Set up the Center display in a convenient area of your classroom.

2. Duplicate a copy of SH25 All-About-Me Contract for each student and store it in the Center.

3. Mount the task cards (1–18) on heavy paper. Cut them in half and laminate for durability. Store all the materials needed to complete the tasks at the Center (these are indicated on the task cards as well as in the list above).

Students may complete the tasks in any order. Upon completion of a task, the student colors in the corresponding task card number on the All-About-Me Contract.

| Grades K–5 | The Gift of Self | SH44 |

Purpose: To develop students' awareness that one of life's greatest gifts is the "self."

Materials: 2 pieces 9" x 12" green construction paper; 5" x 3" brown construction paper; tagboard pattern of a tree; glue, scissors, writing paper.

Procedure for Shape Books:

1. Make a pattern of a tree on tagboard for students to trace around on two pieces of green construction paper.

2. Cut out patterns. Paste scraps of brown construction paper to fit pattern below dotted line for tree trunk.

3. Staple several sheets of plain or writing paper in the shape of a tree to fit inside the two green paper covers.

4. Students use the shape books to draw, write or dictate ideas about what they can give to others—all gifts of the self.

Enlist Suggestions from Students of Nonmaterial Giving Items:

Post suggestions onto a large Giving Tree bulletin board. (Use the same pattern enlarged onto butcher paper.) Write each suggestion on a red apple, made out of construction paper, with the student's name inside.

Suggestions:

- hugs; write a letter; phone call
- kisses; do chores; sing a song
- smiles; say a kind word; do something without being asked...homework, bedmaking
- pick flowers; share something; make a picture for someone

Variation: Make a ditto of a tree shape and run off on green construction paper. Students trace around the apple pattern onto red construction paper and make "apples." In each apple they write a gift they could give and paste the apple on the tree.

Plaster of Paris Tree Branch: Stick a tree branch in a coffee can filled with plaster of Paris. Hang cutout apple shapes on the tree.

SUGGESTED READING FOR THIS ACTIVITY:

For younger students:
Ask Mr. Bear, Marjorie Flack (Collier Books, 1962).
Do You Know What I'll Do? Charlotte Zolotow (Harper & Row, 1958).
Mr. Rabbit and the Lovely Present, Charlotte Zolotow (Harper & Row, 1962).

For all students:
The Giving Tree, Shel Silverstein (Harper & Row, 1964).
Hugs & Shrugs, the Continuing Saga of a Tiny Owl Named Squib, Larry Shles (Jalmar Press, 1988).

For older students:
Charlotte's Web, E.B. White (Harper & Row, 1952).
Stone Fox, John Reynolds (Thomas Y. Crowell, 1980).

ESTEEM BUILDER #4

Enhance Ability to Identify and Express Emotions and Attitudes

The importance and pervasiveness of emotions in our lives hardly needs debating. Emotions are fundamental to human nature; they enrich our lives and, when ignored, may cause problems or lack of interest in life. Exploring their emotions helps students better understand themselves and others.

Include Emotions in the Classroom Curriculum

This would encompass the following:

- Increase students' awareness and sensitivity to the fact that not everyone reacts to the same experience in the same manner.

- Help them explore their own emotions and thereby further develop self-understanding.

- Encourage the use of constructive ways to deal with their feelings.

- Assist in conflict situations (a student who verbalizes feelings will be less likely to use physical means to resolve a relationship problem).

- Increase awareness of what is personally valued.

Emotion education is a critical esteem builder because it helps students clarify and sharpen their self-picture and thus develop a stronger sense of selfhood.

ACTIVITIES: GROUP 4

The following activities are designed to help students access their feelings and consequently clarify their self-image.

Grades K–3 | **Dictionary of Feelings SH45**

Purpose: To help students learn the words that identify emotions and to increase awareness of feelings.

Materials: Colored Xerox paper for dictionary cover; crayons or marking pens; paste or glue; stapler and scissors.

Dictionary Construction:

1. Duplicate the SH45 Dictionary of Feelings sheets (marked 1–14) so that you have one copy of each page for every student. The cover page should be a bright color; the interior pages can be white. Photocopy so that pages 1/14 are on the back of the cover; 3/12 on the back of 13/2; 5/10 on the back of 11/4; and 7/8 on the back of 9/6.

2. Collate, fold in half and staple the book together along the center fold.

Procedure: Introduce the dictionary to the students, perhaps with a discussion about how important emotions are. Students fill out the cover with their name and the copyright date.

On the day that the students write about a specific emotion, discuss it with them and show them pictures that illustrate the feeling. You may also read a story that depicts the subject matter (see SH48 Booklist). Students then work on the page that correlates with the emotion discussed.

For each emotion, the following activities may be performed:

1. The class can formulate their own definition. (Consider having "real" dictionaries on hand as models.) A few ideas to incorporate in the definitions are:
   • angry—mad
   • happy—glad
   • proud—feeling special
   • lonely—being without company
   • sad—unhappy
   • scared—afraid
   • silly—having fun
   Write class definitions next to the emotion word.

2. Students illustrate the emotion by depicting themselves feeling that emotion.

3. Students write about a time they remember when they felt that way. Younger students dictate their stories.

4. On the facing page, students may paste or glue pictures from magazines that illustrate the emotion word.

Grades K-3	Feelings Wheel	SH46

Purpose: To increase students' sensitivity to the emotions of others, as well as make them aware of their own emotional fluctuations.

Materials: Light-colored construction paper or cardstock; two-pronged paper fasteners; hole-punch and scissors.

Procedure: Duplicate the top and bottom sections of SH46 Feelings Wheel onto heavy paper. Cut out the sections, placing them on top of each other. Connect the wheels together with a paper fastener.

Wheels may be kept on students' desks or worn (punch a hole at the top of the bottom wheel section and tie it with a 24" yarn length). Encourage students to identify their shifting emotions by moving the dial. Invite classmates to be sensitive to their peer's feelings by observing each other's wheels. Encourage sympathetic words and gestures when a peer's wheel indicates a troubled time.

Note: This activity also works well with Affiliation, Chapter 5.

Grades 3-8	Sending I Messages SH47

Purpose: To help students learn to cope with the emotions of anger and frustration. To provide opportunities for students to use appropriate emotional language.

Procedure: Explain to students that we all encounter times of frustration and difficulty. There are appropriate and inappropriate ways of dealing with the frustration. How we verbalize our frustrations may make all the difference as to how the situation ends.

Begin by encouraging students to think of incidents among peers that generally cause feelings of anger. List a few of these on the chalkboard. Write additional incidents on a separate piece of paper and keep for future use. Examples may include:

• You're walking in the hall and someone trips you.

• You've been waiting a long time in the cafeteria line. Someone cuts ahead of you.

• You see a student across from you copying all your answers from your test.

• You see a student take your pencil and then walk away.

• Someone makes fun of you and calls you a name.

• Someone pushes you in the hallway.

• Someone walks by and slams your locker closed while you are trying to get books out of it.

• Someone is spreading rumors about you that aren't true.

Invite students to discuss how they usually handle these situations. Continue the discussion for a brief time. Then point out to students that there are alternative methods of responding to the "aggressor" without accelerating the situation to a new level. One way is to send "I" messages.

Sending I Messages

Begin the process of teaching students this strategy by choosing one of the incidents listed above or asking a student to volunteer one. Read the incident aloud and then ask students how it would make them feel if it happened to them.

Example:
Incident: Someone pushes you in the hallway.

Teacher: *How does it make you feel?*

Student: *Angry...mad...frustrated...ticked off...furious...scared.*

Teacher: *Why don't you let him know how it makes you feel. Start with an "I" and tell him how it feels for him to do that.*

Student: *I feel MAD...*

Teacher: *Now tell him why it feels like that. What did he do that made you mad?*

Student: *He pushed me in the hallway.*

Teacher: *Tell him that's why you're mad. Start with "I feel mad..." and then tell him what he did to make you mad.*

Student: *I feel mad because you pushed me in the hallway.*

Continue role-playing incidents until students appear to understand the sequence. You may wish to make a poster depicting the "I Message" sequence as a reference for students.

To Send an I Message:

1. Start the statement with an "I."
2. Tell the person how you feel ("I'm mad..." or "I feel hurt...").
3. Tell the person what he or she did that made you feel that way. ("I'm mad because you took my pencil without asking.")

Make a ditto listing the incidents students suggested and use it in a following session:

Divide students into teams of three to five members. Give each team a copy of the incidents and include, if you wish, a form with the "I Message" sequence. Students take turns sending "I Messages" to one another by role-playing the incidents.

Adapted from Dr. Thomas Gordon, Effectiveness Training, Inc.

Grades K-8 Books to Enhance Identity SH48

Purpose: To gain awareness of how others acquired their selfhood.

Materials: One or more books from the list below appropriate to grade level. Either read aloud or assign as independent reading.

Primary Level:
The Bedspread, Sylvia Fair (William Morrow & Co., 1982).
Benji, Joan M. Lexau (Dial, 1964).
Crow Boy, Taro Yashima (Viking, 1955).
Dandelion, Don Freeman (Viking, 1964).
Faces, Barbara Brenner (Dutton, 1974).
Ferdinand the Bull, Munaro Leaf (Viking, 1977).
Hooray for Me, R. Charlip and L. Moore (Parents, 1975).
I Know What I Like, N. Simon (Albert Whitman, 1971).
I Like to Be Me, Barbara Bel Geddes (Viking, 1963).
The Important Book, Margaret Wise Brown (Harper & Row, 1949).
Leo the Late Bloomer, Robert Kraus (Windmill, 1971).
The Little Rabbit Who Wanted Red Wings, Carolyn Sherwin Bailey (Platt & Munk, 1978).
Max, Rachel Isadora (MacMillan, 1976).
The Mixed-up Chameleon, Eric Carle (Harper & Row, 1987).
Moths & Mothers, Feathers & Fathers, A Story About a Tiny Owl Named Squib, Larry Shles (Jalmar Press, 1989).
Petunia, Roger Duvoisin (Knopf, 1950).
The Rotten Chicken, Letitia Ursa Solomon (Henchanted Books, 1984).
Someday, Charlotte Zolotow (Harper & Row, 1965).
TA for Tots, Alvyn Freed (Jalmar Press, 1975).
TA for Tots, Vol. II, Alvyn Freed (Jalmar Press, 1980).
The Whingdingdilly, Bill Peet (Houghton & Mifflin, 1970).
William's Doll, Charlotte Zolotow (Harper & Row, 1972).

Intermediate Level or Advanced Listener:
Be a Perfect Person in Just Three Days, Stephen Manes (Clarion, 1982).

SELFHOOD

Black and Blue Magic, Zilpha Keatley Snyder (Atheneum, 1972).
Blowfish Live in the Sea, Paula Fox (Bradbury, 1970).
Circles of Fire, William H. Hooks (Atheneum, 1983).
Dear Mr. Henshaw, Beverly Cleary (Morrow, 1983).
The Great Gilly Hopkins, Katherine Paterson (Crowell, 1978).
Hazel Rye, Vera and Bill Cleaver (Lippincott, 1983).
Hoots & Toots & Hairy Brutes, Squib the Owl Saves the Day, Larry Shles (Jalmar Press, 1989).
Lafcadio, The Lion Who Shot Back, Shel Silverstein (Harper, 1963).
Mostly Michael, Robert Kimmel Smith (Dell, 1987).
Nobody's Family Is Going to Change, Louise Fitzhugh (Farrar, Straus & Giroux, 1974).
Nothing's Fair in Fifth Grade, Barthe DeClements (Viking, 1981).
Queenie Peany, Robert Burch (Puffin, 1988).
Shoeshine Girl, Clyde Robert Bulla (Crowell, 1975).
TA for Kids, Alvyn & Marge Freed (Jalmar Press, 1978).
There's a Boy in the Girl's Bathroom, Louis Sachar (Alfred A. Knopf, 1987).
A Time for Watching, Gunilla Norris (Random, 1969).
Tuck Everlasting, Natalie Babbit (Farrar, Straus & Giroux, 1975).
Weird Henry Berg, Sarah Sargent (Dell, 1980).

Books Dealing with Self-Awareness Sensitivity

Primary Level:
Arthur's Eyes, Marc Brown (Avon, 1976).
Arthur's Nose, Marc Brown (Avon, 1979).
Big Enough, Sherry Kafka (Putnam, 1974).
The Big, Fat Enormous Lie, Marjorie Weinman Sharmat (E.P. Dutton, 1978).
Big Little Davy, L. Lenski (Henry Z. Walck, 1956).
Billy, the Littlest One, M. Schlein (Whitman, 1966).
But Names Will Never Hurt Me, Bernard Waber (Houghton Mifflin, 1976).
Danny and His Thumb, Kathryn F. Ernst (Prentice-Hall, 1973).
Eddie and the Fire Engine, Carolyn Haywood (William Morrow, 1949)—about missing teeth.
Fat Elliott and the Gorilla, Manus Pinkwater (Scholastic, 1974).

Green Eyes, A. Birnbaum (Golden, 1973)
Growing Story, Ruth Krauss (Harper & Row, 1947).
Hey, Look At Me! Sandy Grant (Bradbury, 1973).
Hooray for Jasper, B. Horvath (Franklin Watts, 1966).
I Hate to Take a Bath, J. Barrett (Four Winds, 1975).
Katie's Magic Glasses, J. Goodsell (Houghton Mifflin, 1965)—a five-year-old girl needs glasses.
Little Is Nice, Alicia Kaufmann (Hawthorne, 1970).
The Littlest Rabbit, Robert Krauss (Harper & Row, 1961).
A Look at Physical Handicaps, M.S. Purcell (Lerner Publications, 1976).
Rosa Too Little, Sue Fett (Doubleday, 1950).
The Shy Little Girl, Phyllia Krasilovsky (Houghton Mifflin, 1970).
Smallest Boy in the Class, Jerrold Beim (Wm. Morrow, 1949).
Spectacles, Ellen Raskin (Atheneum, 1974)—insecurity about wearing glasses.
Tall Tina, Muriel Stanek (Albert Whitman, 1966).
The Very Little Boy, Phyllia Krasilovsky (Doubleday, 1953).
The Very Little Girl, Phyllia Krasilovsky (Doubleday, 1953).
Who's That in the Mirror? Polly Berends (Random House, 1968).

Intermediate Level or Advanced Listener:
Aliens in My Nest, Squib Meets the Teen Creature, Larry Shles (Jalmar Press, 1988).
Blubber, Judy Blume (Dell, 1974)—overweight fifth-grade girl.
Do Bananas Chew Gum? Jamie Gilson (Lothrop, Lee & Shepard, 1980)—dyslexia.
Edith Herself, Ellen Howard (Atheneum, 1987)—epilepsy.
Freckle Juice, Judy Blume (Scholastic, 1971).
Invisible Lisa, Natallie Honeycutt (Avon, 1986).
Me and Einstein: Breaking the Reading Barrier, Rose Blue (Human Sciences, 1985).
Nothing's Fair in Fifth Grade, Barthe DeClements (Scholastic, 1981).
The Plain Princess, Phyllis McGinley (Lippincott, 1945).
The Real Me, Betty Miles (Avon, 1976).
Sixth Grade Can Really Kill You, Barthe DeClements (Scholastic, 1981).
Someday Angeline, Louis Sachar (Avon, 1983).

Special Books on Emotions Suitable for Classroom Discussions

P = Primary (K–3)
I = Intermediate Level (4–8) or Advanced Listener

Alexander and the Terrible, Horrible, No Good Very Bad Day, Judith Viorst (Atheneum, 1972). [P]

The Bear's House, Marilyn Sachs (E.P. Dutton, 1971)—misfit 10-year-old Fran turns out to be an ace babysitter. [I]

Do Bananas Chew Gum? Jamie Gilson (Lothrop, Lee & Shepard, 1980). [I]

Do I Have to Go to School Today? Squib Measures Up, Larry Shles (Jalmar Press, 1989). [I]

The Do-Something Day, Joe Lasker (Scholastic, 1982). [P]

Feelings, Aliki (Greenwillow, 1984)—illustrated. [P]

Feelings, Judy Blume (Creative Publications, 1971). [P]

Feelings Alphabet: An Album of Emotions from A to Z, Judy Lalli (B.L. Winch & Associates, 1984). [P]

The Gold Cadillac, Mildred D. Taylor (Dial, 1987)—Black prejudice in the '50s. [I]

How I Feel, J. Behrens (Children's Press, 1973). [P]

I Have Feelings, Terry Berger (Human Sciences, 1971). [I]

Immigrant Girl, Becky of Eldridge Street, Brett Harvey (Holiday House, 1987). [I]

Molly's Pilgrim, Barbara Cohen (Lothrop, Lee and Shepard, 1983). [P]

Nobody Listens to Andrew, Elizabeth Guilfoile (Scholastic, 1957). [P]

Rose Blanche, Roberto Innocenti (Creative Education, 1985)—Holocaust. [I]

The Shrinking of Treehorn, Florence Parry Heide (Holiday House, 1971). [P–I]

The Stone-Faced Boy, Paula Fox (Aladdin, 1968). [I]

Today Was a Terrible Day, Patricia Reilly Giff (Puffin, 1980). [P]

Anger:

Boy Was I Mad! Kathryn Hitte (Parents, 1969). [P]

Feeling Angry, Sylvia Root Tester (Children's Press, 1976). [P]

Hating Book, Charlotte Zolotow (Harper & Row, 1969). [P]

I Was So Mad! Norma Simon (Albert Whitman, 1974). [P]

The Quarreling Book, Charlotte Zolotow (Harper & Row, 1963). [P]

Sometimes I Get Angry, J.W. Watson (Golden, 1971). [P]

Temper Tantrum Book, Edna M. Preston (Viking, 1969). [P]

Where the Wild Things Are, Maurice Sendak (Harper & Row, 1963). [P]

Fear:

Buster and the Bogeyman, Anne Rockwell (Four Winds, 1978). [P]

Ira Sleeps Over, Bernard Waber (Houghton Mifflin, 1972). [P]

Night of the Twisters, Ivy Ruckman (Harper & Row, 1984). [I]

Sometimes I'm Afraid, Sylvia Tester (Children's Press, 1979). [P]

There's a Nightmare in My Closet, Mercer Mayer (Dial, 1976). [P]

Sadness:

The Accident, Carol Carrick (Seabury, 1976). [I]

Charlotte's Webb, E.B. White (Harper Trophy, 1974). [I]

The Dead Bird, Margaret Wise Brown (Young Scott Books, 1938). [P]

Mustard, Charlotte Graeber (MacMillan, 1983). [I]

My Turtle Died Today, Edith Stull (Holt, 1964). [P]

Nana, Lyn Littlefield Hoopes (Harper & Row, 1981). [P]

A Taste of Blackberries, Doris B. Smith (Scholastic, 1976). [I]

Where the Red Fern Grows, Wilson Rawls (Bantam, 1985). [I]

SELFHOOD

Name	Date

A Self-Portrait

A Picture of How I Look

Describe your appearance to someone who has never seen you.

"When I look into a full-length mirror I see . . . ."_____

_____

_____

_____

_____

_____

_____

Esteem Builders. Jalmar Press
Rolling Hills Estates, CA

Name	Date

Focus on Me

1. I weigh _____ pounds.

2. I am _____ tall.

3. I have _____ hair.
   _{Color}

4. I have _____ eyes.
   _{Color}

5. I have _____ teeth (_____ on top and _____ on the bottom).

6. I wear _____ do not wear _____ glasses. (Check one)

7. I have _____ do not have _____ freckles. (Check one)

8. I am right handed _____ left handed _____ ambidextrous _____ .

9. My hair is long _____ short _____ curly _____ straight _____ .

10. I think I look best when I wear the color _____ .
    _{Color}

This is a picture of me.

Esteem Builders. Jalmar Press
Rolling Hills Estates, CA

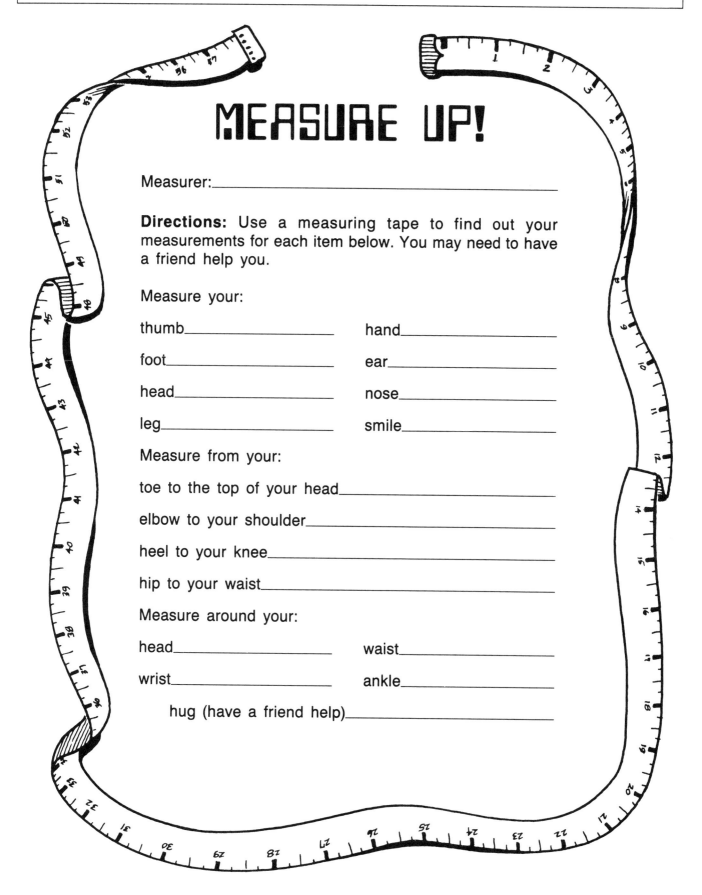

Name_____   Date_____

MEASURE UP!

Measurer:_____

Directions: Use a measuring tape to find out your measurements for each item below. You may need to have a friend help you.

Measure your:

thumb_____   hand_____

foot_____   ear_____

head_____   nose_____

leg_____   smile_____

Measure from your:

toe to the top of your head_____

elbow to your shoulder_____

heel to your knee_____

hip to your waist_____

Measure around your:

head_____   waist_____

wrist_____   ankle_____

hug (have a friend help)_____

Esteem Builders. Jalmar Press
Rolling Hills Estates, CA

Me Doll

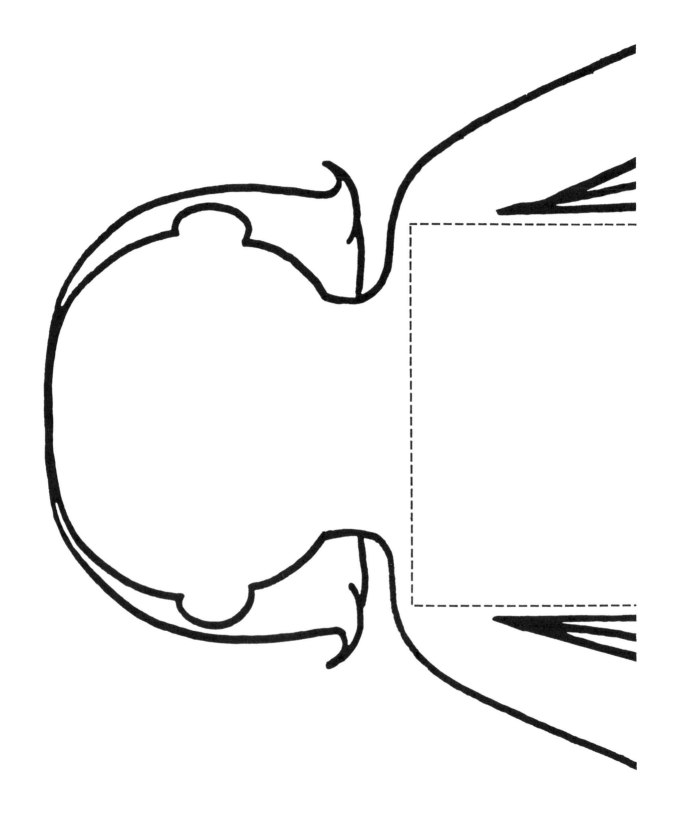

Esteem Builders. Jalmar Press
Rolling Hills Estates, CA

Me Doll

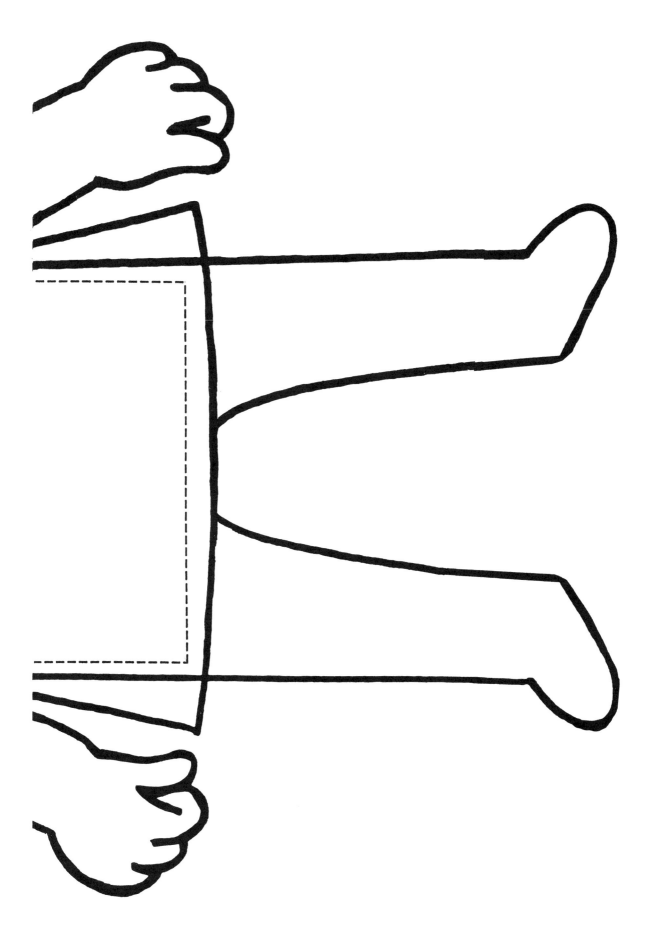

Esteem Builders. Jalmar Press
Rolling Hills Estates, CA

Walking Me Puppet

Esteem Builders. Jalmar Press
Rolling Hills Estates, CA

Paper Bag Face Puppets

Esteem Builders. Jalmar Press
Rolling Hills Estates, CA

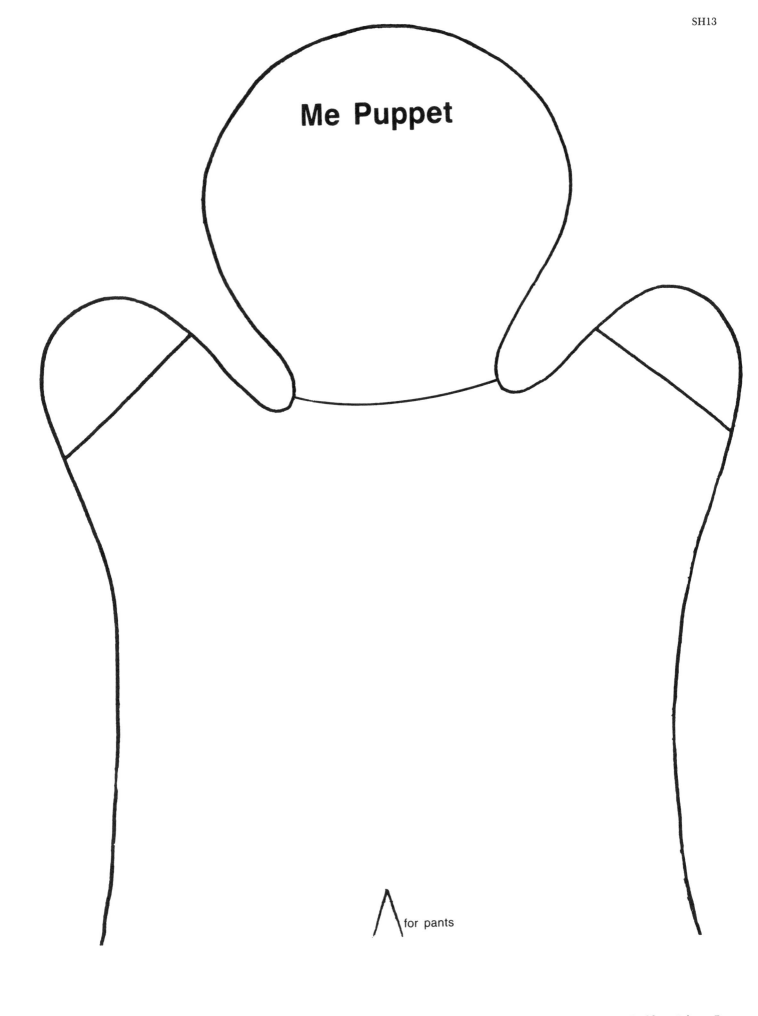

Me Puppet

for pants

Esteem Builders. Jalmar Press
Rolling Hills Estates, CA

Name _____   Date _____

Time Line of Significant Events

Directions: You've had many, many experiences in your life that have helped to make you who you are. Think back and try to decide which events were the most important or special to you. Make checks next to the topics below that you think have been important in your life.

★ **Early Moments**

_____ Birth*

_____ First walked*

_____ First talked*

*Ask your parents about these.

★ **Travel**

_____ Special trips

_____ Outings

_____ Favorite places

★ **Sports**

_____ First sport

_____ Awards

_____ Martial arts

_____ Difficulties

★ **Health**

_____ Illness

_____ Operation

_____ Accident

★ **Family Events**

_____ New baby

_____ Parent's new job

★ **Education**

_____ Start school

_____ Special teacher

_____ Difficulties

★ **Upsetting Events**

_____ Death of a loved one

_____ Family breakup

_____ Moving

★ **Creative Times**

_____ Art

_____ Music lessons

_____ Dance/Gymnastics

★ **Significant Others**

_____ Friendships

_____ Conflicts

★ **Other**

_____   _____   _____

1. Use the paper strips at the Time-Line Center. Write on each about an important event in your life. Where you made a check mark, you must write that event on a strip.

2. Read through the strips you've written. Put them in order as to which event went first, second, third, etc. The last event should be something happening to you now.

3. Now make your time line on the butcher paper. Draw a black line across the bottom edge of the paper.

4. Paste the strips in sequence along the time line.

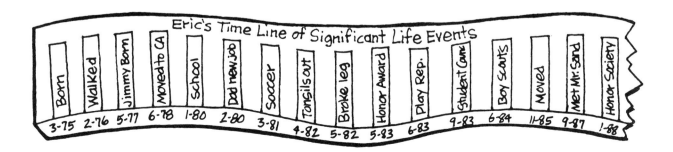

Esteem Builders. Jalmar Press
Rolling Hills Estates, CA

Name	Date

A MOVIE OF MY LIFE

Esteem Builders. Jalmar Press
Rolling Hills Estates, CA

Name	Date

The Many Parts of Me

All of us are made up of many different parts, and special experiences help to form our personality. Each event (either positive or negative) is just one piece of our self.

Directions: On each puzzle piece write a different experience that was significant in your life. If you can remember, write how old you were when the experience happened. Some will be easy to think of and others will be much more difficult. It may help you to quickly review each year of your life. For example, "When I was six, my *grandma* came to *live with us.* Use key words.

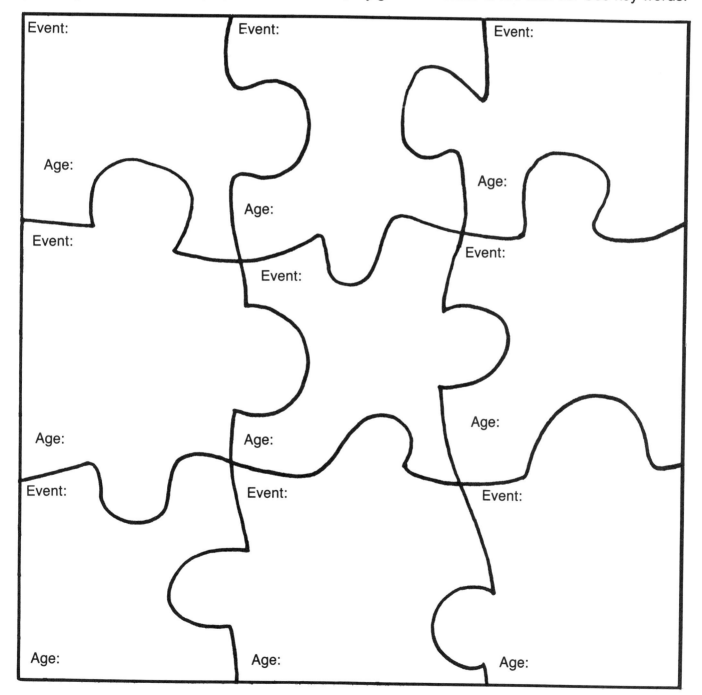

Esteem Builders. Jalmar Press
Rolling Hills Estates, CA

Who Am I?

(cover)

by _____

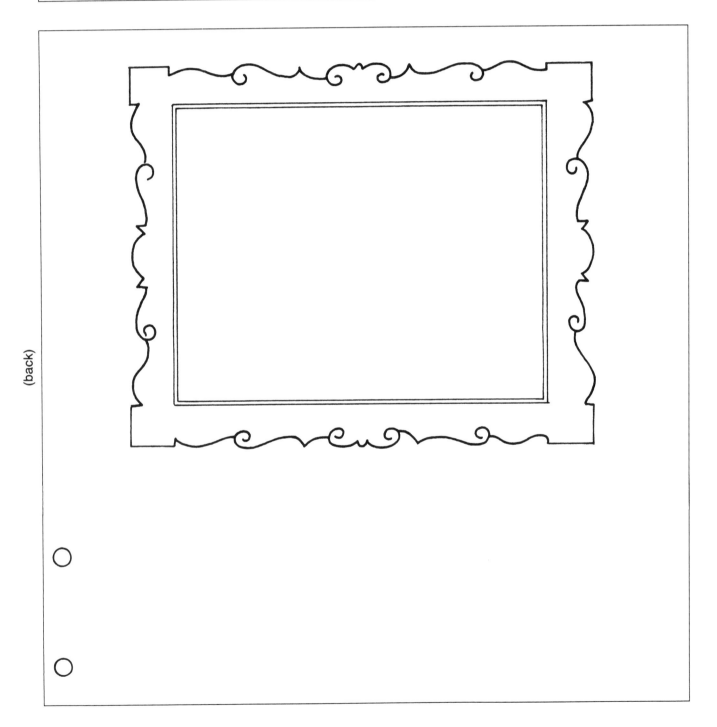

(back)

Esteem Builders. Jalmar Press
Rolling Hills Estates, CA

Who Am I? Comment Strips

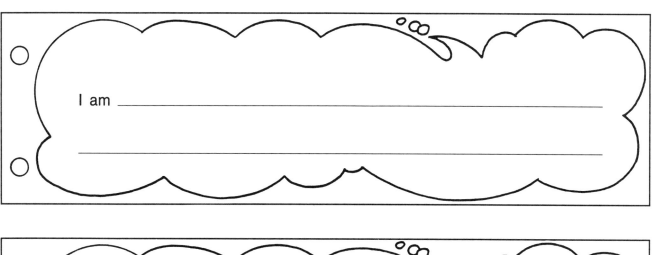

I am _____

_____

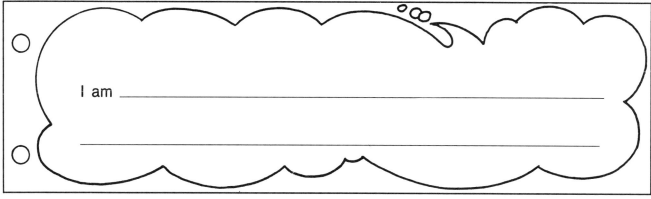

I am _____

_____

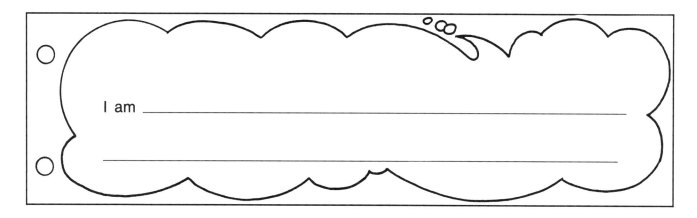

I am _____

_____

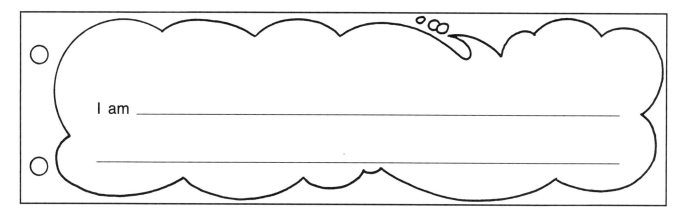

I am _____

_____

Esteem Builders. Jalmar Press
Rolling Hills Estates, CA

Name	Date

My Identity Shield

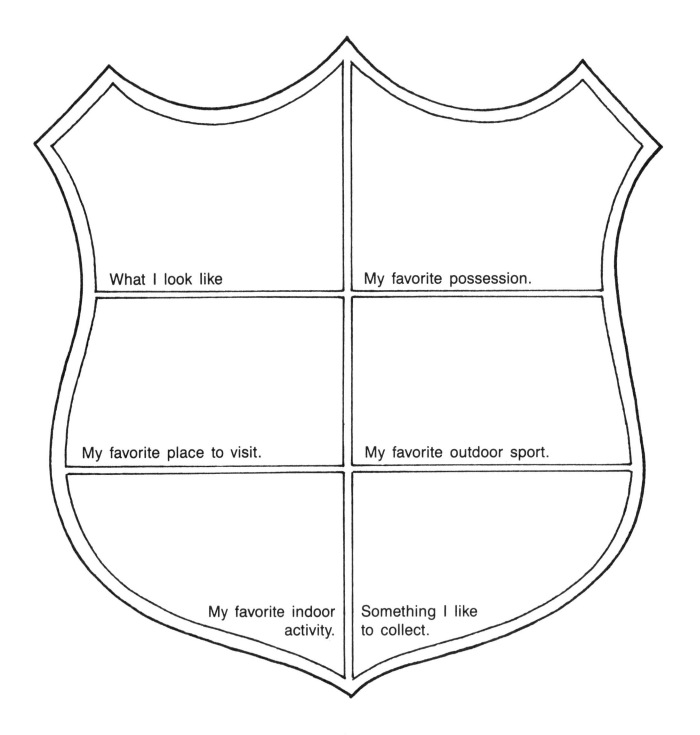

What I look like

My favorite possession.

My favorite place to visit.

My favorite outdoor sport.

My favorite indoor activity.

Something I like to collect.

Esteem Builders. Jalmar Press
Rolling Hills Estates, CA

Name	Date

Playing Favorites

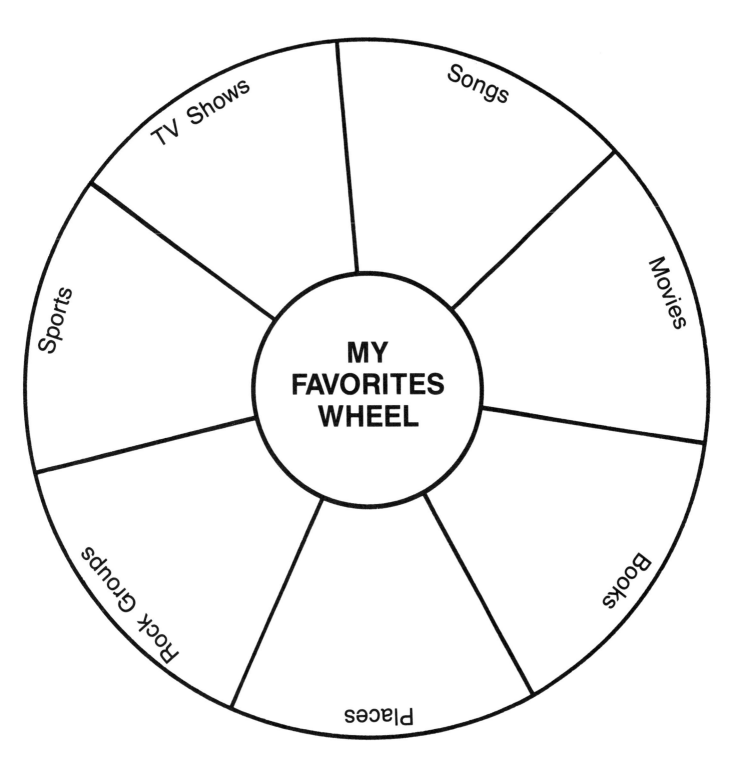

TV Shows

Songs

Sports

Movies

MY FAVORITES WHEEL

Rock Groups

Books

Places

Esteem Builders. Jalmar Press
Rolling Hills Estates, CA

Name _____ Date _____

WANTED

You are wanted by your classmates for being special.

Age: _____

Weight: _____

Height: _____

Eye Color: _____

Hair Color: _____

Most Likely to Be Found: _____

_____

_____

Picture of Wanted Student

Special Skills and Talents: _____

_____

_____

Best Known for: _____

_____

_____

_____

Likes to: _____

_____

_____

Esteem Builders. Jalmar Press
Rolling Hills Estates, CA

Name	Date

Resumé

Address:_____

Current Grade Level:_____

Special Training:_____

_____

_____

Hobbies and Outside Interests:_____

_____

_____

Favorite School Subject:_____

Clubs, Organizations:_____

_____

_____

Contribution You Can Make to This Classroom:_____

_____

What You Want to Be When You Grow Up:_____

Special Duties and Responsibilities:_____
                                        (Home and School)

_____

_____

References:_____
            (People who know you well and would speak highly of you)

_____

_____

Esteem Builders. Jalmar Press
Rolling Hills Estates, CA

Name	Date

My Interests and Hobbies

1. A favorite interest or hobby of mine is_____

   _____

2. I've enjoyed this for_____
   (How Long?)

3. I got started in this_____
   (How Did You Get Started In This Field?)

4. Some things I have done in this hobby or interest are _____

   _____

   _____

5. I enjoy doing this interest or hobby because _____

   _____

   _____

6. I usually do this with _____
   (Name Other People Involved, If Any))

   _____

7. The most interesting thing that has happened while I was doing this is _____

   _____

8. An interest or hobby I'd like to learn more about is:

   ☐ Stamps   ☐ Dinosaurs   ☐ Singing   ☐ Rocks

   ☐ Wild Flowers ☐ Basketball   ☐ Skateboarding   ☐ Sewing

   ☐ Sea Shells   ☐ Calligraphy   ☐ Tennis   ☐ Painting

   ☐ Writing   ☐ Bowling   ☐ Music   ☐ Cooking

   ☐ Insects   ☐ Soccer   ☐ Baseball   ☐ Reading

   ☐ Other: _____

   _____

Use this as an outline to help you give a short talk about your interest or hobby.

Esteem Builders. Jalmar Press
Rolling Hills Estates, CA

Name   Date

All-About-Me Contract

Esteem Builders. Jalmar Press
Rolling Hills Estates, CA

Dioramas

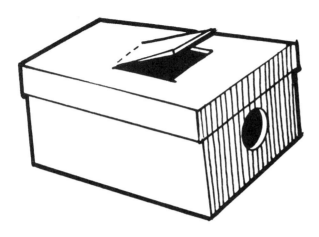

1. Find a box with a removable lid.

2. Cut a small peephole in the end of the box.

3. Make a slot in the top of the box to let in light. Cut along 3 sides of the slot and fold back the flap.

4. Inside the box, make a scene that is a favorite memory from your past.

You need: paper, scissors, marking pens, glue and a box with a removable lid.

Letter to a Friend

1. Write a letter to a person who has been very important in your life. Tell the person how special he or she has been and why.

2. If necessary, use the sample letter below to help.

	(Date)
	(Your address)
	(Your city and state)
Dear _____,	
	Sincerely, (or Love,)
	(Your name)

Esteem Builders. Jalmar Press
Rolling Hills Estates, CA

I Like Mobile

1. Cut out at least 4 shapes from heavy paper. Use the templates to trace around.

2. On the front of each shape, draw or cut out pictures of things you like.

3. On the back of the shape, write why you enjoy your choices.

4. Tie your shapes to the hanger.

You need: paper, paper punch, magazines, templates.

Commercial About Me

On a sheet of writing paper, write a commercial about you. Try to sell yourself so that a stranger would like to meet you. For instance, say something positive about your looks, personality, skills and friendliness.

Esteem Builders. Jalmar Press
Rolling Hills Estates, CA

Measuring Me

You need: measuring tape, writing paper, pencil.

1. Use the tape to measure each part of your body listed below. Write your answers to each measurement on writing paper. Print each body part and then print your answer.

- **head**
- **neck**
- **waist**

- **knee**
- **foot**
- **hand**

- length of your **arm**
- length of your **leg**
- length of your **body**

Me Mask

1. Cut around the circle template onto heavy paper to make a face mask.

2. Cut out a place for the eyes, so that you can look through.

3. Decorate your mask. You could use:

- crayons
- marking pens
- yarn
- ribbons

- noodles
- crepe paper
- buttons
- wallpaper

- cotton
- construction paper
- tissue paper
- paints

Life Story

1. Make a movie of your life.

2. Cut a long strip of butcher paper 3″ × 36″ (or use adding machine tape).

3. Roll each of the ends around a pencil.

4. Tape the ends to the pencil.

5. Use crayons, colored pencils or ink pens to draw scenes from your life.

6. Roll up your movie to tell the story to a friend.

Me Banner

1. Make a banner about yourself. You could make it from cardboard, burlap, material, wallpaper, or construction paper.

2. Decorate your banner with pictures or cut-outs about your life. You could include your interests, hobbies or family. You could use
   - paint • paper cut-outs • stitchery • yarn
   - felt-tipped pens • magazines • crayons

3. Staple or tape your finished banner to a paper tube from a wire clotheshanger. Tie on both ends and hang it up.

Esteem Builders. Jalmar Press
Rolling Hills Estates, CA

I Collage

1. Cut out a large "I" from construction paper.

2. Divide the "I" into sections like a puzzle.

3. Draw a different picture in each section of things you enjoy doing at home.

4. Label each picture with words.

Puppet Bag

1. Take a brown lunch bag and draw part of your mouth on the top flap of the bag and the rest of your mouth on the side under the bottom flap.

2. Add features to your face. You could use:

   - paper
   - yarn
   - pipe cleaners
   - wallpaper samples
   - noodles
   - egg carton pieces
   - fabric
   - bric-a-brac

3. Decorate the rest of the bag to add features to your "body."

Esteem Builders. Jalmar Press
Rolling Hills Estates, CA

My Dreams
11

1. Draw a picture of your head and cut it out. (Or make your silhouette by standing in front of an over-head projector. Have a friend trace the silhouette that appears on a piece of paper taped on the wall.)

2. Cut out your silhouette. What things do you dream about? What things do you wish might happen to you? Draw pictures of your dreams on your cutout.

Want Ad
12

POSITION WANTED

Brown-eyed, red-haired girl wants people to like her. Nine years old and a good sport! Can be found playing tennis. Likes horseback riding.
Be friends with her now!

1. Pretend you are advertising yourself in the newspaper. You'll want people to know things you're good at (strengths) and what you look like (physical characteristics). How will you sell yourself to people?

2. Write your ad on paper. You must limit your ad to 30 words. What will they be?

Sparkles

1. Trace a large star pattern onto yellow construction paper. Cut it out.

2. Draw a picture of yourself in the center of the shape. Color.

3. On each star point, write something about yourself you like (or something you're proud of or think you're good at).

4. You may wish to dab tiny bits of glue on your star and sprinkle it with glitter. Punch out a hole at the top and attach a length of yarn to hang your star.

Special People

1. Using a template, cut out a 2" circle from colored construction paper. Draw a picture of your head in this circle.

2. Cut out 4 more circles from different colors. Each circle should be about 1 1/2" larger than the previous one.

3. Glue the circles inside one another from largest to smallest.

4. On each circle, write the name of a different person who is important to you. Now write next to each name why the person is special to you.

You need:
scissors, paper, glue, templates

Esteem Builders. Jalmar Press
Rolling Hills Estates, CA

Time Capsule

1. Think about your life today. How would you like to be remembered?

2. Use a long strip of butcher paper. Draw or glue cutout pictures of things that are your favorites. You may wish to include:

a handprint	favorite food	favorite book
a footprint	favorite movie	favorite friend
family pictures	front page of the news	

3. Roll it up and give it to a grown-up to store for a few years.

You need: paper towel tube, magazine, glue, scissors, butcher paper 10" × 36"

Like Me

1. Make a folder from 9" × 12" paper. Fold it up about 3" along the 12" side. Staple the folder along both edge sides to make a pocket.

2. Fold the paper in half.

3. Write "Like Me" on one side pocket and "Not Like Me" on the other side pocket.

4. Cut out magazine pictures of things you like and don't like. Glue them onto the cards. Make 12 cards.

5. Now sort the cards into the appropriate pocket in your folder.

You need: magazine, glue, scissors, 12 3" × 5" cards, marking pens, 9" × 12" construction paper, stapler.

Esteem Builders. Jalmar Press
Rolling Hills Estates, CA

Me Hanging

1. Make a paper figure of you and color it.

2. Cut 6'' circles out of paper.

3. On each circle write something about yourself.
   Describe:
   a. what you look like.
   b. your family.
   c. something you're proud of.
   d. an interest or hobby.

4. Punch a hole in the middle of the top and bottom of each circle. Punch one hole in your figure.

5. Tie 5'' yarn pieces in the holes to connect the holes.

You need: hole punch, yarn, marking pens, paper, glue, scissors

Me Poster

1. Cut out pictures from magazines of things that remind you of yourself for your Me Poster.

2. Paste the pictures onto a large sheet of paper.

3. Write your name at the top of the paper.

You need: magazines, scissors, glue, construction paper

Esteem Builders. Jalmar Press
Rolling Hills Estates, CA

Dictionary
of
Feelings

Author_____

Copyright_____

Esteem Builders. Jalmar Press
Rolling Hills Estates, CA

Pictures of others feeling this way:

silly

How I Look:

A time I felt this way was . . .

_____

_____

_____

_____

_____

_____

_____

1

14

Pictures of others feeling this way:

angry

How I Look:

A time I felt this way was . . .

_____

_____

_____

_____

_____

_____

_____

13

2

Esteem Builders. Jalmar Press
Rolling Hills Estates, CA

Pictures of others feeling this way:

scared

How I Look:

A time I felt this way was . . .

_____

_____

_____

_____

_____

_____

_____

3

12

Esteem Builders. Jalmar Press
Rolling Hills Estates, CA

Pictures of others feeling this way:

happy

How I Look:

A time I felt this way was . . .

_____

_____

_____

_____

_____

_____

_____

11

4

Esteem Builders. Jalmar Press
Rolling Hills Estates, CA

Pictures of others feeling this way:

sad

How I Look:

A time I felt this way was . . .

_____

_____

_____

_____

_____

_____

_____

5

10

— 152 —

Esteem Builders. Jalmar Press
Rolling Hills Estates, CA

Pictures of others feeling this way:

lonely

How I Look:

A time I felt this way was . . .

_____

_____

_____

_____

_____

_____

_____

9

6

— 153 —

Esteem Builders. Jalmar Press
Rolling Hills Estates, CA

Pictures of others feeling this way:

proud

How I Look:

A time I felt this way was . . .

_____

_____

_____

_____

_____

_____

_____

7

8

Esteem Builders. Jalmar Press
Rolling Hills Estates, CA

SH45

e lingo Wi 1

How 9 Feel
Wheel

by

_____

Esteem Builders. Jalmar Press
Rolling Hills Estates, CA

F elings Wh l

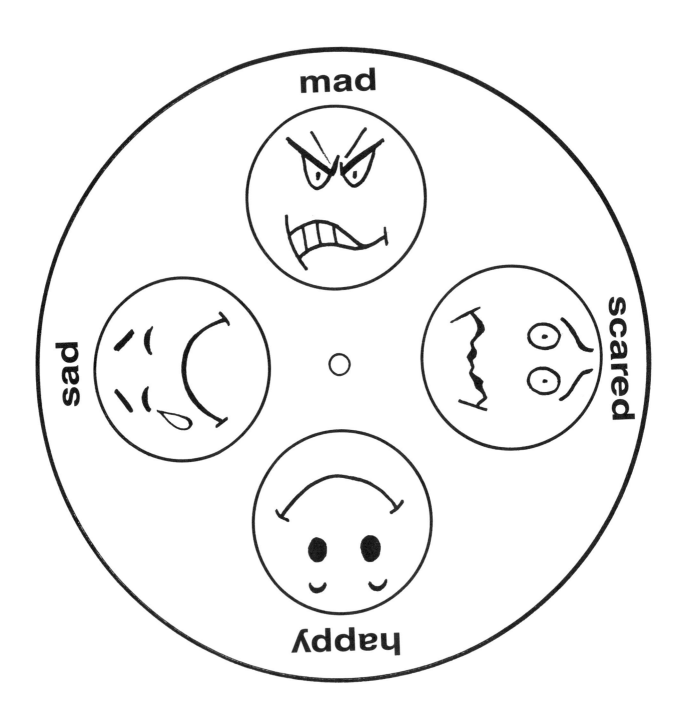

Esteem Builders. Jalmar Press
Rolling Hills Estates, CA

5

A Cooperative Spirit: Building Affiliation

ESTEEM BUILDERS
- Promote Inclusion and Acceptance Within the Group
- Provide Opportunities to Discover the Interests, Capabilities and Backgrounds of Others
- Increase Awareness and Skills in Friendship Making
- Encourage Peer Approval and Support

SUMMARY OF AFFILIATION

Definition: *A feeling of belonging, acceptance or relatedness in relationships that are considered important. Feeling approved of, appreciated and respected by others.*

SUPPORT DATA

- "Self-esteem is related to the recognition we achieve from other people. One of the factors that erodes self-concept is the inability of some children to make and keep friends." James Dobson. *Hide or Seek* (Old Tappan, NJ: Revell, 1974).
- "Shyness tends to go hand-in-hand with low self-esteem. Although shy people may value some skill or special ability they may possess, most are their own worst critics." Philip G. Zimbardo and Shirley L. Radl. *The Shy Child: A Parents Guide to Overcoming and Preventing Shyness from Infancy to Adulthood* (New York: Doubleday, 1982).
- "Children's feelings about themselves have important effects on how successfully they deal with friendships. A feeling of personal significance is necessary for children to reach out to others with confidence: believing in their own competence enables them to resolve social problems; and feeling lovable makes affectionate ties more likely." Charles Smith. *Promoting the Social Development of Young Children* (Palo Alto, CA: Mayfield, 1982).

ESTEEM BUILDERS

- Promote Inclusion and Acceptance Within the Group
- Provide Opportunities to Discover the Interests, Capabilities and Backgrounds of Others
- Increase Awareness of and Skills in Friendship Making
- Encourage Peer Approval and Support

Note: Helping students to function and collaborate as group members is a vital building block to self-esteem; therefore, an entire chapter in ESTEEM BUILDERS is devoted to the topic. See Chapter 8, Concept Circles.

POSSIBLE INDICATORS OF WEAK AFFILIATION

- has difficulty initiating and maintaining friendships;
- connects with objects rather than people;
- is easily influenced by others;
- isolates self from the group, appears to be lonely;
- is uncomfortable working in group settings, which may result in behaviors such as: withdrawal, reticence, bullying, showing-off, being silly, monopolizing, being uncooperative;
- ridicules or rejects others, being insensitive to their emotions and needs;
- feels that others don't value him/her;
- brags and boasts excessively to gain approval;
- relies on adult companionship as sole source of affiliation;
- is seldom sought out by others.

POSSIBLE INDICATORS OF STRONG AFFILIATION

- understands the concept of friendship and initiates new relationships;
- shows sensitivity and compassion toward others;
- demonstrates ability to cooperate and share;
- is comfortable in group settings;
- easily achieves peer acceptance and is sought out by others;
- demonstrates appropriate social skills;
- feels valued by others.

Most students will not conform exactly to the profiles listed above but are more likely to be stronger in some areas and weaker in others. In order to determine the degree to which a student feels affiliated, complete the student self-esteem assessment (B-SET) chart located in Appendix II. The chart may be used periodically or updated as a way of measuring progress. These charts are also useful in determining which activities are appropriate for your class.

Affiliation Activities List

Code	Grade	Title	Soc. Studies	Sci.	Writ. Lang.	Oral Lang.	Math	Art	Lit.
A1	K–8	Books on Belonging and Acceptance	✔			✔			✔
A2	2–6	Common Points			✔	✔			
A3	2–8	Getting to Know You Wheel			✔	✔		✔	
A4	3–8	Paired Name Collage			✔	✔		✔	
A5	K–6	Class Discovery Book		✔	✔				
A6	1–4	Solve the Riddle			✔				
A7	K–4	Friendship Graphs					✔		
A8	K–3	Our Favorite Books			✔	✔	✔		✔
A9	2–6	Mystery Person			✔				
A10	2–8	Friendly Riddles			✔				
A11	1–8	V.I.P. Center			✔	✔		✔	
A12	1–8	Parent Letter	✔		✔				
A13	1–6	Friendly Letter			✔			✔	
A14	K–3	King/Queen for the Day			✔	✔		✔	
A15	K–3	Dandy Lion				✔		✔	✔
A16	2–8	Pen Pals	✔		✔				
A17	K–8	Friendly Class Actions				✔			
A18	K–4	Helping Each Other			✔	✔			
A19	K–8	Friend Interviews				✔		✔	
A20	4–8	What Is a Friend?	✔		✔	✔	✔		
A21	2–5	Friendship Recipes			✔	✔		✔	
A22	K–5	Friendship Wheel			✔	✔			
A23	4–8	Friendship Openers	✔		✔			✔	
A24	1–4	Word Gifts			✔	✔			
A25	K–8	Friendship Pals			✔	✔			
A26	2–8	Friendship Book Reports			✔	✔			✔
A27	2–8	My List of Friendly Deeds	✔		✔				
A28	2–8	Recording Good Deeds	✔		✔				
A29	1–4	My Friendship Book	✔		✔				✔
A30	K–8	Books About Friendship	✔						✔
A31	K–8	Friendship Goal	✔		✔				
A32	K–3	Sunrays	✔		✔			✔	
A33	K–8	Caring Words			✔				
A34	2–8	Calendar of Caring Deeds			✔		✔		
A35	K–6	Card Friendship Center			✔			✔	
A36	2–8	Team Member Center/Certificate	✔		✔	✔		✔	
A37	K–3	Care Ropes	✔						
A38	1–6	Compliment Hanging			✔	✔		✔	✔
A39	2–8	Autographs			✔	✔			
A40	K–8	Books on Caring and Competence	✔			✔			✔

Security Activities That Promote Inclusion and Acceptance

S17	1–8	Time for Friends		S21	2–8	Student Interview
S18	1–5	Name Bingo		S22	K–3	Interest Search
S20	4–8	Personality Trivia		S23	3–8	Find a Friend

Security Activities That Encourage Peer Approval and Support

S24	2–8	Sparkle Statements		S30	3–8	Builder-Uppers
S25	2–5	Smile Book		S31	K–4	Sparkle Line
S26	K–6	Super Sparkle Gram		S32	K–3	Sparkle Compliments
S27	K–8	Secret Friendly Hello Person		S34	2–8	A Special Message to You
S28	K–4	Smile File		S35	3–8	Add a Compliment
S29	K–4	Smile Cans		S37	2–8	A Month of Positivism

Concept Circles Activities That Promote Affiliation

Code	Grade	Title	Grouping
CC25	K–8	Sunshine Statements	Full/Team
CC26	K–5	Sparkle Box	Full
CC27	1–8	Banners	Full/Partner
CC28	2–8	Questions	Full/Team
CC29	2–8	Picture Puzzles	Full/Team
CC30	2–8	We're All Stars	Full/Team
CC31	K–8	Riddles	Full/Team
CC33	K–4	Word Gifts	Full/Team
CC34	3–8	Word Power	Team
CC36	K–5	Sun Rays	Full/Team
CC35	K–3	Glasses Circle	Full/Team
CC37	K–8	Me Bags by Others	Full/Team
CC38	K–8	Me Bag Compliments	Full/Team
CC39	2–8	Name Poster	Full/Team
CC40	K–8	Compliments	Team
CC41	2–8	Compliment Hanging	Team
CC42	K–5	Fuzzy Circles	Full/Team

School-wide Activities That Promote Affiliation

Code	Grade	Title	Element
SW1	K–8	Spirit Tickets	Security
SW2	K–8	Spirit Award	Security
SW3	K–8	Positive Performers	Security
SW4	K–8	Positive Performance Award	Security
SW5	K–8	Gotcha Tickets	Security
SW10	K–8	Friendship Assembly	Security/Affiliation
SW11	K–8	Name Tag Exchange	Security/Affiliation
SW12	K–8	Who's New?	Affiliation

Checklist of Educator Behaviors
That Promote AFFILIATION

Directions: For a self-evaluation of your skills in enhancing your students' feelings of belonging, complete the following items:

Never 1	Sometimes 2	Frequently 3	Always 4	

As an educator:

1. Do I provide the opportunity for every student to feel accepted?

2. Do I provide all students with the opportunity of group entry?

3. Do I allow each student to participate as a functioning, contributing group member?

4. Do I help students acquire special skills in friendship making?

5. Do I provide opportunities for students to gain peer recognition and approval?

6. Do I encourage them to show approval and support toward one another?

7. Do I allow classmates to discover the interests, capabilities and backgrounds of one another?

8. Do I teach students to praise one another for their accomplishments?

9. Do I encourage students' sensitivity toward the needs and feelings of fellow classmates?

10. Do I plan activities that encourage a sense of class/school spirit and pride?

_____ + _____ + _____ + _____ = Total:_____

Areas I could improve in to increase the development of a student's sense of affiliation:

_____

_____

5

A Cooperative Spirit: Building Affiliation

You know where self-esteem comes from?
It comes from peers, from being liked, accepted, connected.
—DAVID JOHNSON

Students with high self-esteem generally possess a sense of affiliation because self-esteem is related to the recognition received in relationship to others. The importance of interpersonal relationships in our lives cannot be overstated. We all need to feel a sense of connectedness to another human being—particularly to those individuals whom we consider to be important and significant. When we feel as though we belong and are connected to those we consider important, and in return we receive respect and approval from them, we gain a sense of affiliation.

Friends have an enormous influence on our students' feelings of self, and because of this, affiliation is a crucial building block toward positive self-esteem. In a struggle for social recognition, peers can provide important avenues for a student's social skill development and sense of affiliation that adults and family experiences alone cannot fulfill.

Peer interactions also provide invaluable lessons that play a critical role in shaping a young person's self-perception or identity. The social comparisons associated with peer interaction enhance self-feedback. Remarks such as: "You sure are a good jumper, Billy" and "I like to be with you" are especially significant when students hear them from their peers.

By contrasting what they can and cannot do with the actions of their peers, students are able to make decisions about their selfhood and formulate opinions on their strengths and weaknesses. "Am I really good at spelling?" "Do others like my ideas?" "Am I too short?" These are types of frequent evaluations students make as they interact with one another. As they win some acceptance and experience a few rejections, students arrive at significant verdicts about themselves.

It is obvious, therefore, that group experiences will develop a sense of affiliation. Damico's research made it clear that peer relations have significant influence on self-concept and school achievement.[1] Yet, 5 to 11 percent of elementary school students are not named as a friend by anyone in their class.[2] Studies on high school dropouts also substantiate that a feeling of being unaffiliated is the second leading cause of leaving school before graduation (U.S. Office of Education, Center for Educational Statistics, 1986). Let's consider the growing number of social maladies that have been correlated with low affiliation. Students who do not feel strongly affiliated are more likely to:

1. Damico, S. *Education by Peers: A Clique Study* (Research Monograph No. 9). P.K. Yonge Laboratory School, University of Florida, August 1974.
2. Gronlund, N.E. *Sociometry in the Classroom.* (New York: Harper & Row, 1959).

- be low achievers in school (Bonney, 1971; Buswell, 1953[3]);

- experience learning difficulties (Amidon and Hoffman, 1965[4]);

- drop out of school (Ullmann, 1957[5]);

- be identified as juvenile delinquents (Roff, Sells and Golden, 1972[6]);

- experience mental health problems in adulthood (Cowen, Pederson, Babigian, Izzo and Trost, 1973[7]).

To sum up, a student who has a weak sense of affiliation:

- has difficulty initiating and maintaining friendships;

- connects with objects rather than people;

- is easily influenced by others;

- isolates self from the group, appears to be lonely;

- is uncomfortable working in group settings which may result in behaviors such as: withdrawal, reticence, bullying, showing-off, being silly, monopolizing, being uncooperative.

- ridicules or rejects others, is insensitive to their emotions and needs;

- feels that others don't value him/her;

- relies on adult companionship as sole source of affiliation;

- is seldom held out others.

On the other hand, a student with a strong affiliation:

- understands the concept of friendship and initiates new relationships;

- shows sensitivity and compassion toward others;

- demonstrates ability to cooperate and share;

- is comfortable in group settings;

- easily achieves peer acceptance and is sought out by others;

- demonstrates appropriate social skills;

- feels valued by others.

All these factors not only enhance self-esteem but make the student a better learner.

SUMMARY

There are four steps the esteem builder can take to increase a student's ability to affiliate:

1. Promote inclusion and acceptance within the group.

2. Provide opportunities to discover the interests, capabilities and backgrounds of others.

3. Increase awareness of and skills in friendship making.

4. Encourage peer approval and support.

3. Bonney, M.E. "Assessment of Efforts to Aid Socially Isolated Elementary School Pupils." *Journal of Educational Research*, Vol. 64, 1971, pp. 345–364.
Buswell, M.M. "The Relationship Between Social Structure of the Classroom and the Academic Successes of the Pupils." *Journal of Experimental Education*, Vol. 22, 1953, pp. 37–52.
4. Amidon, E.J., and Hoffman, C. "Can Teachers Help the Socially Rejected?" *Elementary School Journal*, Vol. 66, 1965, pp. 149–154.
5. Ullmann, C.A. "Teachers, Peers, and Tests as Predictors of Adjustment." *Journal of Educational Psychology*, Vol. 48, 1957, pp. 257–267.
6. Roff, M.; Sells, S.B.; and Golden, M.M. *Social Adjustment and Personality Development in Children* (Minneapolis: University of Minnesota Press, 1972).
7. Cowen, E.L.; Pederson, A.; Babigian, M.; Izzo, L.D.; and Trost, M.A. "Long-term Follow-up of Early Detected Vulnerable Children." *Journal of Consulting and Clinical Psychology*, Vol. 41, 1973, pp. 438–446.

Promote Inclusion and Acceptance Within the Group

"Man finds his fulfillment and happiness only in relatedness to and solidarity with his fellow men."
—ERICH FROMM

Before friends become part of the child's world, the major relationships consist primarily of family—particularly parents and siblings. As the child moves out of the close inner circle of family, however, he/she begins to experience new types of social interactions that are not always possible within the family structure. The child begins to learn basic socialization functions—some pleasant, others not—that are all part of growing with others. The child also learns that being part of a group, and the acceptance that goes along with it, is a crucial part of growing up. As the young person grows so does the circle of friends and the desire for group inclusion.

Unfortunately, many students go through school without friends or with few friends. For example, Gronlund[8] found that about six percent of third-through sixth-graders in one school system were not selected as a friend by any classmate on a sociometric questionnaire, and an additional 12 percent were selected by only one classmate. Hymel and Asher's[9] research revealed that 11 percent of the students studied received no friendship nominations and another 22 percent received only one.

Generally, the first questions students ask as they enter a new classroom have little to do with the academic curriculum. They are more likely to ask themselves: Who is in my class? Who will I sit next to? What are their names? Will they like me? Such concerns point to students' overriding desire for inclusion. Social growth and acceptance dominate their thinking. The need to belong, however, can put enormous stress on a student, particularly if he/she is not considered to be "one of the guys." Students must be given an invitation to be included and affiliated with a group. It is only by gaining access to

a group that they can practice social skills and form an identity as a group member. The learning environment can only be valuable to a student's growing sense as a social being if it provides conditions that promote inclusion and affiliation of its members.

ACTIVITIES: GROUP 1

The following activities promote students' feelings of tolerance toward one another and acceptance within the group.

In addition to those activities listed, several affiliation activities can also be located in Chapter 3, Security. These include S17, S18, S19, S20, S21, S22, S23, which provide opportunities for students to discover the names and interests of their classmates.

Grades K–8	Books on Belonging and Acceptance	A1

Purpose: To promote the awareness that everyone has the need to feel included and accepted.

Materials: One book from the list.

[P] = Primary (K–3)
[I] = Intermediate Level (3–5)
[A] = Advanced Readers (5–8)

Procedure: Choose one of the following books as a class read-aloud or for independent reading. All of the books deal with nonacceptance, cliques or taunting.

Address the following questions either as part of an open-ended discussion or as a written response:

- What problem is the character facing?
- How does the character feel?
- How did the problem happen?
- Has this ever happened to you or someone you know?
- If so, how did you or the other person feel?
- Do you think this ever happens in our school or classroom?
- What could you do to help stop the problem from occurring?

8. Gronlund, N.E. *Sociometry in the Classroom* (New York: Harper & Row, 1959).
9. Hymel, S., and Asher, S.R. "Assessment and Training of Isolated Children's Social Skills." Paper presented at Society for Research in Child Development, New Orleans, 1977. (ERIC Document Reproduction Service No. ED 136 930.)

Blubber, Judy Blume (Dell, 1974). An inside look at how obnoxious some well-to-do, suburban, fifth-grade children can be to each other and to adults. [I–A]

The Changeling, Zilpha Keatley Snyder (Dell, 1970). Even though no one approves of Ivy, Martha accepts her friend without question. Can pressures from other people take the friendship away? [I–A]

Crow Boy, Taro Yashima (Penguin, 1976). The story of a boy who is different and misunderstood by his peers. [P]

Did You Carry the Flag Today, Charley? Rebecca Caudill (Holt, Rinehart and Winston, 1966). No one ever expects Charley to win...after all, he's different. But win, he does! [P–I]

The Hundred Dresses, Eleanor Estes (Harcourt, 1944). School isn't easy for those who are different—especially Wanda. Exquisite! [I]

It's Mine, Leo Lionni (Alfred A. Knopf, 1986). The great one about sharing and taking turns—perfect to use when you hear, "It's mine!" [P]

Molly's Pilgrim, Barbara Cohen (William Morrow, 1983). The girls in third grade laugh at Molly and make fun of her imperfect English and old-country clothes. Touchingly told! [P–I]

Nothing's Fair in Fifth Grade, Barthe DeClements (Scholastic, 1981). Befriending the school outcast can be tough, but sticking by your feelings in the long run is beneficial. [I]

The Outsiders, S.E. Hinton (Viking, 1967). Contemporary issues of in-group, out-group behavior. [A]

The Preacher's Kid, Rose Blue (Watts, 1975). A story of racial prejudice centered around the problems a white minister and his family face in the community. [I–A]

The Stone-Faced Boy, Paula Fox (Aladdin, 1968). Well-told story of a boy's experiences of being taunted in school. To deal with it, he decides to no longer show his emotions and become "stone-faced." [I–A]

The Witch of Blackbird Pond, Elizabeth George Speare (Dell, 1958). Newbery winner. Sixteen-year-old Kit's friendship with a lonely old woman arouses the villager's suspicions: is Kit a witch like her? [A]

Grades 2–6	Common Points	A2

Purpose: To increase students' awareness of their family and individual interests as well as those of their classmates.

Materials: A copy of A2 Common Points form for each student; pencil or other writing instrument.

Procedure: Students write their answers for the six categories as described in each point of the star. They then search for a classmate who shares the same interest. Ask them to find a different friend for each category. When they have found the "right" classmate, he/she signs on the second line.

Grades 2–8	Getting to Know You Wheel	A3

Purpose: To provide the opportunity for students to learn more about each other.

Materials: SH20 Playing Favorites form for each student (see Chapter 4, Selfhood). Using a thin-tipped black marking pen, draw an additional circle, 5" in diameter, around the inner circle containing the words "My Favorites Wheel." Copy the form on light-colored construction or cardstock-weight paper and cut out.

Procedure: Provide each student with a copy of the SH20 Playing Favorites Wheel and explain that it is now going to be used as a "Getting to Know You Wheel." Ask each student to write his/her name in the center wheel under the words "My Favorites Wheel."

In the second circle, each student writes a word or draws a picture that describes each of the categories. Instruct students to now circulate around the room, exchanging wheels with other classmates and the teacher. When a student finds another student with the same words, the student writes his/her name in the area next to the word. Example: If both Ryan and Kevin enjoy reading *Stone Fox*, then under that title on Ryan's paper, Kevin would write his name and vice versa.

Variation: The activity could be adapted in the following manner: Each student begins the activity by completing their wheel with words or pictures that represent their interests. The student then introduces him-/herself by name to another classmate and they exchange wheels. The classmates examine each other's wheels for a few minutes to find out about each other and then each student writes his/her name in any available space on another student's wheel. The activity continues until all available spaces are completed.

Grades 3–8 Paired Name Collage A4

Purpose: To encourage students to find out the names and common interests of one another.

Materials: 12" x 18" (or larger) light-colored construction paper, colored marking pens or crayons; one set of the above per team. *Optional:* large letter stencil patterns.

Procedure: Divide students into pairs (either randomly chosen or use pairs from S17 Time for Friends activity in Chapter 3, Security).

Tell students that *together* on one side of the 12" x 18" drawing paper they are to draw each other's names in large block letters (stencils may be used if available). *Encourage students to draw the letters at least 3" high and 1" wide.* The students now have five minutes (longer for older students) to get to know one another and find out what they have in common. At the end of the five minutes, partners work together filling in their name letters with words or pictures representing the common interests, hobbies or experiences they've discovered about one another. At the conclusion of the activity, students can share their poster with the class and describe what they've learned about each other. The activity can be adapted so that students work in teams of three, four or five.

AFFILIATION

ESTEEM BUILDER #2

Provide Opportunities to Discover the Interests, Capabilities and Backgrounds of Others

"A child's life is like a piece of paper on which every passerby leaves a mark."
—ANCIENT CHINESE PROVERB

If there is any single predictive principle by which children will become friends, it is that "like attracts like." In an extensive review of literature, Hartup[10] discovered dozens of studies documenting the finding that friends choose each other because each is approximately the same age, the same sex, the same size, the same level of intelligence and the same degree of physical maturity. Interviewing kindergarten, third- and sixth-grade students, Berndt[11] found that "shared activities" was one of the most commonly mentioned "friend qualifications." Those pairs of children who become friends and who stay friends—for at least some period of time—are especially likely to have similar activities, styles, interests and values.

Recognizing similarities of interests, capabilities and backgrounds of others contributes to the growth of self-acceptance. Awareness that a peer has shared interests and feelings can be important information to a student—especially when a growing number of students are preoccupied with concerns revolving around the issue that "I must be like everyone else." It is a moment of jubilation to recognize that another student shares the same interest or background: it is a moment of feeling *not alienated* but *accepted* for a shared commonality.

On the other hand, an awareness of differences can be a powerful tool for self-clarification. Through such recognition, students learn that not everyone has the same interests, opinions, feelings, background, capabilities and values as he/she does. Slowly, recognition develops that it "really is all right to be different because that's what makes me unique." Such acknowledgment is much more likely to develop in a respectful, accepting environment, where the awareness of another's differences and similarities is encouraged in a nonjudgmental manner. Providing opportunities for students to look at themselves through others is an important avenue toward the development of a sense of significance.

10. Hartup, W.W. "Peer Interaction and Social Organization," Paul H. Mussen, Ed. *Carmichael's Manual of Child Psychology*, Vol. 2 (New York: Wiley, 1970).
11. Berndt, T.J. "Children's Conception of Friendship and the Behavior Expected of Friends." Unpublished manuscript. Yale University, New Haven, CT, 1978.

ACTIVITIES: GROUP 2

The following activities are designed to enhance students' awareness of each other and to discover shared interests with others.

Grades K-6 Class Discovery Book A5

Purpose: To increase students' awareness about the interests and capabilities of fellow students.

Materials: A5 Class Discovery page for each student; construction paper; stapler or spiral binding.

Discovery Book Construction: Make copies of the A5 Class Discovery page. Be sure to make a copy for yourself. Cut out and staple together to form a book.

Procedure: Display the book to students and explain that it will be used to record discoveries that they make about each other. Tell students that a discovery is something we've never known before and that there are many things we don't know about each other.

For the next week or so, point out your discoveries to students: "I've discovered that Sally really likes to draw," "I've discovered a good friend in Brent because he's willing to help me when I need it."

Write these findings on students' individual discovery pages. Encourage them to write their own discoveries about each other. Or they can wait for a Discovery Circle where they share their discoveries with each other.

Younger or nonwriting students dictate their responses to a cross-age tutor or parent aide.

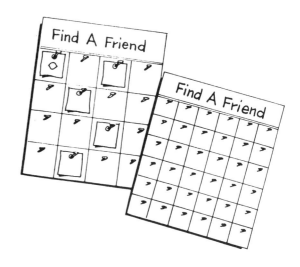

Grades 1-4 Solve the Riddle A6

Purpose: To increase students' awareness of the interests and characteristics of peers. To enhance visual perception skills.

Materials: Permanent grid designed to fit one of your smaller bulletin boards; 20 riddle cards; Student Answer Sheet.

Grid Construction: Cut a piece of white butcher paper the same dimensions as the bulletin board. Draw the grid using a thick black marking pen. Decrease the number of squares and increase the square size for special education and primary students. Gradually increase the square numbers and decrease their sizes for older students. Place a long stickpin or curtain hook in the middle of each square about 1 1/2" from the top line.

Riddle Cards Assembly: Cut 20 cards, 4 1/2" x 4 1/2", from light-colored construction or cardstock-weight paper. Punch a hole 1/2" from the top in the middle of each card. Add more cards as new categories are created. On each card draw or write (depending on students' skill levels) the following categories:

green eyes
brown eyes
blue eyes
black hair
red hair
brown hair
blonde hair
freckles
glasses
missing teeth
braces

a band-aid
likes to swim
plays an instrument
has a nice smile
likes to read
likes hamburgers
likes red
likes football
takes dance lessons
has a baby at home

Student Answer Sheet: Make a ditto of the bulletin board grid in exact square dimensions but reduced to fit the ditto page. Duplicate a large quantity and keep them stocked under the bulletin board grid.

Procedure: Each week place several riddle cards, in random order, on the permanent grid. Hang the cards from the pins or curtain hooks on various squares on the grid. Give each student a Student Answer Sheet and ask them to make it look exactly like the grid. For instance, if the card with blue eyes is in the third square from the top left, the student writes or draws a facsimile of the card in the same place on his/her grid sheet.

When they've completed the answer sheet, students must then find a friend in the classroom to fit each category card. When they find a friend that matches the category (e.g., brown hair) the friend signs the answer sheet in the corresponding box.

Each riddle card should be answered by a different friend. Change the board to add new category cards as often as you like.

Variation: You may also change the board to the A9 Mystery Person, where one student is highlighted. All the cards should be about his/her characteristics. It's up to the class to figure out who the Mystery Person is.

Grades K–4	**Friendship Graphs**	A7

Purpose: To make students more aware of common interests and characteristics. To develop one-on-one correspondence. To provide various counting experiences. To familiarize students with graphs. To develop "greater than/less than" concepts.

Materials: 2 sets of clothespins with a student's name written on each pin (clothespins may also have a Xeroxed photo of each student glued to the

Name_____

Graphing Investigation

Today I graphed [   ]

I discovered:

There are [   ] _____

There are [   ] _____

There are [   ] _____

There are [   ] _____

[   ] is the most   [   ] is the least

HAIR COLOR

	Brown	Yellow	Black	Red
11				
10				
9				
8				
7				
6				
5				
4				
3				
2				
1				

boys / girls 6 5 4 3 2 1

FAVORITE MOVIES

Karate Kid / Peter Pan / Star Wars / Ghost Busters   6 5 4 3 2 1

clip); *or,* 3" x 5" tagboard name cards, each one containing the name and photo of a classmate; Friendship Graph forms—see illustration for examples.

Graph Construction: Make from tagboard strips, cut 6" x 28", and laminate. They may be used over and over again if the categories are not permanently drawn on the graph. You may also make graphs from butcher paper.

Procedure: Graphing experiences for younger students should begin with actual objects plotted on tagboard graphs (or large vinyl sheets divided with masking tape, or butcher paper drawn with marking pen lines).

Student fills out an appropriate Friendship Graph form for the activity. Students should explain each completed graph and state the relationship between the numbers: "There are more boys than girls; 12 is greater than 10."

Begin with experiences in which students only compare two attributes (are there more boys than girls?), then work up to comparisons of three, then four attributes (hair and eye colors, favorite movies and books, kinds of lunch pails, etc.). Each activity helps students to see similarities and differences of peers.

Some graphing topics might include the following:

Number boys/girls	Favorite color
Long hair/short hair	Favorite rock group
Long sleeves/short sleeves	Favorite movie
Tie/velcro/buckle shoes	Type of pet owned
Eye color	Number of siblings
Favorite sport	Favorite indoor game
Favorite football team	Hair color
Favorite book	Month born
Type of lunch pail	State born in

Example: Are there more boys than girls? Use the clothespins to show. Read the name on each clothespin. If it's a girl's name, clip it on the girl's side; if it's a boy's name, clip it on the boy's side.

Grades K–3 · Our Favorite Books · A8

Purpose: To discover common interests in the class through books. To become acquainted with graphs. To experience "more than" and "less than" concepts.

Materials: A8 Our Favorite Books form for each student.

Procedure: Take a poll among students to discover what some of their favorite books are. Students write these titles in the spaces along the bottom column. Now take a tally to find out which is the favorite. Students color in the boxes in the "number column" for each vote.

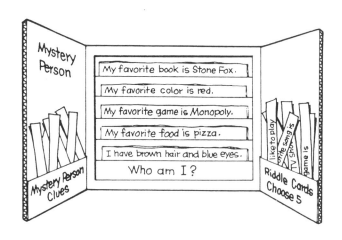

Grades 2–6 · Mystery Person · A9

Purpose: To encourage students to find out about each other's interests, hobbies and characteristics.

Materials: 25" x 26" piece of tagboard backed with similar-sized cardboard; 2 pieces of 13" x 18" tagboard backed with similar-sized cardboard; roll of 1 1/2" reinforced tape; 12 light-colored sentence strips, each 3" x 20"; scissors, black marking pen.

Carrel Construction: Make a pocket chart constructed from 25" x 26" piece of tagboard. (Before folding, make sure the long axis of the sheet is vertical.) Attach 2 pieces of 13" x 18" pieces of tagboard backed with cardboard. Make the large pockets for cards from tagboard. Hinge the carrel together with 1 1/2" tape.

Prepare 12 or more 3" x 20" tagboard sentence strips. On each strip print an open-ended sentence stem using the words "My favorite _____ is _____." Complete the missing word with a riddle category such as interests, characteristics or hobbies. Cover each strip with clear contact paper.

The carrel may easily be adapted to a permanent bulletin board by using a standard class pocket chart.

Procedure: Each week choose a different student to be the "Mystery Person." The chosen student selects five riddle cards and uses a grease pencil to complete the response. Each day a new riddle card is placed in the pocket. Classmates try to guess who the Mystery Person is by these riddles.

At the end of the week, clean sentence strips and place them back in the pocket for the next Mystery Person.

Grades 2–8	**Friendly Riddles**	**A10**

Purpose: To help students focus on the interests of each other.

Materials: Library pockets, 1 per student; large supply of 3" x 5" index cards or paper facsimiles; thin-tipped marking pen; 1" metal ring; 1 1/2" reinforced tape; 3 pieces each of 12" x 26" cardboard and tagboard; small photograph of each student.

Carrel Construction: Build the carrel from 3 pieces of 12" x 26" tagboard backed with cardboard. Make the large pocket for the cards from tagboard. Glue a small photograph of each student on separate library pockets. Write the name of the student below the photo and attach the pockets to the carrel. Hinge the carrel together with tape. Prepare 34 cards (3" x 5") by writing a riddle on each. Punch the cards in the upper left-hand corner and fasten them with a metal ring.

Procedure: At the beginning of each week, students read the riddle, answer it on a separate index card and print their initials on the back, lower right-hand corner of the card. They place completed cards in the large riddle pocket.

Working in small teams or as individuals, students read each answer and place it in the classmate's pocket they think best fits the riddle. When the task is completed, turn the cards over to see if the initials match the pocket. By changing the riddle card each week, it can become a permanent weekly activity.

Riddles for Riddle Cards: Write each of the riddles that appear below on a separate 3" x 5" index card.

Begin each phrase with "What is your. . ." and continue with these words:

1. favorite color?
2. color hair and eyes?
3. height?
4. favorite actor?
5. favorite actress?
6. favorite male singer?
7. favorite female singer?
8. favorite holiday?
9. favorite place to visit?
10. favorite flavor ice-cream?
11. favorite fiction character?
12. favorite possession?
13. proudest achievement?
14. favorite song?
15. favorite flavor drink?
16. month of birth?
17. favorite movie?
18. favorite book?
19. state where born?
20. favorite indoor game?
21. favorite subject in school?
22. favorite musical instrument?
23. favorite pizza topping?
24. favorite hobby?
25. favorite kind of candy?
26. favorite type of pet?
27. favorite TV show?
28. favorite rock group?
29. favorite animal?
30. favorite female sports star?
31. favorite male sports star?
32. most happy/sad/angry/frightening memory?
33. favorite gift to receive?
34. favorite grown-up occupation?

| Grades 1–8 | V.I.P. Center | A11/12 |

V.I.P. activities affirm each student's "specialness" by centering classmates' attention on him/her for several days or a full week. Students will have the opportunity of discovering the V.I.P.'s special characteristics including background, unique qualities, interests and attitudes. Students at any age can benefit from such an experience—we all need a "place in the sun."

Purpose: To emphasize the "specialness" of each student. To allow everyone to be important in the eyes of others. To help students become aware of their positive attributes (and those of others).

Materials: A12 Very Important Pupil parent letter describing the V.I.P. program and student responsibilities for the week; display space for the V.I.P. such as one or more of the following:

- table to display student's possessions;
- bulletin board;
- student-made cardboard carrel (1 piece 12" x 20" tagboard backed with cardboard and hinged together with 2 pieces 12" x 15" tagboard backed with cardboard. Use 1 1/2" reinforced tape to attach cardboard pieces together. (See A10 Friendly Riddles for complete directions.)

Procedure: Begin this continuing activity by choosing a student each week to be the individual in the spotlight. Every student should have an equal chance to be selected. Once the student is chosen, he/she is eliminated from further V.I.P. drawings until all other classmates have had the opportunity. The V.I.P. will be responsible for creating a bulletin board and/or display table featuring himself/herself.

Send the A12 letter home to parents the week before the display explaining the value of this project and the rationale behind it. Ask parents for their support in providing objects, photographs or other material to depict various categories about the student. These should be brought to school a few days before the event.

Variations:

1. One week prior to the student's debut as the V.I.P., send home—along with the A12 letter—9" x 12" colored papers, each with a different topic as below. The student draws, writes or finds photographs/concrete objects to substantiate each category. Post these as borders on the bulletin board for that week.

   Categories for paper borders:
   talents   interests
   family   short biography
   friends   proud moment
   other (student's choice)

2. *All-About-Me Poster.* Give the V.I.P.-to-be student a 28" x 22" piece of tagboard to take home. Student makes up a collage of photographs, drawings and written material that represent the categories mentioned in the A12 letter. The completed poster is brought back to school and displayed.

3. *Interview (older students).* One week prior to the activity, students compile a list of appropriate questions to use in finding out more about their peers. Write the most appropriate questions on a large piece of paper or poster to use every week. Each V.I.P. has a turn to be interviewed by his/her classmates using the list of questions. Tell students that each V.I.P. has the right to "pass" on any questions presented to him/her. You may wish to set a timer to limit the interview time. Consider assigning the role of "reporter" to a different student each time. The reporter summarizes the information in a V.I.P. featured article that is either posted in the room or sent home with classmates.

4. See A13 The Friendly Letter for an additional activity that can be included in the V.I.P. Center.

| Grades 1–6 | The Friendly Letter | A13 |

Materials: A13 Friendly Letter form for each student.

Procedure: Run off copies of the A13 Friendly Letter and envelope so that they are back to back. Include these at the V.I.P. Center.

AFFILIATION

Older students may wish to use notebook paper or design their own stationery for the project.

During the week, each classmate is responsible for writing a letter to the V.I.P. student for that week. (You may wish to give them ideas for letter content.) Send the letters home at the end of the week with the student.

Grades K–3	King/Queen for the Day	A14

Purpose: As per All.

Materials: A crown, chart paper, ribbon.

Procedure: Randomly choose a student to sit on the "throne" (any chair or center of the circle). Classmates take turns in praising the king or queen for his/her positive attributes and strengths. Teacher writes the comments on a large scroll (use chart paper). At the end of the day, roll the scroll up, tie it with a ribbon and present it to the student to take home.

Note: Be sure to keep a permanent record of classmates' comments to each king and queen. At the end of the year, copy them all onto a ditto. Let each student illustrate his/her description on the ditto and run off enough copies so that everyone has a copy. Bind these pages together for a "Class Yearbook."

Grades K–3	Dandy Lion	A15

Purpose: To increase students' awareness of their peers' interests. To emphasize that each student is special.

Materials: A copy of *Dandelion* by Don Freeman (Viking, 1964); 36" of 1/4" cording; clear plastic bag; large safety pin; felt scraps, glue, colored marking pens. *Optional:* puppets.

Jennifer Giraffe Puppet Construction:

Materials: 1 beige knee or tube sock; brown, black and gold felt scraps; glue and scissors; 2 1/2" brown pom poms.

Procedure:

- Use a long sock. Lay it flat, heel side facing you.
- Cut horns and bangs from brown felt.
- Cut eyelashes and eyebrows from black felt.
- Cut ears from gold felt.
- Stitch or glue horns, ears, bangs, eyebrows and eyelashes in place.
- Glue two brown pom poms in place for nose.
- Cut and glue brown spots all over remaining part of sock.

Dandy Lion Puppet Construction:

Materials: 1 beige knee or tube sock; white, gold, brown, red, black felt strips; 16" beige yarn, cut into 4" strands; glue, scissors, needle and thread.

Procedure:

- Lay the sock flat, heel side facing you.

- Cut ears and mouth from gold felt.

- Cut nose, curly mane and mangy mane from brown felt.

- Cut outer eye from white felt.

- Cut inner eye sections from black felt.

- Cut bow tie from red felt, on fold.

- Glue (or stitch) on mouth, ears, eye sections, and bow tie (at the X) to curly mane.

- Glue strands of yarn (whiskers) under nose and attach nose.

- Manes may be slipped on and off Dandy by cutting out middle section.

Procedure:

1. Read to younger students (with or without the aid of puppets) the book *Dandelion*—the story of a lion who is invited to a party by Jennifer Giraffe. Dandelion decides to get all "spruced up" with newly curled hair and a special outfit. When he arrives at Jennifer's house, she slams the door on him because she doesn't recognize him. Downcast, Dandelion stands outside in the wind and rain, which blow away his outfit and uncurl his hair. When he decides to return to Jennifer's house the second time, she lets him in with open arms. Dandelion apologizes for his disheveled appearance, but Jennifer is delighted to see the lion that she knows. She assures him that he's special just the way he is.

2. Now reveal to students the Dandy Lion bag, which has "mysteriously arrived" in the classroom. You can make this from an old pillow case with cording pulled through the hem to open and close the opening. You may wish to decorate the bag with a lion's face made from felt or drawn on with colored marking pens.

3. Explain to the students that the bag is for carrying things special to each student—things from home that normally we in the classroom don't get a chance to see. Each day (or week) a different student will have the chance to bring the bag home, fill it with things special to him/her, and then return with it to school the next day to share. Be the first Dandy Lion yourself to set the tone for the activity.

Letter: Attach a letter in a plastic bag inside the Dandy Lion bag to clue parents in on the project. List any categories appropriate for your students. The letter might read:

Dear Mom/Dad,

Your child will be collecting (with your help) the following things to bring to school on _____ and share with class:
1. a baby picture
2. a family picture
3. favorite thing to take to bed
4. favorite book
5. favorite toy
6. three more things to share (souvenir, favorite outfit, something he/she is proud of).

Thank you!

Grades 2–8	**Pen Pals**	A16

Purpose: To experience the joy of friendships by mail. To learn about others and their interests. To increase letter-writing proficiency.

Note: This activity may easily be adapted to younger, nonwriting students by dictating the letter to a teacher, cross-age tutor or parent aide.

Materials:

1. A pen pal for each student. *Several options are available:*

   - Exchange the names of students in your program with students in another classroom or within your school district.

   - Exchange addresses with a teacher from another district.

   - Purchase addresses through a friendship league:

     International Friendship League
     40 Mt. Vernon Street
     Boston, MA 02108

     For $2.00 service charge you become a member, and they'll send you the name of an international pen pal.

     League of Friendship
     P.O. Box 509
     Mount Vernon, OH 43050

     For $1.00 service charge you'll receive a foreign name. Send a self-addressed, stamped envelope (ages 12–25).

Pen Pals
International Friendship League, Inc.
22 Batterymarch
Boston, MA 02109
Send a self-addressed, stamped envelope and a registration fee of $3.00 (under 19 years). They will send names and addresses from two different countries.

Student Letter Exchange
910 Fourth Street S.E.
Austin, MN 55912
Ages 10–19. $1.00 for a foreign name; $0.50 for an American name. Send self-addressed, stamped envelope.

World Pen Pals
1690 Como Avenue
St. Paul, MN 55108
Enclose a self-addressed, stamped envelope and a $2.00 service fee (or special group fee, $1.75 each for six or more names). Each student will receive a foreign name, a suggestion sheet and a *World Pen Pal* newsletter.

2. *Stationery for each student.* Consider holding a class stationery contest where each student designs stationery on an 8 1/2" x 11" piece of paper. The design with the most votes becomes the stationery pattern. You may add formal letter head, closure and writing lines for the body of the letter. Run off copies for every student. Envelopes may be made, purchased or brought from home.

3. Stamps.

Procedure: Students write to their respective pen pals. First letters should be an exchange of information. They may also include a photograph. Students should be encouraged to exchange letters on their own with their pen pal.

Variation: Letters need not be strictly individual; instead, compose a class letter. It can take several forms:

- Dictate a letter as a class into a tape recorder. Transcribe the letter, which is then sent once all classmates have signed.

- Add on to a single letter. Each student writes his/her own thoughts onto one page and then passes the same sheet to another classmate.

AFFILIATION

ESTEEM BUILDER #3

Increase Awareness of and Skills in Friendship Making

"One of the factors that erodes self-concept is the inability of some children to make and keep friends."
—JAMES DOBSON

Rubin's[12] research on children's friendships asserts that an impressive number of social skills are needed to establish and maintain social relationships, among which are the following:

1. the ability to gain entry into group activities;
2. to be approving and supportive of one's peers;
3. to manage conflicts appropriately;
4. to exercise sensitivity and tact.

These are by no means always easy to learn, and some students never succeed in acquiring them. The result is that many students go through school with few or no friends at all. This also hinders their success in building a sense of significance, or self-worth.

In these cases, adult intervention—such as coaching in a particular friendship making skill—may be desirable. One of the most successful intervention strategies is Oden and Asher's[13] research with socially isolated third- and fourth-grade students.

A MODEL FOR ENHANCING SOCIAL SKILLS

Oden and Asher demonstrate that special social skills can be grasped through adult tutoring. Their findings can be applied to students with poor friendship-making skills by following these steps:

---

12. Rubin, Zick. *Children's Friendships* (Cambridge: Harvard University Press, 1980), p. 47.
13. Oden, Sherri, and Asher, Steven. "Coaching Children in Social Skills for Friendship Making," *Child Development*, Vol. 47, 1977, pp. 495–506.

1) *Identify* **one** *student with poor social skills.*

2) *Identify a* **specific** *social skill the student lacks.* Be sure to break this down into a *particular* aspect of friendship-making. Try to analyze why the student is having this problem with peers. *Example:* You notice the student is always standing on the fringe of the group and never is included. Why? Is he/she capable of initiating a conversation? Does he/she make eye contact? Can he/she play a simple game during recess time? There are any number of reasons why the student may be having difficulty with peers. Isolate one small factor at a time.

3) **Coach** *the student in the skill.* Find a moment to work privately with the student. Demonstrate to him/her the special skill and talk about how it can be successfully performed. Be sure that the student understands what is expected of him/her and exactly what he/she needs to do. Ask the student to demonstrate the skill to you so that you're sure he/she understands the concept.

4) *Provide opportunities to* **practice** *the skill with peers.* Just working one-on-one with the student is not enough. The opportunity to practice the skill with peers must be part of the process. The practice session could be any time during the school day: at recess, during homeroom, in a cooperative learning team or a Concept Circle time. You may also wish to inform the parents of the skill so that the student can practice at home.

5) **Evaluate** *the practice with the student and offer feedback.* Oden and Asher discovered that a critical part of teaching social skills is evaluating the performance with the student. As soon as you can, get back to the student to discuss how the practice session went. Ask questions such as: How did it go? Who did you try it with? How did you feel? What did they do? This helps the student reflect on the process. You may wish to have the student keep an ongoing record of his/her progress by writing about it in a journal. As soon as the student is successful and feels comfortable with the skill, begin the process again by adding a new social skill. If the student is unsuccessful with the skill, analyze why this might be. Perhaps the skill is not broken down into small enough steps.

A sociometric assessment at the end of the four-week training indicated that the coached students increased their friendship skills significantly and were consequently nominated as friends by others more frequently. A follow-up assessment a year later confirmed continued progress in friendship making.

Another way to increase social skills and engender a more positive self-concept is to allow students the opportunity to view and analyze their behavior and that of their peers. Garner[14] videotaped fourth- through sixth-graders and encouraged them to analyze the classroom behavior and patterns of interaction with each other. He found that being able to observe their own behavior resulted in positive changes. To observe and discuss group social skills, therefore, is most beneficial to students' social skill development.

Build Affiliation Through Teamwork

Several researchers working on cooperative learning techniques have found that teams do increase students' self-esteem. Students in cooperative learning classes have been found to have more positive feelings about themselves than do students in traditional classes.[15] One of the reasons cooperative learning has been successful as a technique for enhancing self-esteem is that it allows students the opportunity to be affiliated as well as practice social skills within a comfortable environment. Research by The Johns Hopkins Institute,[16] William Glasser[17] and Roger and David Johnson[18] further support the overall effectiveness of the technique as a method of increasing both self-esteem and

14. Garner, G. "Modifying Pupil Self-Concept and Behavior," *Today's Education*, Vol. 63, 1974, pp. 26–28.
15. De Vries, D.L.; Edwards, K.J.; and Slavin, R.E. "Biracial Learning Teams and Race Relations in the Classroom: Four Field Experiments on Teams-Games Tournament," *Journal of Educational Psychology*, Vol. 70, 1978, pp. 356–362.
Madden, N.A., and Slavin, R.E. "Cooperative Learning and Social Acceptance of Mainstreamed Academically Handicapped Students." Paper presented at the Annual Convention of American Psychological Association, Montreal, 1980.
Blaney, N.T.; Stephan, S.; Rosenfield D.; Aronson, E.; and Sikes, J. "Interdependence in the Classroom: A Field Study," *Journal of Educational Psychology*, Vol. 69, No. 2, 1977, pp. 121–128.
16. *Cooperative Learning: The John Hopkins Team Learning Project*, Center for Social Organization of Schools, The Johns Hopkins University, 3505 N. Charles Street, Baltimore, MD 21218.
17. Glasser, William. *Control Theory in the Classroom* (New York: Harper & Row Publishers, 1986).
18. Johnson, David and Johnson, Roger T. *Learning Together and Alone: Cooperation, Competition, and Individualization* (Englewood Cliffs, NJ: Prentice-Hall, 1975).

feelings of affiliation. Because the results on cooperative learning have been so promising, Chapter 8 in ESTEEM BUILDERS, called Concept Circles, is devoted to providing students the opportunity to enhance their self-perceptions within a group framework.

Build Affiliation Through Cross-Age Tutoring

A technique that many researchers have found to be effective is cross-age tutoring. For more information, refer to Chapter 2, How to Use This Curriculum, in the section, The Esteem Builder's Attitude.

This is a program in which older students—typically two to three grades higher—are trained to tutor younger ones. Typically the best students are sent as the tutors, but keep in mind that *every* student can be a candidate. It may be the only avenue for the socially isolated to gain a feeling of affiliation. Philip Zimbardo[19] in his work on shyness discovered that pairing an older, "shy" student with a younger, responsive student is also an excellent technique for the shy student to practice social skills. The description of the cross-age tutor does not have to be limited to academic tutoring. Consider also having the student perform the following duties:

- school-related jobs such as errands or office help;

- serving as a "friend" for a special or new student;

- school-related projects that demonstrate community leadership;

- assisting school personnel (audio-visual monitor, helping out in the library or cafeteria, teaching games on the playground to younger students).

With a bit of ingenuity and flexibility, almost any student can become a successful tutor.

Research on cross-age tutoring has revealed that not only are friendship-making skills increased but also reading ability,[20] self-esteem of both tutor and tutee,[21] and overall motivation and achievement.

The most successful cross-age tutoring programs are ones that train the tutors. The Allendale School Tutorial Program in the Oakland Unified School District holds four training sessions for perspective student tutors who have been recommended by teachers. The tutors and tutees are then matched one on one for the year. Tutors also meet once a month to share with one another insights and problems. Every two months the teacher trainer meets individually with each tutor to discuss progress. At the end of the school year the trainer gives a written evaluation to each tutor. For a discussion of cross-age tutors, their implementation and available educational resources, see the Introduction.

Conclusion

Popular students are that precisely because they know how to make friends.[22] Through successful interactions with others, these students continue to feel appreciated and accepted. Although this can be developed by tutoring, the end goal is not so much to produce popular students but to help students become confident enough in social encounters to have the opportunity to increase their sense of affiliation.

AFFILIATION

19. Zimbardo, Philip, and Radl, Shirley L. *The Shy Child: A Parents' Guide to Overcoming and Preventing Shyness from Infancy to Adulthood* (New York: Doubleday, 1982).

20. Stern, T.M. "A Study of the Use of Freshman and Sophomore Elementary Education Majors as Reading Tutors to Disadvantaged Elementary Students." Doctoral dissertation, University of Georgia, 1978.

21. Allen, V.L., et al. "Research on Children Tutoring Children: A Critical Review," *Review of Educational Research*, Vol. 46, 1976, pp. 355–385.
Gartner, A.; Kohler, M.C.; and Riessman, F. *Children Teach Children: Learning by Teaching* (New York: Harper & Row, 1971).
Mohan, M. *Peer Tutoring as a Technique for Teaching the Unmotivated: A Research Report* (Fredonia, NY: Teacher Education Research Center, University College, 1972).

22. Gottman, John; Gonso, Jonni; and Rasmussen, Brian. "Social Interaction, Social Competence, and Friendship in Children," *Child Development*, Vol. 46, 1975, pp. 709–718.

ACTIVITIES: GROUP 3

The following activities give students opportunities to practice social skills that will enhance their ability to make friends.

Grades K-8   Friendly Class Actions   A17

Purpose: To increase students' awareness of the friendly deeds of their peers.

Procedure: Begin by posing the question: "Who has had someone do something friendly toward them today?" Usually students who already feel affiliated will raise their hands, but that's all right!

Now ask the volunteer: "How did it make you feel?" The activity draws immediate attention to the students who have performed kind deeds toward one another. It also lets remaining students know that the deeds were appreciated. Students with low self-esteem need to be exposed to repeated friendly acts; point them out as they occur.

Grades K-4   Helping Each Other   A18

Purpose: To increase awareness that words and actions are friendship makers or breakers. To increase awareness of what a friend is.

Materials: Several pieces of construction cardstock-weight paper cut into 3" x 5" or 4" x 6"; marking pens; hat, basket or other container.

Procedure: On index cards, write or draw problem situations a young student might encounter. For example:

- student spills his/her crayons;
- block construction falls down;
- student can't find jacket where all the other clothes are hanging;
- sandwich falls on the ground and is ruined;
- student forgets lunch at home;
- student needs to go to the bathroom urgently;
- student falls down on the playground and is hurt;
- zipper is stuck.

Place the cards in a box or hat. The class sits in pairs in a circle and one member of each team chooses a card. The team acts out a solution to the problem they picked. One partner is the needy one, and the other is the helper.

Younger students enjoy this song:

> *Friends can help each other*
> *Friends are people who care*
> *Friends can help each other*
> *Friends work together and share*
>
> *Now here's a problem*
> *It could happen to you*
> *One of the friends feels bad*
> *What, oh what, could you do?*

Grades K-8   Friend Interviews   A19

Purpose: To provide opportunities to make new friends.

Procedure: Begin with a discussion on things we know about a close friend. Then ask each student to choose as a partner a classmate he/she doesn't know very well. The partners sit together for 3 to 15 minutes and get to know each other. Then students take turns, stand up and introduce their partner to the class. Younger students make a gift (from scrap materials only) at home for their new friend and bring it to school.

For older students you may wish to make a ditto with a few of the following suggestions for partners to ask one another during the interview:

- What do you enjoy doing outside of school?
- What is your favorite hobby or interest?
- Have you ever lived in a different location? If so, where?
- Do you have any brothers or sisters? If so, how old are they?
- Where is your favorite place to visit? Why?
- What is your favorite TV show?
- What kind of music do you enjoy listening to?
- What one thing would you like me to tell the class about you?

Older students may add additional questions to their interview list. Remind them that questions must be answered with more than a simple "yes" or "no."

<table><tr><td>Grades 4–8</td><td>**What Is a Friend?**</td><td>**A20**</td></tr></table>

Purpose: To build an awareness of what are friendly characteristics.

Materials: A20 What Is a Friend? form for each student.

Procedure: Divide students into teams of three or four and provide each student with the What Is a Friend? form. Inform students that as a team they must decide on a list of characteristics they all agree are important in a friend. They list these characteristics on the form.

Secondly, each team must work together to rank the characteristics in order of importance. Remind students that the characteristic they have agreed is most important should be listed as number 1, and so on. Students now complete the remainder of the form by themselves. Tell students to now look over the form and decide which characteristics can best be applied to themselves.

Finally, explain to students that sometimes when people work in a group, positions or ideas have to be compromised so that the group can come to an agreement. Ask students to think about whether that happened to them, and whether they would have come up with the same answers if they had completed the form on their own. If the student has any different answers, he/she describes them on the last question. Remind students that if they choose not to, they need not share the form with anyone.

<table><tr><td>Grades 2–5</td><td>**Friendship Recipes**</td><td>**A21**</td></tr></table>

Purpose: To be able to identify and articulate the characteristics of a good friend.

Materials: Chart paper; marking pen.

Older students: index cards and cookbooks *(optional).*

Procedure: As a group, discuss the characteristics of a good friend. Ask older students to list at least five important friendship attributes, such as: humor, availability, kindness, loyalty and common interests. Write the descriptions that come up on a chart to refer to again and to add to as the class thinks of new descriptions. Using these friend characteristics, encourage students to write their own "recipes" for how to make a friend. You may compile these into a class-made book entitled "Friendship Recipes."

Older students may work in teams to develop a mutually agreed upon recipe. The team's final recipe can written on an index card in a "recipe" format. Use a cookbook as a guide.

<table><tr><td>Grades K–5</td><td>**Friendship Wheel**</td><td>**A22**</td></tr></table>

Purpose: To increase students' awareness of friendly actions.

Materials: 6" circle of A22 Friendship Wheel out of posterboard; dial hand/pointer cut out of whipped cream or other plastic container; paper fastener, washer *(optional).*

Procedure: Make a 6" circle out of posterboard and cut it out. Divide the circle into at least eight segments. Cut a dial hand/pointer from a plastic container. Attach the spinner to the center of the wheel with a paper fastener and secure it with a small washer under the clip.

Ask students to think of ways to be friendly. Write down appropriate deeds in each section of the circle. Extend the activity by asking students to spin the wheel. At some time during the day they are to perform that task to a peer. As a follow-up ask them to evaluate their deeds. You may also make individual wheels by duplicating the pattern.

<table><tr><td>Grades 4–8</td><td>**Friendship Openers**</td><td>**A23**</td></tr></table>

Purpose: To build an awareness that words can create friendships.

Materials A copy of A23 Friendship Openers form; marking pens, crayons or colored pencils.

AFFILIATION

AFFILIATION

Optional: scissors, magazines, glue.

Procedure: Divide students into pairs. (You could use the S17 Time for Friends activity to do this; see Chapter 3, Security.) Provide each pair with a Friendship Openers form. Tell students that the types of words we say to one another can be either friendship makers or breakers. Instruct the teams to take 10 minutes to come up with words, phrases or sentences that would put a smile on another student's face. Each team must then design their own "Friendly Words" poster using the form.

At the end of 10 minutes, each team shares their poster, and a few selected words of their choice, with the rest of the class. Laminate completed posters and use as a bulletin board display.

Variations: As students become comfortable working as partners, do the same activity in groups of three or four. The directions of the activity could be changed each time so that the same form is used a number of different ways. Each way provides students with the opportunity to think about different components of friendship. For instance, in addition to students listing friendly words, ask them to come up with lists of friendly deeds, conversation openers ("hi," "hello," "how are you?"), conversation topics (hobbies, interests, favorite TV shows) or nonverbal friendly actions (hugs, smiles, pats, handshakes, winks, eye contact).

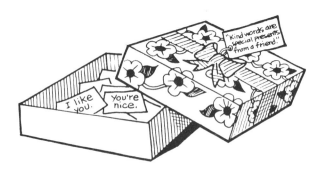

| Grades 1–4 | **Word Gifts** | **A24** |

Purpose: To build awareness in students of the power of kind words. To increase students' repertoire of kind words.

Materials: A small, flat box slightly larger than 3" x 5"; wrapping paper, ribbon; large supply of 3" x 5" cards; clear tape, scissors, marking pen.

Box Construction: Wrap the top of the box only with colorful wrapping paper and bow. Make sure the top can still be removed. Attach to the bow a greeting card with these words: *Kind words are special presents for a friend.*

Procedure: Ask students to tell you words or phrases to say that will put a smile on someone else's face. List these words or phrases on separate index cards. Place the cards inside the Word Gift box.

Tell students that any time they need to give a Word Gift to a friend, they may use the cards for ideas. As you catch students saying "word gifts" to one another, encourage them to add their words to the box.

Variation: Make an individual Word Gift box for a birthday student. Classmates all contribute a Word Gift message on an index card and place it in the box for the student to take home on his/her birthday.

Older students may each create an individual folder of builder-upper words written on index cards.

| Grades K–8 | **Friendship Pals** | **A25** |

Purpose: To provide opportunities to practice friendship making.

Materials: Container such as a basket, hat or bag; students' names printed on strips of paper.

Procedure: Each student pulls the name of a peer out of a hat. This person becomes his/her secret Friendship Pal for the day. Some time during the day, students should secretly do a friendly deed or say friendly words to their pal. At the end of the day, ask each partner to comment on the activities of the day. Did they know who their friend was? What deeds were performed?

| Grades 2–8 | **Friendship Book Reports** | **A26** |

Purpose: To identify characteristics of a friend.

Materials: An assortment of books about friends. See A30 for a partial list according to grade levels.

Procedure: Following a class read-aloud or independent reading, engage the students in a discussion about the characters. In particular, center in on a question such as:

---

1. Who was a friendly character in the book?
2. What made the character a friend? What specific things did the character do that made you feel he/she is a good friend?
3. Would you like to have this character as a personal friend? Why or why not?
4. Describe a particularly friendly part in the story.
5. Do you know anyone who has done deeds similar to those the character performed in the book?

You could also write up the questions on a ditto to which students respond in written form as a book report.

Grades 2–8 — **My List of Friendly Deeds** — **A27**

Purpose: To increase students' awareness of friendly acts.

Materials: A copy of A27 My List of Friendly Deeds form for each student; writing instrument.

Procedure: Tell students that for the next week they are to keep track of their friendly deeds on the form. You may wish to have a quick discussion as to what friendly deeds are, writing some samples on the board. As a final activity each day, students take out their sheets and privately write down what they did that was friendly toward another person that day. These do not have to be shared in class.

Grades 2–8 — **Recording Good Deeds** — **A28**

Purpose: To increase students' awareness that words and deeds are friendship makers.

Materials: A copy of A28 Recording Good Deeds form for each student, duplicated on light-colored construction or cardstock-weight paper. *A28a is for younger students; A28b is for older students.*

Procedure: Explain to students that deeds are powerful deterrents to friendship as well as builders.

Provide each student with the A28 form appropriate for their age. Ask them to keep it handy or store the forms in a convenient place. Older students may include theirs in a journal or notebook. Encourage students to keep track of the friendly deeds they perform for others. They should include the name of the person for whom they performed the "good deed."

Grades 1–4 — **My Friendship Book** — **A29**

Purpose: To provide students an opportunity to think and write about friendships.

Materials: Copies of A29 My Friendship Book pages; light-colored construction paper for covers; stapler or hole-punch and yarn; scissors or paper cutter.

Procedure: Before you begin this project, make a copy of A29 My Friendship Book pages and cover for each student. Cut each duplicated page in half and store in manila folders. Students each have their own set.

Begin this project by enthusiastically announcing that the class will be making a book about friends. You may wish to have library books on hand about the topic (see A30 Books About Friendship). Students start to fill in the interior pages of their books. Introduce no more than one topic per day. You may wish to precede the writing activity with a class discussion. Students then write or dictate their topic statement, in each case completing the sentence.

As a final activity following the last completed page, students bind their finished books together.

Variation: Older students may bind writing paper together for individual Friendship Books. Each writing period students address a different friendship issue in their books. Ask them to focus on topics that deal with conflict in relationships.

AFFILIATION

| Grades K–8 | **Books About Friendship** | **A30** |

Purpose: To enhance students' understanding of friendship. To increase awareness of friendship-making skills.

Materials: Booklist.

Procedure: Choose one of the following books to read aloud or assign as independent reading. Use the book as a discussion guide about the concept of friendship:

- Who was the friendly character in the book?
- Why do you consider the character friendly?
- What did the friendly character do for others in the story?
- How did the other characters feel about the friendly act(s)?

Primary Level

Alexander and the Wind-up Mouse, Leo Lionni (Random House, 1969).

Alfred Snood, Joan Hanson (Putnam & Sons, 1972).

Amigo, Byrd Baylor Schweitzer (Collier Books 1963).

Amos and Boris, William Steig (Penguin, 1977).

Are We Still Best Friends? Carol Barkin and Elizabeth James (Raintree Editions, 1975).

Best Friends, Miriam Cohen (Collier MacMillan, 1973).

Best Friends for Frances, Russell Hoban (Harper & Row, 1969).

Everett Anderson's Friend, Lucille Clifton (Holt, Rinehart & Winston, 1978).

A Friend Can Help, Terry Berger (Raintree Editions, 1974).

A Friend Is Someone Who Likes You, Joan Walsh Anglund (Harcourt Brace Jovanovich, 1958).

Friends, Helme Heine (Atheneum, 1985). Beautifully illustrated, describes friendship in the most concrete terms.

Frog and Toad Are Friends, Arnold Lobel (Harper & Row, 1979).

George and Martha, James Marshall (Houghton Mifflin, 1972). Humorous tale of friendship of two rhinos.

George and Martha Rise and Shine, James Marshall (Houghton Mifflin, 1976).

Good, Says Jerome, Lucille Clifton (Dutton, 1973).

Guinea Pigs Don't Read Books, Colleen S. Bare (Dodd Mead, 1984).

The Hating Book, Charlotte Zolotow (Harper & Row, 1969). Perfect for friendship conflicts and reconciliation.

Hello Henry, I.M. Vogel (Parents, 1965).

It's Mine, Crosby Bonall (Harper & Row, 1964).

It's Mine, Leo Lionni (Alfred A. Knopf, 1985).

Let's Be Enemies, Janice Undry (Harper & Row, 1961).

Little Blue and Little Yellow, Leo Lionni (Astor-Honor, 1959).

Meet M and M, Pat Ross (Pantheon, 1980).

My Friend Charlie, James Flora (Harcourt Brace Jovanovich, 1964).

My Friend John, Charlotte Zolotow (Harper & Row, 1968).

Nannabah's Friend, Marine Perrine (Houghton Mifflin, 1970).

New Friend, Charlotte Zolotow (Abelard-Schuman, 1968).

Rock Finds a Friend, Randall J. Wiethorn (Green Tiger Press, 1988).

Rosie and Michael, Judith Viorst (Atheneum, 1974). Teachers' favorite.

Susan Sometimes, Phyllis Krasilovsky (MacMillan, 1962).

That's What Friends Are For, Florence Parry Heide (Scholastic, 1968).

Thy Friend, Obadiah, Brinton Turkle (Viking, 1969).

Two Is a Team, Lorraine Beim (Harcourt Brace Jovanovich, 1974).

Where Are You, Ernest and Celestine? Gabrielle Vincent (Greenwillow, 1985).

The White Marble, Charlotte Zolotow (Abelard-Schuman, 1962).

Will I Have a Friend? Miriam Cohen (Collier MacMillan, 1971).

Won't Somebody Play with Me? Steven Kellogg (Dial, 1972).

Intermediate and Advanced Level (I = intermediate, A = advanced)

Almost a Hero, Clyde Bulla (Dutton, 1981). [I-A]

A Taste of Blackberries, Doris B. Smith (Scholastic, 1976). Sensitive portrayal of a boy's sorrow and grief over the death of his best friend.

The Bad Times of Irma Baumlein, Carol Ryrie Brink (MacMillan, 1974). [I-A]

Blubber, Judy Blume (Dell, 1974). [I]

Bridge to Terabithia, Katherine Paterson (Avon, 1977). Sensitive character portrayal of a friendship between a boy and a girl. Newbery winner. [A]

Burnish Me Bright, Julia Cunningham (Dell, 1980).

Charlotte's Web, E.B. White (Harper & Row, 1952). A favorite! [I]

Cider Days, Mary Stolz (Harper & Row, 1978). [I]

Cricket in Times Square, George Seldon (Farrar, Straus & Giroux, 1960). Focuses on friendship and personal sacrifice.

Dexter, Clyde Robert Bulla (Crowell, 1973). Story of a promise between two friends, who remain connected by the heart if not by proximity. [I]

Four Miles to Pinecone, John Hassler (Warne, 1977). [A]

Grey Cloud, Charlotte Graeber (Four Winds, 1979). [A]

The Gumdrop Necklace, Phyllis LaFarge (Knopf, 1947). [A]

The Hundred Dresses, Eleanor Estes (Harcourt Brace Jovanovich, 1944). [I]

Killing Mr. Green, Lois Duncan (Dell, 1980). [A]

Meaning Well, Shiel R. Cole (Franklin Watts, 1974). [A]

The Secret Garden, Frances Hodgson Burnett (Dell, 1971). [A]

Shoeshine Girl, Clyde Robert Bulla (Scholastic, 1977). [I]

The Sign of the Beaver, Elizabeth George Spears (Dell, 1983). Story of survival in the wilderness—12-year-old Matt is rescued by an Indian chief and his grandson. [I-A]

The Snailman, Brenda Sivers (Little, Brown, 1978). [I]

Soup, Robert Newton Peck (Knopf, 1974). [I-A]

Thank You, Jackie Robinson, Barbara Cohen (Lothrop, Lee and Shepard, 1974). [A]

You Two, Jean Ure (Morrow, 1984). Two girls of different backgrounds. [A]

Grades K–8	Friendship Goal	A31

Purpose: To aid students in friendship skill improvement.

Materials: A copy of A31 Friendship Goal sheet for each student.

Procedure: First help students isolate one very specific area in which they could improve. Explain the skill to each student, and demonstrate how it can be successfully performed. Then provide opportunities for the student to practice the skill with peers.

For example: Jeffrey knows how to make friends but he doesn't like to share his possessions so he ends up losing friends. As the teacher, show Jeffrey that he has a right to have control over his possessions, but sharing is part of friendship. Have him role-play sharing with a partner—say, letting his friend have something just for a limited time—knowing that he has control over the situation.

Finally, take a few moments to evaluate the student's performance. Discuss why the skill practice was effective or ineffective and what can be done differently to make the skill become a building block in friendship making for the future.

Ask students to write (younger students dictate and draw) their friendship goal and the procedure on the provided form. They must also note whether or not they achieved the goal and how they would do it better next time. This last part would be a follow-up session. These forms become a permanent record of friendship-making progress.

===== ESTEEM BUILDER #4 =====

Encourage Peer Approval and Support

"When two people are friends, even water is sweet."
—CZECH PROVERB

Have you ever stopped to watch students with high self-esteem interact with a peer? It quickly becomes apparent they know exactly what to say and do in order to gain acceptance and approval from others. As a result, other students like to be around them and purposely seek out their company. It is no accident that those who feel significant are judged as popular by classmates.

Popular students are much more likely to verbalize and demonstrate support and approval to fellow

AFFILIATION

classmates than their more unpopular counterparts. Hartup's[23] observations found that the most popular students—those whom their classmates preferred playing with—were also the ones who more often praised other students, showed affection and willingly acceded to their requests. On the other hand, students who frequently ignored others, refused to cooperate, ridiculed, blamed or threatened others were most likely to be disliked by their classmates. Students become popular by initiating and receiving positive interaction with peers.[24]

Praising others is not only helpful in gaining social acceptance, but can also be beneficial to building the sender's esteem. This is in part due to the fact that such gestures are generally met with approval, and "like breeds like." As a result, building self-esteem in others becomes a reciprocal process: to be included and accepted, you must include and accept.

Classroom investigations show that one of the most successful components for enhancing self-concept is teaching students to praise others.[25] Classrooms that encourage students to write positive statements to each other on a daily basis improve self-concept scores for both students with high and low self-esteem.[26] Felker cautions us that though this praise may be difficult to develop, and its results are not always visible in the beginning, continued practice of peer praise can be instrumental in producing more positive self-esteem.[27] This process has already been introduced in Chapter 3, Security (see Esteem Builder #3); it continues at a more complex level here in Affiliation.

Consider also the activities throughout this chapter—all deal on some level with being positive and considerate to others.

23. Hartup, W.W.; Glazer, Jane A.; and Charlesworth, Rosaline. "Peer Reinforcement and Sociometric Status," *Child Development*, Vol. 38, 1967, pp. 1017–1024.
24. Allen, K.E.; Hart, B.; Buell, J.S.; Harris, F.R.; and Wolf, M.M. "Effects of Social Reinforcement of Isolate Behavior of a Nursery School Child," *Child Development*, Vol. 35, 1964, pp. 511–518.
25. Brady, P.J. et al. "Predicting Student Self-Concept, Anxiety, and Responsibility from Self-Evaluations and Self-Praise," *Psychology in the Schools*, Vol. 15, 1978, pp. 434–438.
26. Stilwell, W.E., and Barclay, J.R. "Effects of Affective Education Interventions in the Elementary School," *Psychology in the Schools*, Vol. 16, 1979, pp. 80–87.
27. Felker, D.W. *Building Positive Self-Concepts* (Minneapolis: Burgess, 1974).

ACTIVITIES: GROUP 4

All activities from A32 through A40 are specifically designed to increase students' awareness that they can help themselves and others to grow by showing that they care. The activities also provide opportunities to practice giving approval and support to others. Refer also to Security activities, especially S24, S25, S26, S28, S29, S30, S31, S32, S34, S35.

| Grades K–3 | Sunrays | A32 |

Materials: 8" circle cut from yellow construction paper for each student; 7–8 "rays" cut from orange construction paper (triangles cut from 10" x 5"); glue, scissors.

Procedure: Explain to the students that they can make the sun "shine" by making the world brighter for others through words and actions.

Cut out an 8" circle from yellow construction paper for each student. You may glue a photo of the student to the center. Cut rays from orange construction paper. On each ray students write a kind word or deed they could do for another to show "they care." Glue the rays to the inner center.

Adapted from: Miller, Maureen. *To Share With Your Children—Activities to Help Them Feel Worthwhile* (Argus Communications, 1978).

| Grades K–8 | Caring Words | A33 |

Materials: 12" x 18" light-colored construction paper for each student; crayons or colored marking

construction paper; scissors, glue.

Procedure: Discuss with the students how important
our words can be as an avenue of showing we care
about others. Students each draw a picture depicting how they could show another individual that
they are concerned for them. Cut out statement
bubbles (as seen in comics) and glue to the pictures.
Students write caring words that the helper is saying to the other person in the picture. Younger
students dictate their statements.

Grades 2–8	**Calendar of Caring Deeds**	**A34**

Materials: A copy of a Monthly Calendar; use S37
A Month of Positivism form.

Procedure: In each box of the calendar, students
keep track of the caring deeds they do during a
month. You may wish to do it week by week and
have a debriefing session each Friday in which students share their caring deeds.

Younger students may mark each day with a happy face as they perform a caring deed. Prompt them
so they become aware of what a caring deed is.

Grades 2–8	**Card Friendship Center**	**A35**

Purpose: To provide opportunities for students to
practice friendly actions toward others.

Materials: A permanent, accessible card center in
a convenient location.

Center consists of:

- ink pens and crayons, samples of store-bought cards, glue, magazines
- stickers, stamp pad and stamps
- templates and stencils, scissors
- construction paper scraps, rickrack
- construction paper cut into various sizes: 5" x 8", 7" x 4", 9 x 5"
- Include samples of student-made cards, as well as card topic starters printed on index cards with these types of messages:
  We miss you
  Congratulations!
  Thanks for helping
  You're a nice friend
  Happy Birthday!
  Get well soon
  We hope you feel better
  A special message to you...

Procedure: As occasions arise, encourage students
to write a card to a deserving friend and then send
or present it.

Grades 2–8	**Team Member Center/Certificate**	**A36**

Adapt for younger students.

Purpose: To provide opportunities for students to
encourage and support one another. To recognize
students for positive behaviors such as cooperation,
sharing and friendliness.

Materials: Copies of A36 Team Member Certificate.

Center Construction: Set up a box or carrel display
with materials available for student use such as:
marking pens, scissors, colored pencils, crayons,
stickers, stamp pads and stamps, yarn, hole-punch,
stars, paste or glue.

Place the display in an accessible location along
with a separate small box or folder next to the center
labeled "Team Member."

Procedure: Tell students that an important part of
being a good friend is to recognize friendly actions
of another. Inform them that the Team Member

AFFILIATION

Center is available as a way of recognizing and supporting classmates for friendly deeds.

You may wish to have a discussion in which students tell you kinds of deeds that are friendly and deserving of recognition. These could include: sharing, cooperating, making someone feel good, saying something nice, giving something, receiving something, making something for someone, taking turns and "sticking up" for someone.

Tell students that whenever another individual performs a friendly deed toward someone, the recipient may go to the Team Member Center and either fill out a Team Member Certificate or create an award. In order for the award to be valid, it must have a description of the friendly deed, the name of the "friendly doer" and the signature of the teacher. The award-giving student may choose whether to sign his/her name on the form. However, encourage them to sign their names so that recipients can find out who is recognizing them.

Students place their completed awards in the Team Member folder or small box next to the center. Sometime during the day, the teacher looks through the box or folder and signs appropriate completed awards. The teacher announces the friendly deeds and presents the awards to the recipients.

Grades K–3	**Care Ropes**	**A37**

Purpose: To increase individual awareness of caring/thoughtful deeds.

Materials: A 20" leather strip or rug-yarn length for each student.

Procedure: Ask students to keep track of their caring deeds toward others. Each time they perform a deed, invite them to tie a knot in the rope. Keep ropes in an accessible place, such as a desk.

Grades 1–6	**Compliment Hanging**	**A38**

Purpose: To increase students' positive comments to each other and allow each one the opportunity of feeling special.

Materials: A38 Compliment Hanging card for each student; yarn cut into 6" lengths (1 per student); A38 face pattern (1 for the complimented student).

Face Construction: Choose a different student each day to be complimented. This student creates a self-portrait by coloring in the A38 Compliment Hanging face pattern. Provide a mirror so that physical characteristics are accurate. Then cut out the face pattern.

Procedure: To begin the activity, ask students to sit in a circle with a pre-cut compliment card on their lap and a writing instrument. Each student writes and draws a compliment to the special student and then shares his/her card. Punch compliment cards in the middle of the top and bottom and hang in a continuous length under the face pattern. The cut yarn lengths connect each card.

Note: The activity can be adapted for nonreading, younger students by having them draw the compliment on the card. Adapt the task for older students by eliminating the self-drawn portrait. A photograph or name printed on a card is all that is necessary.

Grades 2–8	**Autographs**	**A39**

Purpose: To provide the opportunity for students to write friendly, caring comments to each other.

AFFILIATION

Materials: For each student, 2 pieces 8 1/2" x 11" construction paper for cover and back; stapler, spiral binding or hole-punch and yarn; several sheets of A39 Autograph form for each student.

Procedure: Make an autograph book for each student by stapling the autograph forms between the construction paper covers. Students may want to decorate the cover with marking pens. Each student asks classmates to "sign" his/her autograph book by filling in the form.

Grades K–8	Books on Caring and Determination	A40

Purpose: To increase students' awareness of the caring deeds of others.

Materials: Any one of the books listed below according to grade level.

Procedure: Choose one book for a read-aloud, or assign as independent reading. Use the literary material as a basis for discussion about caring, compassion and loyalty.

[P] = Primary (K–3)
[I] = Intermediate Level or Advanced Listener

Generally About Caring and Determination
Among the Dolls, William Sleator (Dutton, 1975). [I]
The Bears' House, Marilyn Sachs (Doubleday, 1971). [I]
The Bedspread, Sylvia Fair (Morrow, 1982). [P]
Bridge to Terabithia, Katherine Paterson (Avon, 1979). Newbery winner. A special friendship between a boy and a girl and the lessons they learn from each other. Addresses guilt, death, family, friendship and school. [I]
The Indian in the Cupboard, Lynne Reid Banks (Avon, 1980). An Indian toy given to a nine-year-old boy comes to life, and he learns the lesson of responsibility and caring as well as cultural understanding. Sequel available: *The Return of the Indian*. [I]
Pearl's Promise, Frank Asch (Dell Yearling, 1984). [I]
Sadako and the Thousand Paper Cranes, Eleanor Coerr (Yearling, 1977). A true story about a girl who suffered from leukemia due to the bombing of Hiroshima. Her classmate teaches her to fold a paper crane and tells her: "If a sick person folds 1,000 paper cranes the gods will grant her wish and make her well again." The girl dies, but her classmates keep on making the cranes so that 1,000 could be buried with her. In 1958 they succeeded in their dream of unveiling a monument in her honor. [I]
Stone Fox, John Reynolds Gardiner (Harper & Row, 1980). Ten-year-old Willy enters the dog-sled race with his dog, Searchlight, to win against the legendary Indian Stone Fox so that his grandfather's farm might be saved. [I]
The Trouble With Tuck, Theodore Taylor (Avon, 1981). Helen finds a unique solution to the loss of eyesight of her dog, Tuck. [I]
Where the Red Fern Grows, Wilson Rawls (Bantam, 1985). Exciting, fervent book about a 10-year-old boy who trains two hounds to be the finest hunting team. [I]

On Poverty
A Chair for My Mother, Vera B. Williams (Greenwillow, 1982). [P]
The Hundred Dresses, Eleanor Estes (Harcourt Brace Jovanovich, 1944). [I]
Tight Times, Barbara Shook Hazen (Viking, 1986). [I]

On Old Age and Loneliness
How Does It Feel To Be Old? Norma Farber (E.P. Dutton, 1979). Grandmother describes aging to her granddaughter. [I]
Maxie, Mildred Kantrowitz (Parents Magazine Press, 1970). [P]
A Special Trade, Sally Wittman (Harper & Row, 1978). A beautiful introduction to growing old as a natural progression. [P]
Wilfrid Gordon McDonald Partridge, Mem Fox (Kane/Miller, 1985). Not to be missed! Young boy sets out to "find" his significant other's lost memory. [P]

On Handicaps
A Button in Her Ear, Ada Litchfield (Whitman, 1975). About hearing. [P]
A Cane in Her Hand, Ada Litchfield (Whitman, 1977). About blindness. [P]
Connie's New Eyes, Bernard Wolf (Lippincott, 1976). [P]
Do Bananas Chew Gum? Jamie Gilson (Lothrop, Lee and Shepard, 1980). Dyslexia. [I]

AFFILIATION

Don't Feel Sorry for Paul, Bernard Wolf (Lippincott, 1974). [P]

Howie Helps Himself, Joan Fassler (Whitman, 1975). [P]

Lisa and Her Soundless World, Eda Levine (Human Sciences Press, 1973). [P]

My Brother Steven Is Retarded, Harriet Sobol (MacMillan, 1977). [P]

Now One Foot Now the Other, Tomie DePaolo (Putnam's Sons, 1981). Young boy teaches his paralyzed grandfather to walk again. [P]

The Seeing Stick, Jane Yolen (Thomas Crowell, 1977). [P]

The Summer of the Swans, Betsy Byars (Viking, 1970). Newbery winner. The disappearance of her mentally retarded brother teaches Sara about caring. [I]

Through Grandpa's Eyes, Patricia MacLachlan (Harper & Row, 1980). A grandfather helps his grandson feel blindness. Exquisite picture book. [P]

On Rejection and Taunting

The Bears' House, Marilyn Sachs (E.P. Dutton, 1971). [I]

Bridge to Terabithia, Katherine Paterson (Avon, 1979). [I]

Burnish Me Bright, Julia Cunningham (Pantheon, 1970). [I]

But Names Will Never Hurt Me, Bernard Waber (Houghton Mifflin, 1976). [P]

Crow Boy, Taro Yashima (Viking, 1955). [P]

Daniel's Duck, Clyde Robert Bulla (Harper & Row, 1980). [P]

The Do-Something Day, Joe Lasker (Scholastic, 1982). Family rejection. [P]

The Gumdrop Necklace, Phyllis La Farge (Alfred A. Knopf, 1967). [I]

The Hundred Dresses, Eleanor Estes (Harcourt Brace Jovanovich, 1974). [I]

Molly's Pilgrim, Barbara Cohen (Lothrop, Lee and Shepard, 1983). [P]

The Witch of Blackbird Pond, Elizabeth George Speare (Yearling, 1972). Newbery winner. Teenage girl befriends an old woman out of loneliness and Puritan villagers suspect both she and the old woman are witches. [I]

On Death

About Dying, Sara Bonnett Stein (Walker & Co., 1974). [P]

The Accident, Carol Carrick (Seabury Press, 1976). [I]

Annie and the Old One, Miska Miles (Little Brown, 1971). [P]

Bridge to Terabithia, Katherine Paterson, (Avon, 1979). [I]

Charlotte's Web, E.B. White (Harper & Row, 1974). [I]

The Dead Bird, Margaret Wise Brown (Addison Wesley, 1958). [P]

My Grandson Lew, Charlotte Zolotow (Harper & Row, 1974). [P]

Nana Upstairs and Nana Downstairs, Tomie DePaolo (Putnam, 1973). [P]

A Taste of Blackberries, Doris B. Smith (Scholastic, 1976). Gripping story, looking at death from a child's point of view. [I]

The Tenth Good Thing About Barney, Judith Viorst (Atheneum, 1971). [P]

Where the Red Fern Grows, Wilson Rawls (Bantam, 1985). [I]

On Loyalty

Alexander and the Wind-up Mouse, Leo Lionni (Random House, 1969). [P]

Corduroy, Don Freeman (Puffin, 1976). [P]

Dexter, Clyde Robert Bulla (Thomas J. Crowell, 1973). Story of a promise between two friends. [I]

Mike Mulligan and His Steam Shovel, Virginia Lee Burton (Houghton Mifflin, 1967). [P]

Suggested Reading for Teachers

Arezzo, Diana, and Stocking, Holly S. *Helping Friendless Children: A Guide for Teachers and Parents.* Boys Town Center for the Study of Youth Development, Boys Town, Nebraska 68010.

Asher, Steven, and Gottman John M., eds. *The Development of Children's Friendships* (New York: Cambridge University Press, 1981).

Damon, William. *The Social World of the Child* (San Francisco: Jossey-Bass, 1977).

Flavell, J. "The Development of Inference About Others," T. Mischel, ed. *Understanding Other Persons* (Oxford, England: Blackwell, 1974).

Fox, C. Lynn, and LaVine Weaver, Francine. *Unlocking Doors to Friendship* (Rolling Hills Estates, CA: B.L. Winch & Assoc., 1983).

Hayes, D. "Cognitive Bases for Liking and Disliking Among Preschool Children," *Child Development*, Vol. 49, 1978, pp. 906–909.

Oden, S., and Asher, S. "Coaching Children in Social Skills and Friendship Making," *Child Development*, Vol. 48, 1977, pp. 495–506.

Rubin, Z. *Children's Friendships* (Cambridge, MA: Harvard University Press, 1980).

AFFILIATION

Selman, R. "The Child As a Friendship Philosopher," S. Asher and J. Gottman, eds. *The Development of Children's Friendships* (Cambridge, MA: Cambridge University Press, 1981).

Staub, E. "Use of Role-Playing and Induction in Training for Pro-social Behavior," *Child Development*, Vol. 42, 1971, pp. 805–816.

Varenhorst, Barbara. *Real Friends: Becoming the Friend You'd Like to Have* (Harper & Row, 1983).

Youniss, J., and Volpe, J. "A Relational Analysis of Children's Friendship," W. Damon, ed. *Social Cognition* (San Francisco: Jossey-Bass, 1978).

AFFILIATION

Name	Date

Common Points

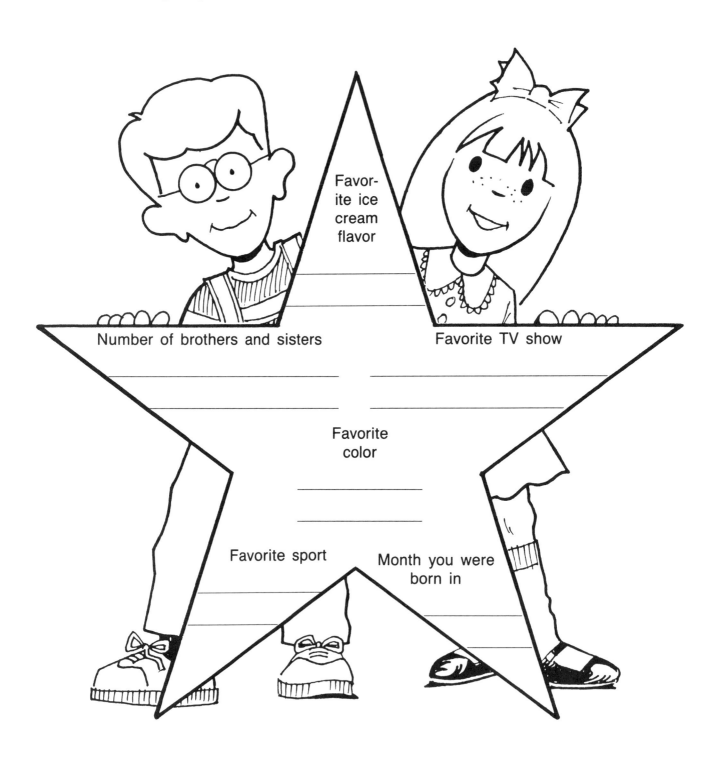

Favor-
ite ice
cream
flavor

Number of brothers and sisters

Favorite TV show

Favorite
color

Favorite sport

Month you were
born in

Directions: Read each point of the star and write your answer to the question.

Now find a friend who has the same interest as you do. Write his/her name on the line below. Find a different friend for each space.

Esteem Builders. Jalmar Press
Rolling Hills Estates, CA

Class Discovery Book

Classmate's Name: _____

Discoveries I've made about my classmate:

_____

_____

_____

_____

_____

_____

_____

_____

_____

_____

_____

_____

_____

_____

_____

_____

_____

_____

_____

_____

_____

. . . and each day we discover even more!

Esteem Builders. Jalmar Press
Rolling Hills Estates, CA

Name   Date

❦ur ℌfavorite ℬooks

The favorite book in our room is_____

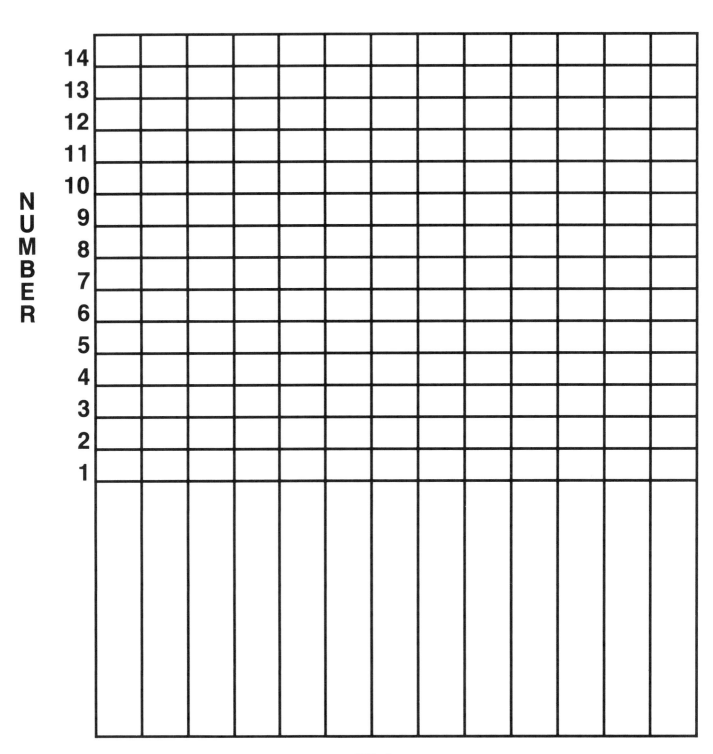

Titles

Take a poll among your classmates to discover what some of their favorite books are. Write these titles in the spaces along the bottom. Now take a tally to find out which is the favorite. Color in one box in the ''number column'' for each vote.

Esteem Builders. Jalmar Press
Rolling Hills Estates, CA

Name	Date

VERY IMPORTANT PUPIL

Dear Parent,

Next week your child will be highlighted in our classroom as the "V.I.P." (Very Important Pupil). Each student will have a turn to be the special person in our class.

This is a time when the class has the opportunity to know your child much better. We particularly hope to find out more about your child's specific interests, talents, background and other unique qualities. To aid us in finding out these facts, a special bulletin board and table has been set aside for your child to create a "self-display." Could you please help your child gather items to represent *some* of the following categories. Not all may be readily accessible. If actual objects are not available, a written description, drawing or photograph of the item is also appropriate. Thank you for your help!

- Special Talents
- Family
- Interests

- Hobbies
- Favorite Possession
- Favorite Book

- Special Collection
- Ancestry Information
- Other (student's choice)

Please place the items in a bag or box marked with your child's name and class number. Please send them on (or before)

_____
(Date)

Thank you.

_____
(Signature)

Please feel free to stop by and see the final display.

Esteem Builders. Jalmar Press
Rolling Hills Estates, CA

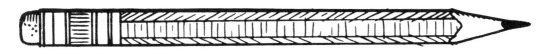

The Friendly Letter

_____
(Your Street)

_____
(Your City)   (Your State)   (Zip)

Dear_____,

                    _____

_____

_____

_____

_____

_____

_____

_____

_____

_____

_____

Your friend,

FRIENDS FOREVER

_____
(Your Name)

Esteem Builders. Jalmar Press
Rolling Hills Estates, CA

Jennifer Giraffe Puppet

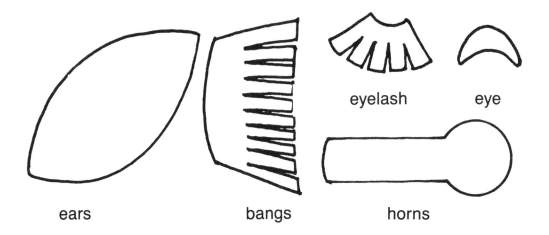

ears   bangs   eyelash   eye   horns

Dandy Lion Puppet

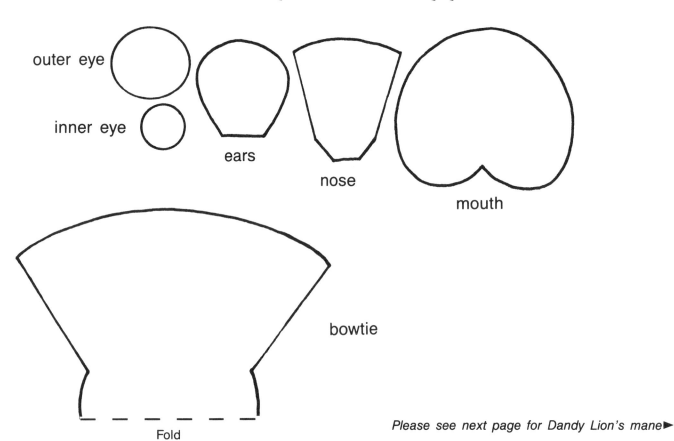

outer eye   inner eye   ears   nose   mouth   bowtie   Fold

Please see next page for Dandy Lion's mane▶

Esteem Builders. Jalmar Press
Rolling Hills Estates, CA

Dandy Lion Puppet

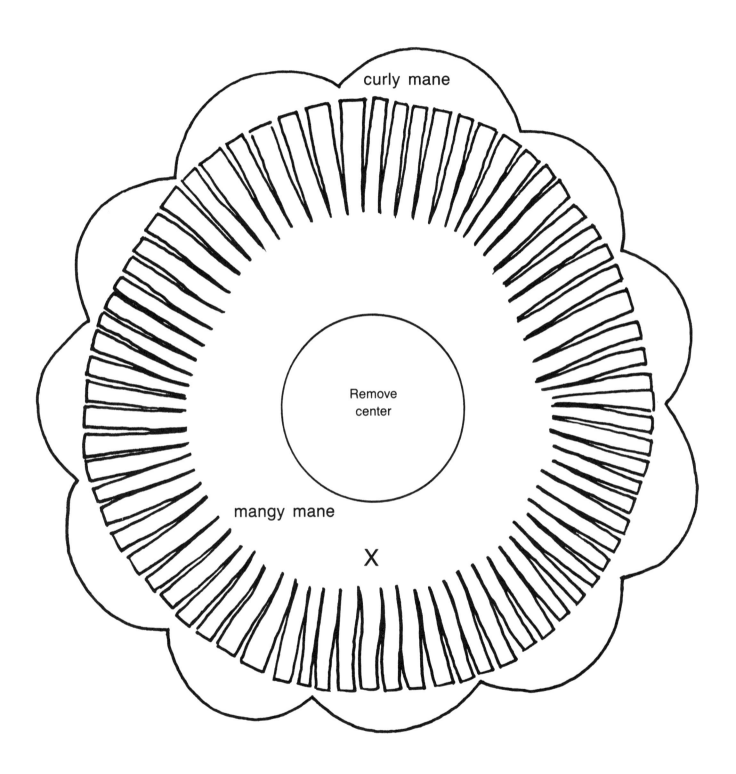

curly mane

Remove center

mangy mane

X

Esteem Builders. Jalmar Press
Rolling Hills Estates, CA

What Is a Friend?

TEAM MEMBERS:

Directions: 1. As a team, decide what are the important characteristics of a friend. List them.
2. As a team, rank the characteristics in order of importance. Place a number 1 by the one your team feels is most important; a number 2 by the next most important, etc.

IMPORTANT FRIEND CHARACTERISTICS	TEAM RANKING	DESCRIBE ME?
1._____	_____	☐
2._____	_____	☐
3._____	_____	☐
4._____	_____	☐
5._____	_____	☐
6._____	_____	☐
7._____	_____	☐
8._____	_____	☐

Now look over your paper alone. You do not need to share this part of the task.

1. Place a checkmark by the friend characteristics you feel describe you.

2. Do you agree with all the team's decisions? If you were to do this form alone, what changes (if any) would you make?_____

_____

_____

Esteem Builders. Jalmar Press
Rolling Hills Estates, CA

Name	Date

Friendship Wheel

Think of ways you can be a friend to someone in this class or school.
Write each friendly deed in a different section.

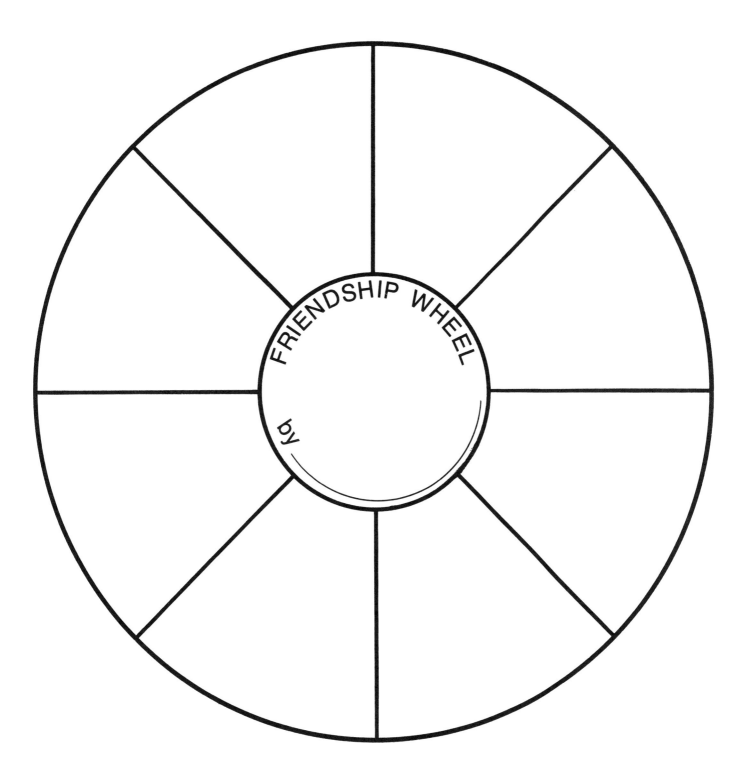

Esteem Builders. Jalmar Press
Rolling Hills Estates, CA

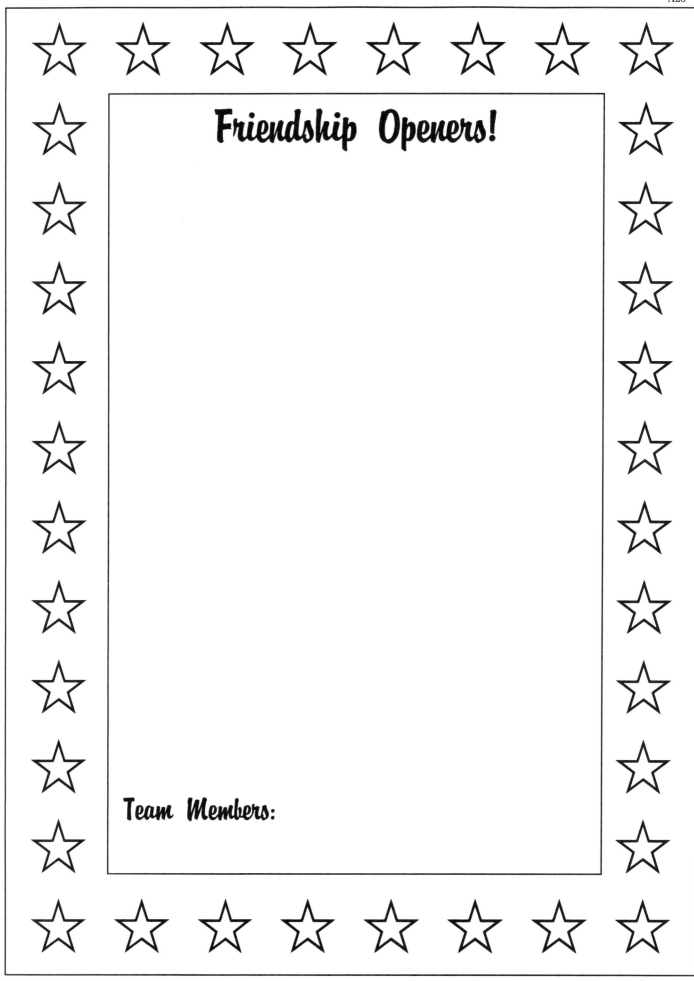

Friendship Openers!

Team Members:

Esteem Builders. Jalmar Press
Rolling Hills Estates, CA

Name	Date

My List of Friendly Deeds

Try to think of a friendly deed you've done for someone else every day for a week and write it down. Maybe it's something you did or said that put a smile on someone else's face.

Monday:_____

_____

_____

Tuesday:_____

_____

_____

Wednesday:_____

_____

_____

Thursday:_____

_____

_____

Friday:_____

_____

_____

Circle your most friendly deed.

What friendly deed will you try next week?_____

_____

Esteem Builders. Jalmar Press
Rolling Hills Estates, CA

Name	Date

RECORDING GOOD DEEDS

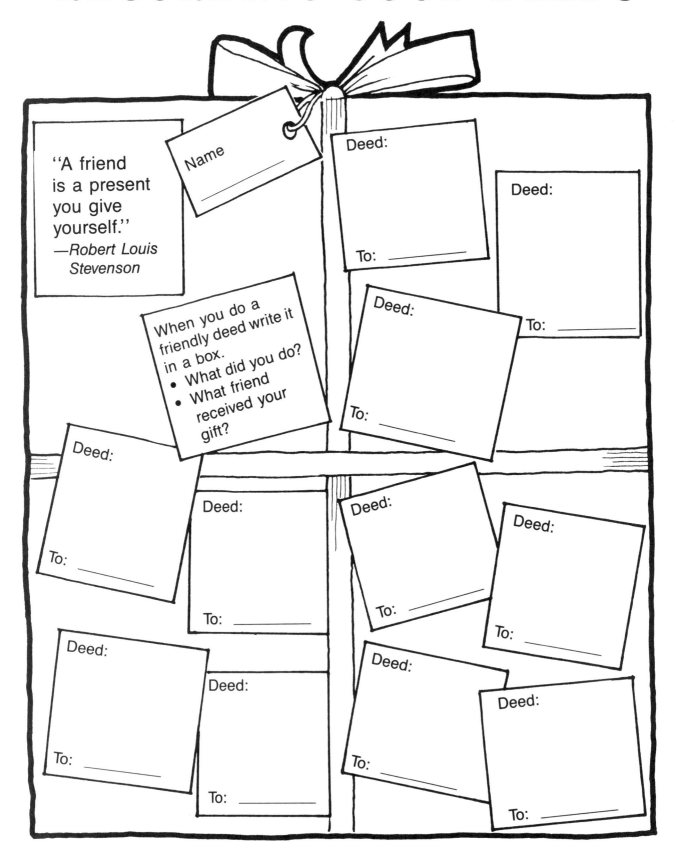

"A friend is a present you give yourself."
—*Robert Louis Stevenson*

Name
_____

When you do a friendly deed write it in a box.
• What did you do?
• What friend received your gift?

Deed:

To: _____

Deed:

To: _____

Deed:

To: _____

Deed:

To: _____

Deed:

To: _____

Deed:

To: _____

Deed:

To: _____

Deed:

To: _____

Deed:

To: _____

Deed:

To: _____

Esteem Builders. Jalmar Press
Rolling Hills Estates, CA

Name		Date	

Recording Friendly Deeds

MY FRIENDLY DEEDS

	Person	My Friendly Action	Their Response
Monday			
Tuesday			
Wednesday			
Thursday			
Friday			

Esteem Builders. Jalmar Press
Rolling Hills Estates, CA

My
Friendship
Book

By _____

Esteem Builders. Jalmar Press
Rolling Hills Estates, CA

The Author and Friends

Author_____

Copyright_____

DEDICATION

My book is for

_____

because

_____

_____

_____

Esteem Builders. Jalmar Press
Rolling Hills Estates, CA

I make new friends by_____

_____

_____

_____

_____

_____

My favorite thing to do with a friend is_____

_____

_____

_____

_____

_____

— 206 —

Esteem Builders. Jalmar Press
Rolling Hills Estates, CA

A29

A friend I like is_____

_____

_____

_____

_____

Friends make me feel_____

_____

_____

_____

_____

Esteem Builders. Jalmar Press
Rolling Hills Estates, CA

I could be a better friend _____

_____

_____

_____

_____

_____

I like my friends because _____

_____

_____

_____

_____

_____

Esteem Builders. Jalmar Press
Rolling Hills Estates, CA

A friend is_____

_____

_____

_____

_____

_____

I'm a good friend when_____

_____

_____

_____

_____

_____

Esteem Builders. Jalmar Press
Rolling Hills Estates, CA

Name _____   Date _____

Friendship Goal

Something I do that makes me a good friend:

Something I'd like to improve in to be a better friend:

How I will do it:

When I will try it:

_____

How did it work?:

What I'll try differently the next time:

Esteem Builders. Jalmar Press
Rolling Hills Estates, CA

TEAM MEMBER CERTIFICATE

presented to

_____

For the following reason:_____
_____
_____
_____

Thanks for being such a great Team Member. I'm glad you're part of our team!

Date_____   Presenter_____

Teacher_____

TEAM MEMBER CERTIFICATE

presented to

_____

For the following reason:_____
_____
_____
_____

Thanks for being such a great Team Member. I'm glad you're part of our team!

Date_____   Presenter_____

Teacher_____

Esteem Builders. Jalmar Press
Rolling Hills Estates, CA

Compliment Hanging

O

A Compliment to: _____

From: _____

Compliment:

O

O

A Compliment to: _____

From: _____

Compliment:

O

O

A Compliment to: _____

From: _____

Compliment:

O

Esteem Builders. Jalmar Press
Rolling Hills Estates, CA

Compliment Hanging

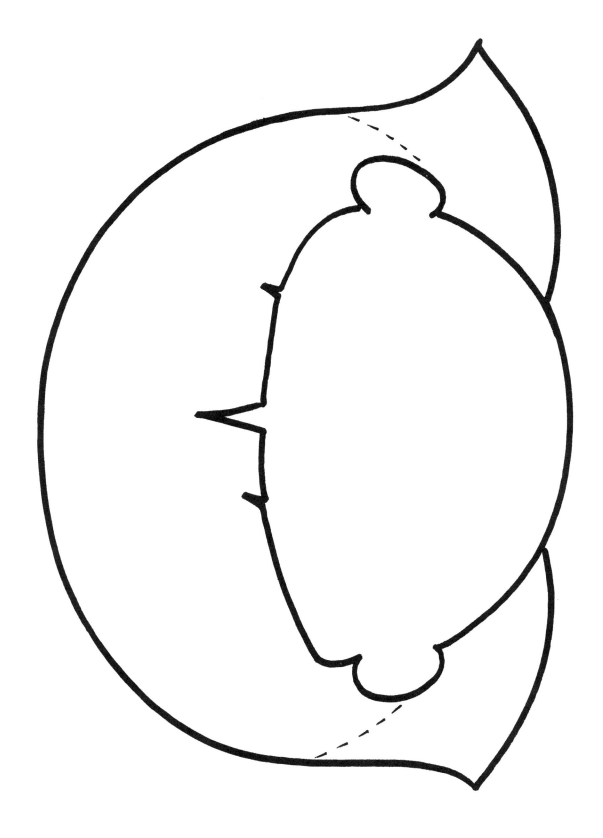

To represent a boy, cut along the dotted lines.

Permission to Reprint for Classroom Use.
© 1989 by Michele Borba

Esteem Builders. Jalmar Press
Rolling Hills Estates, CA

Name	Date

Autographs

A friendly comment:_____

_____

_____

_____

I'll remember you because_____

_____

_____

I think you're good at_____

_____

I like the way you_____

_____

_____

Just a doodle for you...

Signed:_____

Address:_____

Phone number:_____

Esteem Builders. Jalmar Press
Rolling Hills Estates, CA

6

Purpose with Responsibility: Building Mission

ESTEEM BUILDERS

- Enhance Ability to Make Decisions, Seek Alternatives and Identify Consequences
- Aid in Charting Present and Past Academic and Behavioral Performances
- Teach the Steps to Successful Goal-setting

SUMMARY OF MISSION

Definition: *A feeling of purpose and motivation in life. Self-empowerment through setting realistic and achievable goals and being willing to take responsibility for the consequences of one's decisions.*

SUPPORT DATA

- "Goals begin behavior; their consequences maintain behavior." Spencer Johnson and Constance Johnson. *The One-Minute Teacher* (New York: Wm. Morrow & Co., 1986).
- "The key to self-motivation and purposeful behavior is to help children internalize goals for themselves and to work toward their attainment." Robert Reasoner. *Building Self-Esteem: A Comprehensive Program* (Palo Alto, CA: Consulting Psychologists Press, 1982).
- "Each goal success will tend to whet the appetite for doing something a little more ambitious the next time. Along the way, success contributes to the child's sense of accomplishment and builds self-esteem." Gordon Porter Miller and Bob Oskam. *Teaching Your Child to Make Decisions* (New York: Harper & Row, 1984).

ESTEEM BUILDERS

- Enhance Ability to Make Decisions, Seek Alternatives and Identify Consequences
- Aid in Charting Present and Past Academic and Behavioral Performances
- Teach the Steps to Successful Goal-setting

POSSIBLE INDICATORS OF WEAK MISSION

- lacks motivation and initiative;
- cannot see alternatives or solutions;
- feels powerless, therefore may exhibit attention-getting behaviors such as whining or tattling to gain control;
- appears aimless, without direction;
- rarely succeeds due to poor goal-setting (goals are either too high, too low or nonexistent);
- is overdependent on others and feels incapable of being in charge and influencing others;
- avoids taking responsibility for own actions: blames others, denies or inveigles others to do his/her work;
- indecisive: seeks to avoid making own decisions.

POSSIBLE INDICATORS OF STRONG MISSION

- appears purposeful with a clear sense of direction;
- is self-directed and initiating;
- takes responsibility for his/her own actions and recognizes the consequences;
- is decisive because he/she feels sufficiently empowered to have influence over the outcome of decisions;
- seeks alternative solutions to problems;
- sets achievable and realistic goals;
- accurately assesses current capability and skills as well as past performances.

Most students will not conform exactly to the profiles listed above but are more likely to be stronger in some areas and weaker in others. In order to determine the degree to which a student feels a sense of Mission, complete the student self-esteem assessment chart (B-SET) located in Appendix II. The chart may be referred to periodically or updated as a way of measuring progress. These charts are also useful in determining which activities are appropriate for your class.

Mission Activities List

Code	Grade	Title	Soc. Studies	Sci.	Writ. Lang.	Oral Lang.	Math	Art	Lit.
M1	K–8	What I Like... What I Want to Change			✔	✔		✔	
M2	3–8	Problems	✔		✔	✔			
M3	3–8	Problem/Solution Report	✔		✔				
M4	K–2	Pictorial Problem/Solution Report	✔		✔			✔	
M5	4–8	Brainstorming	✔		✔	✔	✔		
M6	5–8	Strategy Sheet of Solution Consequences	✔		✔	✔			
M7	K–8	Booklist to Enhance Mission	✔			✔			✔
M8	1–4	Super Sleuth Book Report	✔		✔				✔
M9	4–8	Problem Map	✔		✔				
M10	K–8	My Progress			✔		✔		
M11	3–8	Graphing Progress			✔		✔		
M12	1–8	Beat the Clock			✔		✔		
M13	2–8	Homework Assignments			✔		✔		
M14	2–8	Goal-setting Step-by-Step	✔			✔			
M15	2–8	Group Goal-setting	✔		✔	✔			
M16	3–8	Goal-setting: Charting the Course	✔		✔				
M17	3–8	Overcoming Obstacles to Goals	✔		✔	✔			
M18	1–6	Climbing High Contract			✔				
M19	2–8	Daily Goal-setting			✔	✔			
M20	2–8	Weekly Goal Card	✔		✔		✔		
M21	4–8	Record of Weekly Goals	✔		✔				
M22	K–3	Goal Wheel			✔			✔	
M23	1–6	Goal Passbook	✔		✔		✔	✔	
M24	1–6	Goal Passbook Cards	✔		✔		✔	✔	
M25	K–8	Goal Results			✔				
M26	K–3	I Think I Can			✔			✔	✔
M27	3–8	Goal Achievement Journal			✔				
M28	2–8	A Month of Goals			✔		✔		
M29	K–5	Goal Award Grams			✔				

Concept Circles Activities That Promote Mission

Code	Grade	Title	Grouping
CC43	K–4	Would You Rather?	Partner/Team
CC44	4–8	Brainstorming Solutions	Partner/Team
CC45	3–8	I Wish I Could	Full/Team
CC46	K–8	Goal Sharing	Full/Team
CC47	K–8	How Will You Make It?	Full/Team
CC48	K–8	Goal Accomplishment	Full/Team

School-wide Activities That Promote Mission

Code	Grade	Title	Element
SW22	1–8	School Problem Report	Mission
SW23	K–6	Koala-T Efforts	Mission

Checklist of Educator Behaviors
That Promote MISSION

Directions: For a self-evaluation of your skills in enhancing your students' sense of mission, complete the following items:

Never 1	Sometimes 2	Frequently 3	Always 4	
				As an educator:
_____	_____	_____	_____	1. Do I aid students in identifying what they want to achieve?
_____	_____	_____	_____	2. Do I take the time to discuss aspirations and goals with students?
_____	_____	_____	_____	3. Do I help students assess their present as well as previous performance capabilities?
_____	_____	_____	_____	4. Do I provide opportunities for students to check their progress regularly?
_____	_____	_____	_____	5. Do I encourage students to acknowledge their goal-setting results?
_____	_____	_____	_____	6. Do I help students to set realistic goals that are attainable?
_____	_____	_____	_____	7. Do I encourage students to consider alternatives in problem solving and make their own decisions?
_____	_____	_____	_____	8. Do I allow students to discover the consequences of their actions?
_____	_____	_____	_____	9. Do I encourage students to influence their own direction in their studies and projects?
_____	_____	_____	_____	10. Do I avoid undue comparison of students' individual performances?

_____ + _____ + _____ + _____ = **Total:**_____

Areas I could improve in that will increase the development of a student's sense of mission:

_____

_____

_____

_____

Esteem Builders. Jalmar Press
Rolling Hills Estates, CA

6

Purpose with Responsibility: Building Mission

*I have found the best way to give advice to your children is
to find out what they want and then advise them to do it.*
—HARRY TRUMAN

Individuals with high self-esteem generally feel self-motivated and have a clear sense of direction. Such individuals usually succeed in life because they have in mind specific aims or intentions of what they want to achieve. In other words, they have a heightened sense of mission. They have taken the time to think about what they want to be and where they want to go. Moreover, they are able to take the necessary actions to accomplish their aim and thus become "achievers." This in turn enhances self-esteem.

Each time a person realizes an intention, he/she attains success and is energized in the process. When each additional attempt is met with further success, it provides fresh ammunition to aim toward other goals. The individual's self-image as an "achiever" is almost a guaranteed outcome. And so the spiral toward higher self-esteem continues. Past performances emit signals that encourage fresh attempts and risks. And why not? The risk is worth the gamble because higher self-esteem is the outcome.

The student weak in mission is quite a different scenario. This individual generally moves through life displaying characteristics of low initiative, as well as lack of motivation and aimlessness. He or she seldom experiences success because there is rarely any attempt to achieve. Along the way frequent failures have turned on an internal red stop light that signals: "Don't try...you won't make it anyway. It's not worth the effort." And so the student stops taking risks, shows little initiative and appears unmotivated. In extreme cases, this type of individual completely relinquishes a feeling of personal mission or of having influence over his/her life.

Students who have a clear sense of mission, who set realistic and achievable goals for themselves, and then take the risks and necessary steps to realize them, are bound to be more self-motivated and self-directed in the classroom.

Several studies point out that feeling able to direct one's life based on individual intentions not only enhances self-esteem but also raises the level of academic performance. The Coleman Report[1], a very comprehensive investigation of American education, concluded that student attitudes regarding their effectiveness as individuals were the most significant determinant of whether they failed or succeeded in the classroom—more than academic performance, class size, yearly expenditure per pupil or level of teacher preparation.

---

1. Coleman, J.S. et al. *Equality of Educational Opportunity* (Washington, D.C.: U.S. Government Printing Office, 1966).

A student with a weak sense of mission can be recognized by the following behavior patterns:

- lacks motivation and initiative;
- cannot see alternatives or solutions;
- feels powerless, therefore may exhibit attention-getting behaviors, such as whining or tattling, to gain control;
- appears aimless, without direction;
- rarely succeeds due to poor goal-setting (goals are either too high, too low or nonexistent);
- is overdependent on others and feels incapable of being in charge and influencing others;
- avoids taking responsibility for his/her own actions: blames others, denies or inveigles others to do his/her work;
- is indecisive and seeks to avoid making own decisions.

On the other hand, a student with a strong sense of mission may be recognized by the following characteristics:

- appears purposeful with a clear sense of direction;
- is self-directed and initiating;
- takes responsibility for his/her own actions and recognizes the consequences;
- is decisive because he/she feels sufficiently empowered to have influence over the outcome of decisions;
- seeks alternative solutions to problems;
- sets achievable and realistic goals;
- accurately assesses current capability and skills as well as past performances.

SUMMARY

Educators can aid students who are lacking in mission by taking the following steps with students:

1. Enhance ability to make decisions, seek alternatives and identify consequences.
2. Aid in charting present and past academic and behavioral performances.
3. Teach the steps to successful goal-setting.

=== ESTEEM BUILDER #1 ===

Enhance Ability to Make Decisions, Seek Alternatives and Identify Consequences

"First, get all the facts. Next, isolate the alternatives. Then weigh them carefully to arrive at the best decision."
—ELWOOD N. CHAPMAN

TEACH PROBLEM-SOLVING SKILLS

The first critical esteem builder for enhancing the feeling of mission involves teaching students how to solve their own problems. This allows the individual to build self-responsibility and gradually exert more and more influence over his/her own actions. Problem-solving activities provide the student with the opportunity to experience the consequences of his/her own decisions in a safe environment and thereby increase skills in finding more viable solutions.

The First Step: What Can I Change?

Many students, however, are not yet aware of what changes they'd like to make and are therefore not able to set accurate and effective goals. It is helpful to introduce goal-setting with a discussion of what we like and don't like about ourselves (see M1

What I Like. . .What I Want to Change), and what can and can't be changed. *A crucial, first step toward goal-setting is for students to recognize what it is about themselves they would like to change.* Then goal-setting becomes a powerful avenue for behavioral change.

With this awareness, skills in making decisions, seeking alternatives and identifying consequences naturally follow. Students who previously floundered when faced with a dilemma now find they have resources to take charge. They are able to make decisions and choose what the outcome will be. In an era filled with rising statistics of adolescent suicide, peer pressure, pregnancy, and drug and alcohol addiction, it is essential that we include in our curriculum the learning of skills that will change helpless feelings to purposeful ones.

For additional problem-solving classroom ideas, refer to *Self-Esteem: A Classroom Affair. More Ways to Help Students Like Themselves, Vol. II.*[2]

_____
2. Borba, Michele and Craig. *Self-Esteem: A Classroom Affair. More Ways to Help Students Like Themselves. Vol. II* (San Francisco: Harper & Row, 1982).

MISSION

ACTIVITIES: GROUP 1

The following group of activities are designed to provide skills for students to use when faced with decisions and/or problems. Along with the performance charts (see M9, M10, M11, M12), they provide a necessary foundation before students start working on actual goals.

Grades K–8	What I Like...What I Want to Change	M1

Purpose: To help students reflect on what they could change about themselves.

Materials:

For older students:
9" x 12" light-colored construction paper folded in half lengthwise, 1 per student; writing instrument.

For younger students:
SH6 Me Doll pattern traced onto 12" x 18" light-colored construction paper, cut out and folded in half lengthwise.

Optional: glue, marking pens, magazines, scissors.

Procedure:

1. Encourage students to think about things they like about themselves and those they wish they could change. Remind them that there are some things we can change (haircut, dress style, study habits, behaviors) and other things that are just "givens" (eye color, race, physical characteristics). At this point, open up the discussion to students by asking them to brainstorm what can and can't be changed. These could be written on the board under the headings "Can Change" and "Can't Change." Write each word or phrase they come up with under the corresponding heading. See M5 for steps to Brainstorming.

2. Direct students to reflect about things they like and things they'd like to change within themselves. Provide the folded construction paper for older students and the cutout Me Dolls for younger ones. On the top left-hand side of the paper, students write the word "Like," and on the top right-hand side "Change." Students write words or phrases or draw pictures or symbols on the two folded halves to depict their

answers. Younger students dictate their answers. Magazine picture cutouts may also be used. Remind students that their work is confidential.

3. At a later date, students look at their answers and choose *one* item that they could change. Tell them to circle the choice. Students now turn over their paper and brainstorm ways that they could make this change. Younger students dictate their answers, which are written on the Me Doll. Older students could also consider what stands between them and the change and what resources they need to help them make the change.
   Note: Encourage students to begin with modest changes. The biggest stumbling block to carrying out any change is that so many of them want to begin with a major change.

4. An effective follow-up activity is for students to bring their completed form to a trusted individual as a homework assignment. The "helper" (who may be an educator) is to comment on the change and work with the student to write an actual goal that could bring about the change.

Grades 3–8	Problems	M2

Purpose: To enhance students' awareness of a problem they are facing. To help them work through the steps toward problem resolution.

Materials: A copy of M2 Problems form for each student.

Procedure: The success of this activity depends on whether the students are willing to discuss any problems they feel are pressing. *A climate of security and trust is essential for this to transpire.* Students will also need to be assured that these issues are confidential. It is best, therefore, to begin with problems that are minor in nature. You may wish to reinforce the concept that problems are normal: everyone has them. Successful people are individuals who have learned to work through their problems.

A good place to begin will be to tell your students about a problem you may have had as a student and how you dealt with it. Assign students the task of interviewing a significant other about a problem he/she had as a youngster and how it was solved. Books that focus on a central character with a problem to solve serve as good models for the students and are catalysts for class discussion. See M7 Booklist to Enhance Mission.

Following a discussion on problems, provide a copy of the M2 Problems form. Students first discuss their problems in small groups. Teammates can then contribute ideas for resolution as well as just being supportive (which is a major component in problem solving). There are specific steps to problem solving that can be taught to students. You may wish to write these on a chart and post them in the room as a reference for students.

Problem Solving Steps:

1. What is the problem?

2. Think of solutions (refer to M5 Brainstorming steps).

3. Select the two or three preferred solutions.

4. What might happen if they were chosen?

5. Choose the best solution after reviewing the consequences.

6. Make a plan.

7. Do it!

---

1. **What is the problem?** Ask the student to identify what the problem is. He/she should be able to briefly describe the problem and explain why they consider it to be a problem.

2. **Think of solutions.** Tell students to brainstorm as many solutions to the problem as they can. No solution should be judged at this point. A good practice is for the student to write all the possibilities down.

3. **Select the two or three preferred solutions.** Students now look through the possibilities and choose two or three "best" choices.

4. **What might happen if they were chosen?** For each best solution, the student now thinks what might be the possible consequence for each choice. The student asks him-/herself, "What are all the things that might happen if I were

to choose this solution?" They may write down the consequences.

5. **Choose the best solution.** Based on their answers to #4, students choose the one solution that promises to be the best.

6. **Make a plan.** The student constructs a plan and then asks him-/herself, "Who or what do I need to help me carry out this plan?" The student also considers when the plan should be started as well as how to deal with any obstacles that may come up along the way.

7. **Do it!** Finally, the student implements the plan after the teacher has reviewed it for workability.

Whether you have your students work individually or in groups for this activity depends upon how familiar they are with teamwork and how secure they are with each other. Students complete their forms and periodically review them to reevaluate their action plan.

Be prepared to hold individual conferences with some students, or bring in a counselor, so that they may receive more personal feedback.

| Grades 3–8 | Problem/Solution Report | M3 |

Purpose: To provide the opportunity for students to identify their problems and generate their own solutions.

Materials: Ample copies of M3 Problem/Solution Report stored in a box or folder in an accessible classroom location.

Procedure: Inform the class that many times students report to staff members problems they could have solved themselves. These relatively insignificant problems take up staff time and lead to ill feelings among classmates because most often this kind of reporting is just "tattling." Tell the class that from now on, there is to be no reporting unless there is an injury (or likelihood of one happening) or the student really can't resolve it him-/herself.

This is the function of the report form: students use this to communicate their problems. Show them the report and where it can be located. Give each student a copy while you talk about it so that they clearly understand what to do. Inform them that when they have a school or class problem that does not fit the categories for reporting permission, they should fill out the entire report. Other members involved in the problem also fill out similar reports. Let them know that you will make time to read the entire report. You will then decide if the "case" still warrants a conference.

The completed reports may also be used as a "discipline form." Before students who are to be disciplined meet with a staff member, they should fill out the form and reflect upon the questions. If you adopt this procedure, be sure to stick to the rules consistently!

Problem/Solution Report designed by Gregory P. Morse; Union School District, San Jose, California.

Grades K–2	Pictorial Problem/ Solution Report	M4

Purpose: To provide the opportunity for students to identify their problems and generate their own solutions.

Materials: Ample copies of M4 Pictorial Problem/ Solution Report stored in a box or folder in a convenient location; crayons or marking pens.

Procedure: This activity is the adapted version of M3, suitable for younger students. Follow the same procedure as before, modifying your approach according to the age of your students. They will be drawing pictures of their "problems" and turning in the report to you.

Grades 4–8	Brainstorming	M5

Purpose: To instruct students in how to generate constructive ideas in a "free" setting.

Materials: A copy of M5 Brainstorming form for each student.

Procedure: Divide the students into small teams for this activity. If teams are new to your class, first read through Chapter 8, Concept Circles, as a guide.

Inform the students that brainstorming is a commonly used creative tool devised to bring about many potential solutions in a short space of time. Once they are familiar with the process, students will be able to do it in groups or to generate solutions on their own.

Instruct them in this step-by-step process:

1. **Wild ideas count.** In fact, every idea stated by a team member counts and will be written down. They must feel free to let their creativity go.

2. **No criticism or evaluation of ideas.** Every idea automatically gets approval. Any criticism will be detrimental to the process as it stifles communication and illumination. Some people may be reticent about sharing; the time would be better spent encouraging them rather than allowing criticism.

3. **It's okay to add on to someone else's idea.** Just ask students to reword it a little so that it now becomes a "new idea."

Following the instruction in brainstorming, you may wish to practice the process as a group. Try posing these problems to the class:

- The schoolyard is in a mess; no one seems to be picking up the trash. What should we do?

- Teachers are complaining that the noise level is far too high after the bell. What should we do?

- Too many students are walking in late to class. What should we do?

Let students suggest problems of their own. Encourage them to brainstorm as quickly as they can. Note the solutions on the chalkboard.

After practicing the brainstorming process in a large group, students will be ready to try the procedure in smaller groups:

1. Divide the students into teams of four. Ask each team to decide which teammates will play the following roles:
   Leader—leads the group, rephrases the questions, keeps team focused on the task.
   Recorder—acts as a secretary and records the major ideas and decisions of the team.
   Timekeeper—keeps the team within their timeframe; lets them know when time is up.

Encourager—acts as a supporter and praiser and encourages all team members to participate in the activity.

2. Each team member receives the M5 Brainstorming form.

3. Students consider several school problems for discussion. Inform the timekeeper to clock them at five-minute intervals. During brainstorming, students jot down their ideas on the top half of the form. A recorder may perform this role for them.

4. At the end of the first five-minute session, students stop and begin the second part of the task. As a group they are now to come to a consensus and choose one problem to consider. When they've chosen, the recorder writes it down on the form.
Note: If brainstorming in teams is new to your class, you may want to save time by giving each group a problem to consider. The team begins with the task of generating solutions (no. 5).

5. Students are now required to generate solutions to the problem they've chosen. Instruct the leader to inform the group what the problem is. The recorder writes down the group's ideas for solution on the form. The timekeeper lets the group know when the five-minute time limit is up. (You may increase time limits as the group becomes more experienced.)

6. Finally, students individually rate their potential solutions as ones they'd either "consider actually doing" or ones they "would not consider." The recorder lists the solutions they rate as worth doing in order of preference: first, second and third choice.
Note: The following activity (M6) continues on to the solution stage. You may choose to do these activities on consecutive days.

Variation: The following may be done in a large group, small teams or in pairs as further practice for problem solving:

- **Dear Abby.** Cut out appropriate problems from newspaper columns. Glue each problem on a separate card. Students take turns portraying the role of "Abby" and brainstorm solutions that are relevant to the issue.

- **Pictorial Problems.** Cut out pictures from magazines, storybooks or other sources that depict problems (choose ones appropriate for students' ages). Glue each picture on a separate Manila envelope.

Instruct students to look at the picture and decide what the problem is. This generally takes a short time.

Secondly, students brainstorm ways to solve the problem. They write each solution down on a separate piece of paper. At the end of the session, students place all the strips inside the envelope. At a future date another team will look at the same pictures and brainstorm their solutions. They compare the two sets of answers and discuss how they differ or are the same.

- **Solution Graphs.** As teams become more proficient in problem solving, they can graph the number of solutions they generate within a set time limit.

Provide each group (or student) with an M11 Graphing Progress form as well as a problem to work on. Set an acceptable limit for the activity (three to five minutes). Students then brainstorm as many solutions as possible. When the time is up, the group adds up their number of solutions and plots it on the graph.

Whenever they conduct this activity, they plot the number of solutions they arrive at. This way they chart their progress in coming up with problem solutions.

- **Problem Box.** The most effective problems for any brainstorming activity are those that are not only suitable for the age of the students, but "real" problems they encounter on a daily basis.

Place a shoe box in a convenient location in the classroom. Cut a small 1/4" x 6" slit in the top of the box. Encourage students to write problems that concern them on slips of paper and insert them in the box. You may wish to suggest that the problems be only classroom/school related. Students do not have to sign the slip of paper. Select problems for future brainstorming sessions.

Grades 5–8	Strategy Sheet of Solution Consequences	M6

Purpose: To help students learn to evaluate the effectiveness and consequences of solutions.

MISSION

Materials: A copy of M6 Strategy Sheet of Solution Consequences for each student; a copy of the completed M5 Brainstorming form from a previous session.

Procedure: This activity succeeds M5 Brainstorming where students learned how to generate solutions to problems. In this activity students will evaluate the three top solutions they have chosen in M5 and now consider the possible consequences to each solution. On the basis of this they will choose the one solution they think will be the best choice.

Step-by-Step Process:

1. Seat students in their previous teams of four. Once again, they take on the roles of leader, timekeeper, recorder and encourager. This time, however, teammates should switch roles from the activity before.

2. Inform students that their task is to choose the best solution to the problem they worked on during their last meeting. Begin by asking them to list their previous top three choices on the Strategy Sheet form.

3. Tell students that they will have three minutes to brainstorm the possible consequences to *each* of the three solutions. The recorder will quickly jot down the ideas generated by the group in the corresponding columns.

4. At the end of the nine minutes, team members now decide on the basis of their findings which solution they think would be the best choice. Everyone fills in his/her form, including the final choice.

Note: Both this activity and Brainstorming may be repeated over time so that students become more proficient at it.

Grades K–8	Booklist to Enhance Mission	**M7**

Purpose: To increase students' awareness of problem-solving strategies used by fictitious characters in children's literature.

Materials: Choice of books from the list below, according to grade level.

Procedure: Read aloud the book to students, or assign as independent reading. Use the following questions as discussion guides to help students access their comprehension of the story and problem strategies:

- Who was the main character in the book?
- What problem(s) was the main character having?
- Did the character have to deal with the problem alone or with other characters?
- How would you have solved the problem?
- How did the character handle his/her problem?

As an extension of this activity, you may want to have older students write their own story with a central character who has a problem to solve.

Primary Level

Alexander, Who Used to Be Rich Last Sunday, Judith Viorst (Atheneum, 1978).

The Blanket That Had to Go, Nancy Evans Cooney (Putnam, 1981).

The Boy with a Problem, Joan Fassler (Behavioral Publications, 1971).

A Chair for My Mother, Vera Williams (Greenwillow, 1983).

The Checker Players, Alan Venable (Lippincott, 1973).

Frederick, Leo Lionni (Pantheon, 1963).

Gorky Rises, William Steig (Farrar, Straus & Giroux, 1980).

The Hating Book, Charlotte Zolotow (Harper & Row, 1969).

Ira Sleeps Over, Bernard Waber (Houghton Mifflin, 1972).

It Could Be Worse, Margot Zemach (Farrar, Straus & Giroux, 1976).

Little Rabbit's Loose Tooth, Lucy Bate (Crown, 1975).

Nobody Listens to Andrew, Elizabeth Guilfoile (Follet, 1957).

Pierre, Maurice Sendak (The Nutshell Library, Harper & Row, 1962).

Sam, Bangs, and Moonshine, Evaline Ness (Holt, 1966).

Sleep Out, Carol and Donald Carrick (Clarion, 1973).

Swimmy, Leo Lionni (Pantheon, 1963).

Take It or Leave It, Osmond Molarsky (Scholastic, 1980).

MISSION

Intermediate Level or Advanced Listener

Abel's Island, William Steig (Farrar, Straus & Giroux, 1976).

Altogether, One at a Time, E.L. Koningsburg (Atheneum, 1971).

The Cat Ate My Gymsuit, Paula Danziger (Delacorte, 1974).

Chocolate Fever, Robert K. Smith (Dell, 1978).

Dear Lovey Hart, I Am Desperate, Ellen Conford (Little, Brown & Co., 1975).

Homecoming, Cynthia Voigt (Atheneum, 1981).

How I Hunted the Little Fellows, Boris Zhitkov (Dodd, Mead, 1979).

Jumanji, Chris Van Allsburg (Houghton Mifflin, 1981).

A Matter of Time, Roni Schotter (Collins, 1980).

My Side of the Mountain, Jean George (Dutton, 1959).

On My Honor, Marion Dane Bauer (Dell, 1986).

One Eyed Cat, Paula Fox (Dell, 1984).

The Shrinking of Treehorn, Florence Parry Heide (Holiday House, 1971).

The Trouble with Tuck, Theodore Taylor (Avon, 1981).

Tuck Everlasting, Natalie Babbit (Farrar, Straus & Giroux, 1975).

| Grades 1–4 | Super Sleuth Book Report | M8 |

Purpose: As per M7.

Materials: Either read aloud a book to the class or instruct students to choose a book, suitable for their level, from the booklist in M7. They write a book report answering these two main questions:

- What was the problem in the book?
- How did the character solve it?

Students not yet proficient in writing may dictate their answers and/or illustrate.

| Grades 4–8 | Problem Map | M9 |

Purpose: To provide students with the opportunity to identify a problem, generate possible solutions and, from these, choose the best solution.

Materials: M9 Problem Map form for each student.

Procedure: This activity is the adapted version of M8, suitable for older students. Follow the same procedure as before where students choose a book from the list in M7. This time, instruct students to read only the part of the book where the problem is described but *not solved.*

Students are to write a book report using the steps in the M9 Problem Map form. Instruct them also to briefly describe the title, setting and main problem of the book. Students then write their four possible solutions to the character's dilemma. Finally, each student chooses the solution that in his/her judgment is the best choice and writes it in the "Statement of the Solution" box. Students may then finish reading the book and compare their solution choices to the decision made by the main character. Students could also do this activity in teams in which they brainstorm solutions.

ESTEEM BUILDER #2

Aid in Charting Present and Past Academic and Behavioral Performances

> *"People with goals succeed because they know where they are going."*
> —EARL NIGHTINGALE

A characteristic of individuals with high self-esteem is that they set achievable and measurable goals. In other words, they set goals in relation to past performances. As a result, any goal-setting is more likely to be attained. This process of looking back in order to go forward appears so logical that the educator may incorrectly assume it to be a common goal-setting practice. But this is often not the case.

Students with low self-esteem make it even harder because they tend to set themselves unattainable goals. Felker's[3] review of self-concept literature revealed that low esteem individuals either set goals that are far too high or so low that achieving them

3. Felker, Donald. *Building Positive Self-Concepts* (Minneapolis: Burgess, 1974).

brings little satisfaction. Sears'[4] investigations of children with poor self-concepts yielded the same results—either overcautious or overexpectant. In neither case will higher self-esteem be the outcome. Furthermore, these individuals view unattained marks as a personal failure, the "not good enough" syndrome.

Self-esteem is built on standards that are realistic and reachable, and aiding students to measure their past performances accurately is a critical esteem builder. This will only enhance students' abilities to achieve goals and give them the opportunities to view themselves as a success.

ACTIVITIES: GROUP 2

Charts are a useful, visual tool for more realistic evaluations of capabilities. When students evaluate their prior performances, more accurate goal-setting will result. The chart is a visual reminder of previous and current progress on selected individual behaviors or academic topics. To be workable, charts should be designed with the following in mind:

1. **Accessible**
   Keep charts in convenient locations so that students may refer to them easily. Many teachers choose to tape the chart on the desk tops for immediate access. Students may also wear the M22 Goal Wheel form. Another alternative is to keep charts in readily accessible folders stored in a box on a classroom counter.

2. **Readable**
   Teach students how to *read* a chart. Show them how to interpret their past performance in order to set a more realistic mark in the succeeding goal attempt. Help them find where their previous scores are to use as a basis for comparison in current and future goal-setting. Younger students can be helped in marking their own charts if the teacher first marks their chart using a light yellow crayon or marking pen. Instruct them to mark over the top of the previous mark with a blue crayon or marking pen to make a green mark. This helps younger students practice the process of scoring.

---

4. Sears, Pauline. *In Pursuit of Self-Esteem* (Belmont, CA: Wadsworth, 1964).

3. **Individual**
   Performance charts should be *individual* so that the student keeps track of *his/her own performance*. There need be no comparison with other students to measure progress.

4. **Measurable**
   For convenience, usefulness and meaning, allocate areas on the charts for:
   a. dates, times, levels or page numbers;
   b. current and previous scores;
   c. topic or goal.
   Students may evaluate both behavior and academic skills on their charts.

Grades K–8	My Progress	M10

Materials: Duplicate a copy of M10 My Progress form for each student; concept/skill evaluation test; yellow and blue crayons or marking pens (younger students).

Procedure: Each student receives a copy of M10 My Progress form, which will be used periodically to evaluate progress in a specific skill—the more frequently the better. This could be any academic area where the same concept is evaluated constantly.

Math timed tests, spelling words or word recognition are three areas that are commonly graphed on a progress chart. Each day (or week) give the same number of math facts, spelling or reading words. Advance the level each week and note this on the level column.

1. Write the name of the subject along with the student's name across the top of the chart.

2. Use the level column for charting levels or dates or page numbers.

3. The numbers across the top of the graph refer to the number of problems, facts or words that appeared on the test. The student colors in the number of facts he/she correctly accomplished in that test. Students may need some help initially not only in coloring in the grid but also in interpreting their scores. *The value of this activity is charting progress by comparing the latest results with previous scores.*

For younger students, you may wish to first color in yellow the correct number of facts. The student

MISSION

goes over the mark with a blue pen to make it green. They will then begin to get the idea of how to fill in the grid so that at a future date they can do it on their own.

Idea adapted from: Reasoner, R. *Building Self-Esteem: A Comprehensive Program* (Palo Alto: Consulting Psychologists Press, 1982).

Graphing Progress M11
Grades 3–8

Materials: A copy of M11 Graphing Progress form for each participating student, duplicated on light-colored cardstock-weight or construction paper; concept/skill evaluation test.

Procedure: Choose a subject area in which one of the skills or concepts is evaluated repeatedly. Fill in the student's name, subject being evaluated and the date the chart was started. Each time they evaluate the skill, students mark the date along the bottom of the form. They mark the number of correct attempts along the vertical column.

Following the second evaluation, students can begin to "plot" their progress by drawing horizontal lines between the plots of previous markings.

Note: See also M5 under **Solution Graphs.**

Beat the Clock M12
Grades 1–8

Purpose: To aid students in keeping track of their academic progress in a particular skill that is timed.

Materials: A copy of M12 Beat the Clock form for each participating student; the timed tests; an egg

timer, stopwatch or other timer; yellow crayons *(optional).*

Procedure: Choose a subject area that can be evaluated repeatedly and timed. The time limit should be the same each time the test is given. Students (or teacher) fill in the top information of the chart, including the date the chart was begun and the subject.

Students note their progress for each timed test. They place the first test score entry inside the circle at the one o'clock position and write the date of the test below the number. Students continue to keep track of their progress by writing their scores and test dates clockwise around the circle. Ask students whether they scored 100 percent within the time limit. Students can show this by coloring in successful time limit scores with a yellow crayon.

Homework Assignments M13
Grades 2–8

Purpose: To increase students' responsibility in keeping track of their individual school assignments that they do at home.

Materials: A copy of M13 Homework Assignments form for each student, 1 per week; manila folders for students to store their forms.

Procedure: Each student fills out his/her assignments for each subject area, including the due date. As the student completes the assignment, he/she checks it off in the "done" column.

Explain to students how important it is to keep on top of their responsibilities. This is part of developing a sense of mission and accomplishing goals.

ESTEEM BUILDER #3
Teach the Steps to Successful Goal-setting

"The most important thing about goals is having one."
—GEOFFREY F. ABERT

A current and common concern of educators is students who exhibit characteristics of low motivation. It is essential to recognize that motivation is an internal impetus that induces us to perform a cho-

sen exercise—the emphasis being on *internal.* The drive for motivation must emanate from within; it is an intrinsic quality that must be generated by the student. The Gallup Poll of Education[5] reveals that only 25 percent of people produce as much as 50 percent of their capability; therefore, it is in order to analyze some aspects of motivation that affect the educational setting.

5. *Executive Educator.* Gallup Poll of Education, December 1982.

An important aspect of motivation appears to be a sense of mission. Self-motivated individuals generally have a clear idea of where they are headed. They have a sense of direction and a purpose in life. Generally, such individuals are successful in school and in life; goals help them know where they want to be. Reflecting on the direction they wish to take provides the impetus to achieve that aim. And the establishment of goals helps to carry those individuals along the road to success.

The use of goals by individuals with high self-esteem has been well documented. Kay[6] states that these individuals tend to use goals as a means of perpetuating their present level of self-esteem. Sears'[7] study found that students who were successful in school tended to set personal goals that were both realistic and reasonable. Garfield's[8] 21-year study of "peak performers" in sports, science and entertainment found that they all shared the common trait of setting goals for themselves—and then not stopping until they achieved them. It is apparent then that goal-setting is a powerful tool for esteem building, which can be enhanced by teaching the steps from start to finish.

HOW TO TEACH GOAL-SETTING

Although goal-setting is such a useful and applicable esteem builder, it is far from a common educational practice. Gardner McCollum[9] from the University of Alabama states that 87 percent of us have no specific goals or plans for our lives, and of the remaining 13 percent, only 3 percent have specific written goals. It is the latter who accomplish 50 to 100 times more than those who have goals but do not write them down.

Students often find goal-setting a difficult task because they are not familiar with the actual goal-setting process. The educator should not assume any student's prior knowledge about the concept. Goal-setting is a skill that is easier to teach in sequential steps, so start at the beginning by defining what a goal is.

6. Kay, R.S. *Self-Concept and Level of Aspiration in Third and Fourth Grade Children.* Doctoral dissertation, Purdue University (Ann Arbor, MI: University Microfilms, 1972, No. 73–6054).
7. Sears, Pauline. *In Pursuit of Self-Esteem* (Belmont, CA: Wadsworth, 1964).
8. Garfield, Charles. *Peak Performers: The New Heroes of American Business* (Avon, 1986).

WHAT IS A GOAL?

Inform the class that you are going to begin a new area of study: goal-setting. Many teachers have found it helpful to equate the concept of goals with sports. Explain that they are something you shoot for. In football and soccer, players try and shoot their ball through the goals to score points. In life we try and improve something about ourself; a goal is something we are trying to achieve. We do it to score internal points for ourself because it helps to improve areas where we would like change.

STEPS TO SUCCESSFUL GOAL-SETTING

Once you've explained to students what a goal is, instruct them in the sequential steps toward reaching a goal, using this model:

Effective Goals
- Conceptualized
- Measurable
- Achievable
- Sequential
- Individual
- Participatory

Conceptualized. Students must be able to picture and understand what it is they want to accomplish.

Measurable. The student must be able to determine if he/she succeeded in attaining the goal. To do so usually requires some type of evaluation in which the goal can be measured in terms of quantity and time.

Achievable. The goal must be challenging but within reach. So often goals are not achieved because the level of aspiration is either too high or too low. In neither case will self-esteem be enhanced. The most successful goals are usually set *slightly higher than the last goal.*

Sequential. Goals are more attainable when they are broken down into small increments. A most valuable component of goal-setting is the awareness of what steps are necessary in order to attain the end product.

9. McCollum, Gardner M. "Goals—Vital to Success," *Ops' Inc*, Vol. II, No. 3 (Cumberland, MD: November 1986), p. 3.

MISSION

Individual. Goals should be set totally on an individual basis in which students are concerned only with their own personal performance. They must not compare goal progress with performances of others.

Participatory. Students must be able to participate in their own goal-setting. Only through personal involvement will commitment toward completion be felt.

ACTIVITIES: GROUP 3

The following activities are designed to familiarize students with what a goal is and the steps involved in reaching it.

Grades 2–8	Goal-setting Step-by-Step	M14

Purpose: To reinforce visually the goal-setting steps.

Materials: Two-page M14 Goal-setting Step-by-Step chart duplicated on light-colored construction paper. (Glue the pages together along the bottom dotted line. Laminate for durability.)

Procedure: Hang the chart in the classroom and refer to it often during the goal-setting process. As you discuss the chart with students, you may wish to define the following points:

1. **Start: What do you want to aim for?**
   What would you like to do better in? A student must first identify what it is he/she wants to achieve. Goals must be achievable, measurable and set in relation to past performance.

2. **Measure: Where are you now, and what is your next step?**
   In order to set realistic goals, students must have an awareness of their current and past capabilities in the area. The goal must be measurable, and should not be too high or too low.

3. **Plan: How will you achieve your goal?**
   Encourage students to think through the entire goal-setting process. They should be able to identify important resources that may be necessary to help them achieve their goal. Suggest to students that they "visualize" (picture) the entire goal-setting plan from start to finish.

4. **Write: How does your goal look on paper?**
   Instruct students to think through the entire goal-setting process. Students write the goal in the present tense, starting with the words, "I am," and followed by their intention. For example, "I am learning how to sew;" "I am scoring a goal in soccer." The statement should be brief.
   Note: Many goal-setting strategists encourage individuals to write goals as if they have already been achieved. This helps form a positive internal picture that says: "I made it." This is a critical distinction when one considers how many students picture "I can't make it."

5. **Time: How long will it take to achieve my goal?**
   Students must set a date/time in which they plan to achieve their goal. It is best to begin with short-term goals that may be attained quickly, because this will positively reinforce the student not yet proficient in goal achievement.

6. **Do: How are you going to make sure you accomplish your goal?**
   The only way to attain a goal is with preparation and practice. Encourage students to take the time to reread their goal statements and visualize themselves achieving their goals. Check progress regularly.

7. **Evaluate: How did you do in your goal-setting?**
   How are the results coming along?
   For those students who were successful, encourage them to:
   a. acknowledge the results and praise themselves;
   b. thank those who helped them.
   For those students who missed their goals, encourage them to:
   a. evaluate why they missed the goal;
   b. think through what they can do differently next time in order to be successful.

8. **New Target: What will you aim for next time?**
   If the goal was reached, encourage the student to aim for a new, slightly higher, target. For those students who did not succeed, help them replan and rewrite their goal so that they may succeed on the second attempt.

| Grades 2-8 | **Group Goal-setting** | **M15** |

Purpose: To reinforce the steps of goal-setting in a group situation.

Materials: A copy of the M14 Goal-setting Step-by-Step chart for each student; copies of M15 Group Goal-setting form for each student; large chart paper *(optional)*.

Procedure: To help students begin the goal-setting steps, it may be beneficial to start with sessions where group goals are set and acted upon. Use the same M14 Goal-setting Step-by-Step chart throughout the process so that students will become familiar enough with the steps to attempt the procedure individually.

You may choose to make your own copies of the M15 Group Goal-setting form on larger chart paper.

Each week choose one goal for the class to work on together. Enlist the ideas of the students and write these down as a resource list. Goal suggestions are:

- decrease the noise level of the room;
- increase friendliness (or decrease put-down statements);
- decrease cleanup time, increase cleanliness, etc.

As a group, go through each of the steps on the Goal-setting Step-by-Step chart. Measure results daily and graph them on the form. This allows students to see and assess their daily progress. Keep weekly completed graphs in a special folder.

| Grades 3-8 | **Goal-setting: Charting the Course** | **M16** |

Purpose: To practice the goal-setting steps in written form.

Materials: Copies of M16 Goal-setting: Charting the Course form for each student; M14 chart as a reference.

Procedure: As students become familiar with the steps in goal-setting, they may use the M16 form when they're ready to commit themselves to an individual goal. Encourage students to use the Goal-setting Step-by-Step chart as a reference. The same steps appear on this form as those listed on the chart.

| Grades 3-8 | **Overcoming Obstacles to Goals** | **M17** |

Purpose: To help students identify any obstacles that may stand between them and success.

Materials: A copy of M17 Overcoming Obstacles to Goals form for each student; M14 chart as reference.

Procedure: After students are familiar with the goal-setting steps, you may introduce this activity by explaining to students that many people don't succeed in their goals simply because of an obstacle, or "roadblock." Thinking through ways to avoid these "roadblocks" before they happen may make the difference between "hit" and "miss."

Encourage students to verbalize their goals and to think about possible obstacles (what stands in the way). Set up brainstorming teams of two's and three's to discuss their goals. Team members each write down their own obstacles before they go on to the next step. Teammates then help the goal-setter find ways around the obstacles. The goal-setter writes down the possible solutions.

| Grades 1-6 | **Climbing High Contract** | **M18** |

Purpose: To help students reflect on the steps required to accomplish goals.

Materials: A copy of M18 Climbing High Contract for each student; M14 chart for reference.

Procedure: Explain to students that goals are made of many small steps. Students then use the worksheet to establish what they need to do to reach their goal. But first they must be familiar with the goal-setting steps.

Note: This worksheet is excellent for any goal-setting. Bind it together with M14, M16 and M17 for a Goal-setting Booklet.

MISSION

MISSION

| Grades 2–8 | **Daily Goal-setting** | **M19** |

Purpose: To set and acknowledge daily goals.

Materials: Several copies of M19 Daily Goal-setting form for each student; stapler; 2 pieces of 8 1/2" x 11" construction or cardstock-weight paper for front and back.

Procedure: Staple several copies of the M19 Daily Goal-setting form between a construction paper cover for each student. Begin the day by having students write what behavior or academic goal they hope to achieve during that study period. Before the end of the class day or period, each student reflects upon his/her performance and writes it down on the second half of the form.

Students who did not make the goal should write why, followed by what can be done differently the next class session. Students who were successful write a new goal for the following day. Encourage students to attempt the same goals, adding on one more step to the process. Example: "I am sitting still in my seat for 5 seconds" now becomes "I am sitting still in my seat for 10 seconds."

| Grades 2–8 | **Weekly Goal Card** | **M20** |

Purpose: To set and acknowledge goals on a weekly basis. To review the goal-setting steps.

Materials: Duplicate M20 Weekly Goal card on light-colored construction or cardstock-weight paper; crayons, marking pens or pencils.

Goal Card Construction: Once you've duplicated the sheet onto construction paper, cut the cards along the outside margins. Fold them in half and distribute one to each student.

Procedure: This activity is suitable for students who have completed at least two or more successful goal-setting activities. Students write individual goals for themselves that will last the entire week. Each day they check their progress in the space provided under "Weekly Progress."

At the end of the week students assess their goal achievements. Those who are successful also draw a picture of themselves making the goal.

| Grades 4–8 | **Record of Weekly Goals** | **M21** |

Purpose: To practice setting goals in a number of different areas and record the progress.

Materials: A copy of M21 Record of Weekly Goals form for each student.

Procedure: This activity is suitable only for students who have successfully completed previous daily goal-setting activities and are familiar with the goal-setting steps.

Present a copy of the M21 Record of Weekly Goals form to each student. First, students write the specific subjects they are taking under the subject column. Encourage them to write a specific goal they wish to achieve for each subject. Instruct students to write the goal so that it can be achieved within a week (or that they can make visible progress within a week). At the end of each week, students check their goal progress in the appropriate column on the right-hand side.

| Grades K–3 | **Goal Wheel** | **M22** |

Purpose: To acknowledge goal-setting on a daily basis. To provide a visual reminder of goal progress.

Materials: Copy of M22 Goal Wheel form duplicated onto light-colored construction paper or tagboard for each student; hole-punch, scissors and 26" yarn lengths; crayons or marking pens.

Procedure: Cut out the Goal Wheel that you've duplicated onto heavy construction or tag paper. Each week students write (or dictate) an academic or behavior goal for themselves and draw a picture that depicts them achieving that goal.

Keep track of goal achievements in the daily space by:
a. the teacher placing a sticker or stamp there;
b. students marking their own progress with check marks.

Younger students may like to wear the wheel: punch a hole near the top and tie with the yarn length.

Note: For younger students, or those with low self-esteem, a day may be too long to sustain a goal. Change the days on the wheel to be times of the day, so that they can see results and receive reinforcement more frequently.

| Grades 1-6 | **Goal Passbook** | **M23/24** |

Purpose: To increase students' sense of competence in goal-setting. To provide opportunities for daily goal-setting practice.

Materials: M23 Goal Passbook for each student; M24 Goal Passbook Cards, minimum 10 per student.

Construction: Use the M23 Goal Passbook pattern. Make copies of the pages, printing back-to-back, on light-colored tagboard, cardstock-weight or construction paper. Fold up at the dotted lines as indicated. Staple on the outside edges to form two pockets. Now fold in half so that the words "Goal Passbook" are on the cover.

Choose one of the two cards shown (see M24) and duplicate on light-colored cardstock-weight or construction paper. Be sure to copy the card so that the printed material appears on the front and back. Cut the card along the outside lines.

Procedure: Introduce the activity by distributing a passbook to each student. Inform them that the passbooks will be used for daily goal-setting (or as often as you wish to set up the activity). The inside pockets will be used for storing goal cards of achievements as well as the current goal-setting card.

Pass out a card (M24) to each student. Ask them what they'd like to aim for. Review the steps for successful goal-setting, which appear on the back of the passbook. Remind students to use the M14 chart as a reference.

Procedure Step-by-Step:

1. Review steps to successful goal-setting.

2. Students fill out both the front and back of their Goal-Setting Card.

3. Students store the card in the pocket marked "Goal" in their passbook, which is sized so that they can easily carry it around with them. Suggest that they refer to it often.

4. At the beginning of each class period, encourage students to pull out their goal card and turn to the picture they have drawn of themselves making the goal. Ask students to spend 30 seconds picturing themselves completing the goal. They must do the visualization frequently as it is a powerful tool in successful goal-making.

5. As students successfully complete their goal, they move the card to the "Achieved" pocket. Goals that they have not yet achieved should remain in the first pocket to be tried again (or rewritten in a more achievable way).

6. Students record each achieved goal in the passbook. On the left-hand side they write the goal in the space marked "Goals." On the right-hand side they make a check under the column marked "Goals Achieved." You may staple additional pages together as space is used up.

ACKNOWLEDGE RESULTS

In order to create personal change it is important that students develop an awareness of how successful (or unsuccessful) they are in the goals they assign to themselves. Activities in this section help students assess their progress and thereby evaluate their goals.

| Grades K-8 | **Goal Results** | **M25** |

Purpose: To increase students' awareness of their success in goal-setting.

Materials: Choose one of the M25 Goal Results cards for your students. The top card is more suited to the younger grades; the bottom card for older grades. Duplicate the cards on light-colored construction paper, or cardstock-weight for more durability. Cut the cards along the outside margins.

Procedure: These two activity cards help students focus on a single goal and keep track of how well they do on a given day. With older students who are proficient in goal-setting, establish a weekly time-frame for the goal.

Students select their goal and write or dictate it on the space provided. Encourage them to keep track of their progress by coloring or marking the space that corresponds to their goal performance. At the end of the day, you may wish to have an evaluation time where students can discuss the results.

| Grades K–3 | I Think I Can | M26 |

Purpose: To aid students in seeing their actual goal successes. To reinforce capability of achieving a goal.

Materials: A copy of M26 I Think I Can form for each student.

You may also refer to *The Little Engine That Could*, Watty Piper (Scholastic, 1979).

Procedure: This activity is designed to help younger students focus on the success of their goal. They write (or dictate) their goal at the top of the page and then color in a car each time they achieve their goal. Encourage students to use the words "I think I can" as they try.

| Grades 3–8 | Goal Achievement Journal | M27 |

Purpose: To enhance students' feelings of achievement when they accomplish goals.

Materials: Several copies of M27 Goal Achievement form (duplicated on the front and back) for each student. Bind the pages between an 8 1/2" x 11" piece of tagboard, construction or cardstock-weight paper; stapler, hole-punch and yarn or spiral binding.

Procedure: Each student receives a Goal Achievement Journal. They may bind their journals by hand and decorate the cover. Encourage students each day to keep a record of their goal achievements inside the journal. This will help them not only acknowledge their achievement but also identify the behavior that helped them attain their goal.

Note: For more activities on journal work, refer to Chapter 9, Journal Writing.

| Grades 2–8 | A Month of Goals | M28 |

Purpose: To allow students to keep track of their goal progress for a month.

Materials: A copy of M28 A Month of Goals form for each student.

Procedure: Provide a form for each student. Instruct them to fill in the dates for the forthcoming month in the upper right-hand corner of each box.

At the beginning of each day, students write their individual goal in the box with the corresponding date. At the end of each day (or class period) encourage them to evaluate their goal progress. If the goal was missed, the student fills in the negative sign. Ask them to think about why the goal was missed. If the student attains the goal, he/she fills in the positive sign.

This activity is particularly beneficial because it allows students to spot their progress instantly and recognize that they must reformulate their goal if they were unsuccessful in attaining it. When they write goals on a daily basis, students are able to refer to past goals as a reference to writing current goals.

| Grades K–5 | Goal Award Grams | M29 |

Purpose: To acknowledge students for their goal accomplishments.

Materials: Duplicate M29 Goal Award Grams onto colorful construction paper and cut out.

Procedure: Following each successful goal achievement, you may wish to acknowledge the student's achievement with an award. To facilitate this, appoint a student each week to be the "Goalkeeper." His/her task would be to ensure that each student who achieves a goal receives an award.

Name _____ Date _____

Problems

Describe a behavior problem of yours that has been getting in your way.

My problem is _____

_____

How does this problem interfere in your life?

1.

2.

3.

How will you change this behavior? What ways can you think of to solve this problem?

1.

2.

3.

4.

5.

Consider your options—the pluses and minuses for each. Which option will you choose?

What resources will you need to help you with this choice? (Friends, teachers, parents, etc.)
How can they help you?

Make a plan and **DO IT.**

When will you begin your plan?

What do you have to do to show that you have achieved your plan?

Student: _____ Teacher: _____

Esteem Builders. Jalmar Press
Rolling Hills Estates, CA

Problem Report

Filed by _____ Date _____

Who was involved? _____

Where did it happen? _____

When did it happen? _____

Did anyone else see what happened? _____

    Who? _____

Tell what happened: _____

_____

_____

How do you feel about what happened? _____

_____

How do you think the other person(s) feel(s) about what happened? _____

_____

_____

Why do you think the person(s) feel(s) this way? _____

_____

Name 2 ways you could have solved the problem: _____

_____

_____

What could you have done so it would not have happened at all? _____

_____

_____

Solution Report

Filed by _____ Date _____

The Problem _____

_____

My / Our Solution _____

_____

_____

Esteem Builders. Jalmar Press
Rolling Hills Estates, CA

Pictorial Problem/Solution Report

 Draw a picture of what happened.

 Draw a picture of how you could have solved it.

Esteem Builders. Jalmar Press
Rolling Hills Estates, CA

Name	Date

BRAINSTORMING

Brainstorming is a way of finding possible solutions to problems. In brainstorming, you let your imagination flow. You try to come up with as many ideas as possible in a short time.

★ **Wild ideas count—let your creativity go!**

★ **No criticism or evaluation of ideas.**

★ **It's okay to add on to someone else's idea.**

First, list some problems you'd like to consider (5 minutes at the most).

1. _____   6. _____

2. _____   7. _____

3. _____   8. _____

4. _____   9. _____

5. _____   10. _____

Pick one of the above problems and brainstorm solutions to it.

PROBLEM:_____

Possible Solutions	I'd Consider	Won't Consider	Rank Order
1.			
2.			
3.			
4.			
5.			
6.			
7.			
8.			
9.			
10.			

Now, go back and check which possible solutions you'd consider doing. Rank order *only the ones you'd really do something about* and mark them in order of your first, second and third choice.

Esteem Builders. Jalmar Press
Rolling Hills Estates, CA

Strategy Sheet of Solution Consequences

In the last exercise, you ranked solutions to a problem you wished to do something about. Then you picked one of the problems and brainstormed solutions. Check to see if your ideas will work. In the spaces below list the top three solutions you chose before. Brainstorm what might happen with each solution if you choose to do it.

Solution 1
_____

Consequences:

1. _____
2. _____
3. _____
4. _____
5. _____

Solution 2
_____

Consequences:

1. _____
2. _____
3. _____
4. _____
5. _____

Solution 3
_____

Consequences:

1. _____
2. _____
3. _____
4. _____
5. _____

After considering the consequences, which solution do you think would be the best choice?

Individual or Team: _____   Date: _____

Esteem Builders. Jalmar Press
Rolling Hills Estates, CA

Super Sleuth Book Report

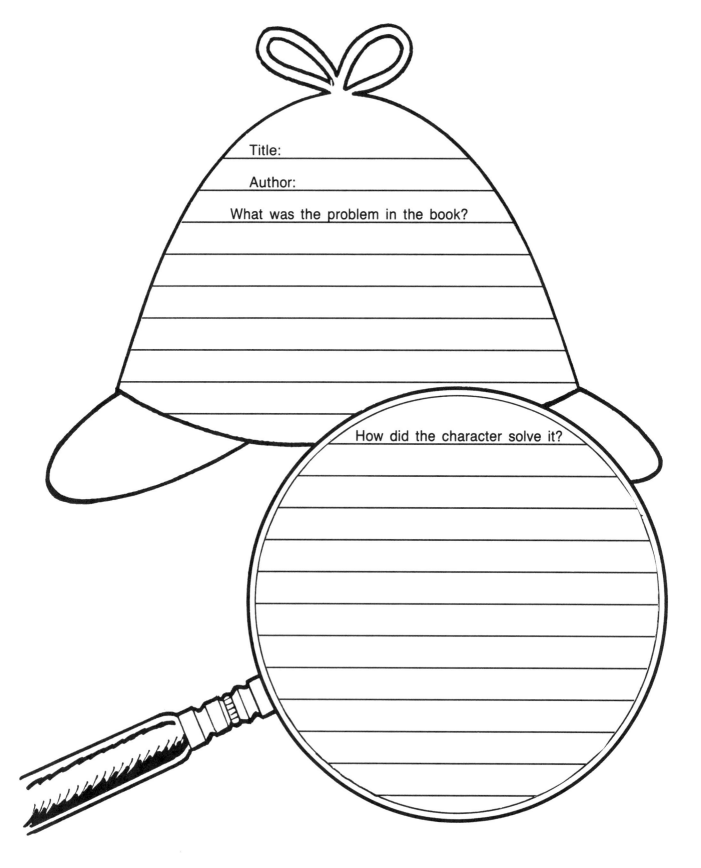

Title:

Author:

What was the problem in the book?

How did the character solve it?

Esteem Builders. Jalmar Press
Rolling Hills Estates, CA

Name   Date

PROBLEM MAP

TITLE:

SETTING:

STATEMENT OF THE PROBLEM:

POSSIBLE SOLUTION 1:

POSSIBLE SOLUTION 2:

POSSIBLE SOLUTION 3:

POSSIBLE SOLUTION 4:

STATEMENT OF THE SOLUTION:

Esteem Builders. Jalmar Press
Rolling Hills Estates, CA

My Progress

Name: _____ Subject: _____

Date	Color in the number you got correct																														
	5	6	7	8	9	10	11	12	13	14	15	16	17	18	19	20	21	22	23	24	25	26	27	28	29	30	31	32	33	34	35

— 244 —

Esteem Builders. Jalmar Press
Rolling Hills Estates, CA

Graphing Progress

Name: _____

Date Started: _____

Subject: _____

Keep a record of your progress. Plot the number correct for each date attempted.

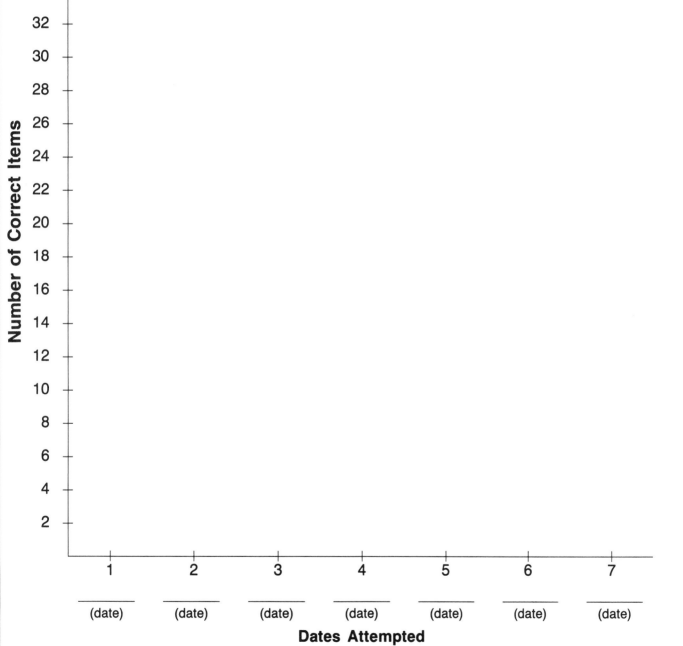

Number of Correct Items

38 +
36
34
32
30
28
26
24
22
20
18
16
14
12
10
8
6
4
2

1	2	3	4	5	6	7
(date)	(date)	(date)	(date)	(date)	(date)	(date)

Dates Attempted

Adapted from: Robert Reasoner *Building Self-Esteem* (Palo Alto: Consulting Psychologists Press, 1982)

Esteem Builders. Jalmar Press
Rolling Hills Estates, CA

Name	Date

Beat the Clock

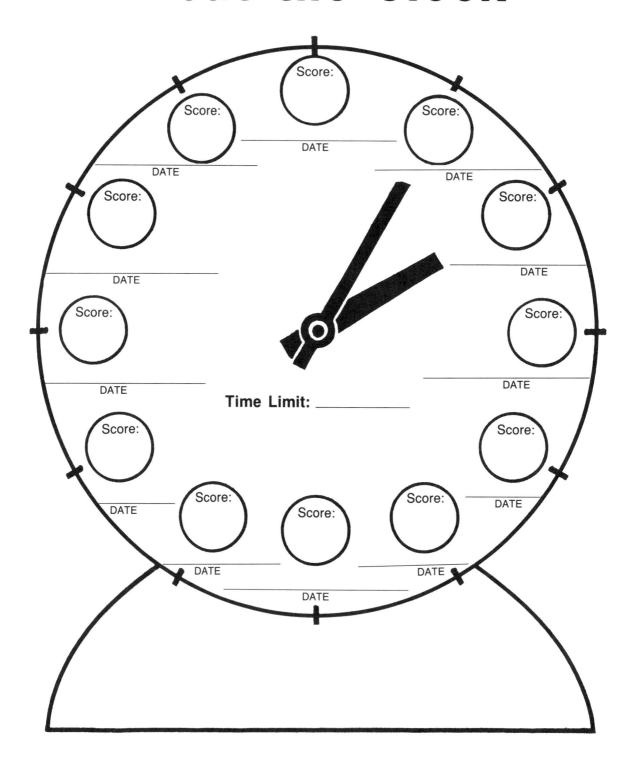

Score:

Score:

Score:

DATE

Score:

DATE

Score:

DATE

DATE

Score:

Score:

DATE

Score:

DATE

Time Limit: _____

Score:

Score:

Score:

DATE

DATE

DATE

Score:

Score:

DATE

DATE

DATE

Keep track of your progress. Begin in the one o'clock position where the minute arrow is pointing. Inside the circle, write the number of correct items you attained within the time limit. Write the date you achieved them on the line provided below the number. Continue to keep track of your progress, moving clockwise around the circle.

Esteem Builders. Jalmar Press
Rolling Hills Estates, CA

Name	Date

Homework Assignments

SUBJECT	ASSIGNMENT	DUE DATE	DONE

Esteem Builders. Jalmar Press
Rolling Hills Estates, CA

GOAL-SETTING
STEP-BY-STEP

1. **Start**
   What do you want to aim for?
   What would you like to be better in?

2. **Plan**
   How will you do it?
   What things will you need to help you?
   Who will you need to help you?
   When will you start?

3. **Measure**
   Where are you now?
   How far do you need to go?
   Can you reach your goal? Or is it too high?
   Too low?

10   20   30   40   5

10   20   30   40   5

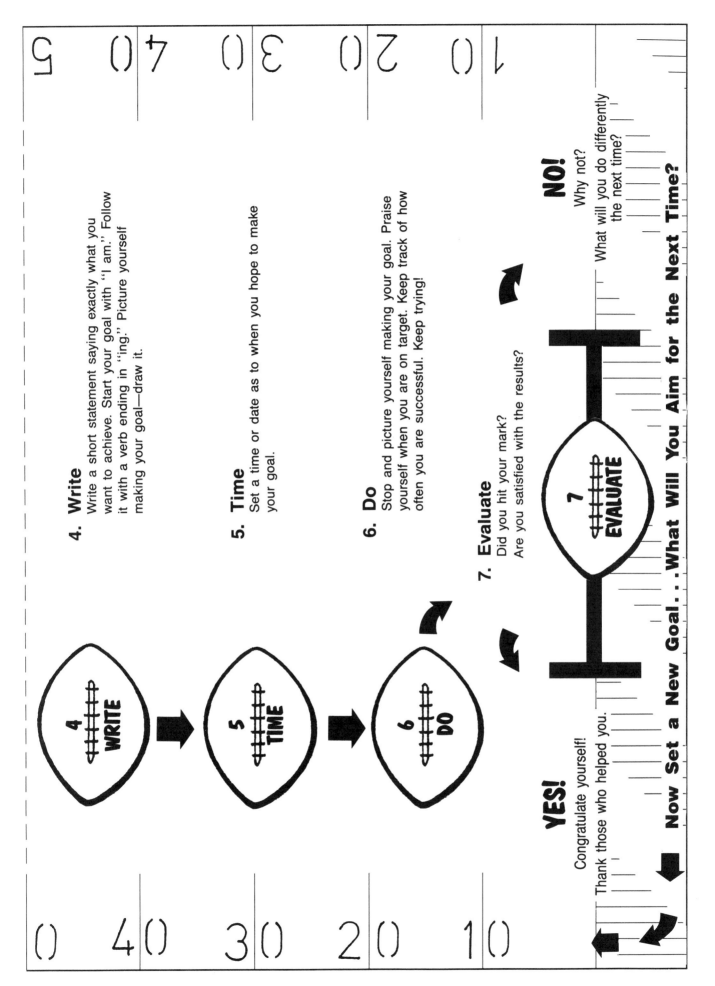

4. Write
Write a short statement saying exactly what you want to achieve. Start your goal with "I am." Follow it with a verb ending in "ing." Picture yourself making your goal—draw it.

5. Time
Set a time or date as to when you hope to make your goal.

6. Do
Stop and picture yourself making your goal. Praise yourself when you are on target. Keep track of how often you are successful. Keep trying!

7. Evaluate
Did you hit your mark?
Are you satisfied with the results?

YES!
Congratulate yourself!
Thank those who helped you.

NO!
Why not?
What will you do differently the next time?

Now Set a New Goal...What Will You Aim for the Next Time?

Group Goal-setting

Team _____

This week our goal

is _____

_____

_____

_____

_____

_____

We think our score

will be _____

_____

Date: _____

How many minutes

did it take us?

_____

	Mon.	Tues.	Wed.	Thurs.	Fri.
10+					
10					
9					
8					
7					
6					
5					
4					
3					
2					
1					

Esteem Builders. Jalmar Press
Rolling Hills Estates, CA

Name _____   Date _____

Goal-setting: Charting the Course

1 START

2 PLAN

3 MEASURE

4 WRITE

5 TIME

6 DO

7 EVALUATE

1. Aim: _____

_____

2. Steps: _____

_____

_____

Help needed: _____

Things needed: _____

Starting date: _____

3. Where I am now: _____

_____

Where I want to be: _____

_____

4. Goal (be specific): I _____

_____

_____

5. I plan to complete my goal by: _____

_____

6. My progress: _____

_____

_____

7. Results: _____

8. Next step: _____

Esteem Builders. Jalmar Press
Rolling Hills Estates, CA

| Name | Date |

Overcoming Obstacles to Goals

1. Reaffirm your goal for yourself. What do you want to shoot for?

   _____

   _____

2. What are the "RED FLAGS" that may stop you from reaching your goal?

   _____

   _____

   _____

3. What can you do to overcome these red flags?

   _____

   _____

   _____

4. **Goal Deadline**

   I will try to make this goal by _____

   _____
   Student Signature

   _____
   Date

Esteem Builders. Jalmar Press
Rolling Hills Estates, CA

Name _____ Date _____

Climbing High Contract

My goal is:

_____
_____
_____
_____

Steps I need to do to get there:

_____
_____
_____
_____
_____
_____
_____

Who or what I need to help me:

_____
_____
_____
_____

I will try to make my goal by_____
                                        Date

Esteem Builders. Jalmar Press
Rolling Hills Estates, CA

Name   Date

Daily Goal-setting

This is my goal for today:

I _____

_____

DATE: _____ SIGNED: _____

This is me making my goal.

This is how I did.

☐ I did not make my goal today.

     This is because I _____

_____

_____

     This is what I can do differently so I will make my goal tomorrow: _____

_____

_____

☐ I made my goal.

     Tomorrow my new goal will be:_____

_____

Esteem Builders. Jalmar Press
Rolling Hills Estates, CA

Weekly Goal Card

Goal: I want... _____ _(what I'm aiming for)_ _____ _____	Weekly Progress	MADE IT	ALMOST!	MISSED
Steps: I will... _____ _(what I must do to make it)_ _____ _____	Monday			
Resources: I need... _____ _(who or what I need to help)_ _____	Tuesday			
_____	Wednesday			
Completion date: _____ _(when I will reach it)_ _____	Thursday			
Signed:_____	Friday			

Front

Goal-setting Steps

1. START: What am I aiming for?
2. PLAN: Steps I take to make it.
              Who and what I need to
              help me get there.
              When will I start?
3. MEASURE: Where am I now?
              How far do I want to go?
4. WRITE: I am brief.
              I start with I.
              I draw myself making it.
5. TIME: When will I make my goal?
6. DO: I must try it.
              I picture myself making it.
              I praise myself.
              I keep trying.
7. EVALUATE: Did I hit my mark?
   Yes: I congratulate myself.
              I thank those who helped.
              I set a new goal.
   No: I ask: Why not? I try again.

Weekly Goal Card

A picture of me making my goal.

Name:_____

Back

Esteem Builders. Jalmar Press
Rolling Hills Estates, CA

Name				Date		

Record of Weekly Goals

SUBJECT	GOALS	Missed It	Almost	Made It

Esteem Builders. Jalmar Press
Rolling Hills Estates, CA

Name   Date

Goal Wheel

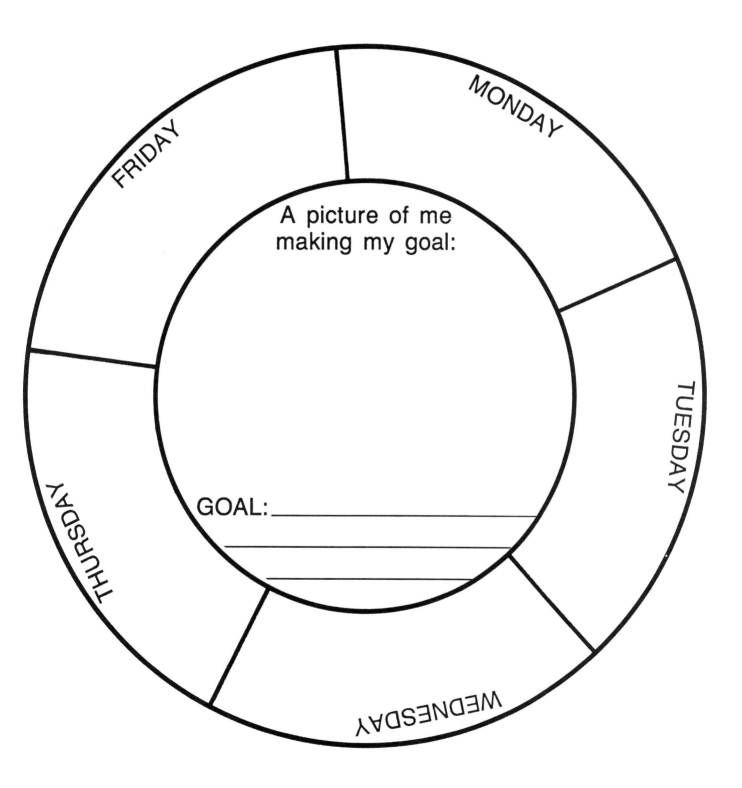

FRIDAY

MONDAY

THURSDAY

TUESDAY

WEDNESDAY

A picture of me
making my goal:

GOAL:_____

_____

_____

Esteem Builders. Jalmar Press
Rolling Hills Estates, CA

Goal-setting Steps

1. **START:** What are you aiming for?

2. **PLAN:** How will you do it?
   Steps: Who and what do you need to help you make it?
   Starting date?

3. **MEASURE:** Where I am now.
   Where I want to go.

4. **WRITE:** Be brief.
   Start with "I am" and include an "ing" verb.
   Draw yourself making the goal.

5. **TIME:** When will you make your goal?

6. **DO:** Try it!
   Stop and picture yourself making it.
   Praise yourself when on target.
   Keep track of your successes.
   Keep trying!

7. **EVALUATE:** Did you hit your mark?
   Yes: Congratulate yourself!
   Thank those who helped you.
   Set a new goal.
   No: Why not?
   What will you do differently next time?
   Try again or set a new goal.

ACHIEVED

GOAL

GOAL PASSBOOK for

Esteem Builders. Jalmar Press
Rolling Hills Estates, CA

GOALS

GOALS ACHIEVED

Fold up

Fold up

— 259 —

Esteem Builders. Jalmar Press
Rolling Hills Estates, CA

Goal Passbook Cards

My Target ◎

I will_____
(tell what you will do)

_____

_____

I will reach my target by: _____
(time or date)

_____

Signed:_____

Date:_____

A picture of me hitting my target.

Front

Goal Card

Goal:_____

_____

Steps:_____

_____

_____

Resources:_____

_____

Completion date: _____

Signed:_____

Date:_____

Goal Picture

This is a picture of myself making my goal.

Back

Esteem Builders. Jalmar Press
Rolling Hills Estates, CA

Name _____ Date _____

GOAL RESULTS

Today I am going to try to _____

_____

Each time I remember, I will color the △ .

Each time I forget, I will color the ○ .

I Remembered	**I Forgot**
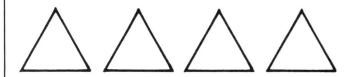  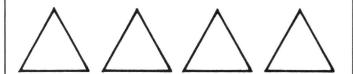	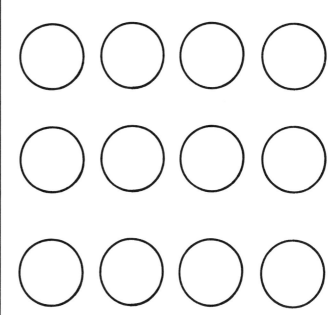
I remembered _____ times.	I forgot _____ times.

GOAL RESULTS

Name _____

Date _____

Goal _____

Each time you are successful in your goal, put a check mark in the "I Made It" column. Each time you are unsuccessful, mark the "I Missed It" column.

I MISSED IT					
I MADE IT					

Esteem Builders. Jalmar Press
Rolling Hills Estates, CA

Name _____ Date _____

I think I can _____

Color a car each time you make your goal.

I Thought I Could!

Goal

Goal Achievement

I made my goal of: _____

To achieve it I had to: _____

When I made it I felt: _____

I (learned, discovered, relearned) this about myself: _____

Signed: _____
Witness: _____
Date: _____

Goal Achievement

I made my goal of: _____

To achieve it I had to: _____

When I made it I felt: _____

I (learned, discovered, relearned) this about myself: _____

Signed: _____
Witness: _____
Date: _____

Esteem Builders. Jalmar Press
Rolling Hills Estates, CA

A Month of Goals

Directions:
1. Fill in the dates for the current month.
2. At the beginning of the day, write your goal in the first available square.
3. At the end of the day, check yourself to see if you made or missed your goal.
4. If you made your goal, write a new goal for yourself tomorrow.
   If you missed your goal, rethink and rewrite your goal tomorrow so you can be successful.

Goalsetter:_____ Month:_____

Goal for the Month:_____

MONDAY	TUESDAY	WEDNESDAY	THURSDAY	FRIDAY
Goal:	Goal:	Goal:	Goal:	Goal:
Goal:	Goal:	Goal:	Goal:	Goal:
Goal:	Goal:	Goal:	Goal:	Goal:
Goal:	Goal:	Goal:	Goal:	Goal:
Goal:	Goal:	Goal:	Goal:	Goal:

Esteem Builders. Jalmar Press
Rolling Hills Estates, CA

Goal Award-O-Grams

Happygram

I am happy to announce that

_____

was right on the mark in making the goal of

_____

_____

Congratulations!!!

Signed _____

Date _____

Award-O-Gram

This award is presented to _____

For achieving the goal of _____

_____

Signed _____

Date _____

**Congratulations on
a job well done!**

Esteem Builders. Jalmar Press
Rolling Hills Estates, CA

7

"I Am A Winner!": Building Competence

ESTEEM BUILDERS

- Provide Opportunities to Increase Awareness of Individual Competencies and Strengths
- Teach How to Record and Evaluate Progress
- Provide Feedback on How to Accept Weaknesses and Profit from Mistakes
- Teach the Importance of Self-Praise for Accomplishments

SUMMARY OF COMPETENCE

Definition: *A feeling of success and accomplishment in things regarded as important or valuable. Aware of strengths and able to accept weaknesses.*

SUPPORT DATA

- "Students who feel good about themselves and their abilities are the ones who are most likely to succeed." William Purkey. *Self-Concept and School Achievement* (Englewood Cliffs, NJ: Prentice-Hall, 1970).
- "Students who are unsure of themselves or who expect to fail are inclined to stop trying and just give up on school." M.C. Shaw and G.J. Alves. "The Self-Concept of Bright Academic Underachievers: Continued." *Personal and Guidance Journal* 42 (1963): 401–403.
- "Self-esteem is the one key factor that affects the level of proficiency in all fields of endeavor, including academic achievement." John Gilmore. *The Productive Personality* (San Rafael, CA: Albion, 1974).
- "Many psychologists and most educators recognize that self-esteem and achievement are related. These two phenomena, in fact, are highly related, and, as a consequence, it is impossible to distinguish the two as completely separate entities." James Battle. *Enhancing Self-Esteem and Achievement* (Seattle: Special Child Publications, 1982).

ESTEEM BUILDERS

- Provide Opportunities to Increase Awareness of Individual Competencies and Strengths
- Teach How to Record and Evaluate Progress
- Provide Feedback on How to Accept Weaknesses and Profit from Mistakes
- Teach the Importance of Self-Praise for Accomplishments

POSSIBLE INDICATORS OF WEAK COMPETENCE

- is reluctant to contribute ideas or opinions;
- is unwilling to take risks;
- acts as if helpless and is dependent in areas where he/she can or should be competent;
- acts out in areas where he/she feels incompetent by displaying frustration, withdrawal, lack of participation, resisting, defying, daydreaming, cheating;
- does not attempt many tasks because of overriding fear of failure or insecurity (displays "I can't" attitude and doesn't try);
- is a poor loser: magnifies any loss or displays poor sportsmanship;
- uses negative self-statements regarding accomplishments and may discount or discredit any achievement.

POSSIBLE INDICATORS OF STRONG COMPETENCE

- seeks out challenges, takes risks;
- accepts weaknesses and uses mistakes as a learning tool;
- is aware of strengths and positive characteristics;
- generally feels successful at things deemed important;
- eagerly shares opinions and ideas;
- displays good sportsmanship, can handle defeat;
- recognizes accomplishments and achievements, and may verbalize or internalize positive self-statements regarding them.

Most students will not conform exactly to the profiles listed above but are more likely to be stronger in some areas and weaker in others. In order to determine the degree to which a student feels competent, complete the student self-esteeem assessment (B-SET) chart located in Appendix II. The chart may be referred to periodically or updated as a way of measuring progress. These charts are also useful in determining which activities are appropriate for your class.

Competence Activities List

Code	Grade	Title	Soc. Studies	Sci.	Writ. Lang.	Oral Lang.	Math	Art	Lit.
C1	K–4	Hobby Day Checklist	✔	✔	✔	✔			✔
C2	3–8	My Interest	✔	✔	✔	✔			✔
C3	K–8	Strength Profile			✔	✔			
C4/5	K–8	Attention!/Strength Awards			✔	✔			
C6	2–8	Class Strength Book	✔		✔	✔			
C7	K–8	Student Strength Book			✔	✔		✔	
C8	K–6	Strength Barbell			✔			✔	
C9	K–8	Recording Progress				✔			
C10	K–8	Favorite Work Folder			✔			✔	
C11	K–8	Friday Timed Writing Task			✔		✔		
C12	K–4	Things I Can Do			✔	✔		✔	
C13	K–8	Mastery Devices			✔		✔		
C14	K–4	Paper Chains			✔		✔	✔	
C15	1–5	Add a New Success			✔			✔	
C16	K–8	I Can			✔	✔		✔	
C17	K–2	I Know I Can!			✔	✔		✔	✔
C18	2–8	Accomplishment Journal			✔				
C19	K–8	Academic Progress Charts			✔		✔		
C20	2–8	Work Contract	✔		✔		✔		
C21	K–3	Reading Garden			✔			✔	✔
C22	1–3	Ollie Owl Book Report			✔			✔	✔
C23	2–8	Student/Teacher Conference				✔	✔		
C24	K–8	Newsflash/Proud Gram			✔				
C25	3–8	Strengths and Weaknesses	✔	✔	✔	✔			✔
C26	K–8	Accomplishment Banner			✔	✔		✔	
C27	K–8	Be a Model of Self-Talk	✔			✔			
C28	K–8	Group Praise Chants	✔			✔			
C29	K–4	Pat-on-the-Back to Me Book			✔			✔	
C30	K–3	Blue Ribbon Book			✔			✔	
C31	2–6	Now Hear This!			✔				
C32	K–8	Pride Center	✔		✔	✔		✔	
C33	K–4	Pat-on-the-Back Handprints	✔		✔	✔		✔	
C34	1–8	Design an Award	✔		✔			✔	
C35	K–8	Badges	✔		✔			✔	
C36	1–6	Fingerprints	✔	✔	✔			✔	
C37	K–4	Blue Ribbon Award	✔		✔			✔	
C38	K–4	Hanging Award	✔		✔			✔	
C39	K–8	Positive Wristbands	✔		✔			✔	
C40	K–8	Pride Center Awards	✔		✔				
C41	K–8	Books to Enhance Competence	✔						✔

Concept Circles Activities That Promote Competence

Code	Grade	Title	Grouping
CC49	K–8	Strength Book	Full
CC50	K–8	Brag Time	Full/Team
CC51	K–3	Strength Circle	Full/Team
CC52	K–3	Blue Ribbon	Full/Team
CC53	K–3	Hooray for Me	Full
CC54	2–8	One Good Thing About Me	Full/Team
CC55	2–8	Me Commercials	Full/Team
CC56	K–8	I'm Proud	Full/Team
CC57	K–3	I Thought I Could	Full/Team
CC58	K–8	I Can	Full/Team
CC59	2–8	Self-Introduction	Full/Team

School-wide Activities That Promote Competence

Code	Grade	Title
SW26/27	K–8	Book of Winners

Checklist of Educator Behaviors
That Promote COMPETENCE

Directions: For a self-evaluation of your skills in enhancing competence in your students, complete the following items:

Never 1	Sometimes 2	Frequently 3	Always 4	
				As an educator:
_____	_____	_____	_____	1. Do I provide opportunities for each student to succeed?
_____	_____	_____	_____	2. Are my expectations of my students realistic—that is, related to what each one can accomplish?
_____	_____	_____	_____	3. Do I provide opportunities for awards and recognition beyond strictly "academic achievement?"
_____	_____	_____	_____	4. Do I invite my students to expand their special talents and interests and share them with their peers?
_____	_____	_____	_____	5. Do I express confidence in my students' ability to learn and give them feedback on how to increase their competence?
_____	_____	_____	_____	6. Do I sequence subject areas in small steps so that every student has the opportunity to achieve?
_____	_____	_____	_____	7. Do I assess my students' knowledge of subject matter so that I am fully apprised of their capabilities?
_____	_____	_____	_____	8. Do I take steps to ensure that students assess their own progress and not compare themselves to others?
_____	_____	_____	_____	9. Do I encourage students to praise themselves for their accomplishments?
_____	_____	_____	_____	10. Do I provide opportunities for students to become aware of their own capabilities and strengths?

_____ + _____ + _____ + _____ = **Total:** _____

Areas I could improve in that will increase the development of competence: _____

_____

_____

7

"I Am A Winner!": Building Competence

He who thinks he can, can,
and he can't who thinks he can't.
This is an inexorable, indisputable law.
—ORISON SWEET MARDEN

The fifth and final component of self-esteem is competence. Generally, individuals acquire this feeling following frequent successes, particularly in areas considered important or highly valued.

Although every individual is a constellation of strengths and weaknesses, those with high self-esteem tend to concentrate on the former. Previous positive experiences have instilled in them a competent self-image and, as the saying goes, "success begets success." This frees up the desire to take risks and go on for more success, the previous taste of achievement still fresh on the palate. Each additional success restimulates their efforts until these individuals are filled with positive reminders that allow them to interpret themselves as winners. They hold the philosophy "I can do it!" and are willing to go the extra mile.

Students with low self-esteem have the reverse configuration: they emphasize their weaknesses and failures. Students with too few successes and frequent failures end up with little incentive to try again. The attitude of "why try, you're just going to fail again" begins to form and once crystallized, it becomes a fixed part of the self-image and hard to remold. These students feel incompetent because they believe their unsuccessful experiences are a sign of personal failure and inadequacy. The message they give to themselves is: "I am a loser."

CLASSROOM EFFECTS

According to Stanley Coopersmith[1], students who have positive feelings about themselves are motivated learners and participate more in the classroom. A student with an inner image of "loser" can hardly maintain a "receptive student" philosophy. Something has to give way during the hours confined to the classroom setting. This affects the whole learning atmosphere in the classroom. Some of the problems that arise from a lack of achievement in the classroom are student disinterest, lack of motivation and a "don't care" attitude. These behaviors are the outcome of students trying to contend internally with their negative self-perceptions.

There is more than enough evidence to show a persistent and significant relationship between self-esteem (and the feelings of competence) and behavior. Students who feel better about their own ability to perform, who generally feel competent in school work and who expect to do well, actually do better in their studies. Competence and self-esteem have an impact on school performance as

---

1. Coopersmith, Stanley. *Developing Motivation in Young Children* (New York: Albion, 1975).

— 273 —

much as on any other areas in life. Self-esteem cannot be separated from the classroom; it is an integrated part of learning itself. Coopersmith succinctly summed up how crucial competence is to eagerness to learn when he said:

Self-esteem is one of the attitudes and beliefs a person brings with him when he faces the world. It includes his beliefs as to whether he can expect success or failure, how long he can put out effort, whether he will be hurt by failure, and whether he will become more capable as a result of his experiences. In psychological terms, self-esteem provides a mental set preparing the person to respond according to expectations of success, acceptance, and personal strength. Since a child's attitudes about his abilities and expectations of success and failure are an integrated part of his school performance, it does not make much sense to treat these attitudes as something separate and unrelated to school.[2]

Winners and losers belong on an athletic field, not in the classroom. This kind of inner-categorization or polarization is far too deadly for learning. Everyone needs to feel success—especially students. All too frequently, however, school becomes another place where many students feel incompetent and inadequate. Students must feel successful in order to have self-esteem. To help create this self-portrait, the school curriculum should address issues of competency and success and how to make these a living reality for students.

A student who feels incompetent may be recognized by the following behavioral characteristics:

- is reluctant to contribute ideas or opinions;

- is unwilling to take risks;

- acts helpless and is dependent in areas where he/she can or should be competent;

- acts out in areas where he/she feels incompetent by displaying frustration, withdrawal, lack of participation, resisting, defying, daydreaming, cheating;

- does not attempt many tasks because of overriding fear of failure or insecurity (displays "I can't" attitude and doesn't try);

- is a poor loser: magnifies any loss or displays poor sportsmanship;

- uses negative self-statements regarding accomplishments and may discount or discredit any achievement.

A student who feels competent, on the other hand, is likely to display the following behaviors:

- seeks out challenges, takes risks;

- accepts weaknesses and uses mistakes as a learning tool;

- is aware of strengths and positive characteristics;

- generally feels successful at things deemed important;

- eagerly shares opinions and ideas;

- displays good sportsmanship, can handle defeat;

- recognizes accomplishments and achievements, and may verbalize or internalize positive self-statements regarding them.

Competence can be taught. The following are the four steps esteem builders may take to increase competency in the classroom:

1. Provide opportunities to increase awareness of individual competencies and strengths.

2. Teach how to record and evaluate progress.

3. Provide feedback on how to accept weaknesses and profit from mistakes.

4. Teach the importance of self-praise for accomplishments.

2. Coopersmith, Stanley. *Developing Motivation in Young Children* (New York: Albion, 1975), p. 96.

COMPETENCE

Provide Opportunities to Increase Awareness of Individual Competencies and Strengths

"In order to succeed, we must first believe we can."
—MICHAEL KORDA

We all need to feel successful and win approval from our peers. Students are no exception. Our society puts an enormous price tag on human worth and categorizes people into "have's" and "have not's." In the classroom it is those who get the gold stars versus those who don't—the reality being that not all students are capable of getting gold stars when their work is compared to students at the upper-end of the spectrum. But when one considers the statistic that the longer a student remains in school, the lower his/her self-esteem becomes, then this way of measuring ability is obviously deficient. Clearly, many students are not getting their needs met. Yet all students need, and deserve, a chance to have gold stars and happy faces decorate their papers. In light of this, one of the most challenging jobs educators face is to find avenues for *every* student to experience success.

WAYS TO PROMOTE FEELINGS OF COMPETENCE

You may find it beneficial in your classroom to provide opportunities for students to demonstrate or display nonacademic skills. This will give every student the chance to feel competent. Some suggestions are:

- *A Young Author's Day*—students display books they have written.

- *Exhibition Hall*—students demonstrate their special talents and skills, which are not necessarily recognized at school.

- *Hobby Day*—students display a special interest or hobby for others to appreciate and learn.

- *Student Teaching Day*—students have the opportunity to teach another student (or students) a particular skill.

- *Science Fair*—a display or demonstration of science projects or experiments.

- *Art Show*—display of everyone's artwork.

- *Musical Activities*—students demonstrate a musical talent, such as voice or skill on an instrument.

- *Talent Show*—students entertain with dancing, acting and comic skills.

Another positive reinforcement is to give awards and recognition for achievements that are not academic. This way every student is assured a chance for glory. These could be awards for sports, music, "most improved," quality work, effort well applied, art, citizenship, friendliness and attitude. Many students have hidden talents; the real skill of a gifted teacher is to find them.

ACTIVITIES: GROUP 1A

Grades 1–8	Hobby Day	C1/2

Purpose: To provide opportunities for students to share their interests and show "another side" of themselves to their classmates.

Materials: A display area for each student such as a long table or bulletin board area; copy of the Hobby Day Checklist (C1) or My Interest (C2) form for each participating student.

Procedure: Begin the activity by sharing a hobby of your own; this will familiarize students with the process. Set up a carrel display (by hinging together three pieces of 12" x 26" cardboard with 1 1/2" reinforced tape) or bulletin board featuring the hobby or interest. Include materials you'll need to demonstrate the skill, reference books, display of collected items, samples, etc., so that each student can interact with your hobby.

Following your demonstration, invite students to share an interest or hobby of their own:

1. Make copies of either C1 Hobby Day Checklist (Grades 1–5) or C2 My Interest (Grades 3–8).

COMPETENCE

2. For younger students, include an explanation for the parents so that they may help at home.

3. Arrange a time when each student can display his/her hobby to the class. All you need is a display table.

You may either have an individual Hobby Day for each student or a combined one when all hobbies are on display. Arrange for students to teach their classmates about their hobby. The student tells why he/she chose the hobby and where to gather information about it. You could invite another class to view the display.

Present a C1/2 Hobby Day award to each student who contributes his/her hobby.

ACTIVITIES: GROUP 1B

These activities are designed to reinforce an inner self-image of "I am capable." It is usually not enough to ask a student, "Tell me what your strengths are," because most students don't know.

To introduce these activities, inform the class that they are going to be studying their strengths. Explain that each of them has special "magic" inside—magic that they might not even be aware of. (Adjust language according to grade level.) This magic is called "strength" because it is what makes us powerful inside. Tell them that every day for the next week or so they will be doing fun tasks to help bring out their strengths, or magic.

| Grades K–8 | Strength Profile | C3 |

Materials: A copy of C3 Strength Profile for each student.

Procedure: A week or two before beginning the class project, make a study of your students' attributes (strengths). Use the Strength Profile to keep an on-going record of each student's strengths and competencies. Try to find at least one strength for each area as noted on the profile. Use other staff members as resources, if needed. You may also want to send home a note to parents asking them what they think are their child's strong points or attributes. You will use all this information to increase the student's awareness. You may do this a number of ways:

1. Verbalize to the student: "I've discovered one of your strengths today, Billy. You really are becoming quite good in your printing. Look how you're staying in the lines." Try to be as specific as possible. Give concrete evidence.

2. Write a comment on a positive discovery you've made about the student in his/her Journal, such as the Teacher-Student Letter Exchange (S1 and J13).

3. Send an Attention! or Strength Award (C4,5).

| Grades K–8 | Attention!/Strength Awards | C4/5 |

Materials: Copies of the Attention! (C4) and Strength Awards (C5).

Procedure: As you discover a student's strength, fill out one of the awards and present it to him/her. Try to be specific in listing the strength so that the student will know exactly to what you are referring. If the strength can be found on a paper the student has done, you may choose to staple the award to the actual paper and then circle the parts that reveal his/her strength.

Encourage students to present awards to one another as well.

| Grades 2–8 | Class Strength Book | C6 |

Purpose: To encourage students to become aware of their own strengths as well as those of others.

Materials: For each book use C6 Strength Book form and 2 pieces of 8 1/2" x 11" light-colored construction paper; stapler or spiral binding.

Procedure:

1. Copy C6 Strength Book form onto light-colored construction paper for the cover. Cut a similar-size page for the back.

2. Laminate the pages for greater durability, or cover with contact paper.

COMPETENCE

3. Insert plain paper (one sheet for each student) between the covers and staple or spiral bind.

4. Print the name of a different student on the bottom left-hand corner of each page.

5. Encourage students to discover their own strengths as well as those of their classmates. They record their discovery on the page with that student's name on it. You may want to do a strength evaluation circle at the end of each day where students disclose their findings. Keep the book accessible for further notations as they occur.

Grades K–8 Student Strength Book C7

Purpose: To increase students' awareness of their individual strengths.

Materials: For each Strength Book:
- a few pages of plain paper (8 1/2" x 11");
- 2 pieces 8 1/2" x 11" light-colored construction paper.

Procedure: Make individual books as per the instructions in C6 Class Strength Book. Older students may wish to make their own. Students record their own strength discoveries inside their private book.

Younger, nonwriting students may dictate or draw their strengths.

Older students may record their strengths on a 5" x 8" index card. Encourage them to keep the card in a convenient folder so that they have access to it at any time.

Grades K–6 Strength Barbell C8

Purpose: To increase students' awareness of their individual strengths.

Materials: C8 Strength Barbell pattern; light-colored construction paper or tagboard (at least 19" long); scissors, thick black marking pens.

Pattern Construction: Trace the half barbell pattern onto heavy tagboard or light-colored construction paper. Extend the pattern by turning the shape in a semicircle so that it matches the dotted lines. Continue to trace the pattern so that you now have a complete 19" barbell. Cut out one for each student.

Procedure: Students edge their barbell with black marking pens. On the left-hand circle of the barbell, students write or dictate their strengths. They print their first and last name along the bar. In the right-hand circle they draw/illustrate one of their strengths. They may also glue a photograph or a cutout from a magazine.

This activity is very suitable for a bulletin board display with the caption, "Look At Our Strengths."

ESTEEM BUILDER #2

Teach How to Record and Evaluate Progress

"Always remember that your own resolution to succeed is more important than anything else."
—ABRAHAM LINCOLN

We all need to think we're improving, getting better at something—progressing! Knowing that we're doing well causes us to forge ahead and make continued efforts. Awareness that we're improving is like a "pat on the back" to keep trying. Students, like adults, need to see improvement, especially in school-related subjects where growth is being measured constantly.

For some students a report card is all that is necessary as a reminder of individual progress. Good grades also act as an incentive as they are very tangible evidence of competence in that area. Those students who consistently get good grades most likely have a sense of worth because they feel rewarded for their efforts.

For other students, however, a report card is just another failure, and once a semester is far too frequent a reminder. Students with a low sense of competence continually come face to face with blocks to progress. The sad fact is that they may indeed be making noticeable growth in a difficult subject

COMPETENCE

— 277 —

area, but the growth is never realized. It's hard to feel competent if your measure of improvement is to compare it to the progress of a top student.

A student with low competence *must be shown progress in highly concrete terms.* A positive comment on a report once a semester is not frequent enough. It's important to break down skills into small components so that students can actually witness their improvement. If students are not improving, they need to be shown how they can turn their weaknesses into strengths. This is the focus in Esteem Builder #3.

Finally, it is crucial that *these students compare their current work only to* their own *previous work—never to the work of their classmates.* Cross comparisons defeat the purpose of the esteem builder's work.

Whether a student has high or low self-esteem, everyone benefits from seeing individual improvement in subject areas. It is fundamental to building and maintaining a self-image of competence and adequacy. Because it is time-consuming to have conferences on a frequent basis, an alternative and powerful esteem builder is to teach each student to record his/her own progress. Students begin to recognize for themselves that they are actually improving!

ACTIVITIES: GROUP 2

The following activities help students record and measure their progress and accomplishments.

| Grades K-8 | Recording Progress | C9 |

Purpose: To allow students to "listen to" their own progress.

Materials: A blank tape cassette per student; tape recorder.

Procedure: Each student brings to school a blank cassette tape from home. Every week students record their progress in an academic area to "hear about" their abilities. Try any area: auditory memory—poetry, rhymes; oral language—reading a passage from a book, original storytelling, interview with a friend, etc.

| Grades K-8 | Favorite Work Folder | C10 |

Purpose: To increase students' visual awareness of their growth both in skill and academics.

Materials: 2 pieces tagboard per folder (10" x 12" for older students; 13" x 19" for younger students), or construction paper if it is laminated; 45" yarn lengths per folder; stapler, hole-punch, crayons or marking pens; glue and construction paper scraps.

Procedure: Staple or punch the tagboard strips along the two short lengths and one long length. If hole-punched, lace through the holes and tie at the end. Older students make their own; younger students require supervision. Students design the cover themselves.

Each week students choose the paper they are most proud of and place it inside the work folder. You may also wish to provide a bulletin board of "Our Proud Moments" where students each place one paper of their choice.

Older students should be required to keep track of their own progress in a particular subject area. They turn in their folders to the teacher at each grading period to show evidence of growth.

COMPETENCE

| Grades K-8 | **Friday Timed Writing Task** | **C11** |

Purpose: To increase students' awareness of their progress in writing skills.

Materials: A folder for each student to store completed weekly task (manila or cardstock is preferred for durability); writing or plain paper according to grade level; timer.

Procedure: At the beginning of the school year, set a goal you'd like each student to work toward. It might be to write his/her name, draw a person with all the body parts, write a sentence with proper punctuation, write a story, etc.

Each Friday, bring out a timer and set it for a particular time (the shorter the better—for example, five minutes). Students do the task until the timer goes off. At the stroke of the bell, the task stops. Students date their work and compare it to the previous week's task, which is stored in the folder.

| Grades K-4 | **Things I Can Do** | **C12** |

Purpose: To enable younger students to keep track of their accomplishments and skill developments.

Materials: Marking pens and crayons; stapler.

For each booklet:

- 12" x 18" piece of colored construction paper folded in half to form a cover;

- several pieces plain drawing paper stapled inside the cover.

Procedure: Students keep track of their progress by dictating, drawing, writing or gluing in photographs of their accomplishments or significant milestones. These could include mastering fractions, finishing reading a book, learning to tie a shoe, remembering to take homework assignments home...whatever is appropriate.

| Grades K-8 | **Mastery Devices** | **C13** |

Purpose: To help students keep track of their own progress in particular academic skills.

Materials: An ample supply of 3" x 5" cards; stapler, marking pens or black crayons. Choose one of the following storing devices for each student:

Alphabet Book. Small spiral-bound notebook divided into 26 parts for the alphabet. Student writes an alphabet letter on the first page of each part. Student prints words that he/she masters under the appropriate letter.

Alphabet/Fact Box. Student brings a shoe box or recipe box from home. Include alphabet dividers if using for spelling/word usage.

Word Pack. A 12" x 9" piece of tagboard folded up 3" from the bottom and stapled along open edges of folded sections for "pockets."

Word Envelope. An 8 1/2" x 11" envelope with 2 stationery-sized envelopes inside.

Procedure: Each time students encounter new concepts—be it math facts, colors, reading vocabulary, sounds or spelling words—they keep track of their progress.

Day One: Students write the new words or facts on pre-cut construction paper or 3" x 5" cards: one fact per card. They put all the facts they need to learn in the Word Pack or Word Envelope on the "To Learn" side. If they don't use a box or envelope, students may keep their cards together with rubber bands—one with a slip of paper saying "To Learn," the other with a slip of paper saying "I Mastered."

Day Two: Each time students have a few spare minutes they practice the facts/words. As they master the facts (can spell, recite from memory) they may transfer the cards to the "I Mastered" (or "I Know") side.

Test Day: As you check (orally or written) each concept and verify that it has been mastered, students may 1) add the concepts alphabetically to their Alphabet Box, 2) store the cards in the Word Envelope or 3) write the words/facts in a spiral bound notebook.

Grades K–4	**Paper Chains**	C14

Purpose: To provide students with visual, tangible evidence of their progress in specific skills (academic or behavior).

Materials: An ample supply of light-colored construction paper cut into 1" x 5" lengths; glue or stapler; writing instrument.

Note: Younger students may wish to draw their accomplishments on paper pre-cut into 3" x 7" strips.

Procedure: Stock an activity center with numerous 1" x 5" paper strips. As students complete academic work, they write on a paper strip the name of the book, the word, the math page completed, the phonics mastered or the project they've finished.

Students then glue the ends of their first paper strip together to form a ring. They pass the next strip through the ring and glue it together to begin a

chain. As students add new links to their paper chains, they will have tangible proof of accomplishments.

Display chains in the classroom at a height each student can easily reach. Encourage students to take responsibility for keeping their paper chains up-to-date.

Grades 1–5	**Add a New Success**	C15

Purpose: To provide students with the opportunity to write or draw their accomplishments.

Materials: 45" length of adding machine tape for each student or strips of butcher paper cut into 45" x 3" lengths (add more lengths by gluing on strips); writing instruments or crayons.

Procedure: Students keep a record of individual achievements on a roll of adding machine tape. As they accomplish a new achievement, they write or draw the success on the next available space on the tape roll. This is kept rolled up (with the writing on the inside) except for the last written record, which is folded back and clipped with a paper clip. Periodically review students' successes by rolling out the length.

Grades K–8	**I Can**	C16

Purpose: To increase students' awareness of their capabilities.

Materials: Soup-size (12 oz.) cans, cleaned and tops carefully removed (1 for each student); copies of larger I Can label for each student; ample supply of smaller I Can tickets; marking pens or crayons, glue, scissors.

Procedure: Begin by collecting clean cans. Students cut out the I Can label and glue it around their can. Students may include a picture of themselves on the label.

Place cans in a convenient location. Have a large supply of I Can tickets on hand. Each time students accomplish something, or recognize a new capability of theirs, they fill out an I Can ticket and place it in the can. This could be done daily or spontaneously when the occasion arises.

COMPETENCE

<table>
<tr><td>Grades
K–2</td><td>I Know I Can!</td><td>C17</td></tr>
</table>

Purpose: To teach students the power of "self-talk." To help students visualize their progress.

Materials: *The Little Engine That Could*, Watty Piper (Scholastic, 1979); colored construction paper cut into 12" x 4 1/2" lengths, several pieces for each student; C17 train patterns; stapler, pencil, scissors and glue; scraps of construction paper.

Procedure: The classic *The Little Engine That Could* is an excellent model for students because it teaches the power of "self-talk."

To show students their progress, make individual scrapbooks by binding together several sheets of similar colored construction paper (12" x 4 1/2"). Cut out the train patterns onto cardstock-weight paper for students to use as templates.

For the cover, glue on a cutout engine pattern, the "smoke" and one additional car pattern next to the engine. Glue the student's photo inside the engine cab.

Each time a student achieves a major classroom goal—such as "I can count to a 100"—he/she traces the train pattern onto bright-colored construction paper and glues it to one of the inside pages of the scrapbook.

Write the goal achieved in pen on the train car. (Older students may write it themselves.) Write the month and date of achievement on the wheels, which have been cut and glued below the car. As the student makes new achievements, add more cars to the train.

<table>
<tr><td>Grades
2–8</td><td>Accomplishment Journal</td><td>C18</td></tr>
</table>

Purpose: To provide students with the opportunity to keep a written log of their accomplishments.

Materials: For each journal: several copies of C18 Accomplishment Journal form; 2 pieces of light-colored 8 1/2" x 11" construction paper; stapler.

Procedure: Staple the C18 Accomplishment Journal form between the construction paper covers. Students may decorate their covers with marking pens. Each day students record their accomplishments and successes by filling out the form.

Note: For more activities on journals, see Chapter 9, Journal Writing.

<table>
<tr><td>Grades
K–8</td><td>Academic Progress Charts</td><td>C19</td></tr>
</table>

Purpose: To aid students in evaluating their own progress in specific academic areas.

Materials: Manila folder for each student; progress charts for each subject area to be recorded; a box to store students' folders.

Procedure: Students like to know they are improving when they're working hard at a task. They should play an active role in charting their own progress. At the beginning of the school year, give each student a manila folder with their name written across the top. Students keep these in an accessible location so they may be used often. Create separate charts for different subject areas (see illustration for ideas).

COMPETENCE

Grades 2–8	Work Contract	C20

Purpose: To increase students' responsibility in keeping track of their individual school assignments.

Materials: A copy of C20 Work Contract form for every student each week.

Procedure: Students write down individual school assignments in the proper columns. As they complete an assignment, they check it off in the appropriate column and the teacher initials it.

Grades K–3	Reading Garden	C21

Purpose: To increase students' awareness of their reading growth.

Materials: Green construction paper; pink, yellow or blue construction paper cut into 9" circles; pins or staples; ditto master of a petal shape run off on bright-colored construction paper; scissors, thin-tipped black marking pen, crayons and pink chalk.

Procedure: "Reading Flowers" are proud reminders to students of their reading successes.

1. On your ditto include the words "title" and "author." Run the petals off on construction paper for students' use.

2. To make the rest of the flower, instruct students to cut out a large construction paper circle. They may decorate it as a flower face, using crayons and cut paper, and adding "cheeks" by smudging pink chalk on the flower face.

3. Students use the green construction paper to cut the stem and the leaves. As students complete a book, they fill out the "flower petal" and attach it to the flower center.

Display the flowers around the room and watch them grow!

Grades 1–3	Ollie Owl Book Report	C22

Purpose: To increase students' awareness of their success in reading.

Materials: Copies of the two C22 Ollie Owl Book Report forms; yellow construction paper; crayons or marking pens; stapler, scissors; paper plates cut in half.

Procedure: Photocopy Ollie Owl onto yellow construction paper. Cut him out for students to color with crayons or markers. Staple half of a paper plate at the staple marks. Each time students read a book, they fill out an Ollie Owl Book Report and put it in Ollie's pocket. (Nonwriting students may dictate their answers.)

COMPETENCE

Provide Feedback on How to Accept Weaknesses and Profit from Mistakes

"Failure is the only opportunity to more intelligently begin again."
—HENRY FORD

How right he was! If we want to improve in a given area, we must first know what we can do better and what we did incorrectly before. Feedback is a major source of help in improving an individual's performance by allowing him/her to identify problems.

Research has shown that when teachers wrote specific comments of encouragement on tests or other written assignments, those students improved on the next test. Students who did not receive comments failed to improve on the next test. This was true for both good and poor students.

By receiving feedback from educators, students know specifically what to do in order to improve. Educators therefore play a significant role in increasing students' sense of competence when they provide them with specific pointers on how to improve in academic or behavior areas. This also helps them learn to profit from mistakes.

WAYS TO PROMOTE TEACHER/STUDENT DIALOGUE

The following guidelines are ways to build rapport between teacher and student with the purpose of improving students' performance and consequently their feeling of competence:

- **Highlight Progress.** A yellow highlighter pen is a useful feedback device. As you correct students' work, highlight the specific parts of the paper that show improvement or growth. Periodically allow a student to use a yellow crayon to highlight what he/she considers was best in the paper and turn it in to you.

- **Feedback Sentences.** As you correct students' work, write specific messages as often as you're able. These messages should tell the student where he/she is improving and what you like about the work. Point out where you see growth occurring.

- **Feedback Conferences.** Set up specific times when you and the student can evaluate school progress together. See C23 Teacher/Student Conference form, which you can use as a guide for feedback discussions. Students need to know where you see them progressing and what they need to do to improve.

- **Feedback Messages.** Make copies of C24 Newsflash award for students and Proud Gram for parents. Periodically write a specific feedback message to the student and/or parents mentioning the progress you've observed.

ACTIVITIES: GROUP 3

The following activities provide opportunities to give feedback to students as well as to assess their strengths and weaknesses.

Grades 2–8	Student/Teacher Conference C23

Purpose: To create a dialogue between student and teacher. To guide students on ways to improve.

Materials: Copy of C23 Student/Teacher Conference form for each student.

Procedure: This activity allows both the student and the teacher not only to track progress but to create a dialogue on how to turn weaknesses into strengths. The teacher reviews the progress made in a particular subject, makes an appropriate comment and offers ways to improve.

The student in turn makes his/her own statement about the work. This way student and teacher are in direct communication.

Grades K–8	Newsflash/Proud Gram C24

Purpose: To give feedback to students and parents in recognition of improvement.

Materials: Copies of Newsflash and Proud Gram.

COMPETENCE

Procedure: Fill in and send to students and parents when appropriate. Keep a record so that each student and their parents receive at least one a quarter.

| Grades 3–8 | **Strengths and Weaknesses** | **C25** |

Purpose: To enhance students' awareness of their own strengths and weaknesses, and help them build on their strengths. To help students reflect on what self-changes they could make.

Materials: A copy of C25 Strengths and Weaknesses worksheet for each student.

Discussion: Begin the activity by discussing that everyone has weak points and nobody can be good at everything, even though it may appear so. Some people are able to turn their weak points into assets that help them accomplish significant things in their life. Consider using the following historical characters to illustrate:

- *Demosthenes (one of the great orators of Ancient Greece)* was said to have a weak voice and a stutter, both of which he overcame.

- *Thomas Edison (an outstanding inventor)* was deaf.

- *Winston Churchill (British prime minister and statesman)* flunked the sixth grade!

- *Albert Einstein (a scientific genius)* only started speaking at age four and didn't learn to read until much later.

Share with students Victor and Mildred Goertzel's *Cradles of Eminence* (Little Brown & Co., 1962), which outlines 400 of the most gifted individuals of the century. According to their discoveries, 300 of these had suffered in some way during their childhood and the remaining 100 were physically handicapped! What made the difference was that some significant other discovered their strengths at an early age and helped them overcome their limitations.

Procedure: Following this discussion, students reflect on their own strengths and weaknesses and then fill out the worksheet. The areas students want to change become future accomplishments. Encourage them to build on their strengths in a follow-up discussion.

| Grades K–8 | **Accomplishment Banner** | **C26** |

Purpose: To provide students with the opportunity to think about things they can do well as well as areas in which they would like to improve.

Materials: For each banner:

- light-colored construction paper;
- tagboard circle patterns: 9", 5 1/2", 3 1/2";
- colored tagboard cut into banner size strips: 12 1/2" x 29 1/2";
- letter stencils;
- scissors, glue, narrow-tipped marking pens or crayons.

COMPETENCE

Procedure: Begin by tracing the 12" x 29 1/2" banner onto colored tagboard. Cut out the pattern. Trace the three circle patterns onto light-colored construction paper and cut them out. Using a thin-tipped black marking pen, students write the following phrases along the border of each circle:

9" circle: Things I'm Good At
5 1/2" circle: What I Want to Get Better At
3 1/2" circle: Me

After reflecting on (and perhaps verbalizing) each topic, students begin to color pictorial representation for the subject. They write a one-word description under each picture, using the marking pen. They glue the circles in descending order of size on the banner. Students may wish to further decorate their banners by including their names made from letter stencils traced and cut onto construction paper.

══════ ESTEEM BUILDER #4 ══════

Teach the Importance of Self-Praise for Accomplishments

"But, dear Biddy, how smart you are!"
"Yes, dear Pip."
"And Joe, how smart you are."
"Yes, dear old Pip, old chap."
—CHARLES DICKENS

There are many strategies and activities that can help to build a student's feeling of competence. However, no esteem builder is as powerful as the one that teaches self-praise for accomplishments. We can provide opportunities for success and praise students' achievements from morning until night, but in the end, the student must become responsible for his/her own self-esteem.

It is important, therefore, to gradually move away from being the external reinforcer so that the student can assume the role of self-reinforcer. Self-esteem must become internalized in order for it to truly take root. Once students are able to see their accomplishments, and praise themselves for them, then competence naturally follows and the five-fold self-esteem cycle is complete.

ACTIVITIES: GROUP 4

The following activities teach students how to praise themselves as well as allow ample opportunities for them to "blow their own horns."

Grades K–8 | **Be a Model of Self-Talk** | **C27**

Purpose: To provide students with an effective model of positive self-talk, which they can then imitate.

Procedure: As a significant other you can do much to help students formulate self-perceptions and

internalize self-esteem. Your students use you as a model every day; it is important that you show them the power of positive self-talk. In front of the students, periodically praise yourself for a well-deserved accomplishment. This also helps to set a tone in the classroom so students recognize that it's safe to praise themselves in front of others.

Grades K–8 | **Group Praise Chants** | **C28**

Purpose: To provide the opportunity for students to practice self-praise in the comfort of a group.

Procedure: For many students this is a less threatening way to introduce them to self-praise. Following a small or large group activity where students did a praiseworthy job, invite them to reward themselves verbally.

If necessary, at first model the chants and have them repeat after you. For example: "You really deserve a lot of praise today for your efforts. Everyone stayed on task and did a great job. Let's tell ourselves that. Ready? WE DID A GREAT JOB!" Chants can gradually be directed more and more by students until they will be reminding you that they deserve a chant.

Grades K–4 | **Pat-on-the-Back to Me Book** | **C29**

Purpose: To increase students' use of positive self-talk.

Materials:

Pat-on-the-Back to Me Book: 3–5 copies of C29 Pat-on-the-Back to Me forms; 2 2" x 7 1/2" pieces of construction paper; stapler.

COMPETENCE

Construction: Cut the "coupons" to form five separate coupons for each page. Staple between the two pieces of construction paper. Make one booklet for each student.

Procedure: Encourage students to fill out a pat-on-the-back coupon each day to congratulate themselves for their achievement that day.

Grades K-3	**Blue Ribbon Book**	**C30**

Purpose: To allow students to practice recording their own accomplishments.

Materials:

Blue Ribbon Book: C30 Blue Ribbon form copied onto light-blue construction paper for front cover; several sheets of plain or writing paper cut into the same shape as the ribbon; piece of light-blue construction paper cut into the same shape as the ribbon for back cover; scissors, stapler.

Construction: Make a Blue Ribbon Book for each student by stapling several sheets of writing paper between the front and back cover.

Procedure: As achievements occur for students, ask them to record the accomplishment by drawing a picture of it inside the ribbon. Hang finished ribbons or bind together as an ongoing Class Blue Ribbon Book.

Grades 2-6	**Now Hear This!**	**C31**

Purpose: To provide students with the opportunity of recording their school accomplishments for at least one week.

Materials: Duplicate the C31 Now Hear This! form for each student.

Procedure: Students write their accomplishments in the space provided for at least one week. Younger or nonreading students may draw or dictate their daily successes.

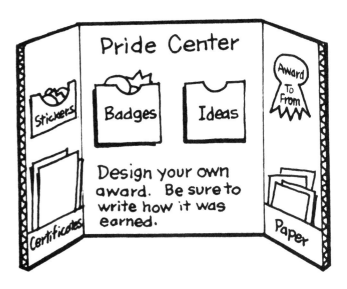

Grades K-8	**Pride Center**	**C32**

Purpose: To provide students with the opportunity to recognize their achievements as well as those of deserving classmates.

To increase positive feelings of caring and concern for one another. To "catch" each other being good.

Materials:
Suggested items:

pens, pencils	carbon paper
scissors	stars, glitter
crayons	pins, double-sided tape
marking pens	samples of awards
glue	letter stamps, stencils
hole-punch	computer certificate maker
stickers	badge maker
magazines	construction paper

Construction: Build the Pride Center onto an existing bulletin board or create one from three 12" x 26" pieces of tagboard backed with cardboard. Hinge the carrel together with reinforced tape. Pockets may be added to store material by stapling the bottom and sides of smaller pieces of cardboard to the carrel or bulletin board.

Make cutout letters to read "Pride Center" and attach to the board. Place the Center in a convenient, accessible location in the classroom. Stock the Center with some of the suggested items mentioned above. From time to time replenish the Center with new materials or suggestions for award making.

Procedure: Inform students that there is a new center available for classroom use called the Pride Center. Using the Pride Center is an earned privilege awarded by the teacher or another student (with teacher permission).

Whenever students are "caught" doing something that the classroom is reinforcing (positive deeds, quality effort, academic achievements, improvement in work or behavior), they will be sent to the Pride Center to make their own certificate or award. Students may also ask to make an award for a deserving classmate.

Pride Center suggested by Jann Bailey: Centennial Elementary School, Littleton, Colorado.

Activities C33 through C40 offer ideas for awards for use in the Pride Center:

| Grades K–6 | Pat-on-the-Back Handprints | C33 |

Materials: Several pieces of 8" x 8" light-colored construction paper; tempera paint—dark colors of thick consistency; small roller or paint brush; pie tins; scissors, double-sided adhesive tape.

Procedure: Students roll tempera paint on the palm of their hands, which they then press firmly onto the middle of the construction paper squares to make prints. Ask them to put their names on their papers.

Allow the prints to dry thoroughly and then stock them at the Pride Center. Encourage deserving students to write a Pat-on-the-Back award to themselves or to make one for a deserving classmate. They use the handprint paper and write in a blank space, "A pat on the back to _____ (name) because _____ (reason)." Nonwriting students may dictate.

Some teachers enjoy taping the award to the recipient's back. You may also punch a hole in the top of the award and string it with a 24" yarn length tied at the top for the student to wear on his/her back.

Variation: Make copies of the C29 Pat-on-the-Back to Me form, cut out and stock at the Pride Center for students to fill in when they've accomplished something special.

| Grades 1–8 | **Design an Award** | C34 |

Materials: Copies of C34 Design an Award form; ample supply of 5 1/2" x 8 1/2" light-colored construction paper; scissors, glue, marking pens, crayons.

Procedure: When students have done a job well, encourage them to create their own award to present to themselves. They cut out borders and paste around the grid shape. They should feel free to add other graphic designs from the page or do their own illustrations.

| Grades K–8 | **Badges** | C35 |

Materials: C35 Badges patterns; construction and cardstock-weight paper; scissors, marking pens.

Procedure: Trace the C35 Badges patterns onto cardstock-weight paper and cut out for templates. Students trace them onto construction paper to design and cut out as badges.

| Grades 1–6 | **Fingerprints** | C36 |

Materials: Stamp pad; ample supply of 3" x 6" pieces of construction paper; thin-tipped marking pens.

Procedure: Students make personalized awards to themselves or classmates by pushing their fingers lightly onto the stamp pad. They then press their inked fingers onto a piece of construction paper. They may also make cards by folding the paper in half. They conclude with a personalized message. Nonwriting students dictate.

COMPETENCE

ESTEEM BUILDERS

| Grades K–4 | **Blue Ribbon Award** | **C37** |

Materials: 3" and 4" oaktag circle patterns; blue construction paper; blue crepe paper or blue ribbon (optional); stapler, scissors.

Procedure: Students use one of the circle patterns to trace onto construction paper and cut out. They staple two strips of crepe paper or ribbon (pointing down diagonally, left and right) to the center back of the circle. The staple may be covered with a sticker, star or photograph of the student.

| Grades K–4 | **Hanging Award** | **C38** |

Materials: 6" and 8" circle oaktag patterns; construction paper; hole-punch; 20" yarn lengths; marking pens, crayons.

Procedure: Students trace one of the patterns onto construction paper and design an award within the circle. They cut out the award and punch a hole near the top of the circle. Using a yarn length, they string it through the hole and tie it securely with a knot. Students wear their awards for all to see.

| Grades K–8 | **Positive Wristbands** | **C39** |

Materials: Ample supply of colored 1 1/2" x 7" construction paper strips; copies of C39 Positive Wristbands form; stapler; marking pens, crayons.

Procedure: Students design awards and write special messages on the strips and then staple them around their wrist.

Idea suggested by Jann Bailey; Centennial Elementary School, Littleton, Colorado.

| Grades K–8 | **Pride Center Awards** | **C40** |

Materials: Copies of C40 awards.

Procedure: Stock a supply of these awards for students to give to deserving classmates. You may also keep a supply yourself to give to students when appropriate.

| Grades K–8 | **Books to Enhance Competence** | **C41** |

Purpose: To increase students' awareness of how others acquire competence.

Materials: Any of the titles listed below according to grade level.

P = Primary (K–3)
I = Intermediate Level (4–8)

Procedure: Read the book to the students or assign as independent reading. You may wish to use the following suggestions as discussion guides or have students write the answers:

- Who was the main character in the book?
- What problem(s) was he/she facing?
- Did the character have to deal with the problem alone or with other characters?
- Did the character grow personally in any way? How?
- How did the character overcome his/her difficulty?

Alexander and the Terrible, Horrible, No Good, Very Bad Day, Judith Viorst (Atheneum, 1976). Alexander learns that everyone has bad days. [P]

Do Bananas Chew Gum? Jamie Gilson (Lothrop, Lee & Shepard, 1980). A boy with learning disabilities receives the special help he needs and finds success. [I]

The Carrot Seed, Ruth Krauss (Scholastic, 1971). A child's faith in the carrot seed she plants holds despite the fact no one believes it will grow. [P]

Castle in the Attic, Elizabeth Winthrop (Bantam Books, 1986). William learns a mighty lesson from the Silver Knight—the power you need to fight any obstacle is within you. [I]

Did You Carry the Flag Today, Charley? Rebecca Caudill (Holt, Rinehart & Winston, 1966). A backward boy finally gains the honor of carrying the flag. [I]

Harry and the Terrible Whatzit, Dick Gackenbach (Scholastic, 1979). Little Harry conquers his fears as he gains competence. [P]

Jake O'Shawnasey, Stephen Cosgrove (Price, Stern & Sloan, 1986). A seagull learns from a wise old owl that if you believe in yourself you will succeed. [P, I]

— 288 —

Katy and the Big Snow, Virginia Lee Burton (Houghton Mifflin, 1974). A modern classic about a brave, persistent snowplow. [P]

Leo the Late Bloomer, Robert Kraus (Windmill Books, 1971). A young lion finally learns to read, draw and talk, much to his parents' delight. [P]

The Little Engine That Could, Watty Piper (Scholastic, 1979). The classic of positive thinking—"I think I can!" [P]

Little Toot, Hardie Gramatky (Putnam, 1978). A small tugboat finally learns to compete with the biggest of them all. [P]

Mrs. Frisby and the Rats of Nimh, Robert C. O'Brien (Atheneum, 1971). A group of rats have become super intelligent through a series of laboratory injections and form a civilization. [I]

Night of the Twister, Ivy Ruckman (Thomas Y. Crowell, 1984). The terrors of a tornado cause Dan to gain a sense of competence. [I]

The Shrinking of Treehorn, Florence Parry Heide (Dell, 1980). A young boy discovers he is shrinking and, ignored by all, must solve the problem himself. [P]

Stone Fox, John Rey Gardiner (Harper & Row, 1980). With grandfather ill, Willy must assume the responsibility of paying off the back taxes. A touching story of compassion and competence. [I]

Whistle for Willy, Ezra Jack Keats (Viking, 1964). A young boy is proud when he learns how to whistle. [P]

COMPETENCE

Name	Date

Hobby Day Checklist

Hobby Topic: _____   Presentation Date: _____

List items you'll be using for your presentation—visual aids (charts, pictures, displays):

_____   _____

_____   _____

_____   _____

_____   _____

Library and Reference Book Titles:

_____

_____

_____

_____

_____

_____

_____

Supplies from Home: Demonstration Materials:

_____   _____

_____   _____

_____   _____

_____   _____

Materials for your Handouts: Special Equipment:

_____   _____

_____   _____

_____   _____

On the back of this sheet draw how you will display your hobby.

Esteem Builders. Jalmar Press
Rolling Hills Estates, CA

Name   Date

My Interest

Think of a favorite hobby or special skill of yours that another classmate might like to know about. Put together a plan to show or explain your hobby or interest to the class. Choose one only.

My hobby / interest is: _____

How did you get started on this interest? _____

_____

What things do you need to get started on this interest? _____

_____

Describe your interest to your classmates. What's special about it? _____

_____

_____

_____

_____

How often do you do it? _____

_____

Do you do this hobby with anyone else? _____

What interesting or unusual things have happened to you because of this interest? _____

_____

_____

_____

_____

Why would you recommend this interest to others? _____

_____

_____

Date of your presentation: _____

Use this outline to aid you in presenting your interest / hobby to the class.

Esteem Builders. Jalmar Press
Rolling Hills Estates, CA

Hobby Day Award

This special RECOGNITION AWARD
is proudly presented to:

_____

for

_____

_____

_____

_____
Signature

_____
Date

AWARD

Thanks for
sharing your skill.
We appreciated
it!

This special RECOGNITION AWARD
is proudly presented to:

_____

for

_____

_____

_____

_____
Signature

_____
Date

AWARD

Thanks for
sharing your skill.
We appreciated
it!

Esteem Builders. Jalmar Press
Rolling Hills Estates, CA

Strength Profile

Student	Talents/Interests	Social Relationships	Academic Competencies	Physical Characteristics

Esteem Builders. Jalmar Press
Rolling Hills Estates, CA

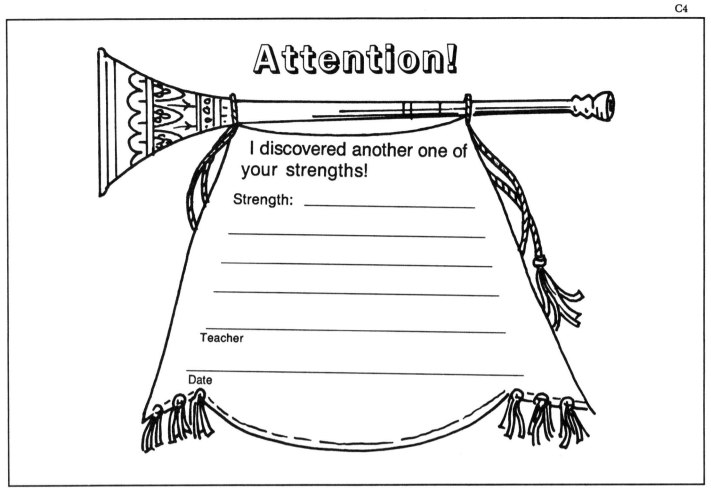

Attention!

I discovered another one of your strengths!

Strength: _____

_____

_____

_____

_____

Teacher _____

_____
Date

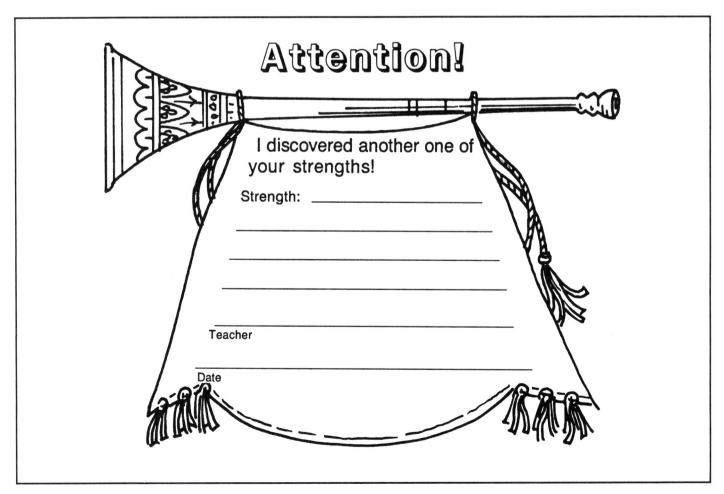

Attention!

I discovered another one of your strengths!

Strength: _____

_____

_____

_____

Teacher _____

_____
Date

Esteem Builders. Jalmar Press
Rolling Hills Estates, CA

STRENGTH ★ AWARD

This award is presented to:_____

for

_____

_____

_____

_____
Signature

_____
Date

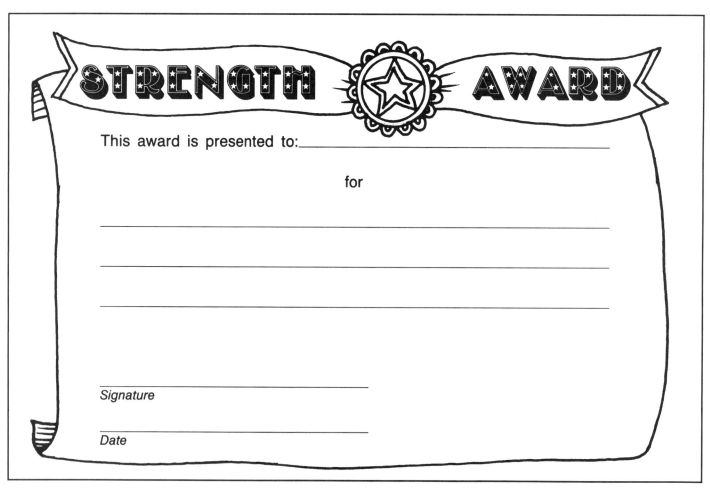

STRENGTH ★ AWARD

This award is presented to:_____

for

_____

_____

_____

_____
Signature

_____
Date

Esteem Builders. Jalmar Press
Rolling Hills Estates, CA

— 297 —

Esteem Builders. Jalmar Press
Rolling Hills Estates, CA

Strength
Barbell

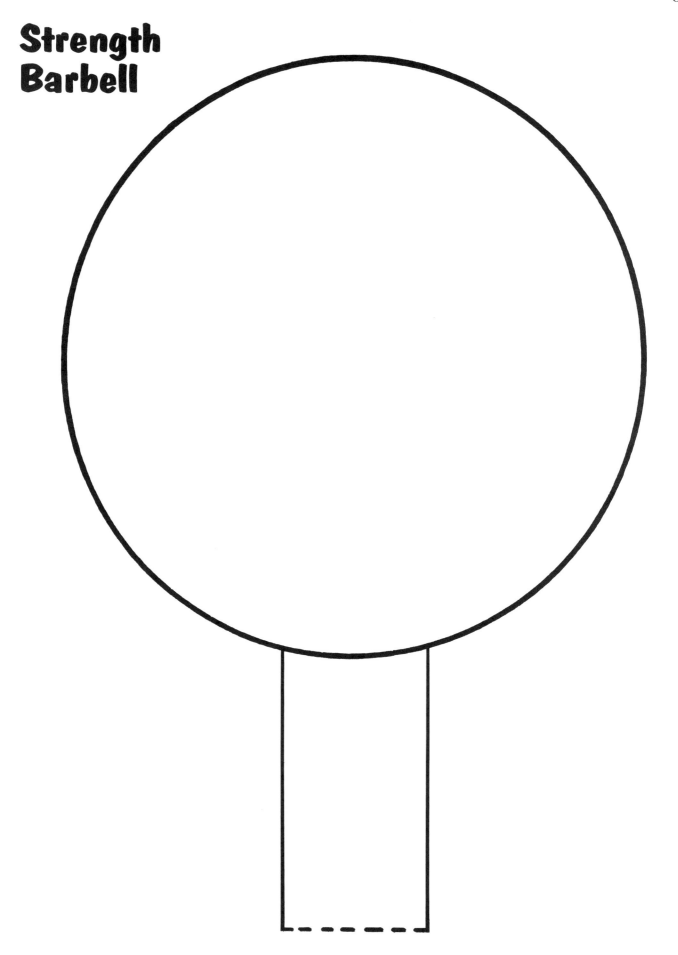

Esteem Builders. Jalmar Press
Rolling Hills Estates, CA

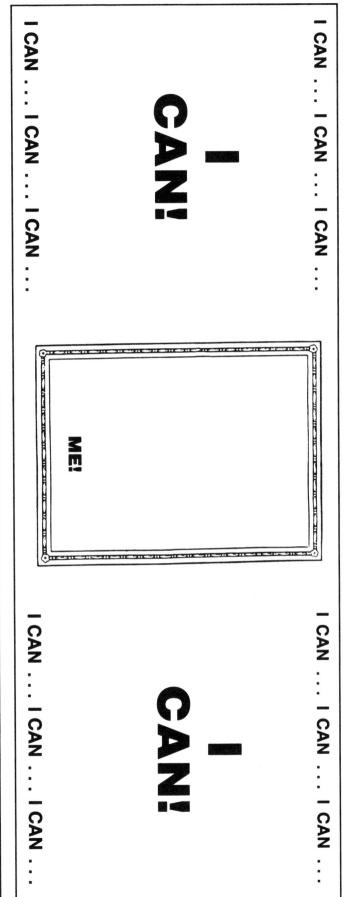

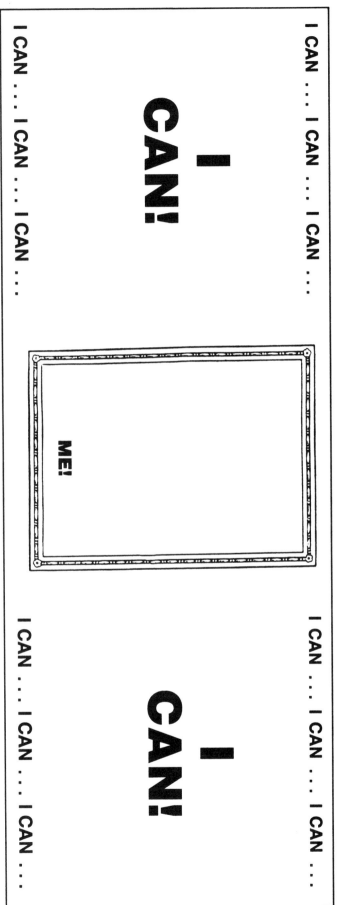

Esteem Builders. Jalmar Press
Rolling Hills Estates, CA

I CAN!

I Can _____

_____

_____

Signed _____ Date _____

I CAN!

I Can _____

_____

_____

Signed _____ Date _____

I CAN!

I Can _____

_____

_____

Signed _____ Date _____

I CAN!

I Can _____

_____

_____

Signed _____ Date _____

I CAN!

I Can _____

_____

_____

Signed _____ Date _____

I CAN!

I Can _____

_____

_____

Signed _____ Date _____

Esteem Builders. Jalmar Press
Rolling Hills Estates, CA

"I Know I Can"

Esteem Builders. Jalmar Press
Rolling Hills Estates, CA

Name	Date

Accomplishment Journal

My accomplishment today was _____

_____

_____

A picture of my accomplishment (How does it look?)

I achieved my accomplishment by _____

_____

_____

_____

When I achieved my accomplishment I felt _____

_____

Esteem Builders. Jalmar Press
Rolling Hills Estates, CA

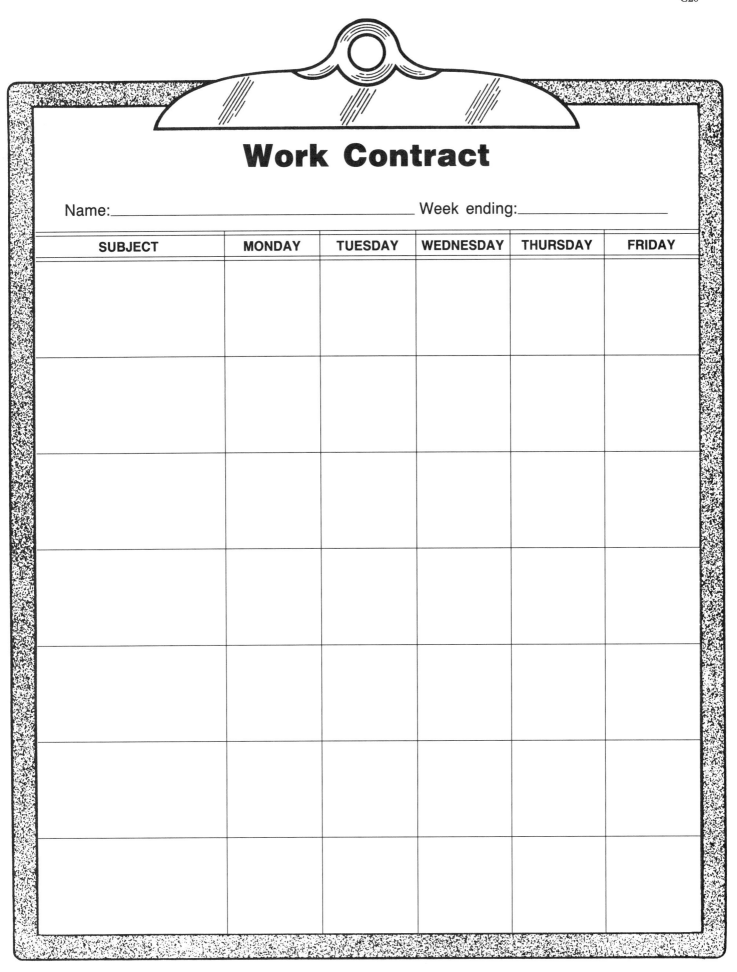

Work Contract

Name:_____ Week ending:_____

SUBJECT	MONDAY	TUESDAY	WEDNESDAY	THURSDAY	FRIDAY

Esteem Builders. Jalmar Press
Rolling Hills Estates, CA

Ollie Owl Book Report

Reader: _____

Title: _____

Author: _____

Book Rating: great so-so not good

Ollie Owl Book Report

Reader: _____

Title: _____

Author: _____

Book Rating: great so-so not good

Ollie Owl Book Report

Reader: _____

Title: _____

Author: _____

Book Rating: great so-so not good

Ollie Owl Book Report

Reader: _____

Title: _____

Author: _____

Book Rating: great so-so not good

Esteem Builders. Jalmar Press
Rolling Hills Estates, CA

Ollie Owl

OLLIE OWL

Esteem Builders. Jalmar Press
Rolling Hills Estates, CA

Student/Teacher Conference

Student: _____

Teacher: _____

Date: _____

Subject	Progress	Ways to Improve
	Teacher Comment	Teacher Comment
	Student Comment	Student Comment
	Teacher Comment	Teacher Comment
	Student Comment	Student Comment
	Teacher Comment	Teacher Comment
	Student Comment	Student Comment
	Teacher Comment	Teacher Comment
	Student Comment	Student Comment

Esteem Builders. Jalmar Press
Rolling Hills Estates, CA

NEWS FLASH

Just to let you know you're doing great!

I really like_____

_____

_____

_____

Keep up the good work!

_____
Signed

_____
Date

NEWS FLASH

Just to let you know you're doing great!

I really like_____

_____

_____

_____

Keep up the good work!

_____
Signed

_____
Date

Esteem Builders. Jalmar Press
Rolling Hills Estates. CA

PROUD GRAM

Dear Parent,

Once again, you can be proud of your child!

_____ has earned this special note

for showing improvement in _____.

Progress was due to _____

_____

_____

Signed:_____ Date: _____

PROUD GRAM

Dear Parent,

Once again, you can be proud of your child!

_____ has earned this special note

for showing improvement in _____.

Progress was due to _____

_____

_____

Signed:_____ Date: _____

Strengths and Weaknesses

by

We all have things we are proud of about ourselves as well as things we would like to change. These could include changes in your appearance, behavior or skills. What things about yourself are you most proud of and what things would you most like to change?

DIRECTIONS: In the first column below, list what you consider to be your most important strengths in each of the three areas. In the next column consider what you'd like to change—in your appearance, behavior and skills. In the third column, list some steps you can take to make these changes occur.

	APPEARANCE How I look	SKILLS How I perform	BEHAVIOR How I act
STRENGTHS			
CHANGES I WANT TO MAKE			
STEPS I CAN TAKE TO MAKE THESE CHANGES	1. 2. 3.	1. 2. 3.	1. 2. 3.

Esteem Builders. Jalmar Press
Rolling Hills Estates, CA

A Pat-on-the-Back to Me

Today I liked the way that I _____

_____

Signed _____ Date _____

A Pat-on-the-Back to Me

Today I'm proud of the way that I _____

_____

Signed _____ Date _____

A Pat-on-the-Back to Me

I congratulate myself today because _____

_____

Signed _____ Date _____

A Pat-on-the-Back to Me

Yes! Today I did a nice job on _____

_____

Signed _____ Date _____

A Pat-on-the-Back to Me

I deserve a pat on the back today because _____

_____

Signed _____ Date _____

Esteem Builders. Jalmar Press
Rolling Hills Estates, CA

Name	Date

Blue Ribbon Book

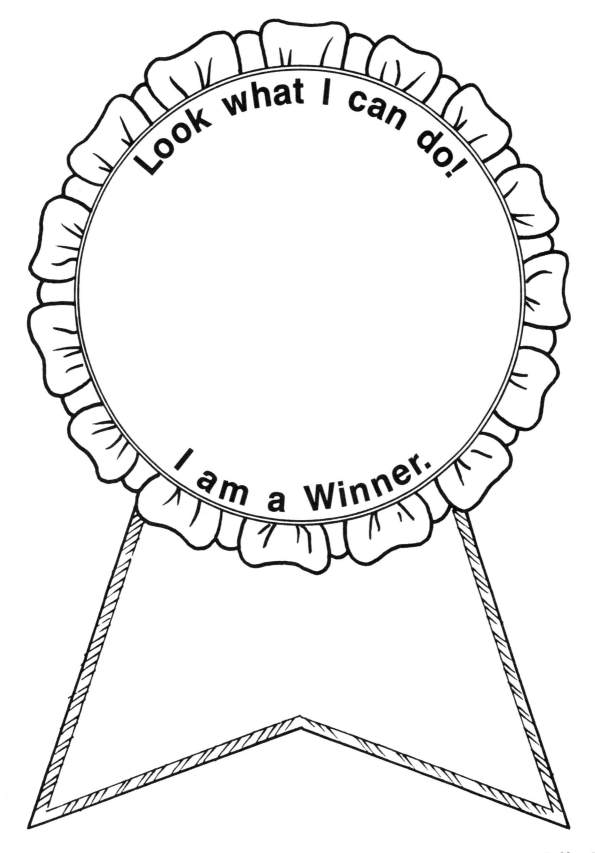

Look what I can do!

I am a Winner.

Esteem Builders. Jalmar Press
Rolling Hills Estates, CA

Name   Date

Now Hear This!

Monday

Tuesday

Wednesday

Thursday

Friday

Every day I have successes.
Here are this week's successes.
I'm proud of myself.

Esteem Builders. Jalmar Press
Rolling Hills Estates, CA

Design an Award

𝔐𝔢

You Are a SUPER KID!

Name

I have a lot of
good qualities:

Presented to:_____

By:_____

Date:_____

1._____

☆ STAR AWARD ☆

2._____

3._____

Awarded to:_____

4._____

For:_____

5._____

Authorized Signature:_____

Graphic Designs and Borders

Esteem Builders. Jalmar Press
Rolling Hills Estates, CA

★ BADGE SHAPES ★

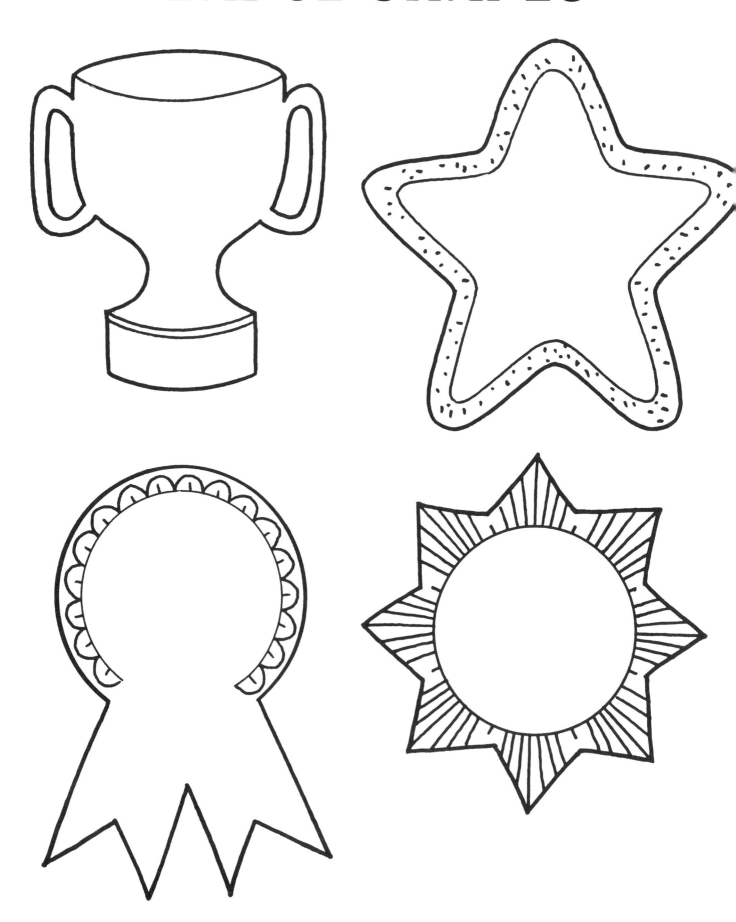

Esteem Builders. Jalmar Press
Rolling Hills Estates, CA

Positive Wristbands

The Helping Hand Award Is Presented to:

Name _____ Date _____

STAR AWARD

Awarded to: _____

Authorized Signature: _____

Blue Ribbon Award

Awarded to: _____

For: _____

Great Kid Award

Awarded to: _____

By: _____ Date: _____

Esteem Builders. Jalmar Press
Rolling Hills Estates, CA

Pride Center Awards

Reading Award

Today I read

_____

Ask me about it!

_____

Signed:

_____

Esteem Builders. Jalmar Press
Rolling Hills Estates, CA

8

Working in Groups: Concept Circles

PURPOSE
- To Enhance Students' Self-Perceptions Using All Five Components of Self-Esteem
- To Increase Students' Awareness of Their Own Strengths and Uniquenesses as Well as Those of Others
- To Build a Positive and Caring Environment
- To Increase Oral Language Proficiency as Well as Build Confidence in Speaking in Front of Groups

SUMMARY OF CONCEPT CIRCLES

Definition: *Students gathering together in a circle and concentrating their thoughts and activities on one specific, designated idea or concept.*

SUPPORT DATA

Concept Circles:

- *Provide students with the opportunity to be heard.* According to many reports, the majority of students are being denied this opportunity, which is fundamental to all the five self-esteem components. One investigation cites that the average amount of time a student is listened to by a non-working mother is 13 1/2 minutes per day. "Children Under Stress," *U.S. News and World Report*, October 1986.
- *Teach students how to make positive self-statements.* The Felker study reports that students with high self-esteem tend to make positive self-statements during and after performing school tasks. D.W. Felker. *Building Positive Self-Concepts* (Minneapolis, MN: Burgess Publishing, 1974).
- *Teach students to praise others.* Brady's study reveals that one of the most effective components for enhancing self-esteem is praise of others. P.J. Brady, et al. "Predicting Student Self-Concept, Anxiety, and Responsibility from Self-Evaluation and Self-Praise." *Psychology in the Schools*, Vol. 15 (1978).
- *Teach students to make positive statements about each other.* In a third, fourth and fifth grade classroom study, each day a different classmate's name was drawn, and everyone was asked to focus on the best qualities of that individual and write them down. The results of the study showed improved self-concept scores for all students. W.E. Stillwell and J.R. Barclay. "Effects of Affective Education Interventions in the Elementary School." *Psychology in the Schools*, Vol. 16 (1979).

PURPOSE

- To Enhance Students Self-Perceptions Using All Five Components of Self-Esteem
- To Increase Students' Awareness of Their Own Strengths and Uniqueness as Well as Those of Others
- To Build a Positive and Caring Environment
- To Increase Oral Language Proficiency as Well as Build Confidence in Speaking in Front of Groups

TARGET AUDIENCE

Concept Circles have been used successfully in a variety of settings for all age levels including regular classrooms (preschool through eighth grade), special education settings and gifted education.

Concept Circles Activities List

Code	Grade	Title	Grouping
Security			
CC1	K–8	Beginning Circle	Full
CC2	K–8	How Do You Do?	Full/Team
CC3	K–8	Listen Up!	Full/Team
CC4	K–3	Ball Pass	Full/Team
CC5	2–8	Partner Interview	Full/Partner
CC6	2–8	Body Tracings	Team
CC7	2–8	The One-Cent Interview	Partner
Selfhood			
CC8	2–8	Names	Partner/Team
CC9	1–8	Design-a-Logo	Team
CC10	K–8	Me Bag	Full/Team
CC11	K–4	I Like	Full
CC12	K–8	Share Yourself	Full/Team
CC13	K–3	I Like to Be Me	Full
CC14	2–8	Identity Bag	Full/Team
CC15	K–8	I'm Great!	Full/Team
CC16	K–6	A Me Hanging	Full/Team
CC17	K–5	Feeling Drawings	Team
CC18	K–2	Happy-Sad Beanbag	Full
CC19	K–2	Emotion Hats	Full
CC20	K–3	Feeling Thermometer	Full
CC21	K–3	Individual Thermometers	Full
CC22	K–3	Feeling Masks	Full
CC23	K–4	Wishes	Full
CC24	3–8	Dreams	Full/Team
Affiliation			
CC25	K–8	Sunshine Statements	Full/Team
CC26	K–5	Sparkle Box	Full
CC27	1–8	Banners	Full/Partner
CC28	2–8	Questions	Full/Team
CC29	2–8	Picture Puzzles	Full/Team
CC30	2–8	We're All Stars	Full/Team
CC31	K–8	Riddles	Full/Team
CC32	K–5	Silent Sparkles	Full/Team

Affiliation (continued)

Code	Grade	Title	Grouping
CC33	K–4	Word Gifts	Full/Team
CC34	3–8	Word Power	Team
CC35	K–3	Glasses Circle	Full/Team
CC36	K–5	Sun Rays	Full/Team
CC37	K–8	Me Bags by Others	Full/Team
CC38	K–8	Me Bag Compliments	Full/Team
CC39	2–8	Name Poster	Full/Team
CC40	K–8	Compliments	Team
CC41	2–8	Compliment Hanging	Team
CC42	K–5	Fuzzy Circles	Full/Team

Mission

Code	Grade	Title	Grouping
CC43	K–4	Would You Rather?	Partner/Team
CC44	4–8	Brainstorming Solutions	Partner/Team
CC45	2–8	I Wish I Could	Full/Partner
CC46	K–8	Goal Sharing	Full/Team
CC47	K–8	How Will You Make It?	Full/Team
CC48	K–8	Goal Accomplishment	Full/Team

Competence

Code	Grade	Title	Grouping
CC49	K–8	Strength Book	Full
CC50	K–8	Brag Time	Full/Team
CC51	K–3	Strength Circle	Full/Team
CC52	K–3	Blue Ribbon	Full/Team
CC53	K–3	Hooray for Me!	Full
CC54	K–8	One Good Thing About Me	Full/Team
CC55	2–8	Me Commercials	Full/Team
CC56	K–8	I'm Proud	Full/Team
CC57	K–3	I Thought I Could	Full/Team
CC58	K–8	I Can	Full/Team
CC59	2–8	Self-Introduction	Full/Team

8

Working in Groups:
Concept Circles

All learning occurs in a social context.
—HANOCH McCARTY

LAYING THE GROUNDWORK

ADAPTING CIRCLES
TO OLDER STUDENTS

Creating circles appropriate for younger students is usually a tough task due to short attention spans. For this reason, there are more circle activities for younger students than for older. It is, however, very easy to adapt a circle activity to older students' needs and interests, as follows:

1. *Eliminate the use of props.* Props are built into many circles to help students with short attention spans anticipate when their turn will be. They also help to motivate the circle; but they may not be appropriate for older students.

2. *Eliminate the jingle.* The use of jingles in many circles is designed to enhance the auditory memory of students as well as provide a motivator for students with short attention spans. However, they are usually not sophisticated enough for older students.

3. *Write the topic on a card and have a permanent card file of topics for students to choose.* These can be placed in a box where students may take turns pulling a card and using it for the circle topic.

4. *Allow students to suggest topics that are appealing to them.* Make a suggestion box

available in the classroom where students add their own topic ideas.

GROUPINGS

Circle activities have been specifically designed to include many different grouping possibilities. The suggested type of grouping for each topic is listed following the circle title:

- **Full.** This means that all students would participate in the circle topic and sit together in one circle. You may wish to consider having cross-age tutors or parent aides participate in the circle as well as facilitate the discussion.

- **Team.** The team approach is based on Robert Slavin and Roger and David Johnson's concepts of cooperative learning.[1] Teams are made up of five to six students representing a broad mix. In one team, for instance, you would place one achiever, one non-achiever, two boys and two girls, one leader and one follower. It is easier to form teams on a permanent basis right from the start so that no time is taken up during the circle activity with planning arrangements.

---

1. Slavin, Robert E. *Cooperative Learning: Student Teams* (Washington, D.C.: NEA Professional Library, 1982).
   Johnson, David W.; Johnson, R.; and Johnson, Edith Holubec. *Circles of Learning: Cooperation in the Classroom* (Edina, MN: Interaction Book Company, 1986).

Some teachers have used the technique of asking students for the names of five students they would like to have on their team. The teacher then forms teams with at least one of the five names on that team. Each team could then design a poster with the names of each member on it. Display the posters during circle time so that students can quickly move into teams.

Teams will need to form an identity for themselves and become comfortable as a group. You may wish to consider doing these activities:

- **Design a name.** Team members brainstorm a team name, take a vote and then introduce themselves to the larger group.

- **Design a logo.** Team members brainstorm a team logo and then draw it on a 12"x 18" piece of construction paper. Team members use it as their identity banner.

- **Create a group collage.** Provide each team with a large piece of butcher paper, magazines, glue, scissors and pens. Each team designs a group collage on the paper: they glue pictures depicting each separate individual (interests, strengths, desires) onto a team collage sheet to represent the whole group. This is then shared with other teams.

- **Partner.** Some activities are designed so that two students have the opportunity to work with each other on a more interactive basis. Initially, students may wish to work with someone with whom they are familiar and therefore feel more comfortable. After a while, ask students to work with another student whom they do not know as well.

Students may be grouped by making a set of name cards (3"x 5" cards with the name of each student written on the card). Print half of the names using one color of ink and the other half with another color ink. Inform each student of their color (it can also be coded on an existing name chart in the room). All of the same color cards are placed in a container. Students with the opposite color are the "pullers." Each student pulls the name of another student from the container. The name refers to his/her work partner for the activity.

(Idea for team grouping suggested by Jean Gibbs in her book, *Tribes.*[2])

2. Gibbs, J. *Tribes: A Process for Social Development and Cooperative Learning* (Santa Rosa, CA: Center Source Publications, 1987).

Clock Pairing. Students could also be instantly paired by using the S17 Time for Friends activity (see Security, Chapter 3). Students fill in the time slots on their clock sheet, each with a different classmate's name. Save the "clocks" for paired sharing activities. On these occasions, the teacher calls a time on the clock (for example, 3 o'clock). Students then pair up with the classmate whose name appears at that time slot.

COOPERATIVE LEARNING TOOLS

The following materials are helpful to facilitate the circle activities. They are merely suggestions and not essential to the activities; however, many facilitators have found them useful.

- **Puppets** (for younger students). Any puppet that is friendly looking will be sufficient. The puppet introduces the circle activities and facilitates the discussion. Students may vote on a puppet name or consider using the name "Sparkles" to remind them to say builder-upper statements to each other.

- **Timer.** This can greatly facilitate circle discussions because it lets students know visually and audibly when the circle time is up. A clock timer is best. Set the timer for the designated time (20 minutes or so) and tell students that when the timer buzzes, the circle is over.

- **Suggestion Box.** A shoe box with a removable top will suffice. Cut a slit 1/2" x 5" along the top of the box. Decorate it with stickers or wrapping paper and write "Suggestions" along the side. Students should be encouraged to place inside the box suggestions for future circle topics, as well as quotes, lyrics, poems and newspaper articles. These are particularly appropriate for older students.

- **Name Cards.** Make a set of name cards on 3"x 5" strips of cardstock-weight material. Print the names of half your students in red ink; the remaining half in another color ink. For younger students, you may wish to paste a Xeroxed photograph of each student on their respective card.

- **Listening Book.** Make a Listening Book ditto like the illustration that appears here. The sheet should have space for each student's name. Make several copies of the sheet and staple

CONCEPT CIRCLES

them between construction paper covers. Use the book during circle time to keep a record of students' comments; it is also an incentive for listening.

On selected circles, name the topic at the top of the form and then quickly jot down the main idea of each student's contribution. At the end of the circle, ask students if they can remember facts about their friends (who was listening?!) *For example,* "Who in this classroom is afraid of the dark?" (Scott) "...of spiders?" (Sally).

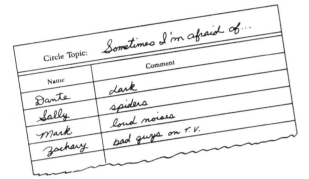

- **Pass-Around-the-Prop.** Several activities suggest a prop featuring the circle's topic to pass around the circle. A prop is particularly helpful for younger students as it instantly reminds them whose turn it is and how much longer it will be until their turn comes. Many teachers keep these props in a large basket or pillow case. Students are more likely to request a particular circle when the prop is in sight. Eliminate props for upper-grade students.

GETTING STARTED

What to Expect at First:

1. Some reticence on the part of students—we're taught to hold back.

2. Students will verbalize very simple, concrete statements, mostly addressing the physical attributes and skills of themselves and others.

3. Those with low self-esteem have a difficult time initially. They may use disguises such as withdrawal, denial or silly behavior to cover up their insecure feelings. For them it's important that you build up a very comfortable, supportive environment.

To Increase Positive Self-Statements You May Wish to:

1. **Point out students' strengths** and uniqueness throughout the day. They won't be able to verbalize their strengths unless they are made aware of them.

2. **Have students keep individual records** of their positive self-statements on their desk. A simple tally will suffice.

3. **Model positive self-statements** yourself! If students hear you saying positive comments periodically about yourself, they'll begin to feel it's safe to do so. *For example,* "I'm really proud of the job I did on this bulletin board today. I worked very hard on it."

4. **Praise and support students** for their use of positive self-statements. You want to create an environment that's caring, nonjudgmental and secure for such growth.

5. **Be supportive of any student** who cannot quickly verbalize a positive self-statement in the circle. Interject with a quick comment of your own, such as: "I've noticed that you are very helpful during cleanup time. You often help the others clean up their places. You could say, 'I'm a good helper.' "

   Following this comment, ask the student to verbalize back to you what you have just provided: "I'm a good helper." (Be careful not to force the statement; let the student first become relaxed in the setting.)

6. **Ask students in the circle for ideas** why _____ (whoever's turn it is) should be happy to be him-/herself. Quickly come to his/her side if no comments surface.

7. **Discuss more concrete subject matter** in the beginning circles. Students are often more comfortable about sharing if they have a possession of their own with them. For the CC56 I'm Proud circle invite students to bring something from home of which they are proud. The CC11 I Like circle can be a similar format.

8. **Invite students to draw a picture** of what they will be saying for the circle. This is particularly helpful for the reticent student: he/she then has the picture to fall back on and can merely show that.

9. **Try using any of the Me Puppets** described in Security and Selfhood, Chapters 3 and 4 (see respective Activity Lists). Students often feel more secure with a puppet on hand to do the talking, which allows them to open up.

10. **For the very shy or retiring student** take a few minutes before the circle begins to discuss the topic and "feed" him/her a possible answer.

11. **Finally, consider using Word Gifts (CC33),** or provide a folder filled with several index cards with builder-upper statements for students to say to one another. Any students who cannot think of an appropriate positive comment to say to another classmate during the circle activity may pull a card from the Word Gifts Box or folder and present it to the classmate.

CONCEPT CIRCLE ACTIVITIES FOR THE FIVE COMPONENTS

There are 59 activities here to use in cooperative learning situations or with high-risk students. These activities are also suitable for the counselor/psychologist.

Some of the activities already appear elsewhere in the book. However, they have been repeated in Concept Circles because they are also relevant to this format. The activities are grouped in the same order as the self-esteem components throughout the book: Security, Selfhood, Affiliation, Mission and Competence.

Concept Circles activities are classified according to whether the group as a whole participates (full), the group is divided into teams (team) or students work in pairs (partner). Look at the beginning of each activity description for the grouping.

CONCEPT CIRCLES THAT INCREASE THE FEELING OF SECURITY

Purpose: To create a positive environment where students are given the opportunity to be heard. To set reasonable limits and rules to build a feeling of security and comfort. To provide opportunities that promote inclusion within the group and trust of others.

Note: Although these activities are primarily focused on Security, they also will enhance students' Selfhood and Affiliation with the group.

Grades K–8	**Beginning Circle**	CC1

Grouping: Full

Note: With younger students it is effective to use a puppet each time to introduce the circle topic and review the rules. Any puppet will work as long as you use it with each circle. You may wish to name him/her "Sparkle." With younger students use the word "sparkles" for builder-upper statements.

Props: *Chart of circle rules,* such as:

1. Remain seated.
2. Say only builder-uppers! (or sparkles!)
3. Take turns.
4. Listen to the comments of others—don't interrupt.
5. Plan your comment.
6. It's OK to pass.

Paper Circle:

1. Cut out one yellow construction paper circle (12" x 16"). With younger students you can call the circle a "sparkle." Sprinkle glitter over glue on the circle and allow it to dry.

2. Cut out yellow construction paper into 6" circles, one for each student as well as for yourself.

   Option: Sprinkle glitter over glue that has been placed around the edge of each circle in the outline of the student's name to make name tags. Divide the circles into four even sections.

Procedure: The Circle Facilitator explains to students what a Concept Circle is: its objective and the rules for the circles. Here is a suggested script to use as an outline:

Please adapt this script to the level and needs of your students. It is meant to serve only as a guide.

"Today is a special day because it is the first time we get to meet in our Concept Circle. This is a time when we will gather together, share our ideas and feelings, and listen to the thoughts and feelings of our friends. This is a time when we want to learn new things about each other and build each other up.

"Just like our classroom and school have rules this circle also has rules. I've written them on this chart to help us remember. [*Show the chart.*] The first rule says '**Remain seated.**' You may choose where you want to sit in the circle. Sometimes I will ask you to sit in a special place. Once you sit down, please stay there; you may not move. [*With younger students this is the time to introduce your 'Sparkle puppet' who 'helps us remember the rules.' Sparkle can sprinkle some pretend glue on the ground each time to help students remember where to sit and not to move.*]

"The second rule says, '**Say only builder-uppers!**' [or sparkles, depending on the age group]. This is the most important rule. In this circle we want to make sure everyone feels included and happy about being here. You can make people feel that way by the kinds of words you say. [*Bring out the large yellow circle.*] I want you to think for a minute just how powerful you can be as a builder-upper [sparkle] to another person. Each of us has feelings about ourself deep inside. These feelings are called our 'self-esteem.' We want everyone to have positive, good feelings about themselves and that's why we have a rule only to say 'builder-uppers' ['sparkles']. Every time someone says a put-down [or 'killer statement' or 'cold pricklie'] to someone it tears a bit of their self-esteem away. [*Demonstrate by tearing a piece through the middle of the yellow circle.*]

"It's hard to mend broken feelings. You may hear other people saying unkind, put-down statements to others. Lots of them. We do know we can change broken feelings by saying lots of builder-upper [sparkle] statements. Put-downs are so powerful, that after hearing one of those a person needs almost 10 positive statements to feel better inside. Remember, we only say builder-upper [sparkle] comments to each other.

"The third rule is to '**Take turns.**' Everyone will have a chance to speak in this circle and everyone's ideas count. All our ideas are equal [the same]—just like the circle we're sitting in. You'll know it's your turn because we shall be passing around a friendly reminder.

"The fourth rule is '**Listen to the comments of others—don't interrupt.**' You will have a chance to speak, so please make sure you allow everyone to have their full turn. You could make the speaker feel more comfortable by looking at him/her and smiling or nodding to show you are really listening.

"The fifth rule asks you to '**Plan your comment.**' Each circle time I will give you a few minutes to think what you'd like to say about the circle topic. Do it then so when it's your turn, you'll know exactly what to say. It will make the circles go much faster.

"The sixth and last rule is '**It's OK to pass.**' We want to hear everyone's ideas; but sometimes you may not want to talk about that topic. You have that option, and all you have to say is 'Pass.' Hopefully you won't choose to do it too often because then we won't have a chance to find out about you." [You may wish to inform the class how often you will be having the circle and how long each circle will take. You could then introduce the timer that is set for the number of minutes you have planned for the circle.]

Procedure 2: Pass a yellow circle to each student (called "sparkles" for the younger grades). Ask each student to write their name on the tag in large letters. (These could be pre-printed for nonwriting students). Students each turn to the student on their right and exchange name tags. These partners are now a team. Tell them that they have three minutes each in which to find out their partner's name and favorite hobby or interest. The interviewer draws a picture in one section of the partner's circle and signs his/her name. The partner now does the same. At the end of six minutes, teams rejoin the circle. Each partner now "introduces" the teammate by stating his/her name and interest. (Encourage reticent students to show the drawing they have made.)

Save the sparkle name tags. They may be used in three other Concept Circles by assigning students *new* teammates. You may want to change the questions each time to:

- What is your favorite TV show?
- What is your favorite color?
- What is your favorite book...movie... food...pet?

Close the circle by thanking students for their participation. Then follow with a quick evaluation by asking students to name one thing they learned about a classmate they didn't know before. For younger students, use the Sparkle puppet to perform this evaluation.

Grades K–8	How Do You Do?	CC2

Grouping: Full/Team

Procedure: Students sit in the circle. The first student begins by introducing himself/herself and states one thing that would describe a physical attribute:

"My name is _____ and I have _____."

Example: "My name is Ryan and I have blue eyes."

The student immediately on the right speaks next and starts by introducing the person who previously spoke.

"This is _____ and he/she has _____."

The circle continues until each student has introduced the person immediately preceding.

Grades K–8	Listen Up!	CC3

Grouping: Full/Team

Procedure: The first student begins the circle by introducing him-/herself and stating one thing he/she enjoys doing. *For example:* "Hi! My name is Zachary, and I like to play baseball."

Continue in this manner all the way around the circle until all students have had the opportunity to introduce themselves. The student who originated the circle then introduces his/her "next-door circle neighbor" by stating the person's name and the interest that was already expressed. *For example:* "This is my friend Brooke, and she likes to dress up."

Continue until all students have introduced the person sitting immediately next to them.

Variation: For younger students, you may want to use their SH12 Paper Bag Face Puppet as a prop.

Grades K–3	Ball Pass	CC4

Grouping: Full

Materials: One medium-sized ball (or beanbag).

Procedure: The first person begins by holding the ball and saying, "My name is _____ and I like to _____." The speaker then tosses the ball to another participant who in turn says, "Hi _____ (repeating the name of the former participant), my name is _____ and I like to _____."

The ball continues to be passed around the room until all participants have had the opportunity to catch the ball.

Grades 2–8	Partner Interview	CC5

Grouping: Full/Partner

Procedure: Encourage students to develop a series of 5–10 questions they could use to find out more about a classmate. As they make suggestions, write them on a chart.

Divide students into partners and tell them they have six minutes as a team to find out about each other. One partner interviews the other using the classroom question list. At the end of six minutes partners return to the circle to introduce each other. (You may wish to give students a sign after three minutes to switch partners.)

Grades 2–8	Body Tracings	CC6

Grouping: Team

Materials: Large sheet of butcher paper measuring the length of the student (1 per student); scissors, marking pens.

Procedure: Divide students into teams of four to five members. Each day one student in the team lies down on the paper and has his/her body outlined by another student. The teammates now have five minutes to ask the student any questions about his/her interests, past, family or competencies. The questioned student has the right to pass on any questions. The questioning period must stop at the end of the set time.

The team now has five minutes to fill in the outline with words, slogans or drawings that represent their findings. Each completed body outline is then "introduced to the class." The team "reads" their findings to all students. This activity will take as many meeting times as the number of team members.

Note: You may wish to consider having upper-grade students team up with partners of the same sex on one circle time meeting. This time could be devoted just to tracing each other's body outline onto butcher paper, cutting them out, and setting them aside for the day of the focused student's turn.

| Grades 2–8 | The One-Cent Interview | CC7 |

Grouping: Partner

Materials: 3 minute egg timer *(optional)*. A penny for each child. Dates on the penny should be from the date of the student's birth to the present; bag or basket.

Procedure: Place all pennies in the basket. Each student randomly chooses one penny. Each partner asks of the other:

1. What is your name?
2. When is your birthday (month, day, year)?
3. Tell me something you remember about the year on the penny. (If possible, this should be something personal of significance.)
4. Why was that event so special for you?

Each partner "shares" the discoveries about the student to either the full circle or team.

Follow-up: Read the book *The Hundred Penny Box*, Sharon Bell Mathis (Viking, 1975).

CONCEPT CIRCLES THAT INCREASE THE FEELING OF SELFHOOD

Purpose: To build pride in self-awareness and identity. To provide students with the opportunity to

clarify their sense of selfhood by recognizing individual characteristics, interests, physical attributes and strengths. To increase positive self-statements.

| Grades 2–8 | Names | CC8 |

Grouping: Partner/Team

Procedure: Students form their teams. Within the teams, each student finds a partner. They have one minute each to interview their partner and find out information about their name. They are to ask:

1. What is your name?
2. Do you have any problems with your name?
3. What is the best thing/worst thing about your name?

Students may then share with their team and the class.

| Grades 1–8 | Design a Logo | CC9 |

Grouping: Team

Materials: 12" x 18" piece of light-colored construction paper for each team of 4 students. (They may also do this on an individual basis.)

Procedure: Students design an insignia or logo for Concept Circles. If students are in a support team of four to five members, they will design a logo for just their team. Each team (or individual) shares their logo. At a later date these could later be placed on T-shirts, banners or posters to encourage team affiliation.

| Grades K–8 | Me Bag | CC10 |

Grouping: Full/Team

Materials: Small lunch bag per student; glue, scissors, magazines.

Procedure: Students write their names at the top of one side of the bag. Tell them to look through the magazines and find slogans, words or pictures that describe themselves. They glue the pictures on one side only of the bag. You may wish to set the timer for a specified time. When the time is up, everyone takes a turn explaining their bag to other students (or to their Support Team). Bags should remain at school for use in additional circle activities.

Note: To save class time the bag could be sent home as an evening home assignment and brought back the following day.

Grades K–4	**I Like**	**CC11**

Grouping: Full

Materials: A shoe box or similar-sized box. Cover with wrapping paper/contact paper and glue a mirror on top of the box.

Rhyme:
Mirror, mirror on the box,
My face in you I see.
There are so many things I like
Just because I'm me!

Each student says the jingle (with the help of other friends) while holding the box and then states one thing he/she likes. It is fun for students to draw a picture of a favorite thing they like before the circle starts. When it is their turn they can then place the drawing inside the box.

Variations: Change the format so that each time the box is used the I Like item becomes specific.

"I like the color _____."

"I like the book _____."

"I like to eat _____."

"I like to watch _____." (TV or movie)

"I like to play _____."

You can easily graph each topic for students to see each other's choices. Students paste their drawings next to their choice on a large piece of butcher paper.

Grades K–8	**Share Yourself**	**CC12**

Grouping: Full/Team

Procedure: Assign the class the task of sharing themselves to their classmates on the following day of school. They are to share with each other a part of themselves they'd like their friends to learn.

Grades K–3	**I Like to Be Me**	**CC13**

Grouping: Full

Materials: *I Like to be Me*, Barbara Bel Geddes (Viking Press, 1963). Read the book to the students. This is a wonderful motivator. The book lends itself to the flannel board.

Procedure: The first student in the circle says "I'm glad to be me because I'm cute." The second student says exactly what the first student stated ("Sally is glad to be Sally because she is cute") and then follows with why he or she likes to be him-/herself ("And I'm glad to be me because I'm a good soccer player").

Continue moving around the circle in this manner.

Note: Write down the students' self-statements exactly as they say them. At a later date print these

Our Favorite Colors

12	11	10	9	8	7	6	5	4	3	2	1	
									John	Brad	Mary	blue
								Tammy	Pam	Carol	David	red
											Mike	green
			Zach	Adam	Jill	Brianne	Burt	Fred	Bill	Ted	Barbara	yellow

CONCEPT CIRCLES

comments surrounded by self-portraits on a large piece of butcher paper for a bulletin board.

Grades 2–8	Identity Bag	CC14

Grouping: Full/Team

Materials: A large grocery bag for each student; a copy of SH18 My Identity Shield with words and directions whited out. Using a black marking pen, print a category in each of the four boxes on the Shield.

Make a copy of the revised shield for each student, who cuts out the shield and glues it to the front of his/her bag.

Procedure: Each afternoon choose one student from the full group or team. He/she takes the bag home and searches for things around his/her house that would depict the following things:

1. his/her family;

2. something he/she is proud of (achievement or accomplishment);

3. favorite interest or hobby;

4. favorite possession.

The student places the actual object or drawing of the object into the bag and brings it to share at school the following day. To share, the student removes each object or drawing from bag to show the class.

Grades K–8	I'm Great!	CC15

Grouping: Full/Team

Materials: Large bag of small food items such as candy, raisins, small marshmallows or cereal; container to hold them.

Procedure: On the first day of this circle, pass the container around the circle with the food items inside. Instruct students to take one piece only. Before eating the food, students must say one statement describing themselves. In the beginning these could include statements about interests (favorite

food, movie, TV show, etc.) or physical characteristics. With each succeeding circle increase the amount of food items by one (for instance, on the fourth circle, each student would take four pieces from the container, say four self-describing comments, and then eat the food).

Note: You may wish to make a chart or words or pictorial representations of the types of describing comments students could say. First circles should always be nonthreatening and focus on concrete descriptions. Favorite things are always safe kinds of topics. Only gradually will students feel secure enough to describe more abstract thoughts and feelings about themselves.

Variation: Consider using non-food items as rewards, such as trinkets, writing accessories, stickers, etc.

Idea suggested by Leona Leist; New Richmond School District, New Richmond, Ohio.

Grades K–6	A Me Hanging	CC16

Grouping: Full/Team

Materials: 5" light-colored construction paper circles—cut 4 for each student; crayons, hole-punch, yarn lengths, glue; magazines.

Procedure:

1. Provide each student with four circles. On each circle students depict an interest or something they like. They may represent their interests with words, phrases, drawings or magazine cutouts. Instruct students to fold completed circles in half.

2. Each circle day, students share one completed circle with the rest of their classmates by stating and showing what they like.

Variation:

1. Take a circle, which is folded in half, and glue one half of it back-to-back to half of another circle. Do this to each circle until all four are joined together to form a sphere.

CONCEPT CIRCLES

2. Punch a hole in the top of the sphere and thread a yarn length through the hole. Tie it securely and hang the sphere from the ceiling to form Me Hangings.

Grades K–5 Feeling Drawings CC17

Grouping: Team

Materials: Record player or tape recorder; 12" x 18" drawing paper, 1 sheet per student; crayons or marking pens.

Records depicting different emotions:
- *Sadness*:
  Anton Dvorak, "Symphony No. 5 in E Minor"
  Peter Ilich Tchaikovsky, "Symphony No. 6 in B Minor"
- *Anger*:
  Modest Mussorgsky, "Night on Bare Mountain"
  Paul A. Dukas, "The Sorcerer's Apprentice"
  Claude Debussy, "The Sea (La Mer)"
- *Happiness*:
  Maurice Ravel, "Bolero"
  Anton Dvorak, "Carnival Overture"
  Peter Ilich Tchaikovsky, "Nutcracker Suite"
- *Fear*:
  Gustav Holst, "Mercury" from "The Planets"
  Edvard Grieg, "Peer Gynt"
- *Playful*:
  Camille Saint-Saens, "Carnival of the Animals"

Procedure: For each circle activity, students listen to a different musical selection that depicts an emotion. Using crayons or marking pens, students express their feelings by moving the crayons across the paper. At the conclusion of the activity, students dictate or write their reactions to the musical selection on the bottom or back of the paper by completing the appropriate sentence stem:
- "I feel (angry, sad, happy, scared) when _____."
- "Something that makes me feel _____ is _____."
- "A time when I felt _____ was _____."
- "When I feel _____ I usually like to _____."

Grades K–2 Happy-Sad Beanbag CC18

Grouping: Full

Materials: Make a circular beanbag (at least 6" in diameter) from plain-colored fabric. Stuff it with beans or rice. Use felt scraps and glue to make a happy face on the front and a sad face on the back.

Procedure: Toss the bag to each student in the circle. They verbalize back to you and the group a situation that causes them to feel the emotion shown face up on the bag. They then toss the bag back to you for a new toss.

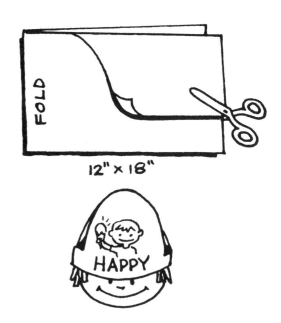

Grades K–2 Emotion Hats CC19

Grouping: Full

Materials: Emotion hat per student: cut the hat from construction paper (12" x 18") and staple the back. On the front, print the emotion term to be discussed that day.

Procedure: Following a discussion about a particular emotion, each student tells what makes him/her feel that way. The student draws a picture on the front of his/her hat to represent a situation that causes him/her to feel that way.

Students wear their hats during circle time when they share their feelings.

Feeling Thermometer CC20

Grouping: Full

Materials: Make a large thermometer from a heavy piece of paper at least 12" x 20". Draw faces (or use cutouts) vertically along the thermometer depicting each of the following emotions: happiness, sadness, fear, anger, pride, etc.

Punch a hole in the middle of the board 2" from the top and 2" from the bottom. Thread large rug yarn (red and white, 9" of each tied together) between the two holes.

Procedure: Pass the thermometer from student to student in the circle and ask them to put the red yarn next to the face that represents how they feel that day. (They pull the yarn until the red comes up to the place they want.)

Variation: Preset the red yarn to a certain emotion and pass it from student to student while asking them to comment on when they felt that way.

Grades K-3 **Individual Thermometers CC21**

Grouping: Full

Materials: Paper plates (for thermometers); glue, magazine pictures, scissors; paper fasteners, black construction paper scraps.

Procedure: Each student makes his/her own thermometer: Students find magazine pictures that depict the different emotions they are studying and glue them around the edge of a paper plate. Cut an arrow from black construction paper and fasten it to the center of the plate with a brad. Students turn their arrow to the emotion that best represents their answer to sentence stems such as those below:

- When I'm in a dark room I feel...
- On the first day of school I feel...
- On my birthday I feel...
- During reading I feel...
- Talking in front of the class makes me feel...
- When I come to school each morning, I feel...
- When it's time for circles, I feel...
- Friends make me feel...
- The people in this classroom make me feel...
- During music time I feel...
- When I get my papers back, I feel...
- During spelling tests I feel...
- When someone tells me they like me I feel...
- When my best friend is sick, I feel...
- When someone smiles at me, I feel...
- At recess time I feel...

Grades K-3 **Feeling Masks CC22**

Grouping: Full

Materials: One set of Feeling Masks for the group cut from 9" x 12" tagboard-weight paper into circles.

Construction: Put on facial features and staple or glue each mask to a ruler, pencil or skewer. The faces illustrated here or those on CC20 Feeling Thermometer could serve as patterns.

Procedure: Use the masks for various purposes in Concept Circles:

- **Role-play:** In turn, students choose one of the masks, place it in front of their face, and act out a time when they felt that way.

- **Individual mask:** Use a different mask for each circle. In turn, students place the mask in front of them and describe a time when they felt that way.

Variation: Students work in pairs or teams to write lines of dialogue that verbalize the expressions on the masks.

Grades K–4	Wishes	CC23

Grouping: Full

Materials:
Wishing Well: make the well from a large ice cream carton (available from ice cream stores). Glue torn pieces of brown and gray construction paper (tear

freely into "stone shapes") onto the carton. Staple a paper handle across the top.

Coins: Cut 6" construction paper circles for each student.

Procedure: Instruct students to draw a self-portrait on one side of the coin and on the flip side draw a picture of something they would like to wish for. Each student in turn tosses his/her coin into the well, which is placed in the middle of the circle, and says the rhyme.

Rhyme:
My wish upon my coin I drew
I'll toss it in for hopes come true.

Variation: Read a book to the students on the theme of wishing:

Alexander and the Wind-up Mouse, Leo Lionni (Pantheon, 1969);
Sylvester and the Magic Pebble, William Steig (Simon & Schuster, 1969);
The Little Rabbit Who Wanted Red Wings, Carolyn Sherwin Bailey (Platt and Munk, 1978).

Grades 3–8	Dreams	CC24

Grouping: Full/Team

Materials: *Dream Cloud:* Each student makes a "cloud" from a 12" x 18" piece of white construction paper cut freeform into a cloud shape.

Optional: glue, magazines.

Procedure: Instruct students to cut a cloud shape from their piece of white paper and write their name inside the shape. Encourage students to think about things they like to dream about both now and in the future. Using words, pictures or symbols, students depict their dreams inside the cloud shape.

Cutout magazine pictures and words may also be glued onto the form.

Each student then shares his/her dreams with team members. The completed forms may later be added to a bulletin board under a caption such as "What We Dream About" or "What's on Our Minds."

CONCEPT CIRCLES THAT INCREASE THE FEELING OF AFFILIATION

Purpose: To encourage students to perform acts of friendliness. To increase students' awareness of the characteristics and attributes of others so that they extend awareness beyond themselves. To teach students to praise others.

Affiliation circle topics generally follow on from those designed to increase students' sense of selfhood. Individuals must feel secure and confident in their identity before they can genuinely compliment others and take pride in their achievements. When students learn to praise themselves, praising others almost comes automatically.

TEACHING STUDENTS TO PRAISE OTHERS

- Expect students' praise of others to be general and non-specific at first. Only gradually will students begin to make comments that are specific and relate to actual experiences.
- No student should ever be expected to say a "Plastic Fuzzy." Statements that they say to each other should be ones they feel comfortable and sincere about. Point out that for a while it will be acceptable to say statements such as "Hello," "How are you?" and "Have a nice day." Later on, however, they will be expected to say something positive and specific, such as: "I like you because you listen to me."
- An essential component in teaching students how to praise others is teaching them how to accept a compliment. You may wish to keep a chart of phrases, such as the ones below, for students to use after receiving a compliment:
  — Thank You!
  — I'm glad you noticed.
  — I appreciate that!
  — I know it! (for the high-powered student)

Many students feel uncomfortable praising another student because compliments may be not part of their repertoire. Let them know that if they need help in thinking of a compliment they may choose one from available sources such as the Word Gifts (CC33) or Sunshine Statements (CC25) board.

Grades K-8 Sunshine Statements CC25

Grades K-1 need teacher's direction.

Grouping: Full/Team

Materials:
1. Cut a large circle (at least 20") from yellow or orange tagboard.
2. Cut 1 "sunray" (a triangle 4" x 6") for each participant from yellow and orange construction paper. Using black marking pen, draw a "sunshine face" inside the large circle. Print the words "Sunshine Statements" on the inside of the circle.

Each student will need a black crayon or marking pen.

Procedure: Review the circle rules with students. Emphasize the importance of saying "builder-upper" or "sparkle" statements because they are like "sunshine" to our self-esteem. Tell them that there will be many opportunities in circles to say "builder-upper" or "sparkle" statements to each other. Not only is it important to say them, but it is also important to accept them: ask them what they could say if someone gave them a compliment.

Using a black marking pen, write the following comments in the center of the large circle and tell students these are a few comments they could say back to accept a compliment:

- Thank you.
- I'm glad you noticed.
- I appreciated that.
- I know it.

Divide students into teams of two (or four, if ready). Ask each team to think of statements they could say to someone in this class or school that would put a smile on his/her face. These statements should be general so that anyone could say it to anyone else ("I like your curly hair" would not be general enough).

Pass a sunray (triangle) to each student and ask them to write or draw (younger students could use the help of a cross-age tutor for each group of four) a builder-upper comment on each triangle. Students then rejoin the circle and present the compliment to the student on their left. The receiving student should be encouraged to say one of the four accepting comments back.

To conclude, display all the sunshine statements around the edge of the large circle. Keep the poster in the room to use with each circle. Students may refer to accepting and giving comments from time to time.

Grades K–5   **Sparkle Box**   **CC26**

Grouping: Full

Materials: A shoe box decorated with "sparkles" (stickers, names of students, etc.); 3" x 5" set of index cards printed with the name of each student (for younger students glue a small Xeroxed photograph next to the student's name).

Procedure: Students take turns drawing names from the box. Instruct them to say a compliment to the person whose name they draw. They should feel free to refer to the CC25 Sunshine Statements poster if they desire. Remind them how they can accept a compliment.

Grades 1–8   **Banners**   **CC27**

Supervise K–1.

Grouping: Partner/Full

Materials: 12" x 18" construction paper, 1 per participant; scissors, crayons or marking pens.

Procedure: Each student cuts out a banner shape. (For directions on how to make banners, see C26 Accomplishment Banner.)

Students form a "partnership" with another student they do not know well. Students each have three minutes to interview their partner, with the purpose of finding out about their partner's interests, background, family, unique competencies, etc. At the end of six minutes total time, each student has 5–10 minutes to construct a banner about his/her partner. The banner should have the student's name printed in large colorful letters as well as words or pictures representing the student's discoveries. Everyone shares the banners with the full group.

Grades 2–8   **Questions**   **CC28**

Grouping: Full/Team

Materials: 3" x 5" cut slips of paper, 2 per student; pencils.

Procedure: Instruct students to think of questions they could ask another classmate to find out more about his/her background, interests or competencies.

Each student writes two questions (the kind of questions you wouldn't mind someone asking you) on a separate piece of paper. Collect all the questions and place them in a bag or container. Students now form into teams. Each team member pulls out two questions and places them face down in the center of the circle.

Team members take turns drawing a question card. Each person reads the question out loud and either answers it or states "pass" and draws another question. The activity continues until the facilitator calls "time."

Grades 2–8   **Picture Puzzles**   **CC29**

Grouping: Full/Team

Materials: 9" x 12" piece of light-colored construction paper per student; red, blue and green crayons; scissors.

Procedure:

1. Provide students with one piece of construction paper each. Ask them to cut the paper to form a puzzle, which, when finished, should consist of three pieces each large enough to contain a picture.

CONCEPT CIRCLES

Give them these directions:

a. In the first piece use red crayon to draw a picture of your favorite food.

b. In the second piece use green crayon to draw a picture of your favorite TV show.

c. In the third piece use blue crayon to draw a picture of your favorite place to be.

These categories may be changed at any time. Ask students to print a word or phrase under each picture to describe their drawing. Students should now form their team, but keep their pieces "secret" from other participants.

2. Instruct students to form three separate piles for each color of their puzzles and place them in the center of their circles. (One for red crayon, one for green...) Pieces should be placed face down.

3. Beginning with the red puzzle pieces, the first person turns one piece over, reads it to the team, and tries to guess which member of the group it represents. The student has one try to guess correctly. If the other student verifies the guess, he/she must keep his/her own piece. If the guess is incorrect (the student in question answers "no, it's not me"), the piece goes back to the color pile. The next person in the circle now has a turn to guess.

4. Guessing continues until all pieces have been returned to each student. The same procedure now follows for the blue pieces and then, finally, the green.

5. You may vary the activity by forming students into new teams or by changing the three questions.

<table><tr><td>Grades 2–8</td><td>We're All Stars</td><td>CC30</td></tr></table>

Grouping: Full/Team

Materials: 8" star figure cut out of yellow construction paper, 1 per student (star figure may be found in A2 Common Points, see Affiliation, Chapter 5); marking pens or crayons.

Procedure:

1. Distribute a cutout star to each student and ask the student to print his/her name across the center of the figure.

2. Moving clockwise from the top point around the figure to the final left-hand point, students write (or draw) answers to each of the following:

- A wish I have for myself.
- My favorite place on earth.
- What I want to be when I grow up.
- A person whom I admire, or would want to be more like.
- My favorite indoor activity.

3. Each student shares his/her star with the rest of the team.

4. Consider adding the stars to a bulletin board under the caption: "All Our Stars."

<table><tr><td>Grades K–8</td><td>Riddles</td><td>CC31</td></tr></table>

Grouping: Full/Team

Materials: Slip of paper 5 1/2" x 8 1/2" for each student.

Procedure: Tell students that their task is to write a riddle about themselves on the paper. The riddle should include clues about:

- personal physical characteristics;
- an interest or hobby;
- where the student is most likely to be found.

Student includes his/her name on the back right-hand corner of the card. To save time, the riddle card should be a homework activity. Students who do not read or write need a parent or aide to help them with the task. Younger students could draw the riddles and provide only one clue on a card.

Students place the completed riddles in a container and pass them counterclockwise around the circle. The first student pulls a card from the container and reads it (or has it read to him/her). He/she then tries to guess who the student may be. If the person guesses correctly, he/she may present the card to the student. If the student chooses incorrectly, however, any two other students may try to guess.

The activity continues around the circle until all the cards are distributed. The game may stop at any time and be continued as time permits. Students who are last to guess will obviously have the advantage. Point out that it is because they had to wait longer.

| Grades K–5 | Silent Sparkles | CC32 |

Grouping: Full/Team

Procedure:

1. Begin by asking participants to think of ways they could put smiles on other people's faces *without saying anything* (mention that these are called actions).

2. List the suggestions on a large piece of chart paper. You may wish to keep the chart in a permanent place so that you can add additional ideas. Action ideas may include:
   • hugs
   • holding hands
   • handshakes
   • pats
   • smiles
   • looking at the person (eye contact)
   • listening to the person
   • sharing something
   • sitting by someone
   • spending time with the person
   • walking up to someone

3. As a follow-up activity you may like to read them *A Book of Hugs,* Dave Ross (Thomas Y. Crowell, 1980).

4. Design a "Class Book of Friendly Actions": Students draw a picture of a friendly action they might do for someone else. Collect the pages and bind them together as a Class Book.

5. Learn the song "Hugs" (or change the words to any of the above-mentioned friendly actions):

   A hug is something if you give it away
   Give it away, give it away . . .
   A hug is something if you give it away
   You end up having more!

   It's just like a magic penny
   Hold it tight and you don't have any
   Lend it, spend it, and you'll have so many
   They roll all over the floor.

   Repeat Chorus (changing hug to smile, pat, handshake. . .).

6. **Silent Circle:** Each student does an appropriate, friendly action toward the student sitting immediately to their right. Note: Some students will be very uncomfortable giving and receiving hugs and that should be respected. Smiles and handshakes are fine!

| Grades K–4 | Word Gifts | CC33 |

Grouping: Full/Team

Materials: 4" x 6" cards, 1 per student; pencils.

Word Gifts Box: Cover the top only of a gift box with wrapping paper in such a way that the top of the box can still be lifted.

Procedure: Ask students as a group to state words, phrases and sentences that would put a "smile on someone's face." Write each comment on a separate 4" x 6" card and place it in the box, which is then passed around the circle. Students take turns choosing a phrase from the box and saying it to their neighbor. Encourage the recipient to accept the comment with an "acceptance phrase."

Periodically add new word gifts to the box as they are stated or suggested by classmates. Remind students that words we say to one another are gifts we can give. You may wish to write a card on the top of the box that reads: "Kind words are special presents from a friend."

Variation: In future circles use the box to ask students to compliment another student. The box may be kept in the middle of the circle. Any time a student wishes to validate another student he/she may use an idea from the gift box.

| Grades 3–8 | Word Power | CC34 |

Grouping: Team

Materials: CC34 Word Power worksheet.

Procedure: Put-down messages can be killers to a class environment. This exercise helps students recognize how deadly put-downs are to others' feelings. It also helps them find ways to change negative messages to more positive builder-upper statements.

Begin by making a copy of the CC34 worksheet and a set of 10 index cards (3" x 5") for each team. Write a different negative statement on each card. Statements that appear below are merely suggestions; you may wish to include ones more commonly used in your setting.

- Shut up!
- Get out of here!
- You're stupid!
- You dummy!
- Quit bugging me!
- You're such a nerd!
- Go away!
- Quit copying me!
- Leave me alone!
- Don't touch me!

Each team elects one member to be the dealer who passes out the cards. Moving clockwise, each team member reads one put-down message to the group. After each reading, the team brainstorms builder-upper statements that could be said instead. The team chooses the best answer to each put-down statement and fills it out on the worksheet.

Grades K-3	**Glasses Circle**	**CC35**

Grouping: Full/Team

Materials: A pair of used eyeglasses with the glass portion removed.

Rhyme:
Glasses, glasses, say what you see.
Say what you like best about me.

Procedure: Students sit in a circle and take turns passing the glasses to the person sitting immediately to their right. The student puts the glasses on and recites the jingle (encourage other students to recite the jingle at the same time). He/she removes the glasses and passes it to the next student, who responds with a compliment to that person.

Grades K-5	**Sun Rays**	**CC36**

Grouping: Full/Team

Materials: Pre-cut 4" construction paper circles (yellow and orange), 1 circle of either color for every

participant; triangles cut 4 1/2" x 5 1/2" (long) from yellow and orange construction paper, 6 of either color per student.

Procedure: Students decorate and print their name on sun centers (4" circle shape). Display the sun centers so that students can easily attach the sunrays to them at a later date. During a series of concept circles, ask each student to share a discovery about a specific classmate, such as: what he/she likes or doesn't like, what he/she does well, friendly things he/she does, etc.

Students print (or draw) their discoveries on the pre-cut sunrays and attach them to the appropriate sun centers. This activity will take six circle sessions to complete.

Grades K-8	**Me Bags by Others**	**CC37**

Grouping: Full/Team

Materials: Me Bags (saved from CC10); magazines, scissors, glue.

Procedure: Students sit in support teams. A different team member is the focus for each concept circle. Other team members cut out magazine pictures, words or slogans that somehow depict the student. These are glued on the remaining side of the bag. Each group then shares the bag with the class explaining what they've learned about that member.

Grades K-8	**Me Bag Compliments**	**CC38**

Grouping: Full/Team

Materials: Me Bags (from previous circle); 3" x 5" index cards (1 card per student); pens.

Procedure: Choose one student to be the recipient of compliments. Give an index card each to the remaining students and ask them to write or draw a compliment to the student. Students sit in a circle with the student's Me Bag in the center and take turns "reading" or saying the compliment before putting it in the bag.

CONCEPT CIRCLES

Note: This is a good closing activity. As it takes a short time to do, each session could end with a compliment-writing (or drawing) finale, focusing on several students in turn.

Name Poster — CC39
Grades 2–8

Grouping: Full/Team

Materials: 12" x 18" piece of construction paper per team; colored marking pens.

Procedure: Each team prints the first initial of every team member down the left side of the paper. Within three minutes, each team is to come up with a positive phrase or word to describe every team member. *The phrase or word must begin with the same letter as the initial.* Students write down the comments on the paper. They reconvene as a full group and discuss their poster and the descriptions of each member. Posters may be saved and used as "Team Posters" for team gatherings.

Compliments — CC40
Grades K–8

Supervise K–1; 3–8 use plain piece of paper instead of doll figure.

Grouping: Team

Materials: Cut a doll figure for each student using the SH6 Me Doll pattern (use construction paper, trace and cut out); marking pens or crayons.

Procedure: Each student writes his/her name in large, colorful letters on the top of the figure. Instruct the students to pass the figure around their small circle so that each student may write (draw) a positive compliment about the student represented by the figure. Continue passing the figures until all students have their original figure.

Compliment Hanging CC41
Grades 2–8

Grouping: Team

Materials: 3" x 6" strip of construction paper for each participant; yarn or string; hole-punch, crayons, scissors.

Procedure: Each day feature one student from the team to sit in the center of the circle. Each team member takes a turn coming up behind the student and placing on his/her back a 3" x 6" card on which a compliment for that student has been written. The "giver" may choose to sign his/her compliment.

At the conclusion of each circle, hang the cards vertically and present them to the recipient. The featured student may design a name card with his/her name in large, colorful letters and hang all other cards from it.

Fuzzy Circles — CC42
Grades K–5

Grouping: Full/Team

Materials: CC42 Fuzzy Balls made up into props.

Optional: Teacher Fuzzy Bag. To store your Fuzzies you may wish to make a cloth Fuzzy Bag. Make it from material and use cording pulled around the top to open and close. The fuzzy on the front of the bag may be cut from bright-colored felt scraps and glued on. (A convenient size is 12" x 15".)

CONCEPT CIRCLES

Optional reading:

Fuzzies, Richard Lessor (Argus Communications, 1975);

The Original Warm Fuzzy Tale, Claude Steiner (Transactional Publications, 1977);

TA for Tots and Other Prinzes by Alvyn M. Freed (Jalmar Press, 1973).

Procedure: The Fuzzy Ball is used as a prop. The first student begins by holding the Fuzzy Ball and saying a "fuzzy" to the student on his/her right side. The receiver then holds the ball and does the same, and so on.

The circle continues until all students have given a fuzzy statement and received one.

CONCEPT CIRCLES THAT INCREASE THE SENSE OF MISSION

Purpose: To help students recognize they have control and influence over their own lives by the actions they take. To provide students with the opportunity to solve their own problems.

Goal-setting is a technique that enhances self-esteem only if goals are set so they are realistic and achievable. You may wish to refer to Mission, Chapter 6, to review the steps for successful goal-setting. Many of the goal-setting forms could be used in these circles.

Grades K–4 | **Would You Rather? CC43**

Grouping: Partner/Team

Materials: Cut out magazine pictures depicting student-centered activities, at least 25 per team; (topics may include: food, interests, games, toys, places of interest, pets, etc.). Glue each picture on a separate card.

Procedure: Read *Would You Rather?* John Burningham (Crowell, 1978) as a motivator to the activity and to provide additional sentence stem ideas for discussion.

Tell students to place the cards face down on the floor in front of each team and gently shuffle them. The student whose last name is the shortest in length goes first. Students then take turns in a clockwise direction. Inform students that there are no right or wrong answers to any decision, and every decision counts.

The first student turns two cards over and quickly completes the sentence stem, "I would rather _____ than _____ because _____" by stating his/her choice and the reason.

Example: "I would rather play ball than swim because I don't know how to swim."

The two cards are then turned over and quickly shuffled into the stack for the next student's turn.

Grades 4–8 | **Brainstorming Solutions CC44**

Grouping: Partner/Team

Materials: "Dear Abby" or "Ann Landers" newspaper columns. Cut out the most appropriate problems and glue to separate index cards. Also cut out the answers, which are glued on different cards. Students may also generate their own problems, or use current events. Encourage students to scan the newspaper and bring in clippings.

Procedure: Provide each group with one problem card for each three minutes of session. Before beginning, quickly review with them the rules of brainstorming (see Chapter 6, M5 Brainstorming):

1. Every idea counts.
2. The more ideas the better.
3. No judging of ideas.
4. It's OK to add on to someone else's idea.

If you haven't already done so, you may wish to make a poster of the rules and post them so all students can see them. Students quickly choose a recorder (or designate the recorder to be the student whose first name is closest to "A" in the alphabet). The recorder quickly reads the problem and writes down solutions as the group generates them. The group has three minutes to complete this task.

At the conclusion of the three-minute time limit, students total their number of solutions, which are graphed each session. Compare the solutions with that of the columnist.

Grades 2–8	I Wish I Could	CC45

Grouping: Full/Partner

Procedure: 3" x 5" index card per student.

Procedure: Ask students to think of one thing they wish they could do or improve in. Tell them it must be something they could change or have power over.

Students write or draw their "wish" on one side of the index card. Each student repeatedly "reads" his/her card to teammates or a partner. Every time the student reads the wish, teammates take turns asking the student: "What do you have to do to have your wish come true?"

Note: There is to be *no* judging of the student's wish or answers.

The student answers the question and then reads the card again. Another teammate repeats the question. The sequence continues until the student has been asked the question four times by either the same partner or a different teammate. After the fourth question, the student takes a moment to stop and write down on the back of the wish card anything he/she would like to remember from the interaction to help him/her reach the goal.

Grades K–8	Goal Sharing	CC46

Grouping: Full/Team

Materials: 5" x 8" card for each student; marking pens or crayons; small rubber football (to use as a pass-around prop for younger students).

Procedure: Tell students to think of something they would like to achieve: it may be something they want to "get better at" or something new to learn. Behavior or academic goals are preferred.

On one side of the card, students draw a picture of what it is they want to achieve. A glued-on magazine cutout would also be acceptable. Students write or dictate their goal under the picture. Each student shares the goal in the circle. Students should continue sharing the same goal in circle sessions until they have achieved it.

Grades K–8	How Will You Make It?	CC47

Grouping: Full/Team

Materials: 5" x 8" card from CC46 Goal Sharing.

Procedure: In turn, students share their goal-setting cards. As a student states his/her goal intention, the person on the right asks, "How will you make it?"

The question is intended to make students think through the goal-setting process:

1. What needs to be done to achieve the goal?
2. What/who needs to help him/her?

The goal-setter must answer back one behavior he/she could do to achieve the goal. Other students may offer suggestions. Students write each idea on the back of the card.

Grades K–8	Goal Accomplishment	CC48

Grouping: Full/Team

Materials: 5" x 8" goal card from previous circle, or other goal card of your choice.

Procedure: Each student who has achieved the goal he/she set shares it and states what was done to achieve it.

Note: Jack Canfield suggests that those who did not complete their goals not be allowed to share with the class during this circle. In his view, if they did, they would be receiving the same reinforcement of peer attention as those who had completed theirs.

Canfield also suggests decorating the bulletin board in the form of a football goalpost. Each day students who have achieved their goal move their card above the crossbar.

CONCEPT CIRCLES THAT INCREASE THE SENSE OF COMPETENCE

Purpose: To help students focus on their strengths and accomplishments. To encourage students to praise their competencies. To recognize the strengths and competencies of others.

Circles that require students to "brag" about their accomplishments work better after group affiliation has been built when students feel comfortable about sharing and participating. For this reason, they are usually the last type of circles to take place. This corresponds to the fact that competence is generally the last feeling to be acquired in the self-esteem model. When students find it difficult to "blow their own trumpet," keep in mind that as a society we are taught to be humble, to make little of our accomplishments.

TEACHING STUDENTS TO PRAISE THEMSELVES

1. Model positive self-talk yourself. If students hear you saying compliments to yourself, they will feel more comfortable doing it themselves.

2. Whenever possible, use concrete evidence to support students' competencies. Initial competence circles, for instance, could be ones in which students bring in paintings, hobbies, etc., that demonstrate their competencies.

3. Whenever a student is hesitant about "bragging," ask other students for suggestions. At this point students will know each other well enough to be able to offer help.

4. You will find it particularly helpful to keep a Class Strength Book handy. See Chapter 7, C6 Class Strength Book for explanation. Whenever a student doubts his/her competence, you can instantly turn to his/her individual page in the Class Strength Book for verification.

| Grades K–8 | **Strength Book** | **CC49** |

Grouping: Full

Materials: Sheet of plain paper for each student stapled between construction paper covers. Finished size book need be no larger than 8 1/2" x 11" (see Chapter 7, C6 Strength Book for cover pattern). Write students' names in alphabetical order, one name per page.

Procedure: Inform students that you will be studying their "strengths." Each time you discover a strength in a student, point it out ("I discovered you are quite a good artist" or "I discovered you share very nicely") and write the strength on the student's strength page.

This process may take two weeks or so, but continue to point out individual strengths on a regular basis. Use the book in a Strength Circle (or in any of the circles that require a student to verbalize his/her competencies). Report the strength discoveries to the class by stating what strengths have been recorded on each student's strength page.

| Grades K–8 | **Brag Time** | **CC50** |

Grouping: Full/Team

Procedure: Students take turns "bragging" about what they're most proud of in themselves. Limit starting circles to bragging about one item. As students continue to learn their competencies, increase the brags up to three items.

| Grades K–3 | **Strength Circle** | **CC51** |

Grouping: Full/Team

Materials: A 3 lb. barbell or paper barbell. (Glue large styrofoam balls to both ends of an empty paper towel tube. Spray paint black.)

Rhyme:

I have many things I'm good at
As good as good can be
I have so many things I'm good at
I'm good at _____
*   (or, my strength is _____)*

Procedure: Each student says the jingle (with the help of other friends) while holding the barbell. The student states one strength he/she has before passing the barbell on to the next person.

Note: Be sure you've prefaced this activity with the Strength Activities mentioned previously. Students must first have an awareness of what a strength is and what theirs are before they can comfortably engage in this circle.

| Grades K–3 | **Blue Ribbon** | **CC52** |

Grouping: Full/Team

Materials: A blue ribbon (teacher-made, see Chapter 7, C37 Blue Ribbon Award, or purchased from trophy store).

Rhyme:

I am a winner
As special as can be
I am a winner
Just because I'm me!

I'm a winner because _____.

Procedure: Each student says the jingle (with the help of other friends) while holding the blue ribbon. He/she then states one reason why he/she is a winner before passing on the ribbon to the next person.

| Grades K–3 | **Hooray For Me!** | **CC53** |

Grouping: Full

Materials: 9" x 12" construction paper, 1 per student; crayons or marking pens, tape, ruler, pencil.

Books:

I'm Terrific, Marjorie Weinman Sharmat (Scholastic Books, 1977)—older students;
Hooray For Me, R. Charlip and L. Moore (Parents, 1975).

Procedure: Read one of the books to the students, after which each student makes his/her own "sign" on the 9" x 12" piece of construction paper. Using marking pens or crayons, students write one reason why they think they're "terrific."

Students tape the completed sign to the back of a ruler, pencil or empty paper towel tube and bring it to the circle.

Rhyme:

Hooray, hooray, hooray for me!
I am terrific because I'm me!

I'm terrific because _____.

Each student says the jingle (with the help of friends) while holding his/her sign and then states one reason why he/she is terrific.

| Grades K–8 | **One Good Thing About Me** | **CC54** |

Grouping: Full/Team

Procedure: Students sit in the circle. Each student takes a turn introducing him-/herself by saying, "My name is _____ and one good thing about me is _____."

| Grades 2–8 | **Me Commercials** | **CC55** |

Eliminate props for older students.

Grouping: Full/Team

Materials: An old tape recorder microphone (many varieties that work off radio frequency are available in toy stores).

Procedure: Prepare for this activity by discussing with the students their favorite television commercials and acting them out.

Ask students to create a commercial about themselves. The student is to describe his/her qualities in the third person. "This person would be a special friend because he is very good at a lot of things including...."

Students then read out their self-commercial to the group.

Grades K-8	I'm Proud	CC56

Grouping: Full/Team

Procedure: Students are to show something of which they are proud. This could be an actual object brought from home, or a drawing or photograph representing the object. Be sure to bring something to share with students about yourself.

Grades K-3	I Thought I Could	CC57

Grouping: Full/Team

Materials: Small toy train engine.

Book: *The Little Engine That Could*, Watty Piper (Scholastic, 1979).

Procedure: Read the story to younger students. Ask participants to think about a time when they tried to do something, thought they wouldn't be successful at it, but succeeded! What was it? Each student uses the sentence stem, "A time when I thought I couldn't do it but I did was when _____."

Grades K-8	I Can	CC58

Eliminate prop with 4–8.

Grouping: Full/Team

Materials: Soup-size can with top removed and cleaned inside. Cover the can with construction paper and print the words "I CAN" around it. (See Chapter 3, S29 Smile Can.) Strips of paper, 1 per student; pencils.

Procedure: Ask students to choose one of the following sentence stems as a topic question and write (or draw) their "answer" on a strip of paper. The I CAN is passed around the circle. Each student states the stem, completes it and then places his/her strip in the can.

- Something I do well is _____.
- I'm glad I can _____.
- Something I learned to do this year that I'm proud of is _____.
- I'm glad I now can _____.
- It was hard but now I can _____.

Grades 2-8	Self-Introduction	CC59

Grouping: Full/Team

Procedure: Ask each student to think about themselves and specific things of which they are proud. For instance, if he/she were to be introduced by someone else, what accomplishments or strengths would he/she like to be mentioned?

Students are to introduce themselves. As students take a turn, going clockwise around the circle, each one stands up and takes one step back before introducing him-/herself. The student speaks from the third person and includes in the introduction an accomplishment.

Example: "This is Robert. He is a very good soccer player. You'll enjoy knowing him because he's fun to be with."

CONCLUSION

By no means do Concept Circles end here. The topics for successful circles are endless. Some of the best ideas will be generated by the students. Any of the activities found throughout ESTEEM BUILDERS could be useful in circles. Journal Writing ideas are also ideal catalysts or starters because they involve the student's own experiences. For a more thorough list of additional circle topic ideas, as well as a lengthy list of sentence completion ideas, refer to Journal Writing, Chapter 9, J5 and J8.

CONCEPT CIRCLES

Word Power

Team Name: _____ Date: _____

DIRECTIONS: Choose one member to be the dealer and pass out all the cards. Moving clockwise, each team member reads one put-down message to the group. After each reading, the team brainstorms builder-upper statements that could be said instead. Now choose the team's best answer and write both the put-down and builder-upper statement on your worksheet. Go on to the next card.

Put-Down Statement	Builder-Upper Statement
1.	
2.	
3.	
4.	
5.	
6.	
7.	
8.	
9.	
10.	

Remember: You can change a put-down to a builder-upper by . . .
1. Starting the message with an "I."
2. Telling the person how you feel ("I'm angry . . .").
3. Telling the person what he or she did that made you feel that way ("I'm angry because you took my pencil").

"You're a dummy Tommy!" ▶ "I'm angry because you kicked me!"

Esteem Builders. Jalmar Press
Rolling Hills Estates, CA

Make Your Own Fuzzy

Materials needed:

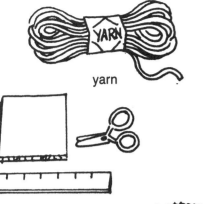

yarn

scissors

cardboard

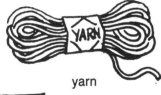

1. Cut a piece of cardboard into a 4" x 4" square.

2. Wrap yarn lengths carefully around the cardboard square 100 times.

3. Carefully remove the yarn from the cardboard onto your finger. Tie a knot tightly around the middle of the lengths. With your scissors begin to snip the yarn along the edges until all the yarn has been fringed. Fluff the yarn ball.

Make Your Own Fuzzy

Materials needed:

yarn

scissors

cardboard

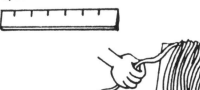

1. Cut a piece of cardboard into a 4" x 4" square.

2. Wrap yarn lengths carefully around the cardboard square 100 times.

3. Carefully remove the yarn from the cardboard onto your finger. Tie a knot tightly around the middle of the lengths. With your scissors begin to snip the yarn along the edges until all the yarn has been fringed. Fluff the yarn ball.

Esteem Builders. Jalmar Press
Rolling Hills Estates, CA

9

Esteem Building Through Written Experiences: Journal Writing

PURPOSE

- To Enhance Students' Self-Perceptions Using All Five Components of Self-Esteem as the Basis for Writing Topics

- To Provide Students with the Opportunity to Formulate More Realistic and Accurate Self-Concepts

- To Enhance Written Language Skills

- To Foster a Written Dialogue Between Teacher and Students

SUMMARY OF JOURNAL WRITING

Definition: *A record of personal experiences. Journals provide an extended opportunity for students to reflect upon different aspects of their self-concepts and then further refine their reflections in writing.*

SUPPORT DATA

- "Journal time is an effort to get students writing and sharing bits of themselves. The purpose is to foster dialogue and invite a meaningful exchange between teacher and child . . . Journals represent a consistent invitation that extends over several months." Chick Moorman and Dee Dishon. *Our Classroom: We Can Learn Together* (Portage, MI: Personal Power Press, 1983).
- "Keeping a journal has several advantages. It allows the student to keep an ongoing account of how he is growing, of what is happening to him, of how he uniquely responds to a given situation. It provides a cumulative statement of who he is, how he sees himself, and how others see him. The more a person learns about himself, the more he will expand his concept of himself." Jack Canfield and Harold C. Wells. *100 Ways to Enhance Self-Concept in the Classroom* (Englewood Cliffs, NJ: Prentice-Hall, 1976).
- "Diaries [sic] is a strategy that enables the students to bring an enormous amount of information about themselves into a class to be examined and discussed." Sidney B. Simon, Leland W. Howe and Howard Kirschenbaum. *Values Clarification* (New York: Hart Publishing Co., 1972).
- "A journal is an ideal way for young children to record their feelings, thoughts, perceptions, and fears." Michael E. Knight, Terry Lynne Graham, Rose A. Juliano, Susan Robichaud Miksza and Pamela G. Tonnies. *Teaching Children to Love Themselves* (Englewood Cliffs, NJ: Prentice-Hall, 1982).

PURPOSE

- To Enhance Students' Self-Perceptions Using All Five Components of Self-Esteem as the Basis for Writing Topics
- To Provide Students With the Opportunity to Formulate More Realistic and Accurate Self-Concepts
- To Enhance Written Language Skills
- To Foster a Written Dialogue Between Teacher and Students

TARGET AUDIENCE

These journal topics have been used successfully in a variety of settings for all age levels, including regular classrooms (kindergarten through eighth grade), special education settings and gifted education. Some adaptation is necessary for the younger, nonwriting student.

Journal Writing Activities List

Code	Grade	Title
J1	K–8	Journal Cover
J2	K–2	Journal Page: Younger Student
J3	3–8	Journal Page: Older Student
J4	K–8	Journal Binding
J5	K–8	Journal Topics
J6	2–6	A Month of Journal Writing
J7	K–8	Class Journal
J8	K–8	Sentence Completion Topics
J9	2–8	Roll-a-Topic
J10	2–5	Writing Center
J11	2–6	Your Thoughts About
J12	2–8	Journal Feedback
J13	2–8	Teacher/Student Letter Exchange
J14	K–8	Teacher/Student Letter Topics
J15	K–8	Journal Booklist

See also:

Code	Grade	Title	Element
M27	3–8	Goal Achievement Journal	Mission
C18	2–8	Accomplishment Journal	Competence

9

Esteem Building
Through Written Experiences:
Journal Writing

My journal...looks like a Beethoven manuscript...leaping
with joy from exclamation marks to dashes that speak more
than the words in between, my journal...dances with the
heartbeat of a process in motion.
—MARION WOODMAN

Regardless of a student's age, keeping a journal can be a valuable tool of self-discovery. The more varied the topics, the greater the student's chance to consider his/her opinions, thoughts and feelings.

If the journal reflections are continued on a daily or weekly basis, this activity can become an ongoing account of self-growth. The final product is a cumulative record of a student's self-picture for that year. This process is also an excellent follow-up to Concept Circles. Make a point of introducing journals to your students as early on in the school year as possible.

ACTIVITIES ON HOW TO CONSTRUCT A JOURNAL

Before beginning the writing process, students make (or you make) their own journal.

Note: Decide whether a full-page or half-page format would best suit your students. J3 and J4 show half-page designs; all other journal pages and instructions in this chapter are for full-page formats. You may want to enlarge or reduce the pages to suit your chosen style or simply use plain writing paper.

Grades K-8	Journal Cover	J1

Duplicate the J1 form on light-colored construction or tag paper, or ask students to make their own. A similar-sized sheet will be required for the back cover. Students fill in the information for the front cover and glue on a photograph or draw a self-portrait. Laminate the front and back covers for durability.

Grades K–2	Journal Page: Younger Student	J2

Grades 3–8	Journal Page: Older Student	J3

Depending on the age of your students, duplicate one of the above Journal Page samples to use for the content of the journal. If you plan for your students to write on a frequent or daily basis, be sure to make enough copies for each student. Bind these sheets inside the journal covers. You could use a hole-punch and yarn, staple, or follow the instructions in J4.

Option: You may include copies of the J13 Let's Write to Each Other form (Teacher/Student Letter Exchange) as part of the journal. Refer to J13 activity for details. Also refer to Chapter 3, for S1 Teacher/Student Letter Exchange.

Grades K–8	**Journal Binding**	J4

There are several ways to bind the journals: stapling, spiral binding or hole-punching sheets together between a journal cover are some examples. Use J4 worksheet on binding as a guide. An attractively bound finished product is most appealing to students; therefore, give them the option to "professionalize" their journal by making a smart binding with colored yarn or gluing a piece of cardstock-weight paper to make a spine.

WRITING A JOURNAL

Introduce journal content by informing the class that they will be writing in the booklets they have just made. Explain that journals are special because the ideas that are written down are different in everyone's book, reflecting each person's particular thoughts and feelings.

Emphasize that journals are private: *no one may read another person's thoughts without his/her permission.* Reinforce the need for confidentiality and make it clear that you are the only person besides the student who will be looking in the books (if books are to be sent home, include parents). Some

teachers like to enforce a policy that if a page is confidential, the student may fold it toward the binding and fasten it closed with a paper clip. No one may read that page. Older students are particularly concerned about privacy and may be inhibited about their writing unless this is addressed.

When journals are first started, many students are hesitant to record their thoughts on paper. You may wish to consider some of the following ways to overcome this:

- **Class Journal.** Begin journal writing as a class activity. Write a topic on the board and enlist the ideas of all classmates. Write these ideas on the board as a joint recording. See Chapter 3, S38 for ideas on a class journal.

  The daily repetition of "communal" writing enables students to conceptualize the format. These group journal recordings may later be transferred to the J7 Class Journal form.

- **Teacher Model.** Consider keeping a journal yourself. You can then model your handling of the topics with the students. They will see you writing and formulating your opinions. Be sure to share your thoughts and feelings on topics so that students will get to know you more personally. At the same time, however, encourage students to come up with their own ideas and responses.

- **Literature Models.** Several good juvenile books address the topic of journal keeping. See J15 Journal Booklist for book titles and short descriptions. These books are an ideal way to model the process to students.

- **Early Journal Topics.** Beginning topics should be easy and nonthreatening, such as: "My Interests," "My Favorites," "Things I Like." At a later date advance to more abstract ideas that require greater self-reflection and the consideration of feelings. Choose, if necessary, from the topic suggestions in J5 and J6.

- **Discussion.** Consider allowing students to discuss the journal topic with a partner, support team or the class before committing their thoughts to writing. Many students in the beginning stages need a chance to first "air" their ideas. This format also allows the classmates the opportunity to hear lots of other students' ideas. Soon they realize there is no one answer to a topic question—in fact, there's no right or wrong answer either. They learn that topic thoughts will not be evaluated and everyone's ideas are important.

- **Student Topic Suggestions.** Encourage students to submit journal topics for future consideration. They write suggestions on slips of paper and place them in an empty Kleenex box or in a large envelope.

- **Topic Suitability.** Make topics more student-centered by using subject matter such as: class problems, popular songs, newspaper articles, parables, fables, TV shows, poetry, quotations or current events.

STEPS TO JOURNAL WRITING:

1. Write the journal topic for the day on the board. Examples of beginning topics are:

   - Tell me something you did this summer.

   - Tell me something you enjoy doing at home.

   - What is your favorite _____.
     (color, TV show, movie, sport, food, friend, etc.)? Tell me about it.

2. Students copy the title in their journals next to the heading (date).

3. Ask students to think a moment about the topic. What will they say? Encourage them to write as soon as anything "pops" into their head.

4. Remind students that they will not be corrected for spelling or grammar. This is sustained writing where ideas count. Any words they are unsure of should be sounded out and written down to the best of their abilities.

5. You may wish to place a timer in the classroom set for a specific amount of time (5, 10, 15 minutes). When the timer goes off, journals go away. This may help to pace some students who are slower at completing work.

6. As students become more proficient in journal writing, they may choose their own daily topics from a provided list or make up their own individual topics for each writing assignment.

Primary or Nonwriting Students

Several options are available for students not yet proficient in writing skills:

- **Cross-Age Tutors.** Ask a teacher of upper-grade students to send a few students to your classroom during journal writing time. Students can be trained to transcribe student-dictated thoughts.

- **Parent Aides.** Enlisting the help of a parent aide or two during journal sessions can also be beneficial. Please remind parents that journal thoughts are confidential and should not be shared beyond the classroom.

- **Small Groups.** For ease of supervision only have a small group of students writing each day. Rotate these groups daily so that at the end of the week each student has had the opportunity to write at least once in his/her journal.

- **Taped Journals.** Each student could tape his/her journal topic on a cassette and transcribe at a later date.

ACTIVITIES TO FACILITATE JOURNAL WRITING

Grades K-8	Journal Topics	J5

Duplicate the J5 list for individual students to work through, or use it as your own reference to randomly pick a daily topic.

- If I could have one wish it would _____.

- My favorite place to go is _____.

- My favorite TV show is _____ because _____.

- When I was younger I enjoyed _____.

- I'm happiest when _____.

- I get angry when _____.

- I feel sad when _____.

- I feel scared when _____.

- I love to _____.

- I love _____.

- When I grow up I want to _____.

- If I were a little kid I would _____.

- If I were the teacher I'd _____.

- I wish I could change _____.

- The hardest part of school for me _____.

- The easiest part of school is _____.
- The funniest part of school is _____.
- I wish I could tell you _____.
- I do my best work when _____.
- The worst thing about being me is _____.
- The best thing about being me is _____.
- My best friend _____.
- I like to be with people who _____.
- I like it when _____.
- At home I wish I _____.
- I'm proud of the time I _____.
- The other students in this class _____.
- After school I _____.
- When I get home I wish _____.
- I'm afraid to _____.
- I'm not afraid to _____.
- Sometimes during the day I wish _____.
- The best thing about home is _____.
- I wish it were easier for me to _____.
- I wish my parents knew _____.
- I'm best when _____.
- I can help people _____.
- I'm a good friend when _____.
- I enjoy being with _____ because _____.
- The best part of this school is _____.
- I wish I could change _____.
- It's easy for me to _____.
- When I get home I _____.
- I don't like people who _____.
- I don't want to _____.
- During the summer I like to _____.
- My family _____.
- I hate it when _____.
- I like to hear people tell me _____.
- Someday I know _____.
- A part of me I like is _____.

Grades 2–6   A Month of Journal Writing   J6

Duplicate the J6 form. Students number the calendar to correspond to the current month. The daily topics are meant as journal ideas to be written in the journal as usual. You could also transfer the calendar topics to a large class calendar. Students then read the date and discover the daily topic to reflect on and write about.

Grades K–8   Class Journal   J7

Duplicate several pages of the J7 Class Journal form. These may be stapled together between two pieces of construction paper to form a Class Journal. Use it to transcribe ideas that have been generated by the class as a whole; it can become a permanent record for that particular class.

Grades K–8   Sentence Completion Topics   J8

The J8 journal topics may be used to further develop each of the five feelings. Choose from the list those that reflect the students' actual experiences, interests and concerns.

Materials: 3" x 5" index cards *(optional)*.

Choose appropriate topics for your students from the choices below. Write each one on an index card. Add new suggestions. You may wish to write all topics pertaining to one feeling on the same color card. This way cards can quickly be shuffled back into the right component. Store sets of feeling topics in separate containers.

Procedure: Choose a topic for the journal entry for that day, or ask students to each pick a card from the container holding the topic suggestions of the component you're working on. Students then complete the sentence according to their feelings and opinions about the subject. Students may then exchange cards three or four times so that they have the opportunity to consider several situations.

Note: The following topics are also suited for Concept Circles, Chapter 8. Students select a card and then verbalize an appropriate ending. Circulate a number of cards this way.

Security:

- Someone who really makes me feel comfortable is _____.
- A special person in my life is _____.
- I can always count on _____ and this makes me feel _____.
- One rule I'd like to change in our home is _____.
- One rule I'd like to change in our school is _____.
- If I were the teacher I'd _____.
- If I were the President I'd _____.
- I would hate to lose _____.
- If I were a parent the advice I'd give my child is _____.
- Something I'd allow my children to do that I'm not allowed to do is _____.
- The best part of school is _____.
- Something that is special to me which I'd hate to lose is _____.
- Something at home I like very much is _____.
- The reason adults set rules is _____.
- Two rules older brothers and sisters should have to follow are _____.
- Two rules younger brothers and sisters should have to follow are _____.
- If I could set any new rule for this classroom (school) it would be _____.
- I think the most important school rule is _____.
- One rule that would make the world (school) a better place is _____.
- The most important rule is _____ because _____.
- People expect me to _____.
- My parents expect me to _____.
- My teacher expects me to _____.
- When I'm in a strange place I _____.
- It bothers me whenever I'm _____.

Selfhood:

- I am best at _____.
- Something I like about myself is _____.
- I like to pretend I _____.
- I'm sure glad I _____.
- When I grow up _____.
- If I were an animal, I'd be _____.
- If I were a building, I'd be _____.
- The place I like best to be is _____.
- Two things I like about myself are _____.
- I feel important when _____.
- I don't like it when _____.
- I look best when_____.
- When I was little _____.
- One of the best things about me is _____.
- After school I _____.
- A famous person I'd like to be is _____.
- My face is _____.
- If I were a little kid I would _____.
- My body is _____.
- The part of me I'd like most to change is _____.
- I can play _____ all day.
- If I were very tiny, I would _____.
- When I look in the mirror the first thing I see is _____.
- I run like a _____.
- I'm as tall as _____.
- I don't want to _____.
- During the summer I like _____.
- During the winter I like _____.
- The way I'd describe my family is _____.
- Someday _____.
- I'm not afraid to _____.
- Two of my favorite things are _____.
- If I had a magic carpet, I'd _____.
- My favorite part of the day is _____.
- I'm sure glad I _____.
- I don't like to _____.
- I like to play _____.

JOURNAL WRITING

- I'd like to say a good thing about _____.
- If I could be invisible, I would _____.
- I love to eat _____.
- I hate to eat _____.
- I wish I could _____.
- I like the sound of _____.
- I'm bigger than _____.
- I'm smaller than _____.
- I hope that _____.
- If I could do anything different, it would be _____.
- If I were a giant, I would _____.
- I really like _____.
- I'll never forget _____.
- I like the way I _____.
- I would not like to have _____.
- If I were a bird, I would _____.
- I would like a magic ring that _____.
- I need more _____.
- I'm the kind of person who _____.
- My favorite pet is _____.
- I am unique because _____.
- I am lucky because _____.
- My favorite thing to wear is _____.
- If I were older, I would _____.
- I wish I could play _____ better.
- The person I'd like most to look like is _____ because _____.
- My favorite sport is _____.
- My favorite place to go is _____.
- When I was younger I enjoyed _____.
- My favorite TV show is _____ because _____.
- I wish I could tell you _____.
- A part of me I like _____.
- I'd sure like it if _____.
- I wish grownups would _____.
- I was really sorry I _____.

Feelings and Emotions:

- I'm happiest when _____.
- I feel so mad inside when _____.
- I felt really proud the time I _____.
- I'm happy that _____.
- I feel great when _____.
- I feel embarrassed when _____.
- I feel sad when _____.
- I feel happy when _____.
- I feel angry when _____.
- I feel proud when _____.
- I feel sleepy when _____.
- Sometimes I'm afraid of _____.
- I hate it when _____.
- I love it when _____.
- I like it when _____.
- I laugh when _____.
- I was really scared when _____.
- I was very happy the time that _____.
- My face has a big smile when _____.
- I would be happier if _____.
- I felt like crying when _____.
- Sometimes I feel _____.
- Sometimes I get scared when _____.
- Right now I feel _____.
- It makes me sad to hear _____.
- The silliest thing is _____.
- The happiest thing is _____.
- When I feel lonely I _____.
- When I'm really angry I _____.
- I sometimes get mad when _____.
- I feel bad when _____.
- After I cry I _____.
- I am afraid to _____.
- I wish someone would give me _____.
- What really bothers me is _____.

ESTEEM BUILDERS

all

WRITING

Affiliation:

- I like to be with _____.
- I like to be with people who _____.
- My best friend is _____.
- I was a friend to someone when _____.
- Someone who makes me feel happy is ___.
- I would like to give a present of _____ to _____.
- A way I could help others is _____.
- My favorite person to be with is _____.
- I feel happy when people _____.
- Things I look for in a friend are _____.
- The best person in the world is _____.
- I could be a better friend if _____.
- Once someone helped me by _____.
- I choose my friends because _____.
- I love to give _____.
- What I can give to others is _____.
- I don't like people who _____.
- The greatest harm someone can do to another is _____.
- When people get angry they should _____.
- I wish people could stop _____.
- I would like to say something nice to ___.
- You can tell someone likes you by _____.
- I don't like it when people _____.
- When people tease me I _____.
- I'm a good friend when _____.
- I like my friends because _____.
- I don't like it when kids _____.
- My friends think I'm good at _____.
- I make new friends by _____.
- When I'm with my friend I feel _____.
- I wish my friends would _____.
- My favorite thing to do with a friend is _____.
- The thing that makes me a good friend is _____.
- Someone I'd like to get to know better is _____.

Mission:

- Something I started but didn't finish was _____.
- When I have a problem I usually _____.
- Something I'd like to get better at is ___.
- Today I'm going to try to _____.
- A problem I sometimes have is _____.
- I have difficulty dealing with _____.
- One thing I would like to organize better _____.
- I wish I could change _____.
- If I could do anything I wanted I would _____.
- I wish I could figure out _____.
- If I had one wish, I would _____.
- If I had a million dollars, I would _____.
- If I were older, I would _____.
- I wish I could _____.
- I'd use a magic wand to _____.
- If I were the teacher, I would _____.
- If I were President, I would _____.
- Sometimes I wonder if _____.
- Someday I would like to help solve the problem of _____.
- The first thing I want to do when I grow up is _____.
- My goal for this year is to _____.
- Every day I look forward to _____.
- I know I have to _____ so that I can be successful in _____.
- The biggest change I can make in myself is _____.
- I would reach my goal of _____ if I _____.

Competence:

- Something I do well in school is _____.
- I do my best work when I _____.
- I taught someone how to _____.
- I'm learning to _____.
- I need help to _____.

— 359 —

- I have accomplished _____.
- Something I like to brag about is _____.
- One of my strengths is _____.
- I'm really proud of my _____.
- Today I learned _____.
- I know how to _____.
- I can _____.
- It's hard for me to _____.
- Something I do well is _____.
- My greatest strength is _____.
- I have power to _____.
- Something I can do all by myself is _____.
- Something I can do now that I couldn't do last year is _____.
- I have accomplished _____.
- I felt really proud the time I _____.
- It's easy for me to _____.
- I'm pretty good at _____.
- I'm glad I learned to _____.
- I once got an award for _____.
- I get discouraged when _____.
- Something I once did all by myself is _____.
- I have the hardest time when I _____.
- The easiest part of the school day is _____.
- The hardest part of the school day is _____.
- I would like to learn how to _____.
- I wish I were better at _____.
- It was hard to do, but I finally _____.
- I would like someone to help me _____.
- I am very good at _____.
- I wish I were really good at _____.
- School would be better if I could _____.
- Something I'd like to learn about is _____.

ADDITIONAL USES WITH SENTENCE COMPLETION TOPICS

| Grades 2–8 | **Roll-a-Topic** | **J9** |

Purpose: To provide additional opportunities for students to reflect upon their feelings and thoughts

related to each of the five components of self-esteem.

Materials: 2 half-gallon milk or juice cartons of the same size; colored wrapping paper or contact paper; glue, scissors, thin-tipped black marking pen; white construction paper, cut into 1/2" x 5" strips.

Cube Construction: Clean and dry both cartons thoroughly. Lay each carton on its side and measure the same length along all four sides. Use a sharp knife to cut across the top of the carton so that each side is the same height, length and width as the others. Do the same to the second carton.

Turn both cartons sideways with both open ends facing each other. Push one carton completely inside the other to form a solid cube that is closed at both ends. Cover the cube with colored paper, wrapping it completely.

Procedure: Choose 12 topic phrases (incomplete sentence stems) from the previous activity. (You may wish to make a cube for each different component of self-esteem and wrap it with paper representing topics that relate to that particular feeling.) Print each sentence stem on a separate white construction paper strip. Glue two strips on each side of the cube with each strip facing a different direction (one will appear "right side up" and the other "upside down").

Journal Starter: Students use the topics on the cube as journal starters. Sitting in a circle, they toss the cube and choose one of the two topics appearing face up to write about in their journal.

Adaptation for a Concept Circle Activity: With everyone sitting in a circle, pass the cube in a clockwise direction. Students take turns tossing the cube. Whichever side lands face up, the student chooses one of the two topics that appear and verbally completes the sentence stem. The cube is then passed to the person on his/her right.

| Grades 2–5 | **Writing Center** | **J10** |

Purpose: To increase self-awareness through written language skills.

Materials: Packages of 3" x 5" index cards in 5 colors; J10 Writing Contract for each student.

Writing Book: Staple 12 writing pages inside a construction paper cover for each student. Glue the J10 Writing Contract on the cover of each book. Students may also use existing journals to record their comments.

Procedure:

1. Using J8, or your own ideas, choose 23 incomplete sentence stems from each of the five self-esteem components.

2. For each component package, print one incomplete sentence stem per index card, using a different color for each component.

   Example: When making a card pack for the Security component, write all the sentences on blue cards. When compiling all the sentences on Selfhood, print them on red cards, and so on. You will end up with 5 different color card packs, each with 23 sentences.

3. Number each card in the pack from 1 to 23 in the upper-right corner.

4. Punch each card within the pack in the upper-left corner and attach them together with a small metal ring.

5. Keep all the card packs in a box, or hang them from metal curtain rings on a bulletin board. You may wish to create a center for the cards and mark it "Writing Center." Stock the Center with writing supplies, card packs and individual student writing books.

Task: Assign each student to a particular pack. Students write the subject of the pack on top of their writing contract. They may choose any card from the pack that has not been previously used.

On the first available writing page in the booklet, students write the sentence stem topic and then complete it with their thoughts and feelings. Students write the number of the card on the top right-hand corner of the page. They then color in the card number on the front of the writing contract. Students continue the activity, each answer on a different page, until all cards have been written about, after which they are assigned to a new pack and a fresh writing book.

<table>
<tr><td>Grades 2–6</td><td>**Your Thoughts About**</td><td>**J11**</td></tr>
</table>

Purpose: To learn how to gather information. To enhance interviewing skills. To gain further understanding of the topics through group feedback.

Materials: Copy of J11 Your Thoughts About form.

Procedure: Use this form as a survey in which a student interviews classmates concerning the daily topic. Each day choose a different student to do the survey. He/she writes the journal topic at the top of the paper and then asks classmates for their opinions, thoughts or feelings regarding the topic. Each classmate to be interviewed has the option to "pass" (not give an opinion). At the end of the day, the interviewer presents the findings to the class.

<table>
<tr><td>Grades 2–8</td><td>**Journal Feedback**</td><td>**J12**</td></tr>
</table>

Purpose: To provide student/teacher dialogue and feedback on journal writing.

Materials: J12 Journal Feedback form.

Procedure: Use this as a follow-up to the journal writing. It can also be used with Concept Circles and cooperative learning activities—see Chapter 8. Students form teams of 2–4 and reflect upon their feelings, thoughts and behaviors during their journal writing. As a team, they hand in their response to the teacher.

<table>
<tr><td>Grades 2–8</td><td>**Teacher/Student Letter Exchange**</td><td>**J13**</td></tr>
</table>

Purpose: To provide the opportunity for ongoing dialogue.

Materials: Copies of J13 Let's Write to Each Other form; construction or cardstock-weight paper; stapler or spiral binding.

Procedure: First make several copies of the J13 Let's Write to Each Other form for each student and bind them between construction paper covers. *For older students, bind in plain writing paper instead.*

Alternatively, you may include these forms in students' personal journals, placing them at the back.

Begin the project by composing a letter to the class telling them something about yourself. This could be a personal letter, in ditto form, written to your students. The idea is to give them information about you as a person outside of your teaching role. You may wish to include information such as:

- what you enjoy doing when you're not in the classroom;

- your family, pets and home;

- where and what you did as a child;

- why you enjoy teaching;

- a special happening for the class at a future date.

Include a copy of the letter on the first page in each student's book. End the letter with a question posed to the student, for example:

- What do you enjoy doing at home?
- What's your favorite place to visit?
- What do you enjoy most about school?

Students then read the letter from you and give their answer on the first blank Let's Write to Each Other page. If you wish, let them end the letter with a question back to you.

The letter exchanges could be sustained on a daily basis. A few suggestions:

- Make it a timed activity so that students write only until the timer goes off. Thus, it won't become a writing "chore."

- This type of activity is more successful if it is done consistently—for example, at the same time every day. This way, students can prepare their thoughts and be ready for the assignment every day.

- Remember, this is a writing activity where the goal is to help students' ideas flow more freely as well as create an open forum for real dialogue. Grammar and spelling should not be corrected.

- Some letters will be confidential and need to be respected as such. Tell students if they wish that page to remain a "secret," they should fold the paper in half toward the binding and paper-clip it shut.

- Use the dialogue to include specific comments of praise for good work, citizenship, behavior or improvement.

- With younger students who require more supervision, you may wish to rotate the activity so that only five or six (one group) write each day instead of the whole class at one time. Nonwriting students can dictate their stories to you and/or the cross-age tutor or parent aide.

- As often as feasible, try to respond back to as many students as possible. Include a different topic question at the end of your response for the next session; or, write new topics on the chalkboard.

Grades K–8	Teacher/Student Letter Exchange Topics	J14

Until students are comfortable with journal writing, concrete and "nonthreatening" ideas work best. Keep a suggestion box handy where students can write their own topic ideas on slips of paper and place them in the box.

Questions for letter exchange:

- If you could have one wish, what would it be?

- What is your favorite place to visit?

- What is your favorite TV show? Why?

- When you were younger what did you enjoy most?

- When are you happiest?

- What makes you angry?

- When do you feel sad?

- What do you want to be when you grow up?

- If you were a little kid, you would. . .?

- If you were the teacher, you would. . .?

- What is the hardest part of school for you?

- What is the easiest part of school for you?

- The most fun part of school is. . . .?

- What do you wish you could tell me?

- What's the worst thing about being you?

- What's the best thing about being you?

- Who's your best friend and why?

- Who are the people you like to be with?

- What do you wish you could do at home?
- What's your proudest moment?
- What do you think of the other students in this class?
- What do you do after school?
- How do you help people?
- Which kind of people do you not like?
- What do you want to do this summer?
- What do you like people to say about you?
- Which people do you have special feelings for?
- What would you like to tell me about your family?
- What would you like to do someday?

To adapt to younger students: For those who don't yet write, let them exchange ideas in picture form. Consider using photographs; a student would only need to write a caption underneath. You may rotate the activity so that a small number of students work in their books each day instead of the whole class. Those who struggle with writing may dictate their stories.

| Grades K–8 | **Journal Booklist** | **J15** |

The following titles all deal with personal diaries or journals and offer positive models for journal writing:

[P] = Primary (K–3)
[I] = Intermediate Level (4–8)

Dear Mr. Henshaw, Beverly Cleary (Dell, 1983). This Newbery Award winner depicts a troubled sixth grader whose parents are divorcing. The book is written as a series of letters to an admired author. The ongoing correspondence eventually helps the boy iron out his inner turmoil. [I]

A Gathering of Days: A New England Girl's Journal, 1830–32, Joan W. Blos (Atheneum, 1979). Winner of the Newbery Award, the book is told in the form of a journal kept by a young girl. She recalls many painful times and makes many self-discoveries. [I]

I'm in Charge of Celebrations, Byrd Baylor (Charles Scribner's Sons, 1986). Written in the first person, the text captures an Indian girl's special experiences of the Southwest desert country. [P–I]

Mostly Michael, Robert Kimmel Smith (Dell, 1987). Much to Michael's chagrin, he receives a diary for his 11th birthday. The more Michael writes in it, the more valuable the diary becomes. It eventually becomes a tool for Michael's selfhood development. [I]

Three Days on a River in a Red Canoe, Vera Williams (Mulberry, 1981). Suitable for the younger student, this pictorial account, narrated in first person, tells of a river raft trip taken by a young child. A good catalyst for describing a personal journey or vacation. [P]

Trumpet of the Swan, E.B. White (Harper & Row, 1970). Written by the author of *Charlotte's Web*, this is a beautifully recorded story of a handicapped swan. A main story character, Ben, befriends the swan. Throughout the book, Ben keeps a diary and always ends each entry with a question addressed to himself to take him to the next step. [I]

For further reference:

Dear Bill, Remember Me? Norma Fox (Dell, 1976). [I]

The Diary of a Young Girl, Anne Frank (Pocket, 1952). [I]

The Diary of a Paper Boy, Jean Jacques Larrea (G.P. Putnam's Sons, 1972). [P]

Go Ask Alice, Anonymous (Avon, 1982). [I]

Harold and the Purple Crayon, Crockett Johnson (Harper & Row, 1955). [P]

Hello God, It's Me, Margaret, Judy Blume (Bradbury, 1970). [I]

The Kids Book of Questions, Gregory Stock (Workman Publications, 1988). [I]

Knots on a Counting Rope, Bill Martin, Jr. (Henry Holt & Co., 1987). [P]

Would You Rather? John Burningham (Thomas Y. Crowell, 1978). [P]

JOURNAL

The Author

Author _____

Copyright _____

Esteem Builders. Jalmar Press
Rolling Hills Estates, CA

Name | Date

Today's Topic: _____

_____

What I Think:

- -

_____

- -

_____

- -

_____

- -

How I Feel:

Esteem Builders. Jalmar Press
Rolling Hills Estates, CA

Topic: _____ Date: _____

I learned/discovered/was surprised that I . . . .

Topic: _____ Date: _____

I learned/discovered/was surprised that I . . . .

Esteem Builders. Jalmar Press
Rolling Hills Estates, CA

Name   Date

Bind Your Own Journal

1

Put the pages neatly in the right order.

2

Fold the pages in half.

3

Hammer five thin nails through the fold of the paper.

4

With a needle and thread, stitch back and forth through the holes. Take out the nails as you sew.

5

Tie off the string and cut off any left over.

6

Cover two pieces of cardboard with fabric, wallpaper or gift wrap. Glue them on.

Leave about 3/4" space between the covers. Join the front and back covers together with adhesive cloth tape.

Esteem Builders. Jalmar Press
Rolling Hills Estates, CA

A Month of Journal Writing

1. Number the days for this month. 2. Use these ideas as a guide for your daily journal writing.

MONDAY	TUESDAY	WEDNESDAY	THURSDAY	FRIDAY
When I grow up...	What I like best about this class is...	I like to...	A friend is...	Right now I feel...
Sometimes I dream...	I would like to...	My best friend is...	Someday I hope...	I like people who...
I feel good when...	I don't like people who...	I'm at my best when...	I wish my parents knew...	If I had a magic wand...
Three words that describe me are...	I like myself because...	I'm proud of myself when...	Sometimes I feel like...	I'm very happy that...

Esteem Builders. Jalmar Press
Rolling Hills Estates, CA

Name _____ Date _____

Class Journal

Topic _____

Thoughts from Classmates	Classmate

Top Ranking: Low | 1 | 2 | 3 | 4 | 5 | High

Esteem Builders. Jalmar Press
Rolling Hills Estates, CA

Name

Date

Writing Contract

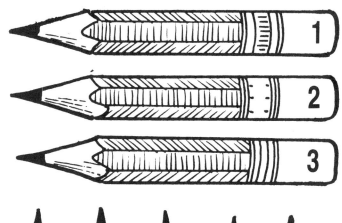

Packet Subject: _____

Directions: Choose from the packet any card you have not used before. Write down your thoughts and feelings about it in your writing book. When you are finished, color in the pencil which shows the card number that you wrote about.

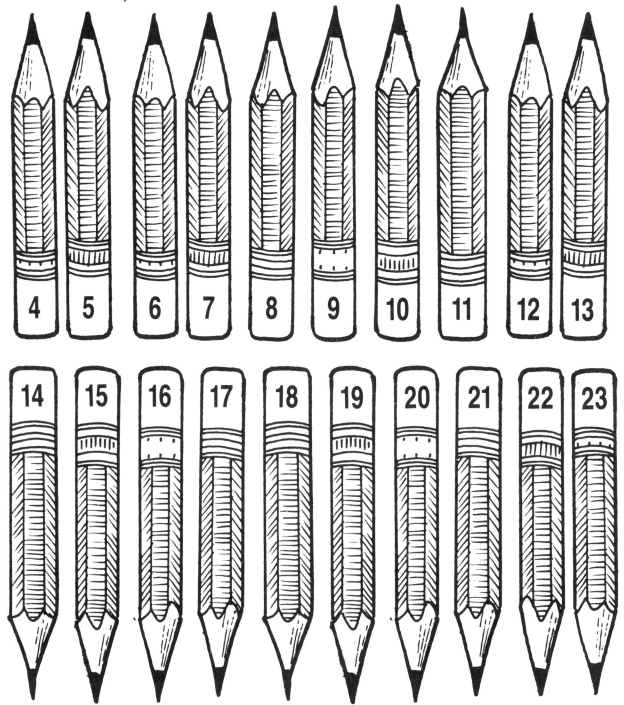

Esteem Builders. Jalmar Press
Rolling Hills Estates, CA

Name   Date

# Your Thoughts About: _____
_(Topic)

Interview several of your classmates about the daily topic. What are their thoughts and feelings?
Write their names and answers in the spaces below.

Esteem Builders. Jalmar Press
Rolling Hills Estates, CA

JOURNAL FEEDBACK

TODAY'S TOPIC:

DATE:

TEAM MEMBERS:

WHAT WE SAID

MEMBER A:

MEMBER B:

MEMBER C:

MEMBER D:

How We Felt About This Topic:

Esteem Builders. Jalmar Press
Rolling Hills Estates, CA

Name _____   Date _____

Let's Write to Each Other...

Student's Turn

Topic: _____

Dear _____,

_____

_____

_____

_____

_____

_____

_____

_____

_____

_____

_____

_____

_____

_____

Signed _____

Teacher's Turn

Dear _____,

_____

_____

_____

_____

Signed _____

Esteem Builders. Jalmar Press
Rolling Hills Estates, CA

10

Creating a Positive School Climate: School-wide Esteem

PURPOSE

- To Foster Feelings of Security and Trust by Setting Clear, Reasonable Guidelines in a Caring Environment

- To Recognize That Each Member is Unique and Special

- To Build a "Cooperative Spirit" Where Members Feel Affiliated and Accepted

- To Provide Opportunities for Members to Share in Decision-Making Processes and Take Cooperative Responsibility for School Goals

- To Enhance Personal Competence by Setting High Yet Achievable Expectations That Build on Personal Strengths and Accomplishments

SUMMARY OF SCHOOL-WIDE ESTEEM

Definition: *A school-wide esteem-building climate is an atmosphere that increases the self-esteem of both staff and students by intentionally paralleling the five components of high self-esteem. The activities and strategies found in this chapter, if instituted on a school-wide basis by staff members, will help create an environment conducive to esteem enhancement.*

SUPPORT DATA

- "The large body of 'effective schools' research leaves little doubt that the school environment in its totality has a powerful impact on student outcomes." Lisbeth B. Schorr. *Within Our Reach: Breaking the Cycle of Disadvantage* (New York: Doubleday, 1988).
- "Evidence strongly suggests that [a posititve school climate] is perhaps the best way educators can encourage students to stay enrolled and to learn. Good schools possess strong leaders who stress academic achievement, maintain an orderly and disciplined environment, and work with staff to instill positive values and self-confidence in students." The OERI Urban Superintendents Network. *Dealing with Dropouts: The Urban Superintendents' Call to Action* (Washington: D.C.: Office of Educational Research and Improvement, November 1987).
- "It was surprising the degree to which the more satisfying schools that were rated positively on characteristics of school climate also were schools in which students viewed their classroom climate positively." John I. Goodlad. *A Place Called School: Prospects for the Future* (New York: McGraw-Hill, 1984).
- "In one sense, the school and class climate serve as the backdrop for everyday living in those settings and thus is a major determinant in the quality of life for learners." James A. Beane and Richard A. Lipka. *Self-Concept, Self-Esteem and the Curriculum* (New York: Teachers' College Press, 1986).
- "The concept of school culture relates to the quality of the school environment which students experience daily. . .However one describes it, the best available evidence shows that where teachers and students experience a given constellation of positive, mutually rewarding behaviors, achievement gains significantly increase." James J. Fenwick. *Caught in the Middle: Educational Reform for Young Adolescents in California Schools*. Report of the Superintendent's Middle Grade Task Force (California State Department of Education, 1987).

PURPOSE

- To Foster Feelings of Security and Trust by Setting Clear, Reasonable Guidelines in a Caring Environment
- To Recognize That Each Member is Unique and Special
- To Build a "Cooperative Spirit" Where Members Feel Affiliated and Accepted
- To Provide Opportunities for Members to Share in Decision-Making Processes and Take Cooperative Responsibility for School Goals
- To Enhance Personal Competence by Setting High Yet Achievable Expectations That Build on Personal Strengths and Accomplishments

EDUCATOR BEHAVIORS THAT INVITE AN ESTEEM-BUILDING CLIMATE

Educator behaviors that create an esteem-building climate are those that parallel the five components of high self-esteem (Security, Selfhood, Affiliation, Mission and Competence).

School-wide Esteem Builders Activities List

Code	Grade	Title	Element
SW1	K–8	Spirit Tickets	Security
SW2	K–8	Spirit Award	Security
SW3	K–8	Positive Performers	Security
SW4	K–8	Positive Performance Award	Security
SW5	K–8	Gotcha Tickets	Security
SW6	K–4	Sparkle Gram	Security/Selfhood
SW7	3–8	Good Guy Award	Security/Selfhood
SW8	K–8	Pass the Buck	Security
SW9	K–6	Spirit Tree	Security/Selfhood
SW10	K–8	Friendship Assembly	Security/Affiliation
SW11	K–8	Name Tag Exchange	Security/Affiliation
SW12	K–8	Who's New?	Selfhood/Affiliation
SW13	K–6	Meet Our Kids	Selfhood/Affiliation
SW14	K–8	Good News Report	Selfhood
SW15/16	K–6	Student of the Week	Selfhood
SW17/18	K–8	Citizen of the Week	Selfhood
SW19	K–8	Birthday Recognition	Selfhood
SW20	K–6	Principal's Birthday Party	Selfhood
SW21	K–8	Birthday Poster	Selfhood
SW22	K–8	Principal's Birthday Card	Selfhood
SW23	K–6	Birthday Pencils	Selfhood
SW24	K–8	School Problem Report	Mission
SW25	K–6	Koala-T Efforts	Mission
SW26/27	K–8	Book of Winners	Competence
SW28	K–8	Principal's Ideas List	All Components
SW29	K–8	Positive Comments Contest	All Components
SW30	K–8	Principal's Award	All Components

Checklist of Educator Behaviors
That Invite an Esteem-Building Climate

Educator behaviors that invite an esteem-building climate are those that parallel the five components of self-esteem (Security, Selfhood, Affiliation, Mission and Competence).

Directions: The statements below describe situations found to promote self-esteem. Read each statement and then check the appropriate number that in your judgment best describes your school's environment.

Never 1	Sometimes 2	Frequently 3	Always 4	
				Security
_____	_____	_____	_____	1. Is the environment perceived as having a sense of caring and trust?
_____	_____	_____	_____	2. Is there effort made to maintain an attractive and pleasing physical environment?
_____	_____	_____	_____	3. Are students clearly aware of the school rules and limits, and do they understand the consequences?
_____	_____	_____	_____	4. Is there in effect a positive discipline policy agreed upon by all staff members?
				Selfhood
_____	_____	_____	_____	5. Are staff members readily accessible to students and other staff?
_____	_____	_____	_____	6. Are changes in students' self-perceptions observed and recorded?
_____	_____	_____	_____	7. Does the school provide opportunities for personal growth?
_____	_____	_____	_____	8. Do individuals receive personal recognition?
				Affiliation
_____	_____	_____	_____	9. Are there deliberate efforts made to help students earn status and affiliate with their peers?
_____	_____	_____	_____	10. Does a positive, sharing atmosphere pervade instead of a negative, critical one?
_____	_____	_____	_____	11. Are feelings of school pride and a cooperative spirit encouraged?
_____	_____	_____	_____	12. Do members feel affiliated and enjoy being together?

(continued on next page)

Esteem Builders. Jalmar Press
Rolling Hills Estates, CA

(continued from previous page)

Mission

_____ _____ _____ _____   13. Do school goals include directives that commit everyone to self-esteem enhancement?

_____ _____ _____ _____   14. Are staff members encouraged to share in the decision-making process, as well as have the opportunity to be listened to and heard?

_____ _____ _____ _____   15. Is there a concerted effort to work together and correct identified problems?

_____ _____ _____ _____   16. Is there agreement on the mission and direction of the school?

Competence

_____ _____ _____ _____   17. Are there opportunities to use individual talents and strengths?

_____ _____ _____ _____   18. Do staff members recognize they can have a significant impact on student perceptions and achievement?

_____ _____ _____ _____   19. Are high yet achievable expectations communicated to both staff and students?

_____ _____ _____ _____   20. Is staff progress monitored and specific feedback given to improve skills and ensure success?

_____ + _____ + _____ + _____ =   Total:_____

Areas we could improve in that would enhance an esteem-building climate in school:

_____

_____

_____

_____

_____

_____

_____

_____

Esteem Builders. Jalmar Press
Rolling Hills Estates, CA

10

Creating a Positive School Climate: School-wide Esteem

*The only way to assure the enhancement of self-concept
and self-esteem is to give careful attention to how
the school affects them.*
—JAMES A. BEANE AND RICHARD P. LIPKA

There is little doubt that the school climate has a powerful impact on students' productivity and the effectiveness of the school as a whole. Schools and classrooms where students show concern for each other, take pride in their environment and display school or class spirit do not come about by mere accident. Creating such an environment requires careful and deliberate planning in which the staff play an integral part. An "esteem-building climate" is one that creates a purposeful feeling of school pride and ownership. It is a place that is physically inviting as well as emotionally supportive. Members immediately feel a sense of belonging and being cared about. It is also a place that has the intent to enhance each of the five components of self-esteem. The following describes the characteristics of an esteem-building school, paralleling the five basic elements of high self-esteem.

1. **A Sense of Security.** A hallmark of the esteem-building school is that it provides an overall feeling of security to all its members—both students *and* staff. This critical need for security has been chronicled by many psychologists including Abraham Maslow and Erik Erikson. Students and staff must feel safe, comfortable and assured in their environment in order to function well. They also must know there are

members available who can be counted on and trusted. Coopersmith[1] states that limits, order and structure are paramount to the feeling of security. According to his research, an enhancing environment is one that has clear and reasonable guidelines that are consistently enforced. Such a framework provides a "security blanket" to its constituents, because they know what is expected of them and can meet the expectations with success. The esteem-building school is by definition a positive, warm place where students and staff feel accepted and included. Everyone feels "cared about."

2. **A Sense of Selfhood.** The esteem-building school sees members as unique and treats them as such. It provides opportunities for staff and students to be recognized for their individual and special qualities. This extends beyond the criteria of grades and performance. It means giving equal importance to attributes such as improvement, effort, quality, friendliness and positive deeds. A characteristic of such an environment is its "student centeredness." Where students' needs are of primary concern, there is a high level of interaction between students

---

1. Coopersmith, Stanley. *The Antecedents of Self-Esteem* (San Francisco: W.H. Freeman, 1967).

and teachers. Moreover, in a school with high self-esteem, staff are accessible to each other and communicate frequently.

3. **A Sense of Affiliation.** Students and staff in an esteem-building school feel like they belong, that they are all part of a "cooperative spirit." Members think of the school as "our school" and "our classroom." In such an environment everyone is encouraged to feel school pride and team spirit. Peers work together to encourage and support one another in group projects, cooperative learning strategies or peer tutoring. Every effort is made to make school members feel as though they are part of a caring and learning community. Perhaps this sense of affiliation can best be illustrated by one elementary student who tried to describe what was special about his school: "My school is the best school because everyone likes everyone. I like to be there because I know they like me."

4. **A Sense of Mission.** In the esteem-building school everyone is expected to take joint responsibility for what happens on the school grounds. If a problem arises, members recognize that it is a communal problem, which requires cooperative decision-making. All "constituents" discuss goals for the school so that everyone has a shared mission.

5. **A Sense of Competence.** Finally, a high priority for the esteem-building school is for its members to gain a feeling of personal competence. In a positive school environment, there are deliberate efforts to help students and staff members recognize personal gains and strengths, and to provide specific feedback. This school stresses high yet achievable expectations. Students who are high-risk are identified early and carefully monitored with the philosophy of "early intervention, not remediation." Everyone recognizes that each individual has untapped potential and therefore must be invited to access his/her own capabilities.

There is certainly no one formula for the creation of an esteem-building school. Each environment takes on unique characteristics as a result of its constituents. In every case, however, the overall atmosphere—regardless of size, staff make-up or economic characteristics—does have one thing in common: enhancement of the self-esteem of its members is a major goal that is not left to chance. The activities in this chapter are ideas that staff members can use on a school-wide basis to help build the five components of self-esteem—and affect their students' self-attitudes and academic progress.

SPIRIT ENERGIZERS

There are many practical ways to create an esteem-building climate. The following ideas are only a partial list of suggestions. Keep in mind that the idea is in no way as powerful as the way individuals interact with each other. Self-esteem is a commodity that can never be given to another person; however, providing the right atmosphere may certainly be instrumental in the enhancement of self-esteem.

- **Develop School Pride.** Early in the school year hold a contest to select an emblem, motto and school colors. You can develop school spirit by using many of the same techniques as athletic teams. Consider forming a "Spirit Committee" consisting of both staff and students.

- **Accentuate the Positive.** Emphasize whatever characteristics you'd like to focus on. Hang up banners, posters and signs all over the school grounds to highlight the message. Encourage class-wide poster contests or ask student council members to donate time to the cause.

- **Keep a Positive Spirit.** So much of self-esteem comes from modeled behavior. Be sure that staff members are modeling the kinds of behavior you want to reinforce. Be an example of positive behavior yourself, and recognize staff and students who display positive behavior.

- **Send Home Positive Messages.** Carry the positive spirit home with the students in written messages to let parents know of the school's goals. Instate a faculty room phone policy: "For every negative phone call home, you must make two positive phone calls." Encourage secretaries to answer the phone in a positive manner.

- **Post Clear Rules and Expectations.** One of the "ingredients" of environments that are successful in building self-esteem is that they convey order with a workable structure—one that's not too strict nor too lax. Form a "Rule Task Force" of students and staff to compose a list of school-wide rules. Coopersmith found that too many rules are overpowering; it is better to create a structure with fewer rules that are achievable and reinforced. Write the agreed-upon rules on posters and display them for all the school to see. Task members should also come up with a list of agreed-upon consequences when the rules are broken.

- **Create a Family Spirit.** Tap the resources of all school personnel to build a feeling of "school community." Everyone should be able to recognize not only the teaching staff but also custodians, secretaries, nurses, librarians, cafeteria workers, bus drivers and other staff personnel. Be sure to acknowledge their efforts and include them in school functions.

- **Promote Positive Public Relations.** Toot your horn about school accomplishments and let the rest of the world know what you're doing. Invite Central Office and Board members and community leaders to school functions. Periodically ask a reporter from the newspaper to feature a school or class happening. Highlight school activities in a newsletter, which is sent home to parents.

- **Take Time Out for Fun.** Every once in a while create events just for fun. Consider having a "Crazy Hat Day," "A Mixed-Up Sock Day," "A Cake Decorating Contest Day," "Dress as Your Favorite Book Character Day," or any other kind of event that allows students and staff to participate just for the fun of it.

- **Set the Tone First Thing.** Encourage staff members to greet students as soon as they set foot on the school grounds. Consider greeting students on the school bus, at the front door or at the carpool lines. This immediately sets a tone that says to students, "I'm glad you're here."

- **Recognize Students and Staff Members' Accomplishments.** Create a special bulletin board in the school just for recognizing individual accomplishments. Encourage all school members to add news articles, photographs or written notations describing special accomplishments of fellow members.

- **Keep the Spirit High.** Print the school motto or emblem on handy items such as banners, pencils and cards. Hand them out periodically to spirited individuals or just as a way of keeping the spirit high. Consider having a "Wear Your School Colors Day" as a set day on the school calendar. Encourage school members to create a school song or adopt a favorite recorded song. Once a week play it over the loudspeaker.

- **Brighten Up the School Appearance.** Develop a feeling of school pride by encouraging everyone to give careful attention to the general appearance of the school environment. If things need to be spruced up, consider having a school-wide Saturday morning painting party, cleanup day or planting spree. Enlist the skills of an artistic staff member to help plan a school mural and then oversee a "structured mural painting" on the outside school walls.

- **Recognize All Members.** Take the time to analyze the current school award system. Ask yourself, "Does everyone have the opportunity to be recognized?" If not, consider ways that more students (and staff) can receive acknowledgment. Behaviors to recognize include: improvement, effort, support, quality, friendliness, cooperation, spirit, positivism and attendance. Print certificates for each area being recognized.

- **Let Members Know You Care.** One of the most prominent characteristics of an effective school environment is that members take the time to let one another know they care. Certificates, personal notes or just personal contact are but a few ways to convey the feeling. Members must feel accepted, appreciated and cared about. Do yours?

BUILDING STAFF ESTEEM

IDEAS FOR FACULTY MEETINGS:

- Consider holding faculty meetings in the rooms of other staff members.

- At each meeting ask staff members to share esteem-building ideas or activities that have been successful with their students.

- Encourage staff members to develop a specialty they can share (and be recognized for) with other faculty members.

- Educators have successfully used many activities in ESTEEM BUILDERS on themselves in an upgraded version. Not only is this technique a fun way for staff members to intermingle and find out about each other, but it also helps build staff esteem. Activities you may wish to try are:

  S28 Smile File (using faculty member names)

  S31 Sparkle Line

  SH18 Identity Shield

  SH33 Me Banner

  A38 Compliment Hanging

  C3 Strength Profile

  C8 Strength Barbell

- Catherine Graham, mentor teacher at Schallenberger School in San Jose, California, suggests doing short activities at faculty meetings:

  Heart on the Back. Cut out a construction paper heart for each participant. Take five minutes to write something nice about each person on their "heart." Tape the corresponding heart to the back of the recipient.

  Whip. Share one special moment you had with your class that day (or during the week). Each staff member takes a few minutes to respond. Or, share something special you have done for yourself during the week. Share favorite vacation spots, books, recipes, restaurants, shopping spots, etc.

- At the beginning of the week, each staff member secretly pulls the name of another staff member. The name puller's job during that week is to watch for positive actions from that person. At the next faculty meeting, each "secret spy" reports their positive findings to the group.

- Add staff suggestions to the faculty meeting agenda. At each meeting, highlight a few staff members who will report to other faculty members what they have done.

STAFF RECOGNITION IDEAS:

- Set up a "Teacher's Pride" bulletin board. Highlight special projects and suggestions currently being used in classrooms.

- Sharon Ough, principal of Longwood School, Hayward, California, keeps a "Good Morning Staff" book, which contains the daily school calendar of events and activities. In addition, it includes special messages and acknowledgments recognizing staff members. Before starting the school day, members individually read the memos and encouraging notes.

- Recognize teacher efforts and happenings as often as possible in the school newsletter. This could also include short biographies on selected staff members and their accomplishments.

- Keep a scrapbook of school- and class-wide happenings that highlight teacher efforts.

- Present to staff members buttons or badges inscribed with: "Significant Other," "Teacher of the Week," "I'm Proud to Teach," etc.

- Purchase a large papier mache egg. Each week choose one deserving staff member to become the egg's recipient ("Good Egg of the Week"). Write a message on a paper strip describing what the recipient did to deserve the award and present it to the honoree. Pass it on to the new recipient each week. (Idea suggested by Catherine Graham, Schallenberger School.)

- Ask the local newspaper to chronicle special school and class happenings as often as possible.

- Cheryl Petermann, principal of Schallenberger School, San Jose, California, writes "Terrific Teacher Notes" for her staff. The bulletin consists of short blurbs about activities and successes staff members are having with students. They are distributed among the staff.

- Create a "Teacher of the Week" board. Each week, highlight a different staff member on a bulletin board display. The recognized individual brings in photographs, articles, objects and short "blurbs" that describe his/her interests, hobbies, background and family.

SUGGESTIONS FOR THE STAFFROOM:

- Create an "Idea Exchange" bulletin board. Encourage teachers to pin up descriptions or samples of successful ideas that have worked for them.

- Tape up a long length of butcher paper to the staffroom wall. With a marking pen, write a caption that reads: "Write Something Nice to a Colleague."

- Create a "Message Center." Glue library pockets to butcher paper. Write the names of each staff member on the pocket cover. Encourage staff members to write notes of acknowledgment to one another.

- Put together a "lunch basket" of donated items from faculty members or parents. These could include: candlesticks, candles, a cloth napkin, tablecloth, silverware and a vase. Each week designate parents, a faculty member or nearby restaurant to fill the basket with a lunch for a different faculty member. Fill the vase with fresh-cut flowers.

- Each staff member pulls the name of another staff member to be their "secret pal." For the duration of the activity, the name puller periodically does secret deeds for the staff member. These could include: purchasing inexpensive gifts, putting flowers or apples on their desk, providing teacher ideas or writing notes of acknowledgment. The activity may last for any length of time. Pals try to keep their identity secret for as long as possible.

- Each staff member designs a Me Poster on a 24" x 28" piece of posterboard. This could also become a staff project, or students could design the poster about their teacher. The poster should include information about the person's interests, hobbies, strengths, background and family life. Hang finished posters to decorate the staffroom.

IDEAS TO SHOW YOU CARE:

- Recognize special events in the life of each staff member (birthdays, special vacations, weddings, anniversaries, illnesses).

- Designate a staff member, parent or cook to bake a cake for each staff member's birthday.

- Contact local florists to see if any will provide special discounts for balloons or flower bouquets. Each week surprise one staff member with a delivered bouquet accompanied by a note of thanks.

- Periodically place an inexpensive treat in each staff member's box with a note attached to let them know they're appreciated. These are some treat suggestions:

  — package of lifesavers: "You've been a lifesaver."

  — Fifth Avenue candy bar: "You're the tops."

  — Three Musketeers bar: "We're all for one and one for all—thanks for the teamwork."

  — Payday candy bar: "You don't need to wait for payday to know you're worth your weight in gold."

  — Hershey's Kiss: "Thanks!"

  — Mr. Goodbar candy bar: "Thanks for the good work."

  — long-stemmed carnation: "Your sweet nature has a powerful effect."

- Ask parents to volunteer to provide weekly faculty treats. Each week a different parent could make the treat and deliver it to the staffroom.

- Provide an ample supply of awards or appreciation grams. Stock them by staff members' boxes along with pens. Place a sign nearby that reads: "Write a Note to a Staff Member" and encourage individuals to thank, congratulate or acknowledge one another on a regular basis.

Staff Warm Fuzzy (see next page) idea suggested by Judy Judd; Elk Grove Unified School District, Sacramento, California.

- Print up a set of business cards for each staff member. The print on the card includes not only their name, school and address, but also the words "I Am Proud to Be an Educator."

- Let teachers know the positive comments you've heard about them from others.

- Send notes acknowledging teacher's accomplishments to the Central Office.

Staff Warm Fuzzy

This is presented to

_____

in recognition for

_____

_____

_____

_____
Presented by

_____, 19_____

ACTIVITIES THAT PROMOTE SCHOOL-WIDE ESTEEM

The following activities will enhance an esteem-building climate; at the same time they will promote the five components of self-esteem: Security, Selfhood, Affiliation, Mission and Competence. These activities may be instituted on a school-wide basis or adapted by teachers for use in individual classrooms.

Grades K-8 Spirit Tickets/Award SW1/2

Purpose: To recognize individual students' gestures of positivism and spirit. To increase school or class positivism.

Materials: 8 1/2" x 11" envelope for each classroom to store earned tickets.

SW1 Spirit Tickets. Photocopy onto light-colored card stock or construction paper and cut out along the lines. For a school-wide activity, you will need at least 30–50 tickets per classroom for each month.

SW2 Spirit Award. Make enough copies for the winning team in each classroom.

Procedure for School-wide Use: Distribute the tickets to each staff member who does **not** have a self-contained room. These could include: principal, vice-principal, secretaries, nurse, resource person, counselor, psychologist, bus driver, custodian, librarian, cafeteria workers, etc.

Inform the staff participants that they are to distribute the tickets to any student they see performing a positive gesture. Students accept the tickets and take them back to their respective home-room teachers who collect them and store them in envelopes or boxes.

At the end of the month the tickets are tallied and then sent to the office. An appointed person (parent, secretary, etc.) then announces the class with the most tickets for that month. In large school settings you may wish to announce two winning classrooms for each month (upper grade and lower grade, or a first and second place).

Distribute SW2 Spirit Awards to the winning class and provide a prize. The contest now starts over for the next month. If desired, award an additional prize at the end of the year to the class with the most tickets. For a list of suggestions for prizes, refer to Chapter 2.

Procedure for Class Use: The activity can easily be adapted for class use by duplicating the tickets just for an individual teacher's use. Throughout the month, the teacher awards spirit tickets to individual students (or student teams) who exhibit positive gestures.

At the end of the month (or week) a set number of students with the most number of points could be awarded certificates or prizes. Many teachers choose to use the ticket distribution for class teams (permanent groups of four to five homogeneously grouped students). The team with the most points each month wins a special treat.

Spirit Ticket idea contributed by Dr. Craig Borba; former Principal, Rucker School, Gilroy Unified School District, Gilroy, California.

Grades K–8	Positive Performers/ Performance Award	SW3/4

Purpose: To recognize positive efforts of classmates. To increase the occurrence of positive deeds.

Materials: Choose a medium-size box with a top for the activity. Students may decorate the box with stickers, wallpaper and paper cutouts, or cover it with contact paper. Cut a 1" x 6" slot across the top of the box. Label it "Positive Performers" with a black marking pen. Place the box in a center supplied with a large quantity of the SW3 Positive Performers tickets. Make ample copies of SW4 Positive Performance Award.

Procedure: Tell the students that for a whole week they are going to keep track of all the positive deeds they do for one another.

Begin the activity by reviewing with students ways to show positivism. Explain that these can be friendly words or actions that put a smile on another person's face. Have students volunteer ways to be positive, or help them recall a time when someone was positive toward them. Students may enjoy role-playing the situations (real or make believe).

Point out the Positive Performance tickets and explain that whenever a student experiences or views a classmate doing something positive, he/she should write the person's name and a description of the performance on the ticket, and then slip it into the box. Encourage students to write exactly what happened. Nonwriting students may draw a picture to describe the experience, or dictate their comments to you.

At the end of the day read aloud the names on the tickets. Be sure that you yourself fill out ones regarding students who may be overlooked by their classmates and add these to the box. Give SW4 Positive Performance Awards to recognized students.

School Activity:

For adaptation as a school-wide activity, each classroom should have a box along with one placed in the office. Encourage students and staff to nominate "positive-performing" individuals throughout the school, write their names on tickets and post them in one of the boxes. The principal (or designated staff member) may recognize positive actions in a variety of ways:

- Place nominated names on a school-wide bulletin board.

- Read the nominated names over a loudspeaker.

- Go to individual classrooms to congratulate recognized students for their positive deeds.

- Provide the homeroom teacher with a signed award from the principal congratulating the person on positive actions.

Grades K–8	Gotcha Tickets	SW5

Purpose: To recognize positive deeds. To increase school-or class-wide positivism.

Materials:

SW5 Gotcha Tickets. Photocopy the ticket onto light-colored construction paper or cardstock. Cut out individual tickets along the outside margins and distribute to participating staff members. (If you use this activity school-wide, it is most effective if all homeroom staff members participate.)

Lottery Bowl. Any large container with a narrow lip at the top is ideal, providing it is large enough for an adult to pull out a winning ticket.

Spirit Prizes. Items for recognizing student positivism should be displayed. These could include: trinkets, school spirit items (pencils, banners), food or restaurant passes (donated by local businesses), movie passes or free-time passes. Look in Chapter 2 for a list of suggestions.

Procedure:

Explain to students that from a certain date their positive gestures will be recognized. Each time you (or a staff member, depending upon whether this is a school- or class-wide activity) see a special display of positivism, you will present that individual with a Gotcha ticket.

Show students that the ticket may be perforated. The long half of the ticket is sent home so that the student's parents can see that he/she was "caught" being positive. The smaller, remaining portion is to go inside the class or school lottery bowl. Every

week, pull four (or more) tickets from the bowl. Read names of the winning students over the loudspeaker and/or include in the school or class newsletter. Award these students a spirit prize of their choice from the display.

Idea adapted from Elmonica School, Beaverton School District, Beaverton, Oregon. Elmonica School calls their tickets "PEP"—People Encouraging People.

Grades K–8	Sparkle Grams/ Good Guy Award	SW6/7

Purpose: To recognize good student acts or positivism.

Materials: Copies of the SW6 Sparkle Gram (Grades K–4) or SW7 Good Guy Award (Grades 3–8).

Procedure: Photocopy the message grams onto light-colored paper and cut out along the outside and center margins. Distribute the grams in large quantity for staff members to use in recognizing positive student (and staff) gestures. Some teachers like to keep these on supply at a convenient class location for students to send to each other.

Grades K–8	Pass the Buck	SW8

Purpose: To recognize positive efforts of classmates. To increase the occurrence of positive deeds.

Procedure: Run off a large quantity of "bucks." Print the copy front and back so that the front of the buck appears to be "money" and the back shows "to" and "from." Cut them into individual bucks and stock them for school or class use.

Inform the school or class that they will have the opportunity to earn "bucks": students earn *two* bucks any time they do or say something positive to someone. The rules for earning them are:

1. The teacher (or staff member who gives them out) has to either hear or witness the kind act; or,

2. The *recipient* of the good deed has to personally inform the teacher of the kind act just performed or said to him/her.

Note: The "doer" will *not* receive the bucks by telling the teacher of the act him-/herself.

When the student receives the "two bucks" from the teacher he/she now has one buck to keep (and save) and one buck to pass. The teacher fills in the back of the first buck:

To: (the name of the student who earns it)

From: (name of staff member received from)

Example:

To: Mike

From: Mrs. Nelson

The second buck *must be passed on by the receiving student to another deserving student.* This buck is also signed on the back:

To: (to be filled in when the student has chosen)

From: (student who originally earned the buck)

Example:

To: _____

From: Mike

As Mike's name is now in the "from" space he can't spend the buck; he must pass it. He gives it to anyone who says or does something nice to him, and fills in the "to" space. The buck now looks like this:

To: Megan

From: Mike

Buck Turn-in: At some appointed time (once a week or so) students may turn in their earned bucks for rewards. These may consist of a variety of different types of rewards appropriate for your setting, ranging from free time to a school movie or trinket. Alternatively, students may keep their bucks to use at a class/school auction/fair at a later date.

Idea suggested by Chris Nelson; Palm Springs Unified School District, Palm Springs, California.

Grades K–6	**Spirit Tree**	**SW9**

Purpose: To recognize special students for different positive features.

Materials:
- *large* tree branch
- plaster of Paris
- tin wastebasket
- hole-punch
- yarn
- construction paper shapes depicting seasons

Procedure: The Spirit Tree is an ongoing symbol recognizing student achievements and positive gestures throughout the school year. Begin the project by finding a tree branch large enough to hold 50–100 paper ornaments. Place the branch in a tin waste paper basket filled with plaster of Paris. Work quickly so the plaster does not dry before you've inserted the branch.

Each month focus on a different feature of positivism. These could include: caring, spirit, friendship, achievement, generosity, etc. Either a staff or student vote could choose which one to feature. Each month, cut out different shapes from construction paper to represent a special theme (e.g., October, pumpkins; November, turkeys; January, snowflakes; February, hearts).

Give each staff member shape patterns and a few pre-cut figures. As staff members see students performing a deed that represents the month's quality, they write the student's name on the shape. Punch a hole at the top of the shape and tie to the tree with a yarn length.

Idea suggested by Marilyn Sweet; Wilder Elementary School, Littleton Public Schools, Littleton, Colorado.

CREATING A MORE PERSONAL ENVIRONMENT

One of the surest ways to become unmotivated is to feel anonymous. When a campus is large, it's often difficult to give personal recognition to individual students. In these instances, special staff planning usually must take place so that individual students feel included. The following ideas are school-wide activities that help students (and staff!) find out more about each other. (See also SW9 Spirit Tree—a month-by-month activity to give public recognition to individual students.)

Purpose: To provide opportunities that promote inclusion, affiliation and acceptance. To recognize individual students. To convey the message that "this is a caring environment where we grow and learn together."

BEGINNING OF THE YEAR ACTIVITIES

Grades K–8 Friendship Assembly SW10

Purpose: To increase students' awareness of their classmates.

Materials: None. (*Option:* decorate the school with student-made posters on friendship.)

Procedure: Assign each new student to the school (or class) a "friend" for the week. During the week, the appointed friend finds out as much as he/she can about the new student. Older students could write a short biographical sketch.

Consider holding a short assembly at the beginning of the year where each new student is introduced to the school by their appointed friend. Display biographical sketches on a bulletin board and later publish in a school or class newsletter.

Ideas suggested by St. Catherine's School, Morgan Hill, California.

Grades K–8 Name Tag Exchange SW11

Purpose: To help students become familiar with the names of classmates.

Materials: Light-colored construction paper cut into 4" x 5" shapes, 1 per student and staff; pins or double-sided adhesive tape; crayons or marking pens.

Procedure: Each student (and staff) designs a name tag for him-/herself on a 4" x 5" cut piece of light-colored construction paper. The individual's name and room number should be clearly visible on the tag. Sometime during the day participants exchange the tag with someone they do not know. The new friend's name and grade level should be written on

the back of the exchanged name tag. As an addition, suggest to students that they find out one additional fact about the person (an interest, favorite sport, state of birth). The exchanged tags are brought back to the students' homeroom and pinned (or glued) to a strip of butcher paper. The activity continues every day for a week; participants find a new friend each day. Encourage students to introduce their new friends to others and to continue to have contact with that friend.

Idea suggested by Alisal School, Pleasanton School District, Pleasanton, California.

Grades K–8 Who's New? SW12

Purpose: To increase school awareness of new students.

Materials: Copies of the SW12 Who's New? form; construction paper frames in which to display the forms; photograph of each new student.

Procedure: Photocopy the SW12 form onto light-colored construction paper or cardstock. Encourage students new to the school or classroom to fill out a "Who's New?" form.

Students may draw a self-portrait or paste their photograph in the open space.

Display completed forms at a central bulletin board for all to see. At a later date include the information in a newsletter.

ONGOING SCHOOL ACTIVITIES TO ENCOURAGE PERSONAL RECOGNITION

Grades K–6 Meet Our Kids SW13

Purpose: To provide the opportunity for students to find out about other students.

Materials: Copies of the SW13 Meet Our Kids form.

Procedure: Every student fills out the SW13 Meet Our Kids form to enable students, staff and parents to find out about them. Rotate a certain number of students on a weekly basis according to the enrollment size of the school. (In a school of 400 students, 11 different students would fill out the form each week.) You may wish to have parent aides or upper-grade students interview the weekly participants.

Display the completed forms in acetate frames on a bulletin board. Each week the previous week's forms are removed and inserted in an ongoing school binder in alphabetical order.

Idea suggested by Kohl School, Bowditch Elementary School District, Bowditch, Colorado.

Grades K–8	**Good News Report SW14**

Purpose: To increase home/school communication. To recognize students for special achievements or behavior.

Materials: Make copies of the SW14 Good News Report on cardstock-weight paper. Copy the top and bottom of the report on the front and back of a 5 1/2" x 4 1/4" card.

Procedure: Type your school address in the upper left-hand corner of the card front. Keep a large supply of cards handy for school and classroom use. Use the cards to send a personal message to students who deserve recognition for behavior or academic improvement. Address the note to the student's home and mail it. Parent volunteers may pre-address cards for you.

Idea suggested by Patricia Ireland-Williams, Principal; Cannon Elementary School, Grapevine, Texas.

Grades K–6	**Student of the Week SW15/16**

Purpose: To give individual recognition to each student on campus.

Materials:

Me Poster. 24" x 28" piece of tagboard for each student to create an individual poster.

SW15 Student of the Week Button. Copy the button form in mass quantity on bright-colored paper and cut them out. Create a button for each student to wear on his/her week by gluing a small photograph of the child in the center of the circle. *Option:* Use a button maker (a great investment!) to create each button, or laminate the finished button and attach a pin to the back.

SW16 Student of the Week Award. Duplicate the award on bright-colored paper to distribute to each Student of the Week.

Procedure: Each week teachers randomly choose one student per class to be the "Student of the Week." Students are chosen with no particular criteria in mind—they are special in themselves.

During the week, assign special duties/tasks/events to the student. These could include:

- Run all office errands.

- Design a personal poster. Provide each student with the 24" x 28" piece of tagboard. During the week, the student's assignment (with parent help as needed) is to design a self-portrait. It may include photographs, drawings, words, magazine cutouts or actual objects that somehow represent the student. The poster should include the student's name and grade level. Hang posters outside the respective classrooms (if the corridor is closed in), in the cafeteria or on the principal's bulletin board. The idea is for all students on campus to see the poster.

- Attend the principal's luncheon. Decorate a "private room" simply with a butcher paper tablecloth, a few balloons and perhaps a flower centerpiece. On a designated day each week, all Students of the Week bring their bag lunch to the room to "dine" with their principal who presents them with their awards. Some schools choose to have bumper stickers made up, which read "My child was Student of the Week at _____ School." You could also provide pencils printed with "I was the Student of the Week."

- Wear their Student of the Week buttons every day that week, after which the button is theirs to keep.

Idea suggested by Darlene Daugherty, Principal; Littleton School District, Littleton, Colorado.

Grades K-8 Citizen of the Week SW17/18

Purpose: To recognize students for behavior denoting outstanding citizenship.

Materials: Copies of the SW17 Citizen of the Week Nomination form sent to each homeroom teacher. Copies of SW18 Citizen of the Week form on light-colored cardstock-weight paper. School photograph or snapshot of each "citizen."

Procedure: Each week the principal randomly chooses one upper-grade and one lower-grade class, or a class from each grade level. These classes are then eliminated from future drawings until all other classes have had a turn to be chosen.

Notify the teacher from each class and ask them to submit the name of the student who, in their opinion, deserves to be recognized for one week as the Citizen of the Week. The student's behavior must exemplify good citizenship and, in addition, the following criteria could also be a factor: that week the student must not have been absent or tardy, turned in any late work or had any behavior problems.

The teacher then fills out the Citizen of the Week Nomination form, describing the specific citizenship behaviors that the student displayed during the week. He/she submits it to the principal, who then fills out a Citizen of the Week award.

The student's photograph is attached to the center of the certificate, which is hung up on a centrally located bulletin board. On a specific day, the principal reads the selected citizens' names over the loudspeaker and gives a brief description of what the students did to earn this honor. The principal also sends notes home to parents.

Idea suggested by Nancy Sheridan, Principal; Southgate School, Hayward School District, Hayward, California.

Grades K-8 Birthday Recognition SW19

Purpose: To celebrate individual student birthdays on a school-wide basis.

Procedure: Recognizing 500 students and staff birthdays can be difficult unless it has been carefully planned. Begin by asking teachers to submit their students' names (and their own) by birth month and date.

Add all the names to a monthly birthday file. To make it simpler, break down the dates into weeks (e.g., January, first week; January, second week; etc.). The following ideas are ways to celebrate individual student's birthdays:

Grades K-6 Principal's Birthday Party SW20

Once a week ask the cafeteria workers (or a parent volunteer whose child's birthday falls on that week) to bake a birthday cake. Decorate a "private room" with a butcher-paper tablecloth, a few balloons and a cake centerpiece.

Those students whose birthday appears during that week are invited to attend the birthday party during lunchtime. Each student (and the principal) brings a bag lunch (or orders from the cafeteria lunch) and celebrates his/her birthday at the "Principal's Birthday Party." Encourage students to wear name tags, or provide some at the party. This is a great opportunity to get to know students better.

Idea suggested by Diane Lewis; Ben Franklin School, Littleton School District, Littleton, Colorado.

Grades K-8 Birthday Poster SW21

Enlist the help of an artistic parent volunteer to make a Birthday Poster for the school. Each month supply the volunteer with a list of students whose birthdays fall during that period.

The volunteer makes a long banner on butcher paper, which reads: "Happy Birthday to Our Friends." The name of each birthday student is written on the banner.

Some schools assign a different classroom each month to make the banner.

| Grades K–8 | Principal's Birthday Card SW22 |

Directions for the Birthday Card:

1. Copy the Birthday Card onto cardstock paper so that the top and bottom of the form is on the front and back of a 5 1/2" x 4 1/4" card.

2. Type your school address in the upper left-hand corner of the front of the Birthday Card form.

3. Keep a large supply of cards handy for school and classroom use. Use the cards to personally send a birthday message to the birthday student. Parent volunteers (or upper-grade students) may pre-address cards.

Each week enlist a parent volunteer to determine which student and staff birthdays need to be recognized. Then address the cards, signed by you (the principal), to the appropriate individuals. Distribute cards in a number of ways, such as:

1. Send the addressed cards in the mail to the students' homes.

2. Send the addressed cards through the teacher-mail. The students' teachers could personally hand the card to each student.

3. Invite all students with birthdays that week to come to the principal's office at a specified time so that they may personally receive their cards.

4. Hand deliver the cards to the birthday students.

| Grades K–6 | Birthday Pencils SW23 |

Pencils with inscriptions printed on them cost very little if obtained through pencil companies.

Order enough pencils for each student to receive one with a message that says "Happy Birthday! You are Special!"

Optional: Include the name of the staff member on the pencil following the message.

| Grades K–8 | School Problem Report SW24 |

Needs adaptation for students in grades K–3.

Purpose: To convey the idea that school problems are a responsibility that should be shared by all. To provide opportunities for problem solving.

Materials: Copies of the SW24 School Problem Report submitted to each homeroom teacher.

Procedure: Ask teachers to convey to students that any school problems are actually problems for everyone to try and solve. Place several copies of the SW24 School Problem Report form in a 9" x 12" envelope and distribute them to each classroom. Tell teachers to keep the forms in an accessible location in the classroom. Teachers should encourage students to fill out a form whenever they recognize a school problem that cannot be solved quickly by individuals. This distinction may need to be discussed with students. Teachers submit completed forms to the principal's office. Consider creating a "Problem Task Force," which consists of staff and students, to review the forms. Take action on any problem whenever the group deems it necessary.

| Grades K–6 | Koala-T Efforts SW25 |

Purpose: To help students focus on the importance of quality efforts. To recognize individual student efforts.

Materials: Large stuffed koala bear (or prize of your choice), available from most toy stores.

SW25 Koala-T tickets. Copy large quantities of the ticket pattern shown onto light-colored construction paper or cardstock and distribute 30 or so to each staff member.

Box for ticket stubs. Choose a box slightly larger than two shoe boxes. It should have a removable top. Cut a slot in the top of the box about 1/2" x 6". Decorate the box with koala bears.

Procedure: Inform students that a major goal of the school is for each student to always do their best at whatever task they have. You may define this as "quality work or behavior."

Each time a student makes an outstanding effort, he/she will be presented with a ticket by a staff member. Part of the ticket will go home with the student so that parents are informed of the good

SCHOOL-WIDE

effort. The remaining shorter portion will stay at school and be kept for the month by the homeroom teacher.

At the end of the month, each classroom tallies the total number of ticket stubs they have earned. They give this number to the office and place ticket stubs inside the Ticket Stub box in the office.

The class with the most tickets keeps the large stuffed koala bear in their classroom for a month. Consider making a large paper "blue ribbon" the length of a door and fix it to the door of the winning classroom.

The stubs remain in the box; four tickets are pulled every week. Read the name of each winning student over the loudspeaker. Those students may be awarded predetermined prizes such as ice cream, popsicles or other items from the Spirit Award List, see Chapter 2.

Idea suggested by Diane Lewis, Principal; Ben Franklin School, Littleton School District, Littleton, Colorado.

Grades K-8 Book of Winners SW26/27

Purpose: To recognize individual student achievements.

Materials: A large ledger book, available at most stationery stores. Write "Book of Winners" on the outside of the ledger and place it in a convenient location where students may comfortably sign in.

SW26 Official Pass. Photocopy the pass in mass quantity.

SW27 You Are a Winner! award. Photocopy the award in mass quantity.

Procedure for School-wide Use:

Distribute a large quantity of Official Pass tickets to each staff member who will be working on academic-related subjects with students. Inform the staff that they may give any deserving student a pass at any time during the day. Students who receive passes should earn them for academic achievement. This could be for either quality work or improvement.

Students take their passes to the office and sign the book in the first available space. Then they receive a You Are a Winner! award before returning to their classrooms. Consider printing the names of the weekly "winners" in the school newsletter.

Procedure for Class Use:

This activity may easily be adapted for class use. Passes are not necessary. Teachers keep a Book of Winners in the classroom and instruct students to sign it when appropriate. Deserving students receive awards.

Idea suggested by Mike Robinson, Principal; Helen Keller Elementary School, Lake Washington School District, Washington.

Grades K-8 Principal's Ideas List SW28

The following are additional suggestions that the principal or other staff member can implement for school-wide esteem builders:

Personal Greeting. Set a tone of welcome for students by personally greeting them at the bus stop, office door, on the playground or in the car pool line.

Business Cards. Have a set of business cards printed with your name, school name and school address included. These could also include one sentence such as "I like having you at this school." Carry them with you always (along with a pen). Whenever the occasion arises, sign your name and hand the student a card.

Printed Pencils. Have a large supply of pencils printed up with a personal message from you such as "Hooray from M.L.B." Hand them out when the need comes. Don't forget to give them to your staff.

Printed Stickers. Pre-printed stickers are very effective with younger students. "Hot dots" (colored circle stickers) can be printed for a minimal fee. Include the school emblem or mascot along with a short message: "Hooray," "Have a great day," or "A great student from _____ (school)." Keep supplies on hand so that at key moments they can be "stuck" onto a deserving student.

Personally Delivered Certificates and Awards. Whenever the occasion arises, try to personally present awards and certificates to students who have earned them. Either call them to the office or hand deliver to each classroom.

Send Students to the Office...for being good! Encourage teachers to send deserving students to you for a pat on the back. Too often students associate the office with "bad times." Have on hand a jar of sugarless lollipops, stickers, pencils or awards to present to each deserving student. (**Note:** One principal from Michigan is so adamant about having each student from the school come to his office at least one time during the year that he keeps an ongoing record of visiting students. Teachers who do not send students to the office are written up on their evaluation.)

Positive Phone Calls. A middle school in Riverside, California, makes it a school policy that for every negative phone call, the staff member must make two positive phone calls. The policy is written on masking tape and attached to each school phone.

Remember that parents need excuses to praise their children. Try to make at least two positive phone calls home to deserving students' parents every day.

Bumper Stickers. These can be very effective for recognizing student efforts as well as building parent relationships with the school. Have a large quantity printed up with a message such as: "My kid was Student of the Week at _____ School," "My child is on the honor roll at _____ School," "My kid was caught being good at _____ School."

Principal's Pride Bulletin Board. Encourage teachers to submit deserving work that shows either quality or improvement. Display on a Principal's Pride Bulletin Board and rotate weekly or biweekly. Present each honoree with a sticker or award and remember to include his/her name in the Principal's Newsletter.

School Scrapbook. Keep an ongoing scrapbook of student achievements and activities. Place it in a highly visible location in the office.

Principal's List of Positive Kids. Display a large strip of butcher paper near the front office. Each week

teachers (and other staff) "sign in" students who have performed positive deeds for others. Include these names in the Principal's Newsletter or give another form of recognition (that is, read their names over the loudspeaker, sit at a "table for positive kids" in the cafeteria, have an extra recess on Friday, or attend a school movie showing).

I Spotted a Friendly Kid at _____ School. Cover a box with wrapping paper and decorate it with stickers. Make a slit 1/2" x 6" in the box top. (Try to find a box with a top that can be easily removed.)

Each day (week) any staff member (and/or students) submit names of students who were caught being friendly on campus. Write the name on a slip of paper and place in the box. At the end of the week pull a few names for "winners" who receive a predetermined prize.

Principal Read-Aloud. Consider going into classrooms and personally reading a book (or beginning chapter) aloud. Many principals report it is one of their favorite things to do because the students look forward to the occasion with such anticipation.

Grades K–8 Positive Comments Contest SW29

Purpose: To foster positive statements in the school.

Materials: Copies of SW29 Positive Comments Contest forms.

Procedure: Sponsor a school-wide contest in which classrooms suggest positive, builder-upper statements they could say to someone at the school or classroom. Each week classrooms send phrases, sentences or one-word comments on the SW29 Positive Comments Contest forms to the principal's office.

Arrange for forms to be stored in a large box marked "Builder-Upper Statements." Each day pull a statement randomly from the box and read it over the loudspeaker. Give credit to the student (and classroom), who may choose a predetermined spirit prize.

You may wish to include the builder-upper statement in your Friday notes and/or attach a large piece of butcher paper to the wall to display a running list of builder-upper statements.

| Grades K-8 | **Principal's Award SW30** |

Purpose: To praise students for their accomplishments. To give recognition to students. To promote pride in students' work.

Materials: Copies of SW30 Principal's Award. Custom stamp saying, "This paper was read by your principal."

Procedure: Every two weeks the principal randomly chooses a class and then personally reads a paper written by each student. The students themselves may choose the paper, or the teacher may submit them. The principal stamps each paper and returns it to the student.

For nonwriting students, the principal may instead evaluate art papers.

Variation: Terrific 10 Papers. Form a "Quality Paper Review Board" at your school consisting of a few staff members and an administrator. Each month every teacher submits to the board 5–10 papers written by students that fulfill one of the following categories: neatness, effort, quality or improvement. Change the category each month so that a different work quality is stressed. The committee reads each submitted paper and chooses the top 10. These papers are then posted on a school bulletin board entitled "The Terrific Ten." A specially printed "Terrific Ten Paper" sticker or other appropriate award could be attached to each paper. The principal reads over the loudspeaker the students' names and sends recognition notes to the parents. In addition, the students could each receive a certificate.

Idea suggested by Nancy Sheridan, Principal; Southgate School, Hayward Unified School District, Hayward, California.

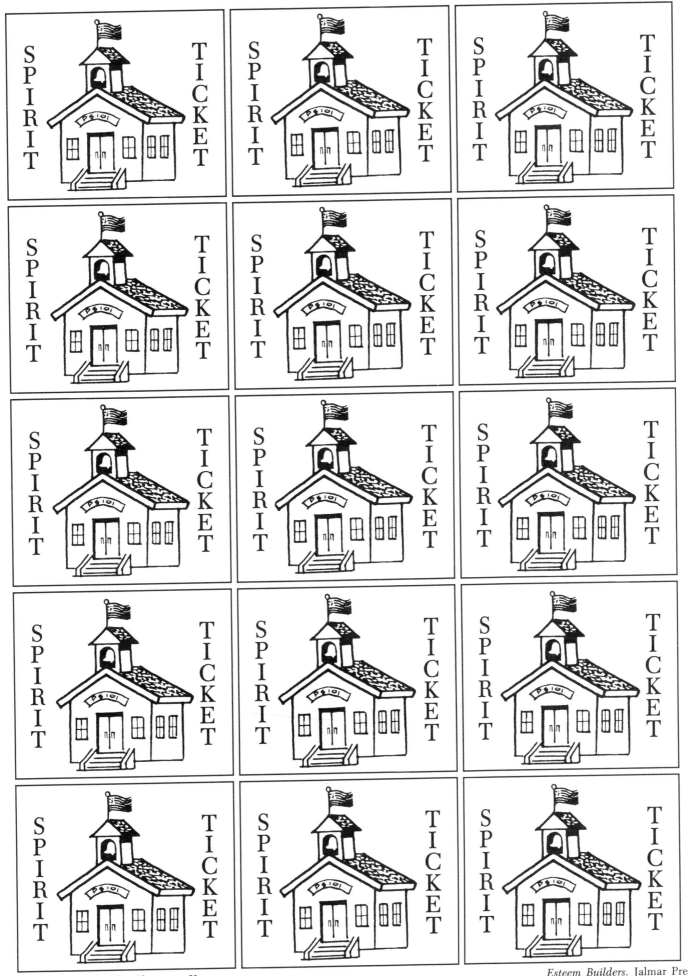

Esteem Builders. Jalmar Press
Rolling Hills Estates, CA

Spirit Award

This certificate is proudly awarded to the students of

Room _____ , _____ Teacher _____ ,

in recognition of outstanding effort in maintaining our school

spirit for the month of _____ 19 _____

Congratulations!

_____
Authorized Signature

Esteem Builders. Jalmar Press
Rolling Hills Estates, CA

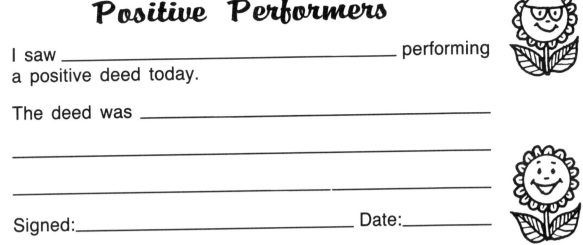

Positive Performers

I saw _____ performing
a positive deed today.

The deed was _____

_____

_____

Signed:_____ Date:_____

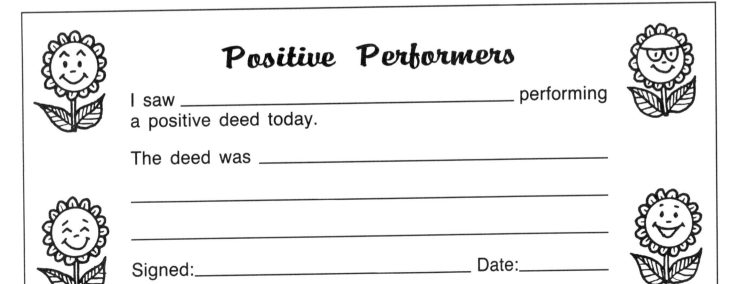

Positive Performers

I saw _____ performing
a positive deed today.

The deed was _____

_____

_____

Signed:_____ Date:_____

Positive Performers

I saw _____ performing
a positive deed today.

The deed was _____

_____

_____

Signed:_____ Date:_____

Esteem Builders. Jalmar Press
Rolling Hills Estates, CA

Positive Performance Award

Esteem Builders. Jalmar Press
Rolling Hills Estates, CA

Name:

GOTCHA!

Name:

GOTCHA!

Name:

GOTCHA!

Name

Congratulations!

We GOTCHA in the
act of being positive!
And we're glad we did...Keep it up!

Staff

Name

Congratulations!

We GOTCHA in the
act of being positive!
And we're glad we did...Keep it up!

Staff

Name

Congratulations!

We GOTCHA in the
act of being positive!
And we're glad we did...Keep it up!

Staff

Esteem Builders. Jalmar Press
Rolling Hills Estates, CA

Sparkle Gram

Date:_____

To:_____

From:_____

Message:_____

_____

_____

_____

_____

Good Guy Award

Date:_____

To:_____

From:_____

Message:_____

_____

_____

_____

_____

Esteem Builders. Jalmar Press
Rolling Hills Estates, CA

Pass the Buck

To: From:	To: From:	To: From:
To: From:	To: From:	To: From:

Esteem Builders. Jalmar Press
Rolling Hills Estates, CA

Pass The Buck

Esteem Builders. Jalmar Press
Rolling Hills Estates, CA

Who's New?

_____ is a _____ grader

from _____ .

_____ likes to _____

_____

_____

_____

_____

_____

_____

_____

_____

Esteem Builders. Jalmar Press
Rolling Hills Estates, CA

Name	Date

Meet Our Kids

Grade: _____

Teacher: _____

Date and place of birth: _____

_____

Members of your family: _____

_____

_____

_____

_____

(Paste your photo here.)

Special interests outside of school: _____

_____

_____

_____

_____

Favorite school subjects: _____

_____

_____

_____

_____

_____

Pets: _____

_____

_____

Kind of music you like best: _____

_____

TV program you enjoy most: _____

_____

Esteem Builders. Jalmar Press
Rolling Hills Estates, CA

From:

_____

_____

_____

To:

_____

_____

_____

_____

(Front)

GOOD NEWS REPORT

Keep up the good work! It's great!

(Back)

Esteem Builders. Jalmar Press
Rolling Hills Estates, CA

Student of the Week Buttons

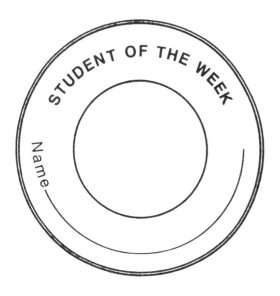
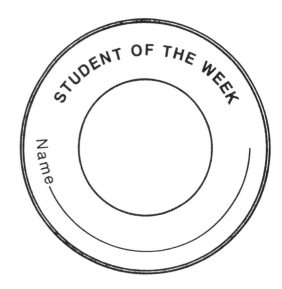
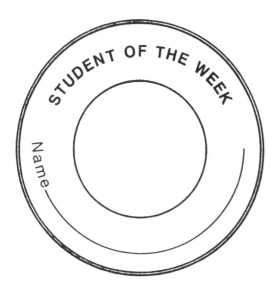
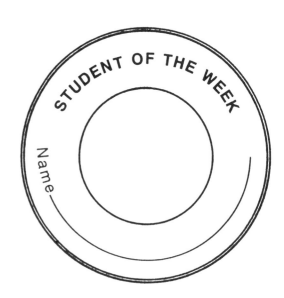

Esteem Builders. Jalmar Press
Rolling Hills Estates, CA

Student of the Week

Awarded to:_____

Date:_____

Authorized Signature:_____

Congratulations!

We're glad you're part of our school.

Student of the Week

Awarded to:_____

Date:_____

Authorized Signature:_____

Congratulations!

We're glad you're part of our school.

Esteem Builders. Jalmar Press
Rolling Hills Estates, CA

CITIZEN OF THE WEEK NOMINATION

Room _____   Date _____

My nomination for Citizen of the Week is _____

because _____

_____

_____

This week the student has had no absences, tardies, late work, or behavior infractions.

Teacher_____

CITIZEN OF THE WEEK NOMINATION

Room _____   Date _____

My nomination for Citizen of the Week is _____

because _____

_____

_____

This week the student has had no absences, tardies, late work, or behavior infractions.

Teacher_____

CITIZEN OF THE WEEK NOMINATION

Room _____   Date _____

My nomination for Citizen of the Week is _____

because _____

_____

_____

This week the student has had no absences, tardies, late work, or behavior infractions.

Teacher_____

Idea suggested by Nancy Sheridan; Principal, Southgate School, Hayward Unified School District, Hayward, CA.

Esteem Builders. Jalmar Press
Rolling Hills Estates, CA

Citizen of the Week

awarded to

_____

_____   _____
grade   room

_____
date

_____
principal

Esteem Builders. Jalmar Press
Rolling Hills Estates, CA

From:

_____

_____

_____

To:

_____

_____

_____

You are special because you are you!

HAPPY BIRTHDAY!
From

Esteem Builders. Jalmar Press
Rolling Hills Estates, CA

School Problem Report

A problem I noticed at our school is _____

_____

_____

_____

When does this problem usually happen? _____

_____

_____

Who is involved when it happens? _____

_____

_____

A way we could solve the problem is: _____

_____

_____

_____

_____

_____

Submitted by _____

Room _____ Date _____

Esteem Builders. Jalmar Press
Rolling Hills Estates, CA

 Another **KOALA-T Effort!**

Name:_____

Room #:_____

 **Congratulations!**

Your child was caught in a KOALA-T effort. Keep up the good work!

_____
Name

_____
Staff

 Another **KOALA-T Effort!**

Name:_____

Room #:_____

 **Congratulations!**

Your child was caught in a KOALA-T effort. Keep up the good work!

_____
Name

_____
Staff

 Another **KOALA-T Effort!**

Name:_____

Room #:_____

 **Congratulations!**

Your child was caught in a KOALA-T effort. Keep up the good work!

_____
Name

_____
Staff

 Another **KOALA-T Effort!**

Name:_____

Room #:_____

 **Congratulations!**

Your child was caught in a KOALA-T effort. Keep up the good work!

_____
Name

_____
Staff

Esteem Builders. Jalmar Press
Rolling Hills Estates, CA

Official Pass

For
_____

To sign
the "Book
of Winners"

Date:_____

_____
Authorized Signature

Official Pass

For
_____

To sign
the "Book
of Winners"

Date:_____

_____
Authorized Signature

Official Pass

For
_____

To sign
the "Book
of Winners"

Date:_____

_____
Authorized Signature

Official Pass

For
_____

To sign
the "Book
of Winners"

Date:_____

_____
Authorized Signature

Official Pass

For
_____

To sign
the "Book
of Winners"

Date:_____

_____
Authorized Signature

Official Pass

For
_____

To sign
the "Book
of Winners"

Date:_____

_____
Authorized Signature

Esteem Builders. Jalmar Press
Rolling Hills Estates, CA

Congratulations!

This is to certify that

_____

has signed the "Book of Winners" for the following

reason:_____

_____

Signed and authorized by:

_____

You
Are a
Winner!

Congratulations!

This is to certify that

_____

has signed the "Book of Winners" for the following

reason:_____

_____

Signed and authorized by:

_____

You
Are a
Winner!

Idea suggested by Mike Robinson, Principal; Helen Keller Elementary School, Lake Washington School District, Washington.

Esteem Builders. Jalmar Press
Rolling Hills Estates, CA

POSITIVE COMMENTS CONTEST

Positive Comment:_____

_____

Name:_____ Room:_____

POSITIVE COMMENTS CONTEST

Positive Comment:_____

_____

Name:_____ Room:_____

POSITIVE COMMENTS CONTEST

Positive Comment:_____

_____

Name:_____ Room:_____

POSITIVE COMMENTS CONTEST

Positive Comment:_____

_____

Name:_____ Room:_____

Esteem Builders. Jalmar Press
Rolling Hills Estates, CA

Principal's Award

Presented to

_____

Enjoy this special day honoring your accomplishment.

Keep up the good work...it's great having you here!
I'm proud of you!

Date_____ Principal_____

Principal's Award

Presented to

_____

Enjoy this special day honoring your accomplishment.

Keep up the good work...it's great having you here!
I'm proud of you!

Date_____ Principal_____

Esteem Builders. Jalmar Press
Rolling Hills Estates, CA

Conclusion

*The future belongs to those who believe
in the beauty of their dreams.*
—ELEANOR ROOSEVELT

Although this section is called the "conclusion" to ESTEEM BUILDERS, it isn't the ending of actual esteem enhancement. The building of positive self-perception is an ongoing process that should never be confined to the boundaries of any set curriculum. The purpose of ESTEEM BUILDERS is to create a framework for educators to improve each of the five critical feelings of self-esteem. The enhancement of these feelings (Security, Selfhood, Affiliation, Mission and Competence) lays a foundation that students can carry with them in all of life's endeavors.

There are many advantages for students with high self-perceptions. Such individuals, for instance, are usually better equipped to cope with life's adversities; they are more resilient to problems and defeats. In general, these students are more content and self-fulfilled; as a result, they are more willing to risk the unknown. They are able to acknowledge personal successes and triumphs as well as to accept weaknesses and failures. The higher the self-esteem, the more likely it is that students will engage in nourishing relationships instead of destructive ones. Self-feelings can also determine whether students capitalize on their skills and capabilities, and use them to the fullest in the classroom and in life.

Self-esteem can be the ignitor for a student's highest learning potential. Moreover, research tells us that a solid foundation of self-esteem is also a powerful deterrent to such social undesirables as dropping out, truancy, juvenile delinquency, teen-age pregnancy, chemical dependency, gang affiliation and adolescent suicide. The potential of self-esteem is much too far-reaching to confine it to thought on paper. Acting on these principles must extend beyond these pages. Self-esteem is a powerful tool that can no longer be ignored in educational settings.

A critical point in esteem building is that self-esteem is only self-empowering when it is *applied*. For individuals merely to have good feelings about themselves can be ineffective, unless those feelings are used to their advantage. One of the key reasons why individuals with high self-esteem are so effective in life is that they are also able to make feelings work for them and thereby increase their potential even further. Webster defines the verb "to mobilize" as meaning "to put into action." High self-esteem students use this same principle, and that's one of the main reasons why these students are so capable. *They have learned to empower themselves.* Here are students who can use their potential to the fullest because they internally reinforce and acknowledge themselves. Acquisition

Self-empowered Internalist (High self-esteem)	Other-empowered Externalist (Low self-esteem)
Internally driven	Externally driven
Self-reinforced	Other-reinforced
Self acknowledges successes	Others acknowledge successes
Self-motivated	Other-motivated
Purposeful	Aimless
Decisive	Indecisive
Powerful	Powerless
Secure	Superficial

and development of the five self-esteem feelings provides all the necessary elements to achieve one's full capacity.

THE DIFFERENCE BETWEEN INTERNAL AND EXTERNAL MOTIVATION

There are a number of other distinctions between self-empowered, high self-esteem students and externally motivated, low self-esteem students. One of the biggest differences is that self-empowered individuals recognize they have responsibility as well as control over their own actions. They are willing to take risks and extend personal boundaries because they have a reserve of previous successes. On the other hand, those who seek reinforcement externally often feel they are not responsible for what happens and are likely to position themselves as victims. This allows them to escape the responsibility for their own failure. Following are other differences between the two quite distinct groups of individuals:

Self-empowered students are individuals who say "I'll try"; whereas, *other-empowered* individuals say "Why bother?" Internally driven students meet setbacks with a "What can I do now?" attitude because they see problems as opportunities in disguise. Externally driven students, on the other hand, see any problem as grounds for quitting. They often say to themselves, "I give up." The difference with internalizers is that they constantly acknowledge their successes inside their heads by telling themselves, "What should I try next?" They have a sense of purpose and direction in their lives.

Unfortunately, externalizers wait for the tangible awards, stickers and verbal approval of others. They rely on others to program them and give them a course of direction. Instead of comparing their achievements with their own goals and potential, they always compare themselves with others. Self-empowered students stand on their own two feet, while other-empowered students wait for external forces to create their "successes."

However, students do form their self-concept in the first three feelings (Security, Selfhood, Affiliation) primarily through external relationships and the environment. As they acquire a more accurate and realistic self-picture, and Mission and Competence are developed, external controls become less essential. At this level, self-esteem no longer depends on the forces of others. Instead, it becomes more internally directed. Students recognize their own worth and achievements without the constant need for approval from the outside.

Becoming internally empowered is by no means an overnight accomplishment. In reality, it is derived from personal interpretations triggered by events or significant others in each of the five critical feelings of self-esteem. It is especially important that early needs of Security, Selfhood and Affiliation be acquired by the student. As a trio of critical emotional needs, these feelings serve as the foundation to future esteem building. They help develop self-assuredness, as well as an accurate and realistic self-concept. Recognition of personal strengths and capabilities serves as a powerful coping and buffer strategy for any obstacles that might be met as well as a compensation tool to use for any weaknesses or setbacks.

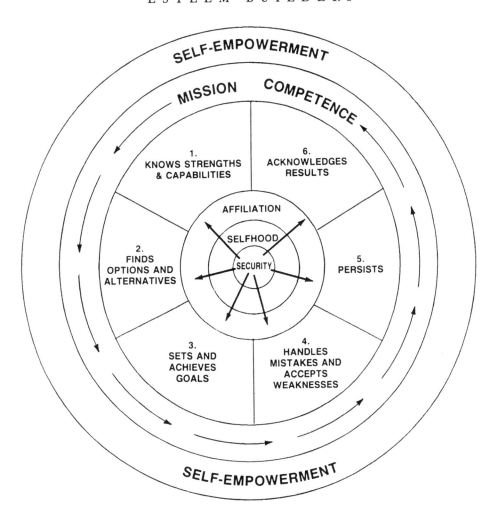

EMPOWERMENT CYCLE

The acquisition of the final two feelings, Mission and Competence, expands the individual's sense of self and sets the empowerment cycle spinning in a forward motion. One of the most important skills that develops is an individual's ability to recognize that there are alternative solutions to problems. Development of problem-solving strategies is also invaluable for another reason—it helps individuals become more effective and successful goal-setters. Internalizers are beings with a sense of purpose: their life has aim and direction; they constantly set goals for themselves. What separates self-empowered individuals from other-empowered individuals is that the former actually achieve their goals. Each successful goal is another internal validation that "I'm a worthwhile individual," and so self-esteem is further enhanced. When an internal self-picture focuses on strengths, successful goal achievements, and knowledge of alternatives and options, mistakes and weaknesses can be accepted without undue self-devaluation. In fact, mistakes and difficulties are often seen as tools for learning

instead of reasons for quitting. When individuals have a reserve of tools and knowledge to call on during setbacks, they are able to persist on their chosen course, and this in turn affects motivation and productivity. And when such individuals do reach their goal, they do not have to depend on others for approval. Instead, they are able to say to themselves, "I did a good job!" These individuals have now become internalizers who are self-sufficient and self-directed. Self-esteem is therefore a cumulative process of acquiring fundamental feelings...this is what ESTEEM BUILDERS is all about.

SELF-ESTEEM ENHANCEMENT WITH A SUPPORT SYSTEM

Unfortunately, the path toward improving self-esteem is not always a smooth road. For this reason, it is often helpful to join with other educators and form a self-esteem network to maximize support and resources. Members generally consist of individuals living in the same geographical location who share the common interest of enhancing student self-esteem. These group gatherings provide opportunities to share successful ideas, resources and research. Members also serve as invaluable resources to schools, agencies or individuals interested in finding out further information about self-esteem. Past experiences with effective self-esteem support groups have shown that the formation of one group frequently leads to additional group networking. If you are considering starting such a group, or need assistance, the National Council on Self-Esteem[1] is an extremely helpful agency. An extensive bibliography of self-esteem resources is included in Appendix I.

If your building site has instituted self-esteem as a yearly goal, consider forming a school-wide coordinator team as part of your self-esteem implementation procedure. My personal experience in conducting seminars nationwide has demonstrated repeatedly that the coordinator team is one of the most effective ways to maintain staff momentum in the topic. Teams may consist of any number of members; generally they are comprised of two to six individuals. Members may include staff, administrators and parents. Most effective coordinators are not necessarily knowledgeable about the topic; however, they are committed and enthusiastic about implementing a self-enhancing educational philosophy. Team roles may vary, but their basic duty is to serve as a school resource in esteem-building to staff members. Distributing copies of self-esteem activities or techniques to individual staff members, displaying idea samples on a designated faculty bulletin board or making short presentations at faculty meetings are just three approaches team members can take to disseminate information. Teams can also plan school-wide esteem projects as well as keep staff members informed on the latest research or resources in self-esteem. As neighboring schools develop similar esteem-building goals, coordinator teams can network.

Schools cannot take on the vast task of improving the self-esteem of their students alone. For maximum effectiveness, every available helping agency needs to be utilized. Ideally, every significant source or person who touches the life of a child should have an active part. The community offers rich resources and invaluable support; the home is another area that should not be ignored. For esteem enhancement to be most effective, the home must be an active partner in the esteem-building process. The reality is, unfortunately, that too many parents are not prepared to be esteem builders. Recognizing the critical need for a solid parent-school esteem-building relationship, a companion volume to ESTEEM BUILDERS entitled HOME ESTEEM BUILDERS was created. The publication includes 40 weekly home esteem builders—activity sheets to photocopy and send home for parents to use with their children in a family context. Each activity is designed to help parents become more familiar with each of the five esteem components as well as provide them with strategies or activities to use with their children to enhance the component.

Whether your efforts to enhance student self-esteem are as a district, school or individual, they are significant. The beauty of self-esteem enhancement is that it is contagious. Educators over and over report that though they began the effort singly, others in no time caught the spirit and joined forces. Their combined efforts have had a powerful effect. This is how we will turn the tide for countless students. Perhaps your local area is just waiting for someone to begin the process. That someone must be you.

Glenn van Ekeren[2] tells a story that so aptly depicts the significance educators can have in the lives of students. An old man happened to be walking along a beach one day and saw a most peculiar sight. Ahead on the beach he observed a young boy surrounded by hundreds of beached starfish. The old man gazed in wonder as the young boy again and again picked up a small starfish and threw it into the water. Finally, the old man could contain himself no longer and approached the boy to ask him why he was spending so much time on a task that appeared to be an obvious waste of time. The young boy bent down and picked up one more small starfish, and as he threw it safely into the sea, he said: "Well, it made a difference to that one."

The conclusion is that you, too, can make a tremendous difference in the lives of your students.

1. National Council on Self-Esteem, P.O. Box 3728, Palo Alto, CA 94303-3728.

2. Van Ekeren, G. *The Speakers' Sourcebook—Quotes, Stories, and Anecdotes for Every Occasion* (Englewood Cliffs, NJ: Prentice-Hall, 1978).

Appendix I

Self-Esteem Bibliography

The following materials are available as resources for school or classroom application to develop self-esteem. They are designed to be used in ongoing self-esteem programs.

Allred, Carol. *Positive Action Self-Concept Curriculum*. Twin Falls, ID: Positive Action, 1986. Designed for kindergarten through seventh grade, the curriculum takes only 15–20 minutes per day through the year.

Anderson, Jill. *Pulsmy: In Pursuit of Excellence*. Eugene, OR: Timberline Press, 1987. A cognitive approach to increasing self-esteem. Designed for primary grades.

_____. *Thinking, Changing, and Rearranging: Improving Self-Esteem in Young People*. Eugene, OR: Timberline Press, 1987. A cognitive approach to increasing self-esteem for upper-grade students.

Canfield, Jack. *Self-Esteem in the Classroom: A Curriculum Guide*. Pacific Palisades, CA: Self-Esteem Seminars, 1987. The guide includes over 225 activities, most of which can be used at any grade level.

Dembrowsky, Connie. *Affective Skill Development for Adolescents*. Lincoln, NE: Selection Research, 1979. A highly structured curriculum to help students in grades 6–12 develop self-esteem and interpersonal skills. The program focuses on the social/behavioral skills of communication, assertiveness, self-responsibility and problem solving/decision-making.

Dinkmeyer, Don. *Developing Understanding of Self and Others (DUSO)*. Circle Pines, MI: American Guidance Services, 1978. A program specifically designed to help younger children improve in social and emotional behavior.

Durfee, Cliff. *More Teachable Moments*. San Diego, CA: Live, Love and Laugh, 1987. This guide contains 10 lessons designed to introduce basic communication skills and includes 140 topics for sharing feelings. For elementary- and junior high age-students.

Gibbs, Jeanne. *Tribes: A Process for Social Development and Cooperative Learning*. Santa Rosa, CA: Center Source Publications, 1987. The manual is a plentiful source of team activities that can be used to enhance the communication and interrelationship abilities of students. Appropriate for elementary- and junior high-age students.

Kluth, Margo, and McCarty, Dorothy. *Smile: You're Worth It!* La Canada, CA: Me and My

Inner Self, 1987. Designed for middle- and upper-grade students, the program focuses on goal-setting, self-esteem and 10 additional concepts. Two one-hour sessions each week are devoted to each concept.

McDaniel, Sandy, and Bielen, Peggy. *Project Self-Esteem: A Parent Involvement Program for Elementary-Age Children*. Rolling Hills, CA: B.L. Winch & Associates, 1986. The program is designed to be taught in the classroom by a team of four parent volunteers or teachers for grades 2–6. The program has twelve 40-minute lessons designed to be taught on an alternate-week basis.

Pike, Graham, and Selby, David. *Global Teacher, Global Learner*. London: Hodder and Stoughton, 1988. The book develops the theory and practice of global education as well as offering an extensive range of activities for the primary and secondary classroom.

Reasoner, Robert. *Building Self-Esteem: A Comprehensive Program*. Palo Alto, CA: Consulting Psychologists Press, 1982. Designed for grades K–8, this manual includes 125 worksheets and 500 suggestions. The program builds self-esteem using the same five esteem components as covered in ESTEEM BUILDERS, with three components named differently, and is therefore quite compatible as a companion volume.

Skills for Adolescents. Columbus, OH: Quest National Center, 1985. Produced by Lions Club International, this book helps junior high-age students deal with change and personal decision-making, thereby reducing drug and alcohol abuse. Includes a curriculum guide for an 18-week course.

Practical Handbooks

The following materials are helpful as supplementary classroom resources to increase student self-esteem.

Borba, Michele and Borba, Craig. *Self-Esteem; A Classroom Affair; Volume 1: 101 Ways to Help Children Like Themselves*. San Francisco: Harper & Row, 1978. An abundance of practical, classroom-tested activities to increase elementary children's self-esteem. Many activities are in reproducible form.

_____. *Self-Esteem; A Classroom Affair; Volume 2: More Ways to Help Children Like Themselves*. San Francisco, CA: Harper & Row, 1982.

More than 100 ideas that are different from Volume 1. The activities develop social skills such as brainstorming and problem-solving, role playing, practicing friendship-making skills, and handling disagreements.

Canfield, Jack, and Wells, Harold C. *100 Ways to Enhance Self-Concept in the Classroom: A Handbook for Teachers and Parents*. Englewood Cliffs, NJ: Prentice-Hall, 1976. Plentiful supply of excellent ideas and techniques, appropriate for all ages.

Chase, Larry. *The Other Side of the Report Card: A How-to-Do-It Program for Effective Education* Glenview, IL: Scott, Foresman and Co., 1975. A smorgasbord of ways for teachers to affect the social and emotional growth of elementary and junior high-age students.

Clark, Aminah; Clemes, Harris; and Bean, Reynold. *Raising Teenagers' Self-Esteem*. Sunnyvale, CA: Enrich Div., 1978. A simple text describing techniques for increasing the self-esteem of adolescents.

Clemes, Harris, and Bean, Reynold. *How to Raise Children's Self-Esteem*. Sunnyvale, CA: Enrich Div., 1978. An easy-to-use manual describing techniques for enhancing elementary students' self-esteem.

Elkins, Don Peretz. *Glad to Be Me: Building Self-Esteem in Yourself and Others*. Englewood Cliffs, NJ: Prentice-Hall, 1976. A booklet packed full of passages and vignettes about the power of self-esteem as written by famous individuals.

Fox, C. Lynne, and Weaver, Francine Lavin. *Unlocking Doors to Friendship*. Rolling Hills, CA: B.L. Winch & Assoc., 1983. Activities are designed to be easily integrated with secondary or junior high curriculum "subject blocks."

Johnson, Spencer, and Johnson, Constance. *The One Minute Teacher: How to Teach Others to Teach Themselves*. New York: William Morrow and Co., 1986. An easy-to-use source describing the teaching principles of effective praising, goal-setting and recovery.

Keyahan, Alex. *Sage: Self-Awareness Growth Experiences*. Rolling Hills, CA: B.L. Winch & Assoc., 1983. A guide presenting 126 strategies designed to facilitate personal growth and social development in eight content areas.

Knight, Michael E. *Teaching Children to Love Themselves.* Englewood Cliffs, NJ: Prentice-Hall, 1982. A collection of activities for young children to enhance a new awareness of self.

Moorman, Chick, and Dishon, Dee. *Our Classroom: We Can Learn Together.* Englewood Cliffs, NJ: Prentice-Hall, 1983. Targeted for K–6 teachers. Provides specific activities and strategies to create a cooperative learning environment.

Purkey, William Watson, and Novak, John M. *Inviting School Success: A Self-Concept Approach to Teaching and Learning.* Belmont, CA: Wadsworth, 1984. An invaluable manual for self-esteem building within all school settings. Appropriate for all grade levels.

Reider, Barbara. *A Hooray Kind of Kid: A Child's Self-Esteem and How to Build It.* El Dorado Hills, CA: Sierra House, 1988. Practical strategies to identify students with low self-esteem and increase their positive feelings about themselves.

Simon, Sidney B. *I Am Lovable and Capable.* Allen, TX: Argus Communications, 1977. A delightful tale that vividly describes the immense destructiveness of put-down messages.

Simon, Sidney B.; Howe, Leland W.; and Kirschenbaum, Howard. *Values Clarification: A Handbook of Practical Strategies for Teachers and Students.* New York: Hart, 1972. An invaluable and timeless guide with over 79 classroom exercises designed to help students clarify their values.

White, Earl. *Nourishing the Seeds of Self-Esteem: A Handbook of Group Activities.* Santa Cruz, CA: Educational and Training Services, 1980. Group activities for any grade level to enhance self-esteem.

Resources for Parents

The following sources are particularly valuable for helping parents learn the skills of self-esteem enhancement. They are also excellent for teachers.

Borba, Michele. *Home Esteem Builders.* Rolling Hills, CA: Jalmar, 1989. The companion volume to ESTEEM BUILDERS, this manual presents an abundance of easy-to-use activities and strategies to build student self-esteem in the home.

Briggs, Dorothy. *Your Child's Self-Esteem: The Key to His Life.* New York: Doubleday, 1970. A self-esteem classic: a readable and invaluable source describing how self-esteem is literally the key to a child's life.

Clarke, Jean I. *Self-Esteem: A Family Affair.* San Francisco, CA: Harper & Row, 1978. Creative ways to help self-esteem flourish using theory and techniques based on Transactional Analysis.

Dobson, James. *Hide or Seek.* Old Tappan, NJ: Revell, 1974. A very readable book about self-esteem and its relevance to youth today.

Dyer, Wayne. *What Do You Really Want for Your Children?* New York: Avon, 1985. Straightforward advice about raising children and increasing their self-esteem.

Elkind, David. *The Hurried Child: Growing Up Too Fast Too Soon.* Reading, MA: Addison Wesley, 1981. An outstanding source for parents and teachers describing the dilemma of today's stressed-out youth.

Eyre, Linda and Eyre, Richard. *Teaching Children Responsibility.* New York: Ballantine, 1986. A guide to help children learn self-responsibility.

Faber, Adele, and Mazlish, Elaine. *How to Talk So Kids Will Listen and Listen So Kids Will Talk.* New York: Avon, 1980. A helpful guide presented in an appealing format dealing with effective techniques to increase communication between parents and children.

Ginott, Haim. *Between Parent and Child.* New York: Macmillan, 1965. Published over 20 years ago, but still a very pertinent book.

Gordon, Thomas. *Parent Effectiveness Training: The Tested Way to Raise Responsible Children.* New York: McKay, 1970. Proven communication techniques packed with examples and exercises to enhance parent-child relations.

Greene, Lawrence J. *Smarter Kids.* New York: Ballantine, 1987. A sourcebook to increase students' organizational, coping and decision-making skills.

Lickona, Thomas. *Raising Good Children from Birth Through the Teenage Years.* New York: Bantam, 1983. Presents the predictable stages of moral development from birth to adulthood as well as down-to-earth advice and guidance for each stage.

Nelsen, Jane. *Positive Discipline: Teaching Children Self-Discipline, Responsibility, Cooperation, and Problem Solving Skills.* Fair Oaks, CA: Sunrise, 1981. A straightforward, valuable guide to discipline with a positive approach.

Pappas, Michael G. *Prime Time for Families: Over 50 Activities, Games and Exercises for Personal and Family Growth.* Minneapolis: Winston Press, 1980. Easy-to-use ideas for family esteem building.

Zimbardo, Philip G., and Radl, Shirley L. *The Shy Child: A Parent's Guide to Overcoming and Preventing Shyness from Infancy to Adulthood.* New York: Doubleday, 1982. Written by the expert on shyness, the manual presents not only research and theory on shyness but excellent strategies for intervention and prevention.

Self-Esteem Research or Reference Books

The following publications are excellent sources about self-esteem. While the list is just a very small biography compared to all the books published on the subject, these are some of the most useful.

Axline, Virginia. *Dibs: In Search of Self.* New York: Ballantine, 1964.

Ball, Samuel. *Motivation in Education.* Orlando, FL: Academic Press, 1977.

Beane, James, and Lipka, Richard P. *Self-Concept, Self-Esteem and the Curriculum.* New York: Teachers College Press, 1986.

Bloom, Benjamin. *Developing Talent in Young People.* New York: Simon & Schuster, 1987.

Branden, Nathaniel. *The Psychology of Self-Esteem.* New York: Bantam, 1982.

Clemes, Harris, and Bean, Reynold. *Self-Esteem: The Key to Your Child's Well Being.* New York: Kensington Publishing, 1981.

Coopersmith, Stanley. *The Antecedents of Self-Esteem.* San Francisco: W.H. Freeman, 1967.

_____. *Developing Motivation in Young Children.* San Francisco: Albion, 1975.

Damon, William. *The Social World of the Child.* San Francisco: Jossey-Bass, 1977.

Elkind, David. *Miseducation: Preschoolers at Risk.* New York: Alfred A. Knopf, 1987.

Felker, Donald. *Building Positive Self-Concepts.* Minneapolis: Burgess, 1974.

_____. *Helping Children to Like Themselves.* Minneapolis: Burgess, 1973.

Glasser, William. *Control Theory in the Classroom.* New York: Harper & Row, 1986.

_____. *Schools Without Failure.* New York: Harper & Row, 1969.

Goertzel, Victor and Goertzel, Mildred. *Cradles of Eminence.* Boston: Little Brown & Co., 1962.

Goodlad, John. *A Place Called School.* New York: McGraw-Hill, 1984.

Hamacheck, Donald. *Encounter with the Self.* New York: Holt, Rinehart & Winston, 1971.

Hill, Napoleon, and Stone, W. Clement. *Success Through a Positive Mental Attitude.* New York: Pocket Books, 1977.

Jersild, Arthur. *In Search of Self.* Columbia University, New York: Teachers College Press, 1952.

Kash, Marilyn, and Boric, G.D. *Teacher Behavior and Pupil Self-Concept.* Reading, MA: Addison-Wesley, 1978.

Kegan, Robert. *The Evolving Self.* Cambridge, MA: Harvard University Press, 1982.

Loevinger, Jane. *Ego Development.* San Francisco: Jossey-Bass, 1976.

Martin, Robert. *Teaching Through Encouragement.* Englewood Cliffs, NJ: Prentice-Hall, 1970.

Maslow, A.H. *Toward a Psychology of Being.* New York: Van Nostrand Reinhold, 1968.

McKay, Matthew, and Fanning, Patrick. *Self-Esteem.* New York: St. Martin's Press, 1987.

Mitchell, William. *The Power of Positive Students.* New York: William Morrow & Co., 1986.

Peale, Norman Vincent. *The Power of Positive Thinking.* New York: Fawcett Crest, 1956.

Purkey, William W. *Self-Concept and School Achievement.* Englewood Cliffs, NJ: Prentice-Hall, 1970.

Rosenberg, Morris. *Conceiving the Self.* New York: Basic Books, 1979.

Rosenthal, Robert, and Jacobsen, L. *Pygmalion in the Classroom: Teachers' Expectations and Pupils' Intellectual Development.* New York: Holt, Rinehart & Winston, 1968.

Samuels, Shirley. *Enhancing Self-Concept in Early Childhood.* New York: Human Science Press, 1977.

Schorr, Lisbeth. *Within Our Reach: Breaking the Cycle of Disadvantage.* New York: Anchor/Doubleday, 1988.

Sears, Pauline. *In Pursuit of Self-Esteem.* Belmont, CA: Wadsworth, 1964.

Silvernail, David L. *Developing Positive Student Self-Concept.* Washington, D.C.: NEA, 1977.

Silverstein, B., and Krate, R. *Children of the Dark Ghetto: A Developmental Psychology.* New York: Prager, 1975.

Wylie, Ruth. *The Self-Concept: A Critical Survey of Pertinent Research Literature.* Lincoln, NE: University of Nebraska Press, 1961.

Yawkey, Thomas. *The Self-Concept of the Young Child.* Provo, UT: Brigham Young University Press, 1980.

References for Cooperative Learning

Cooperative Learning: The Johns Hopkins Team Learning Project, Center for Social Organization of Schools, The Johns Hopkins University, 3505 N. Charles Street, Baltimore, MD 21218.

Glasser, William. *Control Theory in the Classroom.* New York: Harper & Row Publishers, 1986.

Johnson, David, and Johnson, Roger T. *Learning Together and Alone: Cooperation, Competition, and Individualization.* Englewood Cliffs, NJ: Prentice-Hall, 1975.

Johnson, David; Johnson, Roger; and Johnson, Holubec. *Circles of Learning: Cooperation in the Classroom.* Edina, MN: Interaction Book Company, 1985.

Roy, Patricia A., ed. *Structuring Cooperative Learning: The 1982 Handbook.* Minneapolis: Cooperative Network Publications, 1982.

Slavin, Robert. *Cooperative Learning: Student Teams.* Washington, D.C.: National Education, 1982.

Journals and Periodicals

Allen, V.L., and Feldman, R.S. "Learning Through Tutoring: Low Achieving Children as Tutors." *Technical Report,* No. 236. Madison, WI: University of Wisconsin, 1972.

Aronson, E.; Blaney, N.; Sikes, J.; Stephan, C.; and Snapp, M. "Busing and Racial Tension: The Jigsaw Route to Learning and Liking." *Psychology Today* (Feb. 1975): 43–50.

Aspy, David N., and Buhler, June H. "The Effect of Teachers' Inferred Self-Concept Upon Student Achievement." *The Journal of Educational Research,* 47 (1975): 386–389.

Brady, P.J., et al. "Predicting Student Self-Concept, Anxiety, and Responsibility from Self-Evaluation and Self-Praise." *Psychology in the Schools,* 15 (1978): 434–438.

Brookover, Wilbur B., and Thomas, Shailer. "Self-Concept of Ability and School Achievement." *Sociology of Education,* 37 (1964): 271–279.

Brophy, Jere. "Teacher Praise: A Functional Analysis." *Review of Educational Research,* 15, No. 1 (Spring 1981): 5–32.

Bruck, M., and Bodwin, R.F. "The Relationship Between Self-Concept and Presence and Absence of Scholastic Underachievement." *Journal of Clinical Psychology,* 19 (1962): 181–182.

Cloward, R.D. "Studies in Tutoring." *Journal of Experimental Education,* 36: 14–25.

Cohen, A.R. "Some Implications of Self-Esteem for Social Influence." *Personality and Persuasibility,* eds. C.I. Howland and I.L. Janis. New Haven: Yale University Press, 1957, 102–120.

Davidson, H.H., and Lang, G. "Children's Perceptions of Their Teachers' Feelings Toward Them in Relation to Self-Perception, School Achievement, and Behavior." *Journal of Experimental Education,* 29 (1960): 107–118.

Edeburn, Carl E. "Teacher Self-Concept and Student Self-Concept in Grades Three, Four, and Five." *Journal of Educational Research,* 69 (July/August, 1976): 372–375.

Felker, Donald W., and Stanwyck, Douglas J. "General Self-Concept and Specific Self-Evaluations After an Academic Task." *Psychological Reports,* 29 (1971): 60–62.

Felker, Donald W., and Thomas, Susan Bahlke. "Self-Initiated Verbal Reinforcement and Positive Self-Concept." *Child Development* (1971): 1285–1287.

Frager, S., and Stern, C. "Learning by Teaching." *The Reading Teacher*, 23:5 (1970): 403–406.

Garner, G. "Modifying Pupil Self-Concept and Behavior." *Today's Education*, 63 (1974): 26–28.

Gartner, A.; Kohler, M.C.; and Riessman, F. *Children Teach Children: Learning by Teaching.* New York: Harper & Row, 1971.

Good, Thomas L. "Teacher Expectations and Student Perceptions: A Decade of Research." *Educational Leadership* (February 1981): 415–420.

Good, Thomas L., and Brophy, Jere E. "Behavioral Expressions of Teacher Attitudes." *Journal of Educational Psychology*, 63 (1972): 617–624.

Hogan, Ermon D., and Green, Robert L. "Can Teachers Modify Children's Self-Concepts?" *Teachers College Record*, 72, No. 3 (February 1971): 423–426.

Jason, M.H., and Dubnow, B. "The Relationship Between Self-Perception of Reading Abilities and Reading Achievement," ed. W.H. MacGinitie. *Assessment Problems in Reading.* Newark, DE: International Reading Assoc., 1973, 96–101.

Kerman, Sam. "Teacher Expectations and Student Achievements." *Phi Delta Kappan*, 60 (June 1979): 716–719.

Kokovich, S. "A Study of the Relationship Between Perceptions of Leadership Behavior and Certain Dimensions of Teacher Morale." *Dissertation Abstracts International*, 31 (3–A).

Lewis, G.M. "Interpersonal Relationship and School Achievement." *Children 2* (1964): 235–236.

McMillan, James H. "The Effect of Effort and Feedback on the Formation of Student Attitudes." *American Educational Research Journal*, 14, No.3 (Summer 1977): 317–330.

Morgan, R.F., and Toy, T.B. "Learning by Teaching: A Student-to-Student Compensatory Tutoring Program in a Rural School System and Its Relevance to the Educational Cooperative." *Psychological Record*, 206 (1970): 159–169.

Morse, W.G. "Self-Concept in the School Setting." *Childhood Education*, 41 (1964): 196–198.

Quandt, I.J. "Relationships Among Reading, Self-Concept, First-Grade Reading Achievement, and Behaviors." Bloomington, IN: Indiana University, 1971.

Roth, Robert. "The Role of Self-Concept in Achievement." *Journal of Experimental Education*, 27 (June 1959): 265–281.

Shavelson, R.J.; Hubner, J.J.; and Stanton, G.C. "Self-Concept Validation of Construct Interpretations." *Review of Educational Research*, 46, 3 (1976): 407–441.

Silberman, Melvin L. "Behavioral Expression of Teachers' Attitudes Toward Elementary School Students." *Journal of Educational Psychology*, 60, 5 (1969): 402–407.

Smith, D.M.; Dokecki, P.R.; and Davis, E.E. "School-Related Factors Influencing the Self-Concepts of Children with Learning Problems." *Peabody Journal of Education*, 54 (1977): 185–106.

Staines, J.W. "The Self-Picture as a Factor in the Classroom." *British Journal of Educational Psychology*, 18 (1958): 97–111.

Steiner, I.D. "Self-Perception and Goal-Setting Behavior." *Journal of Personal and Social Psychology*, 57 (1957): 344–355.

Stilwell, W.E., and Barclay, J.R. "Effects of Affective Education Interventions in the Elementary Schools." *Psychology in the Schools*, 16 (1979): 80–87.

Wattenberg, William W., and Gifford, Clare. "Relation of Self-Concepts to Beginning Achievement in Reading." *Child Development*, 35 (1964): 461–467.

Appendix II

B-SET
(Borba Self-Esteem Tally)

Numerous studies have linked self-esteem with successful school adjustment and mental health status.[1] Although definitions of self-esteem vary in the mental health literature, most include the components Security;[2] Identity;[3] Connectedness;[4] Self-Direction, Goal-Setting or Purpose;[5] and Competence.[6]

The goal of B-SET is to provide a diagnostic-prescriptive tool to help educators decide which interventions from ESTEEM BUILDERS will be effective in promoting self-esteem for a particular student. The tally, which is appropriate for grades K–8) is designed to be administered by classroom teachers as well as psychologists and counselors who have sufficient knowledge about the evaluated students.

This condensed version should only be considered a guide for self-esteem evaluation. A technical manual for B-SET will be available on completion of the field study.

B-SET consists of five individual components: Security, Selfhood, Affiliation, Mission and Competence. These components are defined in detail in ESTEEM BUILDERS and are described as the essential components of self-esteem. To use the evaluation, make a copy of the assessment charts and the Component Scale Summary for each student. The evaluator has the option of assessing a random sample of students in order to evaluate the overall effectiveness of the program, or selecting certain individual students who are considered at risk. The examiner therefore may evaluate program effectiveness as well as esteem enhancement of individual students.

Prior to completing an individual assessment form, the evaluator should first be familiar with the five esteem-building components—Security, Selfhood, Affiliation, Mission and Competence. Refer to the introductory pages in Chapters 3–7. It is strongly

1. Battle, J. *Enhancing Self-Esteem and Achievement* (Seattle: Special Child Publications, 1982).
   Coopersmith, S. *The Antecedents of Self-Esteem* (San Francisco: W.H. Freeman, 1967).
   Purkey, W.W. *Self-Concept and School Achievement* (Englewood Cliffs, NJ: Prentice-Hall 1970).
   Silvernail, D.L. *Developing Positive Student Self-Concept* (Washington, D.C.: NEA, 1985).
2. Erikson, E. *Identity, Youth and Crisis* (New York: Norton, 1968).
   Maslow, A. *Towards a Psychology of Being* (New York: Van Nostrand Reinhold, 1968).
3. Clemes, H., and Bean, R. *Self-Esteem: The Key to Your Child's Well-Being* (New York: Kensington Pub., 1981).
4. Felker, D. *Building Positive Self-Concepts* (Minneapolis: Burgess, 1974).
   Samuels, S. *Enhancing Self-Concept in Early Childhood* (New York: Human Sciences Press, 1977).
5. Clabby, J.F., and Elias, M.J. *Teach Your Child Decision-Making* (New York: Doubleday, 1987).
6. Borba, M. *Esteem Builders: A Self-Esteem Curriculum For Grades K–8* (Rolling Hills Estates, CA: Jalmar Press, 1989).
   Reasoner, R. *Building Self-Esteem: A Comprehensive Program* (Palo Alto, CA: Consulting Psychologists Press, 1982).

recommended that these be read in their entirety. Educators who deal with students on a daily, personal basis or in intimate, small counseling sessions are in the best position to accurately assess students' self-perceptions. They are often highly sensitive and aware of students' feelings and struggles. Many professionals consider self-esteem difficult to measure; yet most educators seem quite aware of the quality of students' self-image and are effective evaluators.

Scoring the B-SET should not be based on mere opinion. An evaluator should know the behavioral facts that reveal the extent of a student's performance on each item. Do not be misled by the apparent simplicity of the tally. It requires that you also obtain accurate information about the student's behavior from sources intimately familiar with the student. This could include the mother, father, teacher, a close relative or guardian, etc.

Multiple Evaluation Assessments

The B-SET is designed for multiple evaluations of individual students. Multiple assessments provide ongoing and overall feedback on individual students' esteem behaviors. Begin by deciding when the esteem-building activities are to be initiated and culminated. Evaluate before you begin activities and again at the end. You could also evaluate during the interim—for instance, at the midpoint—and make adjustments to your program based on your findings. Two types of evaluations are:

Pre-evaluation	Interim Evaluation	Post-evaluation
1. September	February	June
2. September	November	January

You may find that some students are very low in the first three esteem component areas, particularly in Security. This would reflect in a total score of 26 or less. In this case, the entire assessment could be given in September and a re-tally of observed behaviors conducted in Security each month. Gains in the components of Mission and Competence will be slim until the student feels more secure.

To Assess Results

Make a copy of the *B-SET: Component Scores Summary* for each evaluated individual. Following the evaluation, record the student's total component scores in total scores column. Next, plot the total scores from each esteem component on the *Self-Esteem Component Profile*. For clarity, use a different colored pen or pencil for each separate evaluation period recorded on the profile. Now evaluate the results for each assessment period so that you can prescribe effective and appropriate activities. To illustrate, the following are two different students' profiles:

Student #1: Summary of Total Component Scores

Esteem Component	Date Sep 24	Date Jan 5	Date May 30
Security	17	19	23
Selfhood	16	18	22
Affiliation	16	16	22
Mission	14	14	20
Competence	12	14	18

Student #1 Results

The above summary indicates that the student improved in all five esteem areas by the final assessment on May 30. By the interim assessment in January, the student made no growth in Affiliation and Mission; however, the student did acquire new esteem-building behaviors by the final May 30 assessment date. Many behaviors moved from the "never" category to the "sometimes" category. The goal of B-SET is to document any increase in behaviors regarded as esteem building. In some cases, there might only be minimal growth. But any growth must be seen as positive growth.

Student #2: Summary of Total Component Scores

Esteem Component	Date Sep 24	Date Jan 5	Date May 30
Security	25	26	27
Selfhood	23	24	26
Affiliation	23	23	25
Mission	17	20	24
Competence	16	20	25

Student #2 Results

This student began with significantly higher scores than those of the first student. The overall scores indicate fewer self-esteem deficit areas than the first example. Consequently, the diagnosis for an increase in esteem behaviors is much more positive.

Assessment Precautions

A few cautions should be noted with regard to the behavior-tally approach as a self-esteem evaluation device. The first is that the initial evaluation should be conducted only after you feel you have sufficient information about the student being assessed. Several days prior to assessing, take any available opportunity to observe the student in different settings.

Secondly, keep in mind that behavior fluctuates in different settings. Any given evaluation period does not necessarily indicate the most truthful self-perceptions. Everyone has his/her insecurities or personal problems that can affect behavior. Evaluation will be more accurate if based on the student's most typical daily behavior. Any inconsistent behaviors should be recorded as observations only.

The B-SET is designed to assess only *observed* student behavior. For example, the Affiliation component deals primarily with a student's relationships with peers and in groups. If the evaluator is not in a position to observe the student in a daily context as he/she interacts with peers, any evaluation is not a reliable or accurate assessment of that student's affiliation behavior. The more information you collect, the better your assessment will be. If you have no way of verifying the behavior yourself, use other reliable sources to provide the information you need. These may be parents, former teachers, counselors, coaches or the student.

Fourth, keep in mind that self-esteem is often situational. A student who displays confidence at school may be reserved and hesitant at home, or vice versa. The limitation of this tally is that it is restricted to the locality in which the observations are gathered. In a school setting, it means that the scores are only reflective of esteem behaviors at school. Any conclusions should, therefore, be limited to the school environment.

Finally, the B-SET is meant to be viewed only as a means for assessing student needs in each of the five components and the effectiveness of esteem-building activities to enhance those components.

Prescriptive Esteem-Building Plan

A *Self-Esteem Prescriptive Plan* form is provided in this Appendix to organize and coordinate individual student esteem enhancement. Duplicate the form so that you have one for each student with particular needs in self-esteem. Use the data on the Component Scores Summary to assist you in formulating a plan for the student. (These forms are for your use, not the student's.)

Student Assessments

The emphasis in this section has been on evaluating esteem behaviors based on the perceptions of others; however, data collection need not be limited to this technique. Student self-perceptions are obviously critical and can prove to be highly valuable. J.C. Nunnally stated this position succinctly when he said, "Generally, the most valid, economical, sometimes the only way to learn about a person's sentiments is simply to ask him."[7] Some of the activities in this book are geared toward collecting information directly from the student. These include:

Journal Writing. Journals, written logs or diaries provide valuable insights about students' self-perceptions. Chapter 9 has complete sections on daily journal topics, worksheets and implementation suggestions. Journal writing provides an extended opportunity for students to reflect on different aspects of their self-concepts as well as formulate more accurate and realistic self-pictures. Recorded information should always be regarded as confidential.

Activity Sheets. Several activity sheets in the book are also effective evaluation measures. Copy forms you think may be useful for evaluation and ask students to complete them. Mark completed forms "Self-Esteem"; they can now serve as a pre-assessment for the relevant component. To evaluate students' gains in that area, have them complete the same form at another date following an instruction period.

7. Beane, J. and Lipka, R.P. *Self-Concept, Self-Esteem and the Curriculum* (New York: Teachers College Press, 1986).

B-SET (Borba Self-Esteem Tally)
Component Scores Summary

Student's Name_____

School_____ Grade_____

Assessment Dates_____ Teacher_____

STEP 1: Enter the student's TOTAL component scores in each of the boxes as determined on the Student Self-Esteem Component Scale.

SUMMARY OF COMPONENT TOTAL SCORES			
ESTEEM COMPONENT	DATE_____ TOTAL SCORES	DATE_____ TOTAL SCORES	DATE_____ TOTAL SCORES
Security			
Selfhood			
Affiliation			
Mission			
Competence			

STEP 2: Plot the TOTAL SCORES from each Esteem Component on the Self-Esteem Component Profile.
For the FIRST ASSESSMENT draw lines _____ to connect the scores.
For the SECOND ASSESSMENT draw dashed lines ---- to connect the scores.
For the THIRD ASSESSMENT draw dotted lines .... to connect the scores.

SELF-ESTEEM COMPONENT PROFILE

TOTAL COMPONENT SCORES

© Drs. Craig & Michele Borba, 1989   *This B-SET is designed as a guide to implement the Esteem Builder curriculum and is not a measure of self-esteem.*

B-SET (Borba Self-Esteem Tally)
by
Drs. Craig and Michele Borba

Student's Name_____ Date_____

School_____ Grade_____ Teacher_____

INSTRUCTIONS: This form is a tool to assess student needs in each of the five esteem components. Read each statement below. Circle the appropriate number in each box that in your judgment best describes the student's behavior according to the scoring code.

SCORING INSTRUCTIONS: Read each behavior and circle the appropriate number. Add all of the circled numbers for the **total score** for that esteem component.

1 = Always or Often   2 = Sometimes   3 = Never or Rarely

SECURITY

A student with a strong sense of Security conveys a feeling of assuredness. The individual generally feels comfortable and safe.

Behavior	Always	Sometimes	Rarely
1. Displays difficulty in separating for brief periods from trusted sources and/or environments.	1	2	3
2. Exhibits possible indicators of stress or anxiety, such as: nail biting, thumb sucking, hair twirling, teeth grinding, shaking, crying without reason, extreme nervousness.	1	2	3
3. Exhibits possible indicators of physiological stress, such as: headaches, bed wetting, ulcers, stomach aches, sweating.	1	2	3
4. Is generally unsure of what others expect of him/her.	1	2	3
5. Resists taking on new experiences.	1	2	3
6. Displays excessive and/or unfounded fears.	1	2	3
7. Has difficulty in forming trusting relationships.	1	2	3
8. Is uncomfortable with close physical contact from known sources.	1	2	3
9. Handles change or spontaneity with difficulty.	1	2	3
10. Lacks knowledge of sources that can be counted on.	1	2	3

SECURITY SCORE [ ]

Total all circled numbers equals Security Score

This B-SET is designed as a guide to implement the Esteem Builder curriculum and is not a measure of self-esteem.

SELFHOOD

A student with a strong sense of Selfhood conveys self-knowledge. Such an individual has an accurate and realistic self-description in terms of roles, attributes and physical characteristics.

Behavior	Always	Sometimes	Rarely
1. Is uncomfortable with physical appearance.	1	2	3
2. Has difficulty in accepting praise: denies; undermines; disregards; acts embarrassed.	1	2	3
3. Conforms or mimics others; is unwilling to express self in own way or risk being different.	1	2	3
4. Dresses inappropriately, such as eccentric or excessive clothing, to draw undue attention to self.	1	2	3
5. Has difficulty in expressing and identifying emotions appropriately.	1	2	3
6. Lacks accurate self-information (roles, attributes, physical characteristics, interests); poor self-knowledge.	1	2	3
7. Is over-anxious to please others; displays over-dependence in relationships.	1	2	3
8. Frequently uses negative statements regarding others; criticizes, but is hypersensitive to criticism.	1	2	3
9. Is uncomfortable with fine or gross motor activities (not due to any physical impairment).	1	2	3
10. Feels inadequate; not good or special enough. May adopt defensive behaviors, such as: negative self-statements, silliness, reticence, sullenness, defiance, showing-off, crying without reason or engaging in fantasy.	1	2	3

Total all circled numbers equals Selfhood Score

**SELFHOOD
SCORE**

AFFILIATION

A student with a strong sense of Affiliation has a feeling of belonging or connectedness. This is generally achieved in relationships that are considered important by the individual.

Behavior	Always	Sometimes	Rarely
1. Has difficulty in initiating friendships; lacks appropriate social skills.	1	2	3
2. Feels others don't value him/her.	1	2	3
3. Demonstrates a sense of connectedness with objects in lieu of people.	1	2	3
4. Has difficulty in relating to others. May resort to behaviors such as: bullying, showing-off, excessive bragging or boasting, monopolizing, acting silly, being uncooperative, teasing, smoking or taking drugs.	1	2	3
5. Withdraws, rejects or isolates self from peers and groups.	1	2	3
6. Has few friends; is seldom sought out by others.	1	2	3
7. Displays insensitivity to the emotions and needs of others; lacks empathy.	1	2	3
8. Lacks understanding of the concept of friendship.	1	2	3
9. Has difficulty in maintaining friendships.	1	2	3
10. Relies on adult companionship as the sole source of affiliation.	1	2	3

AFFILIATION SCORE [ ]

Total all circled numbers equals Affiliation Score

© Drs. Craig & Michele Borba, 1989   *This B-SET is designed as a guide to implement the Esteem Builder curriculum and is not a measure of self-esteem.*

MISSION

A student with a strong sense of Mission takes responsibility for the destiny of his/her decisions. Such an individual generally sets realistic and achievable goals, is self-directed, and has a strong feeling of influence and control over life's circumstances.

Behavior	Always	Sometimes	Rarely
1. Is unmotivated; takes little initiative; appears aimless; shows minimal effort.	1	2	3
2. Cannot see alternatives or solutions.	1	2	3
3. Feels powerless; may exhibit attention-getting behaviors such as whining or tattling to gain control.	1	2	3
4. Is unable to complete tasks or work; has diminished attention span; is careless; acts bored or indifferent.	1	2	3
5. Poor goal-setting results in lack of success: goals are either too high, too low or are nonexistent.	1	2	3
6. Feels helpless and incapable of influencing others or self.	1	2	3
7. Depends on others for direction and encouragement.	1	2	3
8. Avoids taking responsibility for own actions—looks to outside sources as cause; blames others or denies.	1	2	3
9. Is indecisive, incapable or unwilling to make own decisions.	1	2	3
10. Has difficulty in correctly evaluating present or past performance level in skills or competencies.	1	2	3

Total all circled numbers equals Mission Score

MISSION SCORE [   ]

COMPETENCE

A student with a strong sense of Competence generally feels successful and capable. Such an individual knows his/her strengths and can accept individual weaknesses. He/she feels successful, particularly in things regarded as personally important or valuable.

Behavior	Always	Sometimes	Rarely
1. Is reluctant to verbalize ideas or opinions.	1	2	3
2. Acts helpless or dependent in areas where he/she should be competent.	1	2	3
3. Does not attempt many tasks because of an overriding fear of failure or making a mistake.	1	2	3
4. Gives up on tasks when confronted with difficulty.	1	2	3
5. Has difficulty in identifying personal strengths.	1	2	3
6. Is a poor loser; magnifies any loss or displays poor sportsmanship.	1	2	3
7. Displays an "I can't" kind of attitude; does not try.	1	2	3
8. Displays frequent behavior flare-ups in areas where incompetence is felt, such as: frustration, withdrawal, resistance, defiance, acting out, daydreaming or cheating.	1	2	3
9. Has difficulty in accepting weaknesses.	1	2	3
10. Discounts or discredits any achievement. May use negative self-statements regarding accomplishments.	1	2	3

COMPETENCE SCORE [ ]

Total all circled numbers equals Competence Score

Competence	Mission	Affiliation	Selfhood	Security		Student:
					Strengths	
					Weaknesses	
					Strategies for Growth	Dates:

Self-Esteem Prescriptive Plan

Esteem Builders. Jalmar Press
Rolling Hills Estates, C

Things I've Tried That Worked

Please share your activities with us!

Name:_____

Position:_____

Address:_____

_____

Phone #:_____

Activities:

1. _____

_____

2. _____

_____

3. _____

_____

4. _____

_____

Please mail to: Dr. Michele Borba
840 Prescott Drive
Palm Springs, CA 92262

PRACTICE prevention rather than intervention!
DEVELOPING positive self-esteem is our best weapon against drug and alcohol abuse!

Project Self-Esteem, Expanded (Gr. K-6)

Innovative parent involvement program. Used by over 2000 schools/400,000 participants. Teaches children to repect themselves and others, make sound decisions, honor personal and family value systems, develop vocabulary, attitude, goals and behavior needed for successful living, practice responsible behavior and avoid drug and alcohol use.

Sandy McDaniel & Peggy Bielen

0-915190-59-1, 408 pages, **JP-9059-1 $39.95**
8½ x 11, paperback, illus., reprod. act. sheets

Esteem Builders (Gr. K-8)

Teach self-esteem via curriculum content. Best K-8 program available. Uses 5 building blocks of self-esteem (security/ selfhood/ affiliation/ mission/ competence) as base. Over 250 grade level/curric. content cross-correlated activities. Also assess. tool, checklist of educator behaviors for modeling, 40 week lesson planner, ext. bibliography and more.

0-915190-53-2, 464 pages, **JP-9053-2 $39.95**
8½ x 11, paperback, illus.,reprod. act. sheets

Michele Borba, Ph.D.

NEW

Self-Esteem: The"Affiliation" Building Block (Gr. K-6)

Making friends is easy with the activities in this thoroughly researched book. Students are paired, get to know each other, produce a book about their new friend, and present it in class. Exciting activities help discover commonalities. Great self-esteem booster. Revised after 10 years of field testing. Over 18 activities.

C. Lynn Fox, Ph.D.

0-915190-75-3, 128 pages, **JP-9075-3 $14.95**
8½ x 11, paperback, illustrations, activities

NEW

6 Vital Ingredients of Self-Esteem: How To Develop Them In Your Students (Gr. K-12)

Put self-esteem to work for your students. Learn practical ways to help kids manage school, make decisions, accept consequences, manage time, and discipline themselves to set worthwhile goals...and much more. Covers developmental stages from ages 2 to 18, with implications for self-esteem at each stage.

0-915190-72-9, 208 pages, **JP-9072-9 $19.95**
8½ x 11, paperback, biblio., appendices

Bettie B. Youngs, Ph.D.

Feelings Alphabet: An Album of Emotions from A to Z (Gr. Pre.K-4)

Watch self-awareness and self-acceptance grow page-by-page as you use this delightful book. Teaches children the alphabet and about themselves and their feelings. Once they can express their feelings, they can learn. And when they learn, they feel good about themselves. An enabling book. "One-of-a-kind" photos.

Judy Lalli, M.S.

0-915190-82-6, 72 pages, **JP-9082-6 $7.95**
6 x 9, paperback, 33 B/W photos

Learning The Skills Of Peacemaking: Communicating/Cooperation/Resolving Conflict (Gr.K-8)

Help kids say "No" to fighting. Establish WIN/WIN guidelines for conflicts in your classroom. Over fifty lessons: peace begins with me; intregating peacemaking into our lives; exploring our roots and interconnectedness. Great for self-esteem and cultural diversity programs.

0-915190-46-X, **JP-9046-X $21.95**
8½ x 11, paperback, illus.,reprod. act. sheets

Naomi Drew, M.A.

REVISED

He Hit Me Back First: Self-Esteem Through Self-Discipline (Gr. K-8)

By whose authority does a child choose right from wrong? Here are activities directed toward developing within the child an awareness of his own inner authority and ability to choose (will power) and the resulting sense of responsibility, freedom and self-esteem. 29 separate activities.

Eva D. Fugitt, M.A.

0-915190-64-8, 120 pages, **JP-9064-8 $12.95**
8½ x 11, paperback, appendix, biblio.

NEW

You & Self-Esteem: The Key to Happiness & Success (Gr. 5-12)

Comprehensive workbook for young people. Defines self-esteem and its importance in their lives; helps them identify why and how it adds or detracts from their vitality; shows them how to protect it from being shattered by others; oulines a plan of action to keep their self-esteem positive. Very useful.

0-915190-83-4, 128 pages, **JP-9083-4 $14.95**
8½ x 11, paperback, biblio., appendices

Bettie B. Youngs, Ph.D.

Self-Awareness Growth Experiences (Gr. 7-12)

Over 593 strategies/activities covering affective learning goals and objectives. To increase: self-awareness/self-esteem/social inter-action skills/problem-solving, decision - making skills/coping ability/ ethical standards/independent functioning/ creativity. Great secondary resource. Useful in counseling situations.

V. Alex Kehayan, Ed.D.

0-915190-61-3, 224 pages, **JP-9061-3 $16.95**
6 x 9, paperback, illus., 593 activities

Unlocking Doors to Self-Esteem (Gr. 7-12)

Contains curriculum content objectives with underlying social objectives. Teach both at the same time. Content objectives in English/Drama/Social Science/Career Education/ Science/Physical Education Social objectives in Developing Positive Self-Concepts/ Examining Attitudes, Feelings and Actions/Fostering Positive Relationships.

0-915190-60-5, 224 pages, **JP-9060-5 $16.95**
6 x 9 , paperback, illus., 100 lesson plans

C. Lynn Fox, Ph.D. & Francine L. Weaver, M.A.

ORDER FROM: Jalmar Press, 45 Hitching Post Drive, Bldg. 2, Rolling Hills Estates, CA 90274-5169
CALL TOLL FREE — 800/662-9662. IN CALIF. CALL COLLECT — 213/547-1240. FAX — 213/547-1644

DISCOVER books on self-esteem for kids.
ENJOY great reading with Warm Fuzzies and Squib, the adventurous owl.

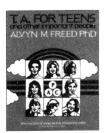

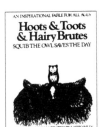

DISCOVER materials for positive self-esteem.

CREATE a positive environment in your classroom or home by opening a world of understanding.

Good Morning Class - I Love You (Staff)

Contains thought provoking quotes and questions about teaching from the heart. Helps love become an integral part of the learning that goes on in every classroom. Great for new teachers and for experienced teachers who sometimes become frustrated by the system. Use this book to begin and end your day. Greet your students every day with: "Good morning class - I love you."

Esther Wright, M.A.

0-915190-58-3, 80 pages, **JP-9058-3 $6.95**
5½ x 8½ , paperback, illust./Button $1.50

NEW

Enhancing Self-Esteem: A Guide for Professional (K-12) Educators (Staff)

For the educator, a healthy self-esteem is job criteria No. 1! When high, it empowers us and adds to the vitality of our lives; when low it saps energy, erodes our confidence, lowers productivity and blocks our initiative to care about self and others. Follow the plan of action in this great resource to develop your self-esteem.

0-915190-79-6, 144 pages, **JP-9079-6 $16.95**
8½ x 11, paperback

Enhancing Self-Esteem: A Guide for Professional Educators
Bettie B. Youngs, Ph.D.

I Am a Blade of Grass (Staff)

Create a school where all — students, teachers, administrators, and parents — see themselves as both learners and leaders *in partnership*. Develop a new compact for learning that focuses on results, that promotes local initiative and that empowers people at all levels of the system. How to in this collaborative curriculum. Great for self-esteem.

Elaine Young, M.A.
with R. Frelow, Ph.D.

0-915190-54-0, 176 pages, **JP-9054-0 $14.95**
6 x 9, paperback, illustrations

NEW

Stress Management for Educators: A Guide to Manage Our Response to Stress (Staff)

Answers these significant questions for educators: What is stress? What causes it? How do I cope with it? What can be done to manage stress to moderate its negative effects? Can stress be used to advantage? How can educators be stress-proofed to help them remain at peak performance? How do I keep going in spite of it?

0-915190-77-X, 112 pages, **JP-9077-X $12.95**
8½ x 11, paperback, illus., charts

STRESS MANAGEMENT FOR EDUCATORS A Guide To Manage Our Response To Stress
Bettie B. Youngs, Ph.D.

Peace in 100 Languages: A One-Word Multilingual Dictionary (Staff/Personal)

Accepted by the Guiness Book of Records as simultaneously the largest/smallest dictionary ever published. Envisioned, researched and developed by Soviet peace activists. Ancient, national, local and special languages covered. A portion of purchase price will be donated to joint US/USSR peace project.

Alexander Lapitsky, Ph.D.

0-915190-74-5, 48 pages, **JP-9074-5 $14.95**
5 x 10, glossy paperback, full color

Feel Better Now (Staff/Personal)

Teaches people to handle stress *as it happens* rapidly and directly. This basic requirement for emotional survival and physical health can be learned with the methods in this book. Find your own recipe for relief by *letting go* with Relaxers, Distractors and Releasers. Foreword: Ken Keyes, Jr. "A mine of practical help" — says Rev. Robert Schuller.

0-915190-66-4, 180 pages, **JP-9066-4 $9.95**
6 x 9, paperback, appendix, biblio.

FEEL BETTER NOW
Chris Schriner, Rel.D.

Learning to Live, Learning to Love (Staff/Personal)

Important things are often quite simple. But simple things are not necessarily easy. If you are finding that learning to live and learning to love are at times difficult, you are in good company. People everywhere are finding it a tough challenge. This simple book will help. "Shows how to separate "treasure" from "trash" in our lives.

Joanne Haynes-Klassen

0-915190-38-9, 160 pages, **JP-9038-9 $7.95**
6 x 9, paperback, illustrations

Present Yourself: Great Presentation Skills (Staff/Personal)

Use *mind mapping* to become a presenter who is a dynamic part of the message. Learn about transforming fear, knowing your audience, setting the stage, making them remember and much more. Essential reading for anyone interested in communication. This book will become the standard work in its field. Easy to understand and use.

0-915190-51-6, 128 pages, **JP-9051-6 $9.95**
6 x 9, paperback, illus., mind maps

Present Yourself!
By Michael J. Gelb
Michael J. Gelb, M.A.

The Two Minute Lover (Staff/Personal)

With wit, wisdom and compassion, "The Two-Minute Lovers" and their proteges guide you through the steps of building and maintaining an effective relationship in a fast-paced world. They offer encouragement, inspiration and practical techniques for living happily in a relationship, even when outside pressures are enormous. Done like the "One Minute Manager".

Asa Sparks, Ph.D.

0-915190-38-9, 160 pages, **JP-9038-9 $9.95**
6 x 9, paperback, illustrations

Reading, Writing and Rage (Staff)

An autopsy of one profound school failure, disclosing the complex processes behind it and the secret rage that grew out of it. Developed from educational therapist's viewpoint. A must reading for anyone working with the learning disabled, functional illiterates or juvenile delinquents. Reads like fiction. Foreword by Bruce Jenner.

0-915190-42-7, 240 pages, **JP-9042-7 $16.95**
5½ x 8½, paperback, biblio., resources

READING, WRITING AND RAGE
The terrible price paid by victims of school failure
Dorothy Ungerleider, M.A.

D. Ungerleider, M.A.

ORDER FROM: Jalmar Press, 45 Hitching Post Drive, Bldg. 2, Rolling Hills Estates, CA 90274-5169
CALL TOLL FREE — 800/662-9662. IN CALIF. CALL COLLECT — 213/547-1240. FAX — 213/547-1644

OPEN your mind to whole brain thinking and creative parenting.
GROW by leaps and bounds with our new ways to think and learn.

Bob Samples, M.A.

Openmind/Wholemind: Parenting and Teaching Tomorrow's Children Today (Staff/Personal)

Can we learn to treat the brain/mind system as open rather than closed? Can we learn to use all our learning modalities, learning styles, creativities and intelligences to create a product far greater than the sum of its parts? Yes! This primer for parents and teachers shows how.

0-915190-45-1, 272 pages, **JP-9045-1 $14.95**
7 x 10, paperback, 81 B/W photos, illust.

Unicorns Are Real: A Right-Brained Approach to Learning (Gr. K-Adult)

Over 100,000 sold. The alternate methods of teaching/learning developed by the author have helped literally thousands of children and adults with learning difficulties. A book of simple ideas and activities that are easy to use, yet dramatically effective. Video of techniques also available: VHS, 1½ hrs., **JP-9113-0 $149.95**

0-915190-35-4, 136 pages, **JP-9035-4 $12.95**
8½ x 11, paperback, illus., assessment

Barbara Meister Vitale, M.A.

REVISED

Bob Samples, M.A.

Metaphoric Mind: A Celebration of Creative Consciousness (Revised) (Staff/Personal)

A plea for a balanced way of thinking and being in a culture that stands on the knife-edge between catastrophe and transformation. The metaphoric mind is asking again, quietly but insistently, for equilibrium. For, after all, equilibrium is the way of nature. A revised version of a classic.

0-915190-68-0, 272 pages, **JP-9068-0 $16.95**
7 x 10, paperback, B/W photos, illus.

Free Flight: Celebrating Your Right Brain (Staff/Personal)

Journey with Barbara Meister Vitale, from her uncertain childhood perceptions of being "different" to the acceptance and adult celebration of that difference. A how to book for right-brained people in a left-brained world. Foreword by Bob Samples-"This book is born of the human soul." Great gift item for your right-brained friends.

0-915190-44-3 , 128 pages, **JP-9044-3 $9.95**
5½ x 8½, paperback, illustrations

Barbara Meister Vitale, M.A.

NEW

Lane Longino Waas, Ph.D.

Imagine That! Getting Smarter Through Imagery Practice (Gr. K-Adult)

Understand and develop your own seven intelligences in only minutes a day. Help children do the same. The results will amaze you. Clear, step by step ways show you how to create your own imagery exercises for any area of learning or life and how to relate imagery exercises to curriculum content.

0-915190-71-0, 144 pages, **JP-9071-0 $12,95**
6 x 9, paperback, 42 B/W photos, biblio.

NEW

Becoming Whole (Learning) Through Games (Gr. K-Adult)

New ideas for old games. Develop your child's brain power, motivation and self-esteem by playing. An excellent parent/teacher guide and skills checklist to 100 standard games. Included are auditory, visual, motor, directional, modality, attention, educational, social and memory skills. Great resource for care givers.

0-915190-70-2, 288 pages, **JP-9070-2 $16.95**
6 x 9, paperback, glossary, biblio.

Gwen Bailey Moore, Ph.D. & Todd Serby

Harold Bessell, Ph.D. & Thomas P. Kelly, Jr.

The Parent Book: Raising Emotionally Mature Children (Ages 3-15)

Improve positive bonding with your child in five easy steps: listen to the feelings; learn the basic concern; develop an action plan; confront with support; spend 1 to 1 time. Ideas for helping in 4 self-esteem related areas: awareness; relating; competence; integrity. 69 sub-catagories. Learn what's missing and what to do about it.

0-915190-15-X, 208 pages, **JP-9015-X $9,95**
8½ x 11, paperback, illus., diag/Rx.

Pajamas Don't Matter: What Your Baby Really Needs is Love (Ages Birth-3)

Worried about your new baby? Lots of unanswered questions? It's simple, really. What your baby needs most is for you to be nice to him. Experts talk about love and security and praise and recognition and bonding and new experiences. What it boils down to is loving him. Here's how in a delightfully illustrated book.

0-915190-21-4, 52 pages, **JP-9021-4 $5.95**
8½ x 11, paperback, illus., 4-color

Trish Gribben & Dick Frizzell (illust.)

Cheryl Foote Gimbel & Wendelin Maners

Why Does Santa Celebrate Christmas? (Ages 5-105)

What do wisemen, shepards and angels have to do with Santa, reindeer and elves? Explore this Christmas fantasy which ties all of the traditions of Christmas into one lovely poem for children of all ages. Beautifully illustrated in watercolors by this mother/daughter team. Great gift book for families.

0-915190-67-2, 36 pages, **JP-9067-2 $12.95**
8½ x 11, hardcover, full color illustrations

The Turbulent Teens: Understanding Helping, Surviving (Parents/Teens)

Come to grips with the difficult issues of rules and the limits of parental tolerance, recognizing the necessity for flexibility that takes into consideration changes in the adolescent as well as the imperative need for control, agreed upon expectations and accountability. A must read! Useful in counseling situations.

0-913091-01-4, 224 pages, **JP-9101-4 $8.95**
6 x 9, paperback, case histories

James E. Gardner, Ph.D.

ORDER FROM: Jalmar Press, 45 Hitching Post Drive, Bldg. 2, Rolling Hills Estates, CA 90274-5169
CALL TOLL FREE — 800/662-9662. IN CALIF. CALL COLLECT — 213/547-1240. FAX — 213/547-1644

6/91

ESTEEM BUILDER TRAINING
Offered by Dr. Michele Borba

A wide variety of Esteem-Building inservice training presentations are offered by Dr. Borba. Programs include keynote addresses, seminars, workshops and long-term comprehensive programs designed to meet the needs, goals and objectives of your setting and staff.

☑ **You Are the Door Opener: You Hold the Keys to Self-Esteem: A Keynote for Educators.** This motivating and inspiring keynote address explains why educators have the power to turn the keys in students' lives by helping them reach their potential as learners.

☑ **Increasing Student Achievement and Behavior Through Self-Esteem: Classroom Esteem Building.** This "hands-on" inservice is designed for the classroom teacher. Strategies for identifying high-risk students, a model for esteem building based on the five components of self-esteem as well as dozens of classroom-proven techniques and activities for esteem building will be demonstrated and displayed.

☑ **"Every Child Can Be a Winner": A Parent Address on Building Esteem.** Practical esteem-building techniques that can be done at home.

☑ **Esteem Building: A Total Staff Effort.** Designed especially for administrators, this inservice covers specific strategies to build staff esteem, recognize staff members with low self-esteem and identify administrator practices that increase staff esteem.

☑ **School Esteem Building.** This workshop is for those who wish to implement either a school or classroom program that addresses the needs of students-at-risk by building self-esteem, motivation and responsibility.

☑ **Coordinator Training for Esteem Builders.** An indepth-training of chosen personnel who will aid in the implementation of the self-esteem framework at the school/district site on a regular basis.

☑ **Self-Esteem for Young Adolescents (7-12).** A seminar designed to assist educators in building positive student attitudes, promoting academic excellence, encouraging student responsibility and creating a positive climate for learning in classrooms for young adolescents. Specific strategies for high-risk students are offered.

☑ **Paired Associations, Cooperative Learning and Esteem Building.** Participants will have the opportunity to experience dozens of cooperative learning techniques based on the Esteem-Building model of the five components of self-esteem.

☑ **Developing Esteem-Building Materials; A Make and Take Session.** An opportunity to make or develop "esteem builders" appropriate to your program and student needs.

☑ **Self-Esteem and Literature.** Building self-esteem through literature and the daily language arts curriculum—a program for integrating esteem enhancement into the existing language curriculum.

To contact Dr. Borba, call or write:
840 Prescott Drive
Palm Springs, California 92262
(619) 323-5387